Sunset

QUICK

LIGHT

AND

HEALTHY

By the Editors of Sunset Books

Sunset Publishing Corporation
Menlo Park, California

SUNSET BOOKS

President & Publisher: Susan J. Maruyama
Director, Sales & Marketing: Richard A. Smeby
Director, New Business: Kenneth Winchester
Editorial Director: Bob Doyle
Production Director: Lory Day

SUNSET PUBLISHING CORPORATION

Chairman: Jim Nelson
President/Chief Executive Officer: Stephen J. Seabolt
Chief Financial Officer: James E. Mitchell
Publisher: Anthony P. Glaves
Director of Finance: Larry Diamond
Vice President, Manufacturing: Lorinda B. Reichert
Editor, Sunset Magazine: William R. Marken
Senior Editor, Food & Entertaining: Jerry Anne Di Vecchio

Quick, Light, and Healthy was produced
in conjunction with Rebus, Inc., New York, NY.

Editor and Publisher: Rodney M. Friedman
Associate Publisher: Barbara Maxwell O'Neill
Editor in Chief: Charles L. Mee, Jr.

Staff for this Book

Executive Editor: Marya Dalrymple
Developmental Editor: Linda J. Selden
Design: Timothy Jeffs
Writer: Bonnie J. Slotnick
Illustrations: Kathleen Edwards
Production Coordinator: Patricia S. Williams

QUICK MEALS THE LOW-FAT WAY

■ ■ ■

We're all facing the same dilemma these days: Sure it would be wonderful to serve our families lighter, more healthful meals, but who has the time to search for easy, low-fat recipes or to experiment with quick cooking techniques? Fret no longer. The recipes you've been seeking—from taste-tempting appetizers to sin-free desserts—can all be found in this book. And the suggestions on the following pages, and with each recipe, will make cooking the quick, light, and healthy way easier than you ever imagined.

Every recipe included in the book conforms to the American Heart Association's recommendations for fat intake; in each, fat provides no more than 30 percent of the total calories. In addition, every recipe is accompanied by a nutritional analysis (see page 5) prepared by Hill Nutrition Associates, Inc., of Florida. We are grateful to Lynne Hill, R.D., for her advice and expertise.

We also provide preparation and cooking times for each recipe. Keep in mind that these times are approximate and will vary depending on your expertise in the kitchen and on the cooking equipment you use.

All of the recipes were developed in the Sunset test kitchens. If you have comments or suggestions, please let us hear from you. Write to us at:

Sunset Books/Cookbook Editorial
80 Willow Road
Menlo Park, CA 94025

If you would like to order additional copies of any of our books, call us at 1 (800) 634-3095 or check with your local bookstore. For special sales, bulk orders, and premium sales information, call Sunset Custom Publishing & Special Sales at (415) 324-5547.

FRONT COVER
Top right, Vermicelli with Turkey (page 136); bottom left, Island Pork with Coconut Couscous (page 107). Design by **Vasken Guiragossian;** photography by **Chris Shorten;** food styling by **Susan Massey;** art direction by **Susan Bryant Caron.**

PHOTOGRAPHY CREDITS
Pages 49, 70–72, 91, 92, 125, 126, 128, 161, 163, 164, 181–184, 202, 204, 240: photography by **Allan Rosenberg;** associate photographer, **Allen V. Lott;** photo styling by **Sandra Griswold;** food styling by **Heidi Gintner;** assistant food and photo styling, **Elizabeth C. Davis.** Pages 50, 90, 162: photography by **Kevin Sanchez;** photo styling by **Susan Massey.** Pages 51, 52, 89, 201, 203: photography by **Nikolay Zurek;** photo styling by **Susan Massey.** Pages 69, 127, 237–239: photography by **Keith Ovregaard;** photo styling by **Susan Massey;** food styling by **Cynthia Scheer.**

CONTENTS

Guidelines for Healthy Eating 4   Cooking Quick, Light, and Healthy 6
Staples for a Healthy Kitchen 8   Tools for a Healthy Kitchen 10
Quick Low-Fat Menus 12

APPETIZERS & SOUPS 15

SALADS 35

SEAFOOD 57

POULTRY 85

MEATS 103

PASTA 117

MEATLESS DISHES 143

SIDE DISHES 169

DESSERTS 193

WEEKEND COOKING 217

INDEX 252

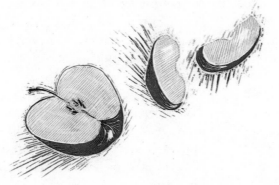

GUIDELINES FOR HEALTHY EATING

Once you've decided to try to eat more healthfully, you should know what nutrients your body requires, which foods supply those substances, and how to choose nutritious foods. What follows are some basic guidelines for a healthy diet.

Striking a Balance

"Moderation in all things" is hardly a new concept, but it's the perfect description of a healthy eating plan. The idea is to eat a wide variety of foods, focusing on vegetables, fruits, grains, and legumes (beans, peas, and lentils). These low-fat or fat-free foods supply nearly all the important nutrients you need and are relatively low in calories (compared with meat, for example).

Avoid foods that derive a high proportion of their calories from fat. These include cheese, mayonnaise, and salad dressings, as well as candy bars, snack chips, cookies, and pastries. Many of these fatty foods are now available in lower-fat forms, but are often high in sugar and calories.

The energy-in/energy-out balance is critical in controlling your weight: If you don't consume more calories than you burn, you won't put on pounds. So as you're watching what you eat, consider adding exercise to your life as well (just walking 15 minutes a day is a good start).

The Basics

Based on current findings, we recommend the following:

• Get at least 55 percent of your total caloric intake from carbohydrates; about 15 percent from protein; and no more than 30 percent from fats. This balance will keep you energetic, enable your body to repair itself, and help you maintain a healthy weight. Most carbohydrates you eat should be *complex* (starches) rather than *simple* (sugars).

• Minimize consumption of saturated fats, which raise blood cholesterol and increase the risk of heart disease. Saturated fats are found mainly in meat, whole-milk dairy products, and solid fats such as butter.

• Consume no more than 300 milligrams of cholesterol per day. Cholesterol is found only in foods from animal sources—meat, poultry, fish and shellfish, dairy products, and eggs. There is cholesterol in the lean portion as well as the fat and skin of meat and poultry. An excessive intake of cholesterol is a contributing factor in elevated blood cholesterol and heart disease; saturated fat, however, has a greater effect than dietary cholesterol—so limit *both*.

• Consume 25 to 35 grams of dietary fiber each day. Fiber is the indigestible portion of plant products—vegetables, fruits, grains, legumes, nuts, and seeds; it is not found in any food from animal sources. The two types of dietary fiber are *insoluble* and *soluble*. Insoluble fiber ("roughage"), found in foods such as wheat bran, keeps your digestive tract healthy, helping you avoid constipation; it may work to prevent certain types of cancer as well. Soluble fiber, in citrus fruits, barley, and oats (among other foods), aids in controlling the body's cholesterol and blood-sugar levels.

• Keep your intake of sodium below 2,500 milligrams per day. For people who are sodium-sensitive, too much dietary sodium can result in elevated blood pressure. But even if your blood pressure is fine, there is some evidence that excessive sodium intake may contribute to other health problems, such as osteoporosis. Most of the sodium Americans consume comes not from the salt shaker but from processed foods and fast foods.

• Be sure to get enough calcium, especially if you're a woman. Sufficient dietary calcium intake during the teenage years will help prevent osteoporosis, the bone-thinning disease that often strikes older women. Young people ages 11 to 24, and pregnant women, need 1,200 milligrams of calcium per day; women over 50 should get 1,500 milligrams; others require 800 milligrams per day. Dairy products are the best sources of calcium, but you can also get your calcium from broccoli, kale, spinach, canned salmon and sardines (eaten with the bones).

• Keep an eye on your iron intake, especially if you are a vegetarian or if you're a woman. Until menopause, women need more iron than men (15 milligrams for women, 10 milligrams for men). Choose lower-fat iron sources, such as oysters, mussels, tuna, turkey, tofu, oatmeal, soybeans, spinach, and artichokes.

• Drink plenty of water. Water helps you digest your food, enables your body to deal with changes in temperature, and keeps your skin healthy. The old eight-glasses-a-day rule is a good one, but remember that you also get water from foods you eat, especially vegetables and fruits. Drink extra fluids in hot weather and when you're exercising.

Smart Shopping

Read the nutrition labeling when shopping for packaged foods. Nearly everything from brown rice to candy bars now carries a standardized "Nutrition Facts" label, which gives the calorie count; total calories from fat; and total fat, saturated fat, cholesterol, sodium, carbohydrate, dietary fiber, sugars, and protein. Four vitamins and minerals—vitamin A, vitamin C, calcium, and iron—must be listed on the label; inclusion of other vitamins and minerals is optional.

The ingredients list on a product is also helpful, especially if you are aware that the ingredients are listed in descending order by weight. If the label on a box of "Healthy Mountain Bran Muffins" reads, "Flour, sugar, corn oil, brown sugar, molasses, whole eggs, honey, bran . . ." you'll know that bran is not really a major ingredient.

The recipes in this book call for lots of fresh produce, which should also be selected with care. The best supermarkets stock an amazing variety of fresh fruits and vegetables. If your local market doesn't offer a wide selection of quality produce, look around for a greengrocer or ethnic market that does.

About Our Nutritional Data

For each recipe, we provide a nutritional analysis stating calorie count; percentage of calories from fat; grams of total fat and saturated fat; milligrams of cholesterol and sodium; grams of carbohydrates, fiber, and protein; and milligrams of calcium and iron. Generally, the analysis applies to a single serving, based on the number of servings given for each recipe and the amount of each ingredient. If a range is given for the number of servings and/or the amount of an ingredient, the analysis is based on the average of the figures given.

The nutritional analysis does not include optional ingredients or those for which no specific amount is stated. If an ingredient is listed with a substitution, the information was calculated using the first choice.

Cooking Quick, Light, and Healthy

Acook who wants to prepare quick, light, and healthy meals must not only be aware of the basics of a healthy diet, but also must be organized and efficient. As you'll see from the suggestions that follow, forethought, a well-ordered kitchen, and the knowledge of a few low-fat cooking tricks can help a lot when you want to turn out nutritious, delicious meals in no time.

Think ahead, think light

Fast, low-fat meals begin long before you peel an onion or turn on the oven: They begin with advance planning. Setting down a week's dinner menus on paper may sound like a chore, but it will save you lots of time (and fat) in the long run. And it's easy to do. Choose main dishes first, then select suitable side dishes that offer contrasts of taste, texture, and color. Appetizers are nice for festive dinners (though unnecessary for every day), and desserts don't have to be an issue—serve fruit, store-bought low-fat cookies, frozen yogurt, and the like, saving homemade treats for special occasions. Be sure to plan a few meatless meals each week, and serve seafood and skinless poultry often.

Shop smart

A healthy menu plan will lead naturally to a well-organized shopping list. Keep up your stock of kitchen staples (see pages 8–9) so that your weekly supermarket run will mainly be for fresh produce, meat, poultry, seafood, and dairy products. With your shopping tailored to your weekly menu plans, you won't end up dashing to the market for an overlooked ingredient—and you'll be less likely to randomly toss tempting high-fat foods into your shopping cart.

When choosing fresh vegetables and fruits, be flexible according to what's in season and looks freshest: Why waste time searching for the Brussels sprouts for Wednesday's dinner, when broccoli will do just fine?

And if you need to put together a meal on really short notice, consider the packaged ready-to-use, prewashed salad and slaw mixtures now sold in many markets. Or take advantage of the precut, sliced, and chopped vegetables available at salad bars.

Store it right

Cooking goes more smoothly and quickly if you store things logically. Stack canned goods so that the labels are visible; line up spices alphabetically. If you do a lot of baking, shelve all the appropriate ingredients in one place. You can transfer some foods to different containers to simplify their use: Pour cooking oil into a squeeze bottle (a catsup dispenser is just right) to make it easier to measure small amounts; store granulated sugar, cereal, and healthy staples such as rice, dried beans, and lentils in large, covered plastic pitchers, which make for tidy dispensing and measuring when you need them.

Order on the counter

Keep favorite seasonings—salt, pepper, cinnamon, and liquid hot pepper sauce, for instance—within easy reach. Utensils, too, should be placed where you can grab them quickly: Cooking spoons and forks, pancake turners, tongs, and the like should hang near the stove; implements such as wooden spoons, measuring spoons, rubber spatulas, whisks, and peelers are handy if kept in a countertop crock. Infrequently used utensils and appliances, such as a waffle iron or ice-cream maker, are best stashed away in high cupboards. The more counter space you can clear, the better.

Ready, set, go!

Always read the recipe through to familiarize yourself with the order of the steps. If you have a few moments free the night before (or in the morning), do some of the "prep work": You can mix dry ingredients, chop vegetables, wash greens, or marinate meat or poultry. When it's time to make dinner, lay out all your ingredients and utensils before you start. If boiling water is needed for pasta or vegetables, put the pot on to boil first thing. As you finish with a pan or utensil, wash it on the spot, or set it in the sink to soak, if necessary (soak greasy pans and those from starchy foods like rice in hot water; pans from protein foods like eggs or cheese should be soaked in cold water).

Double duty

A little planning can allow you an occasional night off from cooking—without resorting to high-fat takeout meals. If your weekend schedule is light, you can cook for the week ahead (see the Weekend Cooking chapter, pages 217–251). Many dishes can be refrigerated for a few days, or frozen. To freeze soups or stews, cut the top off a half-gallon milk carton; place a heavy-duty plastic bag in the carton, then ladle in the food. When frozen, remove the bag and you'll have a cube-shaped package that stacks neatly in the freezer.

Quick and healthy tricks

Here are some chefs' tricks especially suited to preparing quick, low-fat meals:
• For an oil sauté, heat the nonstick skillet or wok before putting in the oil (you need only a tablespoon to sauté vegetables). The food will absorb less oil than if you start with cold oil.
• Briefly chill canned broth in the can in the freezer; you can then lift any fat right off.
• Don't add oil to pasta cooking water. Just add the pasta slowly and stir to separate. Once the pasta is cooked, add the sauce as soon as possible to prevent sticking.
• For mashed potatoes, beat the hot potato cooking water into the potatoes rather than butter and milk. It makes them fluffier, and fat free. You could also use fat-free broth.
• Coat the blade of your knife with no-stick spray before chopping sticky dried fruit or sun-dried tomatoes.
• Before eating an orange or tangerine, or juicing a lemon, grate the zest or remove it with a vegetable peeler and save it for future use: Wrap it in foil and freeze it until needed.
• Wash sandy greens like spinach in tepid, not cold, water: The grit will rinse out faster.
• Slice large mushrooms in an egg slicer.

Staples for a Healthy Kitchen

Fast, slimmed-down meals require some fresh thinking about ingredients. Because fat enhances flavor, lower-fat meals made with lean meats, poultry, fish, grains, beans, and pasta require heightened seasonings. Here are some healthy staples and high-impact flavorings to keep on hand.

Beans, canned and dried Canned beans come in many varieties—garbanzos, black beans, red kidney beans, cannellini, pinto beans, and more—and are great time-savers. Rinse and drain before using to remove the high-sodium canning liquid. Dried beans require presoaking and must cook for about an hour, but you may prefer their firmer texture and fresher flavor. Cook a big batch and refrigerate to use over the course of a week.

Bread It's best to purchase fresh bread as needed, but breadstuffs freeze well if wrapped airtight; warming before serving enhances flavor. Keep a variety of low-fat breads on hand —whole wheat, rye, pumpernickel, pitas, bagels, corn and flour tortillas, English muffins, French and Italian bread are options.

Broth Homemade broth (carefully defatted) is best, but making it is a time-consuming process. Canned fat-free reduced-sodium chicken broth and canned beef broth are great time-savers and flavor boosters. Freeze leftover broth in small containers.

Cheese Think of full-flavored (often high-fat) cheeses as seasonings. Some useful varieties are feta (a salty Greek cheese), Parmesan and romano (sharp Italian grating cheeses), Gorgonzola (an Italian blue cheese), and jalapeño jack (mellow jack cheese with chile bits). Some cheeses come in convenient pregrated form, but freshly grated cheese has a superior flavor.

Chiles and hot sauces Fresh jalapeños and serranos give salsa a real kick; canned diced green chiles add milder flavor. Liquid hot pepper seasoning is a potent sauce made from chiles; add it a few drops at a time, to taste.

Chutney Mango chutney, a sweethot Indian condiment, is often served with curries; it also adds a lively note to poultry dishes and is a tasty fatfree sandwich spread.

Citrus zest The outermost colored layer of citrus peel, called zest, is powerfully fragrant; strip it off with a vegetable peeler, or use a handy, inexpensive tool called a zester.

Cocoa powder Chocolate in its lowest-fat form, cocoa is great for healthy desserts; it also adds depth of flavor to savory sauces.

Cornstarch This finely powdered corn flour lets you create glossy thickened sauces with no additional fat.

Fruit, dried Intensely sweet dried apricots, cranberries, currants, and raisins are delightful in desserts and hot cereals and with poultry and meats. Store them in airtight containers.

Garlic Smashing whole garlic cloves under the flat side of a knife blade to break the skin makes them much easier to peel. Mince the cloves with a knife or put them through a press, as you prefer. Store garlic in a cool, dark, airy place. Garlic powder and garlic salt are pale imitations of the real thing and not worth the little time they save.

Ginger Hot and pungent, fresh ginger is a must for many Asian dishes. Store it in the freezer—frozen, it grates beautifully. If the skin is thin, you don't even need to peel it.

Grains Converted rice takes a few minutes longer to cook than regular long-grain white rice; Indian basmati, jasmine, and other flavored rices are nice for a change. Brown rice takes about 45 minutes to cook, but if you presoak it overnight, it will cook in about half the time. Bulgur is a special form of cracked wheat that is presteamed so that it cooks quickly. Look for protein-packed quinoa at a health-food store if your supermarket doesn't carry it.

Herbs and spices You'll want to stock a full complement of dried herbs, but parsley, basil, cilantro, and mint are widely available fresh, and their flavor is terrific. Stand fresh herbs in a glass of water, like a bouquet, and refrigerate them. Dried herbs and spices lose their flavor over time, so replace them if they're years old.

Jams and jellies Strawberry, raspberry, and plum jam and orange marmalade are wonderful additions to sauces for poultry and meat; use them to sweeten desserts, too.

Milk products, low-fat These wonders include evaporated skim milk; low-fat cottage cheese; part-skim ricotta and mozzarella; reduced-fat Cheddar; low-fat and nonfat yogurt; Neufchâtel (reduced-fat cream cheese); and nonfat sour cream. Use nonfat (skim) milk and 1% milk whenever possible; 2% milk has almost as much fat as whole milk.

Mushrooms, dried Powerhouses of savory flavor, dried mushrooms range from the inexpensive "generic" type sold at supermarkets to pricier porcini, shiitakes, and chanterelles.

Mustard Prepared Dijon mustard seasons and thickens sauces and dressings but adds no fat. Try herbed Dijon in salad dressings.

Oils Use a vegetable oil, such as corn or safflower, or a mild olive oil for most cooking purposes; dark, toasty-flavored Oriental sesame oil is for seasoning. To make flavored oils, see pages 46 and 48, as well as pages 54–56.

Pasta Choose a dried pasta made from semolina flour for the best texture. Fresh filled pastas such as tortellini are sold in the dairy case. Couscous, a tiny, beadlike pasta, is a versatile side dish. It requires only brief steeping in boiling water.

Soy sauce This salty Asian sauce comes in many styles and strengths; our recipes use reduced-sodium soy sauce because regular soy is extremely high in sodium.

Tofu Incredibly versatile, tofu (bean curd) can stand in for many high-fat ingredients. Use the firm type for slicing or dicing, and soft tofu for dips and spreads.

Tomatoes, sun-dried Buy dry-packed (not oil-packed) tomatoes; soak them in hot water to soften and plump them.

Vinegars Choose from rich, mellow balsamic, mild rice, fruity raspberry, tangy cider, and classic red- and white-wine vinegars.

Wines, liqueurs, liquors Dry red and white wine are cooking basics; sherry, brandy, marsala, and vermouth add a lovely "bouquet." Rum and fruit liqueurs go into desserts and sauces.

Tools for a Healthy Kitchen

Appliances, utensils, and gadgets can be a great boon to a healthy kitchen if they're well designed, sturdy, and carefully chosen. The tools described here will help you turn out nutritious, low-fat meals in the shortest possible time.

Food processor Both full-size and mini processors are useful for creating quick, low-fat meals: Use the big machine to chop meat (make your own lean ground turkey from skinless turkey breast); to slice, chop, or julienne raw vegetables for salads and stir-fries; and to purée cooked beans and starchy vegetables for thickening soups without added fat. The mini is great for chopping a single onion or carrot, fresh herbs, or a few nuts. To cut down on clean-up time, process any dry ingredients first; then, without washing the bowl, chop vegetables and other moist foods.

Blender For whirling nonfat yogurt and fruit into a nutritious shake, or blending low-fat cottage cheese into a savory dip, nothing beats an old-fashioned blender. A new twist is the immersion blender, a hand-held device that's like a streamlined electric mixer with a single bladelike beater. It can be used right in a pot on the stove to mash potatoes or purée chunky soups. An immersion blender, used in a deep, narrow bowl, can also churn icy cold low-fat or nonfat milk

into a healthy whipped topping for pies, cakes, and other desserts (add powdered sugar and vanilla to your taste).

Gravy strainer This ingenious tool, which looks like a liquid measuring cup, makes it easy to defat stock, soup, sauce, or gravy. When you pour the liquid into the cup, the fat rises to the top; you can then pour off the defatted portion through the spout, which is set at the base of the cup. There are also various models of skimmer-ladles, which serve the same purpose but work by lifting the fat from the surface of the soup or sauce.

Grill topper The healthiest barbecue meals feature skinless poultry, fish or shellfish, and plenty of vegetables—foods that can be difficult to cook on a regular wire grill rack. A smooth sheet-steel grill topper, perforated with small holes, allows you to cook and turn delicate foods without destroying them.

Kitchen scale It's easy to fool yourself about how much cheese or chocolate you're adding to a dish; only a scale will give you the facts. Although cooks in the United States are accustomed to measuring dry ingredients in cups, Europeans (and professional chefs) more often *weigh* flour, sugar, and the like. (Both types of measurements are given in our recipes, so you can use the method you prefer.) The most useful kitchen scales have a reset function that allows you to place a bowl or other container on the platform, and to weigh several ingredients, one after another, in a single bowl.

Kitchen shears Flavorful, fat-free ingredients such as sun-dried tomatoes, dried fruit, and dried mushrooms can be tricky to chop; kitchen shears with sturdy stainless blades are the perfect solution. They're great for mincing fresh herbs, too: Hold the herb sprigs right over your bowl or pan and snip away. It's also a snap to "chop" tomatoes right in the can.

Knives Perhaps the most important accessories for efficient cooking are good, sharp knives. The basics are a small paring knife, a utility knife with a 6-inch blade, and an 8- or 10-inch chef's knife. You might like to have a bread knife and a serrated slicing knife (good for delicate foods like angel food cake) as well. High-carbon stainless-steel knives are most practical for the home cook: They hold a good edge and will not rust or discolor. There are manual knife sharpeners available that make home sharpening nearly foolproof. Store knives in a block or on a wall-mounted magnetic rack to protect the blades from damage.

Measuring cups and spoons Accurate measurements are important for good results, particularly in baking. You can also use these tools to educate yourself about portion sizes of familiar foods: Exactly what does a cup of breakfast cereal or a tablespoon of peanut butter look like? You'll need a set of dry measuring cups in graduated sizes as well as a liquid measuring cup of clear glass or plastic, with measurements marked on the side. The most accurate measuring spoons are narrow and deep rather than wide and flat.

Nonstick pans These indispensable utensils have been tremendously improved since they were first introduced. The pans can be used over higher heat, and their surfaces are more durable (although it's still a good idea to use nylon or wooden tools with nonstick cookware). In addition to stovetop utensils, you can buy nonstick baking and broiling pans. High-quality, heavy-weight nonstick pots and pans cost more, but they absorb and retain heat much more evenly than thin utensils.

Pressure cooker You can save lots of time by cooking dried beans and dense root vegetables (like turnips) in a pressure cooker rather than by conventional methods. Since pressure cookers tend to be large, this pot (with a different lid) can double as a soup or pasta pot. If you've ever heard alarming tales about pressure cookers being dangerous, rest assured that the newer pots have improved safety features.

Rotary cheese grater Low-fat meals call for small amounts of rather sharp cheeses, like Parmesan and romano, and the more finely the cheese is grated, the more flavorful the dish will seem. A rotary grater quickly cranks out fine, fluffy particles of cheese that melt instantly on contact with hot food.

Steamer Whether it's a folding metal basket or a Chinese-style bamboo model, a steamer is a necessity. Use this healthful cooking method for all sorts of vegetables, as well as fish and thin cuts of poultry. You don't need to add any fat at all, and the food retains its nutrients because it is not immersed in water.

Yogurt cheese funnel Plain low-fat and fat-free yogurt can be transformed into a healthy substitute for sour cream, mayonnaise, or cream cheese if drained in this special gadget, available at housewares stores. You can also fashion your own "funnel": Line a strainer or colander with dampened cheesecloth, or use one of the funnel-shaped drip coffee filters that sit atop a cup.

Wok Stir-frying is a centuries-old technique, and the wok is the traditional and most efficient pan for this quick, low-fat way of cooking. Choose a heavy, nonstick wok and get one with a lid, so it can also be used for steaming. An optional metal ring will keep the wok steady over an electric burner.

QUICK LOW-FAT MENUS

GAME-DAY BUFFET

■ ■ ■

You'll give football fans plenty to choose from with this delightful brunch: chicken or shrimp salad, a selection of fresh fruit, and—for those breakfast diehards—eggs, bagels, and hash browns with apples and cheese. Everything but the eggs and hash browns can be prepared ahead.

Litchi, Penne & Chicken Salad (page 39)

Shrimp & Orzo with Pesto Dressing (page 46)

Scrambled Eggs & Bulgur (page 154)

Cheese & Apple Hash Browns (page 176)

Tossed Green Salad with Strawberry Tarragon Dressing (page 41)

Bagels with Reduced-Fat Cream Cheese

Soft Rolls

Carrot and Celery Sticks

Fresh Fruit

Seltzer, Orange Juice, Tomato Juice, Mimosas

FEAST FROM THE SHORE

■ ■ ■

This meal is a seafood-lover's delight. Creamy white bean soup studded with shrimp is followed by garlicky scallops. To save time, make the soup base a day in advance.

Shrimp & White Bean Soup (page 29)

Scallop Scampi (page 75)

Lemon-Caper Rice (page 171)

Mediterranean Squash (page 190)

Hard Rolls

Peach Shortcakes (page 211)

Beer or Zinfandel

MEATLESS CHILI SUPPER

■ ■ ■

This hearty meat-free menu is perfect for a cool autumn night. Follow the delicious Poppy Seed Cake with a night of board games or cards.

Creamy Guacamole (page 24)

Vegetable-Bean Chili (page 147)

Corn Bread

Wilted Spinach Salad with Oranges (page 43)

Lemon Poppy Seed Cake (page 209)

Light or Nonalcoholic Beer

EASY DINNER FOR TWO

■ ■ ■

When it's just the two of you for dinner, chicken breasts over baked apples served with a tomato-spiked pasta side dish are a winning combination. Halve the Pasta Pilaf recipe, or simply save the leftovers for tomorrow's lunch.

Mixed Greens with Shallot Dressing (page 45)

Chicken Breasts Calvados (page 94)

Pasta Pilaf (page 171)

Sesame Breadsticks

Chardonnay

AN ITALIAN LUNCHEON

■ ■ ■

Cheesy ravioli contrast with hearty sautéed kale and white beans in this lunch with an Italian touch. For dessert, offer strawberries sprinkled with freshly squeezed orange juice and grated orange peel, with biscotti alongside.

Endive & Radicchio Salad

Ravioli with Gorgonzola (page 120)

Sautéed Kale with Cannellini (page 187)

Focaccia

Orange Strawberries

Currant Biscotti (page 196)

Seltzer or White Wine

Espresso

A BIRTHDAY DINNER

■ ■ ■

A celebration calls for celebratory dishes: a shrimp salad, salmon fillets in a tangy sauce, garlicky cauliflower and zucchini, and a rich fudge torte for dessert!

Watercress, Butter Lettuce & Shrimp Salad (page 47)

Salmon Sauté with Citrus Sauce (page 64)

Herbed Cauliflower and Zucchini Stir-Fry (page 179)

French Bread

Mocha Almond Fudge Torte (page 207)

White Wine

Espresso or Cappuccino

EARLY SUMMER SUPPER

■ ■ ■

Big bright peppers, red juicy cherries, and tender green snow peas . . . Look for the best produce the season has to offer for this refreshing meal.

Red & Yellow Pepper Salad (page 36)

Lamb Chops with Cherries & Orecchiette (page 110)

Snow Peas with Bacon & Mint (page 190)

Dinner Rolls

Ginger Bars (page 200)

Seltzer or Iced Tea

CASUAL MEXICAN DINNER

■ ■ ■

These informal but delicious dishes will have everyone cheering *"¡Ole!"* The menu serves four with plenty of leftovers; if more guests are expected, double the burrito recipe.

Cherry Tomato Salsa (page 22)

Water-Crisped Tortilla Chips (page 25)

Roasted Bell Pepper & Black Bean Salad (page 40)

Chile Beef Burritos (page 114)

Cocoa-Glazed Carrots & Onions (page 186)

Drunken Cake (page 210)

Beer and Soft Drinks

VEGETARIAN'S DELIGHT

■ ■ ■

When you have invited both vegetarians and omnivores for dinner, try this healthful meal. Even dyed-in-the-wool meat-eaters will dig into the hearty bean cakes.

Mixed Green Salad

Pinto Bean Cakes with Salsa (page 150)

Couscous with Ratatouille & Feta Cheese (page 145)

Roasted Garlic & Broccoli (page 192)

Sourdough Rolls

Frozen Lemon Yogurt with Fresh Berries

PASTA FOR A CROWD

■ ■ ■

Perfect for low-key entertaining, this filling, low-fat meal is sure to please everyone. Double the bruschetta and chard recipes to make a meal for eight.

North Beach Bruschetta (page 17)

Sausage, Basil & Port Fettuccine (page 134)

Italian-Style Swiss Chard (page 188)

Crusty Italian Bread

Fresh Fruit Platter

Hearty Red Wine

A QUICK MEAL FOR THE KIDS

■ ■ ■

This meal will appeal to kids who are slightly adventurous eaters. Tell them the burgers are nut burgers and be sure to leave the pepper flakes out of the corn marinade.

Chicken Noodle Soup (page 31)

Double Wheat Burgers (page 159)

Seasoned Sweet Corn (175)

Chocolate Chip Cookies (page 198)

Low-Fat Milk or Cider

Appetizers
& Soups

Tomato-Crab Quesadillas

Preparation time: **About 15 minutes**
Cooking time: **20 to 30 minutes**

Warm crab, fresh tomatoes, and jack cheese make a great filling for quesadillas. Offer a cool fresh-chile sauce to heat up each serving.

4 medium-size fresh green Anaheim chiles or other large mild chiles (about 7 oz./200 g total)

¼ cup (60 ml) dry white wine

2 small shallots

1 tablespoon (15 ml) lemon juice

1 cup (40 g) firmly packed cilantro leaves

½ cup (58 g) peeled, coarsely chopped jicama

¼ cup (60 ml) fat-free reduced-sodium chicken broth

1 tablespoon (15 ml) honey

2 medium-size firm-ripe tomatoes (about 12 oz./340 g total), finely chopped

4 ounces (115 g) cooked crabmeat

¾ cup (85 g) shredded jack cheese

1 cup (100 g) sliced green onions

10 flour tortillas (each 7 to 9 inches/ 18 to 23 cm in diameter)

Cilantro sprigs

1. To prepare chile sauce, place chiles on a baking sheet. Broil 4 to 6 inches (10 to 15 cm) below heat, turning often, until charred all over (about 8 minutes). Cover with foil and let cool on baking sheet; then remove and discard skins, stems, and seeds.

2. In a blender or food processor, whirl chiles, wine, shallots, and lemon juice until smooth. Pour into a 2- to 3-quart (1.9- to 2.8-liter) pan. Bring to a boil; boil, stirring, until reduced to ⅓ cup (5 to 10 minutes).

3. Return mixture to blender or food processor. Add cilantro leaves and jicama. Whirl until smooth; scrape sides of container several times. With motor running, slowly add broth and honey and whirl to blend. Serve sauce cool or cold. (At this point, you may cover and refrigerate for up to 4 hours. It makes about 1 cup/240 ml.)

4. Place tomatoes in a fine wire strainer and let drain well; discard juice.

5. In a bowl, mix crab, cheese, and onions. Gently mix in tomatoes. Place 5 tortillas in a single layer on 2 lightly oiled large baking sheets. Evenly top tortillas with crab mixture, covering tortillas to within ¾ inch (2 cm) of edges. Top each tortilla with one of the remaining tortillas.

6. Bake in a 450°F (230°C) oven until tortillas are lightly browned (7 to 9 minutes), switching positions of baking sheets halfway through baking.

7. Slide quesadillas onto a serving board; cut each quesadilla into 6 wedges. Garnish with cilantro sprigs. Add chile sauce to taste.

Makes 8 to 10 servings

NUTRIENTS

Per serving: 209 calories (27% calories from fat), 6 g total fat, 2 g saturated fat, 23 mg cholesterol, 308 mg sodium, 29 g carbohydrates, 2 g fiber, 9 g protein, 150 mg calcium, 2 mg iron

GARLIC CHICKEN BITES WITH TOMATO-RAISIN SAUCE

Preparation time: **About 10 minutes**
Baking time: **18 to 20 minutes**

Serve these tender, garlicky chunks of skinless chicken hot from the oven, with a spicy-sweet tomato-raisin sauce.

- 3 tablespoons minced cilantro
- 2 teaspoons coarsely ground pepper
- 8 cloves garlic, minced
- 1 pound (455 g) skinless, boneless chicken thighs, cut into 1½-inch (3.5-cm) chunks
- ⅓ cup (80 ml) tomato sauce
- 1 tablespoon firmly packed brown sugar
- 1 tablespoon (15 ml) distilled white vinegar or cider vinegar
- ½ cup (73 g) raisins

1. In a small bowl, mix cilantro, pepper, and three-fourths of the garlic; rub mixture over chicken. Place chicken pieces well apart in a lightly oiled 10- by 15-inch (25- by 38-cm) rimmed baking pan.

2. Bake in a 500°F (260°C) oven until chicken is lightly browned and no longer pink in center; cut to test (18 to 20 minutes).

3. Meanwhile, in a food processor or blender, whirl remaining garlic, tomato sauce, sugar, vinegar, and raisins until raisins are chopped.

4. Serve chicken hot, with tomato-raisin sauce.

Makes 4 servings

NUTRIENTS

Per serving: 221 calories (18% calories from fat), 5 g total fat, 1 g saturated fat, 94 mg cholesterol, 225 mg sodium, 22 g carbohydrates, 2 g fiber, 24 g protein, 42 mg calcium, 2 mg iron

NORTH BEACH BRUSCHETTA

Preparation time: **About 20 minutes**
Cooking time: **About 7 minutes**

These cheese-and-pastrami-topped appetizers are named for the section of San Francisco where great Italian food can still be found. Keep an eye on the baking time so that the little open sandwiches don't dry out.

- ⅔ cup (150 g) nonfat ricotta cheese
- ¼ cup (25 g) shredded carrot
- ¼ cup (35 g) dried currants or raisins
- 2 tablespoons thinly sliced green onion
- 1 tablespoon (15 ml) Dijon mustard
- ½ teaspoon dried basil
- 8 ounces (230 g) unsliced crusty bread
- 4 ounces (115 g) thinly sliced pastrami
- ⅓ cup (40 g) shredded part-skim mozzarella cheese

1. In a medium-size bowl, combine ricotta, carrot, currants, onion, mustard, and basil. Set aside.

2. Cut bread in half horizontally. Set halves crust side down; if needed, cut a thin slice from cut side of halves to make each piece about 1 inch (2.5 cm) thick. Trim crust side of each piece so bread sits steadily. Then cut each piece in half crosswise.

3. Spread cut sides of bread with ricotta mixture. Loosely pleat pastrami over ricotta mixture, covering bread. Sprinkle with mozzarella. Arrange bread on a 12- by 15-inch (30- by 38-cm) baking sheet and bake in a 400°F (205°C) oven until mozzarella is melted (about 7 minutes).

Makes 4 servings

NUTRIENTS

Per serving: 271 calories (12% calories from fat), 3 g total fat, 1 g saturated fat, 15 mg cholesterol, 880 mg sodium, 38 g carbohydrates, 3 g fiber, 19 g protein, 345 mg calcium, 3 mg iron

CORN PANCAKES WITH BLACK BEAN SALSA

Preparation time: **About 20 minutes**
Cooking time: **About 6 minutes**

A zesty black bean salsa, tangy with lime and feta cheese, accompanies savory cornmeal pancakes studded with whole corn kernels and diced bell pepper.

BLACK BEAN SALSA:

1 can (about 15 oz./425 g) black beans, drained and rinsed well

1 cup (115 g) peeled, finely chopped jicama

¾ cup (100 g) crumbled feta cheese

3 tablespoons (45 ml) lime juice

⅓ cup (15 g) chopped cilantro

2 tablespoons sliced green onion

2 teaspoons honey

¼ teaspoon crushed red pepper flakes

CORN PANCAKES:

1 tablespoon butter or margarine

1 package (about 10 oz./285 g) frozen corn kernels, thawed and drained

1 large egg

⅓ cup (50 g) diced red bell pepper

⅓ cup (80 ml) nonfat milk

3 tablespoons yellow cornmeal

⅓ cup (40 g) all-purpose flour

1½ teaspoons sugar

1½ teaspoons baking powder

GARNISHES:

Cilantro sprigs (optional)

Lime wedges

1. To prepare salsa, in a large bowl, combine beans, jicama, cheese, lime juice, chopped cilantro, onion, honey, and red pepper flakes. Cover and set aside; stir occasionally.

2. To prepare pancakes, melt butter in a wide nonstick frying pan over low heat. Remove pan from heat. Transfer butter to a large bowl (do not wash frying pan) and add corn, egg, bell pepper, and milk; mix well. In a small bowl, stir together cornmeal, flour, sugar, and baking powder. Add

20 MINUTES OR LESS

2 cans (about 27 oz./765 g each) fava beans, drained and rinsed; or 3 cans (about 15 oz./425 g each) butter beans, drained and rinsed

⅓ cup (35 g) minced red onion

¼ cup (15 g) coarsely chopped fresh oregano or 1½ tablespoons dried oregano

2 tablespoons (30 ml) olive oil

¼ cup (60 ml) red wine vinegar

Salt and pepper

Sliced crusty bread; or miniature pita bread rounds (each about 3 inches/8 cm) in diameter

FAVAS WITH HERBS

1. In a bowl, mix beans, onion, oregano, oil, and vinegar. Season to taste with salt and pepper. (At this point, you may cover and refrigerate for up to 1 day; serve at room temperature.)

2. To serve, spoon onto bread or use bread for dipping.

Makes about 5 cups (1.2 liters)
About 12 servings

Per serving: 107 calories (21% calories from fat), 3 g total fat, 0.3 g saturated fat, 0 mg cholesterol, 205 mg sodium, 17 g carbohydrates, 0.1 g fiber, 5 g protein, 34 mg calcium, 2 mg iron

cornmeal mixture to corn mixture and stir just until dry ingredients are evenly moistened.

3. Place frying pan over medium-high heat. When pan is hot, drop batter into pan in 3-tablespoon (45-ml) portions, spacing portions of batter about 3 inches (8 cm) apart. Use a spoon to spread each portion into about a 3-inch (8-cm) circle. Cook pancakes until tops look dry and bottoms are lightly browned (1 to 2 minutes); turn pancakes with a wide spatula and continue to cook until lightly browned on other side (about 1 more minute). As pancakes are cooked, transfer them to a platter and keep warm.

4. Garnish pancakes with cilantro sprigs (if desired) and lime wedges; serve with black bean salsa to add to taste.   *Makes 6 servings*

NUTRIENTS

Per serving: 240 calories (30% calories from fat), 8 g total fat, 1 g saturated fat, 56 mg cholesterol, 571 mg sodium, 35 g carbohydrates, 5 g fiber, 11 g protein, 204 mg calcium, 4 mg iron

White Bean Pâté with Tomato Relish

Preparation time: **About 20 minutes**
Cooking time: **15 to 20 minutes**

When guests arrive unexpectedly, don't despair: Whip up this easy bean pâté in the blender or food processor and serve it on crisp toasts.

BAGUETTE TOASTS:

1 long, slender baguette (about 8 oz./230 g, about 25 inches/63 cm long), cut diagonally into 24 slices

TOMATO RELISH:

1 large tomato (about 8 oz./230 g), chopped and drained well

1 to 2 tablespoons chopped parsley

1 tablespoon (15 ml) balsamic vinegar

1 tablespoon drained capers

½ teaspoon sugar

Pepper

WHITE BEAN PÂTÉ:

1 can (about 15 oz./425 g) cannellini (white kidney beans), drained and rinsed

1½ teaspoons Oriental sesame oil

¾ teaspoon chopped fresh thyme or ¼ teaspoon dried thyme

¼ teaspoon grated lemon peel

4 teaspoons lemon juice

1 clove garlic, peeled

¼ teaspoon salt, or to taste

GARNISH:

Thyme sprigs

1. Arrange bread slices in a single layer (overlapping as little as possible) in shallow 10- by 15-inch (25- by 38-cm) baking pans. Bake in a 325°F (165°C) oven until crisp and tinged with brown (15 to 20 minutes). Transfer toast to a rack to cool.

2. In a small bowl, stir together tomato, parsley, vinegar, capers, and sugar; season to taste with pepper. Set aside; stir occasionally.

3. In a blender or food processor, combine beans, oil, chopped thyme, lemon peel, lemon juice, garlic, and salt. Whirl until almost smooth. Spoon bean pâté into a small serving bowl or crock and garnish with thyme sprigs.

4. Offer bean pâté to spread over toast. Spoon tomato relish over pâté, using a slotted spoon.
                              Makes 8 to 12 servings

NUTRIENTS

Per serving: 86 calories (14% calories from fat), 1 g total fat, 0.2 g saturated fat, 0 mg cholesterol, 224 mg sodium, 15 g carbohydrates, 2 g fiber, 4 g protein, 25 mg calcium, 0.9 mg iron

CURRY BEEF IN LETTUCE

Preparation time: **About 15 minutes**
Cooking time: **About 15 minutes**

Pears flavor the curry in this Asian-inspired beef appetizer. If you like, roll the filling in the lettuce to eat out of hand.

1 teaspoon cornstarch

6 tablespoons (90 ml) cider vinegar

3 large firm-ripe pears (about 1½ lbs./680 g total)

12 ounces (340 g) lean ground beef

4 ounces (115 g) mushrooms, chopped

½ cup (75 g) golden raisins

¼ cup (55 g) firmly packed brown sugar

2 tablespoons curry powder

2 tablespoons tomato paste

½ teaspoon ground cinnamon

¼ cup (25 g) sliced green onions

2 tablespoons chopped parsley

½ cup (120 ml) plain nonfat yogurt

1 head butter lettuce (about 6 oz./ 170 g), separated into leaves, rinsed, and crisped

Salt

1. In a large bowl, blend cornstarch with 2 tablespoons (30 ml) of the vinegar. Peel, core, and finely chop pears; gently stir into vinegar mixture and set aside.

2. Crumble beef into a wide nonstick frying pan or wok; add mushrooms and raisins. Stir-fry over medium-high heat until meat is browned (about 8 minutes). Add water, 1 tablespoon (15 ml) at a time, if pan appears dry. Spoon off and discard fat from pan.

3. Stir in sugar, ¼ cup (60 ml) water, remaining ¼ cup (60 ml) vinegar, curry powder, tomato paste, and cinnamon. Bring to a boil; then stir until almost all liquid has evaporated (about 3 minutes).

4. Add pear mixture; stir until mixture boils and thickens slightly. Transfer to a serving bowl; stir in onions and parsley.

5. To serve, spoon meat mixture and yogurt into lettuce leaves; season to taste with salt.

Makes 4 to 6 servings

NUTRIENTS

Per serving: 319 calories (21% calories from fat), 8 g total fat, 3 g saturated fat, 43 mg cholesterol, 129 mg sodium, 50 g carbohydrates, 6 g fiber, 18 g protein, 101 mg calcium, 4 mg iron

CUCUMBER & JICAMA SALSA

Preparation time: **About 25 minutes**

Crisp and fresh, this pale green-and-white salsa is best if served within 6 hours after it's made, or it loses its crispness. Look for jicama in stores that sell fine-quality produce.

1 medium-size cucumber (about 8 oz./ 230 g), peeled, seeded, and diced

About 1 pound (455 g) jicama, peeled, rinsed, and diced

⅓ cup (15 g) chopped fresh basil

⅓ cup (35 g) sliced green onions

¼ cup (60 ml) lemon juice

¼ cup (60 ml) plain nonfat yogurt

1 small fresh jalapeño chile, seeded and minced

Salt

1. In a nonmetal bowl, mix cucumber, jicama, basil, onions, lemon juice, yogurt, and chile; season to taste with salt. (At this point, you may cover and refrigerate the salsa for up to 6 hours.)

Makes about 6 cups (1.4 liters)

NUTRIENTS

Per ¼ cup: 11 calories (2% calories from fat), 0.03 g total fat, 0 g saturated fat, 0 mg cholesterol, 4 mg sodium, 2 g carbohydrates, 0.4 g fiber, 0.5 g protein, 15 mg calcium, 0.2 mg iron

Nachos with Pita Chips

Preparation time: **About 20 minutes**
Cooking time: **About 25 minutes**

Garlicky hummus sweetened with carrots is an unusual and colorful topping for nachos, with pita chips as the base.

4   whole wheat pita breads (each about 5 inches/12.5 cm in diameter), cut crosswise into halves

1   pound (455 g) carrots (about 8 small carrots), cut into 1-inch (2.5-cm) lengths

2   cans (about 15 oz./425 g each) garbanzo beans, drained and rinsed

¼   cup (60 ml) lemon juice

3   or 4 cloves garlic, peeled

4   teaspoons (20 ml) Oriental sesame oil
    Salt

1   jar (about 7 oz./200 g) roasted red peppers, drained, rinsed, and chopped

1   cup (about 4 oz./115 g) shredded reduced-fat jack cheese
    Lemon wedges

1   cup (240 ml) plain nonfat yogurt

1. Carefully peel pita bread halves apart; stack halves, then cut stack into 3 equal wedges. Spread wedges in a single layer on 2 large baking sheets. Bake in a 350°F (175°C) oven until browned and crisp (about 15 minutes), switching positions of baking sheets halfway through baking. Let cool on baking sheets on racks.

2. Meanwhile, in a 2- to 3-quart (1.9- to 2.8-liter) pan, combine carrots and 4 cups (950 ml) water. Bring to a boil over medium-high heat; then reduce heat, cover, and simmer, stirring occasionally, until carrots are tender when pierced but still bright in color (about 15 minutes). Drain well.

3. Pour carrots into a food processor or blender and add beans, lemon juice, garlic, and oil. Whirl until smoothly puréed. Season to taste with salt. Spoon bean mixture onto a large ovenproof rimmed platter; spread out to make an oval. Top with red peppers and sprinkle with cheese.

4. Bake in a 400°F (205°C) oven until bean mixture is hot in center (about 10 minutes). Remove from oven. Tuck some of the pita chips around edge of platter; serve remaining chips alongside. Serve with lemon wedges to squeeze to taste, and offer yogurt to spoon over nachos to taste.

Makes 8 servings

NUTRIENTS

Per serving: 267 calories (24% calories from fat), 7 g total fat, 3 g saturated fat, 10 mg cholesterol, 491 mg sodium, 38 g carbohydrates, 7 g fiber, 14 g protein, 224 mg calcium, 2mg iron

Lime Salsa

Preparation time: **About 25 minutes**

Tomatillos add tartness to this salsa. Remove their papery husks and rinse off the sticky coating before using them.

1   large ripe red or yellow tomato (about 8 oz./230 g), finely diced

8   medium-size tomatillos (about 8 oz./230 g total), husked, rinsed, and chopped

¼   cup (38 g) minced red or yellow bell pepper

2   tablespoons minced red onion

1   teaspoon grated lime peel

1   tablespoon (15 ml) lime juice

1. In a nonmetal bowl, mix tomato, tomatillos, bell pepper, onion, lime peel, and lime juice. (At this point, you may cover and refrigerate for up to 4 hours before serving.)

Makes about 4 cups (950 ml)

NUTRIENTS

Per ¼ cup: 9 calories (11% calories from fat), 0.1 g total fat, 0 g saturated fat, 0 mg cholesterol, 2 mg sodium, 2 g carbohydrates, 0.3 g fiber, 0.4 g protein, 3 mg calcium, 0.1 mg iron

CHERRY TOMATO SALSA

Preparation time: **About 25 minutes**

For the very best flavor, use fully ripe, juicy tomatoes in this mild salsa. Try some in the Salsa Fish Soup (page 27).

- 2 cups (about 12 oz./340 g) red cherry tomatoes, cut into halves
- ⅓ cup (15 g) lightly packed cilantro leaves
- 2 fresh jalapeño chiles, seeded
- 1 clove garlic, peeled
- 2 tablespoons (30 ml) lime juice
- 2 tablespoons thinly sliced green onion
  Salt and pepper

1. Place tomatoes, cilantro, chiles, and garlic in a food processor; whirl just until coarsely chopped (or chop coarsely with a knife).

2. Turn mixture into a nonmetal bowl; stir in lime juice and onion. Season to taste with salt and pepper. (At this point, you may cover and refrigerate for up to 4 hours.)

Makes about 2 cups (470ml)

NUTRIENTS

Per ¼ cup: 12 calories (9% calories from fat), 0.1 g total fat, 0 g saturated fat, 0 mg cholesterol, 5 mg sodium, 3 g carbohydrates, 0.7 g fiber, 0.5 g protein, 6 mg calcium, 0.3 mg iron

SPINACH-BEAN ROLL-UPS

Preparation time: **About 25 minutes**

A spinach-flecked cheese spread and a zesty bean filling are wrapped inside flour tortillas for this refreshing meal-starter. Try them as part of a light lunch on a summer day, followed by a fresh fruit salad.

- 1 package (about 10 oz./285 g) frozen chopped spinach, thawed and squeezed dry
- 1 large package (about 8 oz./230 g) nonfat cream cheese or Neufchâtel cheese, at room temperature
- ½ cup (40 g) grated Parmesan cheese
- 2 tablespoons (30 ml) nonfat mayonnaise
- 1 teaspoon prepared horseradish, or to taste
- ⅛ teaspoon ground allspice, or to taste
- 1 can (about 15 oz./425 g) cannellini (white kidney beans)
- 1 tablespoon (15 ml) seasoned rice vinegar (or 1 tablespoon/15 ml distilled white vinegar plus ½ teaspoon sugar)
- 2 teaspoons honey
- ¾ teaspoon chopped fresh thyme or ¼ teaspoon dried thyme
- ⅓ cup (35 g) thinly sliced green onions
- ⅓ cup (20 g) finely chopped parsley
- 6 reduced-fat flour tortillas (each about 7 inches/18 cm in diameter)
  About 48 whole fresh spinach leaves, rinsed and crisped
  Thyme sprigs (optional)

1. In a medium-size bowl, combine chopped spinach, cream cheese, Parmesan cheese, mayonnaise, horseradish, and allspice. Mix well; set aside.

2. Drain beans, reserving liquid. Rinse beans well, place in another medium-size bowl, and add vinegar, honey, and chopped thyme. Coarsely mash beans with a spoon; add enough of the reserved bean liquid to give mixture a spreadable consistency (do not make it too thin). Set aside. In a small bowl, combine onions and parsley; set aside.

3. To assemble roll-ups, divide spinach mixture equally among tortillas. With a spatula, spread spinach mixture to cover tortillas evenly. Then top tortillas equally with bean filling; carefully spread to cover spinach mixture. Sprinkle with onion mixture. Roll up each tortilla tightly to enclose filling. (At this point, you may cover tightly and refrigerate for up to 3 hours.)

4. Line 6 individual plates with spinach leaves. With a serrated knife, carefully cut each tortilla diagonally into 4 equal slices (wipe knife clean between cuts, if desired); arrange on spinach-lined plates. Garnish with thyme sprigs, if desired.

Makes 6 servings

NUTRIENTS

Per serving: 230 calories (17% calories from fat), 4 g total fat, 1 g saturated fat, 9 mg cholesterol, 964 mg sodium, 33 g carbohydrates, 7 g fiber, 15 g protein, 388 mg calcium, 3 mg iron

1 cup (about 4 oz./115 g) shredded jalapeño jack cheese

About 12 cups (250 g) Water-Crisped Tortilla Chips (page 25) or purchased tortilla chips

Cilantro leaves

1. Prepare Lime Salsa and refrigerate.

2. Prepare Lean Refried Black Beans. Spoon beans onto a large, ovenproof rimmed platter; spread out evenly to make an oval. Top beans evenly with corn, then sprinkle with cheese. Bake in a 400°F (205°C) oven until hot in center (about 10 minutes).

3. Remove bean mixture from oven. Tuck some of the tortilla chips around edge of platter; serve remaining chips alongside. Garnish with cilantro.

4. To serve, spoon bean mixture onto plates; top with some of the Lime Salsa. Offer chips for dipping; add more salsa to taste.

Makes 12 servings

NUTRIENTS

Per serving: 159 calories (27% calories from fat), 5 g total fat, 2 g saturated fat, 13 mg cholesterol, 243 mg sodium, 23 g carbohydrates, 4 g fiber, 8 g protein, 108 mg calcium, 1 mg iron

Mexican-Style Corn Nachos

Preparation time: **About 20 minutes**
Cooking time: **About 25 minutes**

Though created north of the border, this colorful appetizer was inspired by three Mexican staples: black beans, corn, and flour tortillas. Here the tortillas come as chips.

About 1½ cups (360 ml) Lime Salsa (page 21)

Lean Refried Black Beans (page 172)

4 cups (665 g) cooked yellow or white corn kernels (from 6 to 8 ears corn); or 2 packages (about 10 oz./285 g each) frozen corn kernels, thawed

CORN SALSA

Preparation time: **About 30 minutes**

Enjoy the season's best fresh corn in a sweet-sharp salsa flavored with orange peel and juice, chiles, and mint. Offer it with Water-Crisped Tortilla Chips (page 25).

3 medium-size ears corn (about 1½ lbs./680 g total), about 8 inches (20 cm) long, husks and silk removed

½ cup (73 g) finely chopped European cucumber

⅓ cup (80 ml) lime juice

¼ cup (25 g) thinly sliced green onions

1 tablespoon grated orange peel

3 tablespoons (45 ml) orange juice

2 tablespoons chopped fresh mint or 1 teaspoon dried mint

1 teaspoon cumin seeds

1 or 2 fresh jalapeño chiles, seeded and minced

Salt

1. In a 5- to 6-quart (5- to 6-liter) pan, bring about 3 quarts (2.8 liters) water to a boil over high heat. Add corn, cover, and cook until hot (4 to 6 minutes). Drain; then let cool. With a sharp knife, cut kernels from cobs.

2. In a nonmetal bowl, mix corn, cucumber, lime juice, onions, orange peel, orange juice, mint, cumin seeds, and chiles; season to taste with salt. (At this point, you may cover and refrigerate for up to 4 hours.)

Makes about 3 cups (710 ml)

NUTRIENTS

Per ¼ cup: 32 calories (9% calories from fat), 0.4 g total fat, 0.1 g saturated fat, 0 mg cholesterol, 6 mg sodium, 7 g carbohydrates, 1 g fiber, 1 g protein, 7 mg calcium, 0.3 mg iron

---

20 MINUTES OR LESS

1 teaspoon grated lemon peel

2 tablespoons (30 ml) lemon juice

1 medium-size soft-ripe avocado

1 cup (210 g) low-fat (1%) cottage cheese

2 to 4 cloves garlic, peeled

⅛ teaspoon salt

2 tablespoons minced cilantro

1 fresh jalapeño or serrano chile, seeded and minced

1 tablespoon thinly sliced green onion

2 small tomatoes (about 8 oz./230 g total), finely chopped and drained well

Cilantro sprigs

About 8 cups (180 g) Water-Crisped Tortilla Chips (page 25), purchased tortilla chips, or bite-size pieces of raw vegetables

CREAMY GUACAMOLE

1. Place lemon peel and lemon juice in a blender or food processor. Pit and peel avocado; transfer avocado to blender along with cottage cheese, garlic, and salt. Whirl until smoothly puréed.

2. Spoon guacamole into a serving bowl and gently stir in minced cilantro, chile, onion, and half the tomatoes. (At this point, you may cover and refrigerate for up to 2 hours; stir before serving.)

3. To serve, garnish with remaining tomatoes and cilantro sprigs. Scoop guacamole onto tortilla chips.

Makes about 3 cups (830 ml)
About 8 servings

Per serving: 138 calories (23% calories from fat), 4 g total fat, 0.7 g saturated fat, 1 mg cholesterol, 215 mg sodium, 21 g carbohydrates, 3 g fiber, 6 g protein, 90 mg calcium, 0.9 mg iron

BLACK BEAN SALSA WITH CRISP VEGETABLES

Preparation time: **About 25 minutes**

Canned black beans seasoned with fresh lime juice, cilantro, green onions, and tomatoes make a quick, satisfying dip.

1 can (about 15 oz./425 g) black beans

2 tablespoons (30 ml) lime juice

⅓ cup (15 g) coarsely chopped cilantro

½ cup (50 g) thinly sliced green onions

3 small pear-shaped (Roma-type) tomatoes (about 6 oz./170 g total), seeded and chopped

   Salt and pepper

1 small jicama (about 1 lb./455 g)

1 small English cucumber (about 10 oz./285 g), thinly sliced

   Cilantro sprigs

1. Drain beans, reserving 1 tablespoon (15 ml) of the liquid. Place reserved liquid and half the beans in a medium-size bowl. Add lime juice, then mash beans with a fork or potato masher until smooth. Stir in remaining beans, chopped cilantro, onions, and tomatoes. Season to taste with salt and pepper. (At this point, you may cover and refrigerate for up to 4 hours.)

2. Peel and rinse jicama; cut in half lengthwise, then thinly slice each half. Arrange jicama and cucumber slices on a platter and set aside. If made ahead, cover and refrigerate for up to 2 hours.

3. Spoon bean salsa into a serving bowl; garnish with cilantro sprigs. Serve bean salsa with jicama and cucumber slices to taste.

Makes about 30 servings

NUTRIENTS

Per serving: 20 calories (6% calories from fat), 0.1 g total fat, 0 g saturated fat, 0 mg cholesterol, 46 mg sodium, 4 g carbohydrates, 1 g fiber, 1 g protein, 10 mg calcium, 0.4 mg iron

WATER-CRISPED TORTILLA CHIPS

Preparation time: **About 5 minutes**
Baking time: **About 6 minutes**

Making your own tortilla chips is an easy way to cut down on fat. A cup of these flour chips has just 2 grams of fat (the corn chips have even less). Compare this amount with the 8 grams of fat you typically find in just an ounce of packaged tortilla chips.

6 corn tortillas (each 6 inches/15 cm in diameter) or 6 flour tortillas (each 7 to 9 inches/18 to 25 cm in diameter)

   Salt (optional)

1. Dip tortillas, one at a time, in hot water; drain briefly. Season tortillas to taste with salt, if desired. Stack tortillas; then cut the stack into 6 to 8 wedges.

2. Arrange wedges in a single layer on large baking sheets. Do not overlap wedges. Bake in a 500°F (260°C) oven for 4 minutes. With a metal spatula, turn wedges over; continue to bake until crisp and browned, about 2 more minutes. (At this point, you may let cool; then store airtight at room temperature for up to 5 days.)

Makes about 4 cups (80 g) corn chips
Makes about 6 cups (125 g) flour chips

NUTRIENTS

Per cup of corn chips: 83 calories (10% calories from fat), 0.9 g total fat, 0.1 g saturated fat, 0 mg cholesterol, 60 mg sodium, 17 g carbohydrates, 2 g fiber, 2 g protein, 66 mg calcium, 0.5 mg iron

Per cup of flour chips: 114 calories (20% calories from fat), 2 g total fat, 0.4 g saturated fat, 0 mg cholesterol, 167 mg sodium, 19 g carbohydrates, 1 g fiber, 3 g protein, 44 mg calcium, 1 mg iron

SWEET POTATOES WITH CAVIAR

Preparation time: **About 15 minutes**
Baking time: **About 25 minutes**

Crisp slices of baked sweet potato are a delectable base for sour cream and crunchy golden caviar. Use inexpensive caviar, such as flying fish roe *(tobiko)*, crab roe *(masago)*, or lumpfish, whitefish, or salmon caviar. Many are available at your supermarket.

2   pounds (905 g) sweet potatoes (each about 2 inches/5 cm in diameter), scrubbed

Vegetable oil cooking spray

¼   cup (64 g) caviar

⅓   to ½ cup (80 to 120 ml) light sour cream

1. Cut off and discard ends of unpeeled potatoes, then cut potatoes crosswise into ¼-inch-thick (6-mm-thick) slices. Spray two 10- by 15-inch (25- by 38-cm) rimmed baking pans with cooking spray. Arrange potato slices in a single layer in pans. Spray with cooking spray.

2. Bake in a 400°F (205°C) oven until slices are golden brown on bottom (about 15 minutes); turn slices over and continue to bake until browned on top (about 10 more minutes). Potatoes at edges of pans brown faster, so move these to centers of pans when you turn slices.

3. While sweet potatoes are baking, place caviar in a fine wire strainer and rinse under cool running water; drain well, then refrigerate until ready to use.

4. Lift potato slices onto a platter in a single layer. Dot each slice with sour cream, then with caviar.
Makes about 60 appetizers

NUTRIENTS

Per appetizer: 22 calories (23% calories from fat), 0.6 g total fat, 0.1 g saturated fat, 7 mg cholesterol, 19 mg sodium, 4 g carbohydrates, 0.5 g fiber, 0.6 g protein, 3 mg calcium, 0.1 mg iron

CRAB & RICE CHOWDER

Preparation time: **About 15 minutes**
Cooking time: **20 to 25 minutes**

Bright bell pepper, broccoli, and corn help extend less than half a pound of crabmeat into a nourishing soup for six.

1   tablespoon (15 ml) vegetable oil

1   small onion, finely chopped

8   ounces (230 g) mushrooms, thinly sliced

½   teaspoon dried thyme

2   cups (145 g) coarsely chopped broccoli flowerets

1   small red bell pepper, finely chopped

2   cups (470 ml) fat-free reduced-sodium chicken broth

2   cups (470 ml) low-fat (2%) milk

1   can (about 17 oz./480 g) cream-style corn

6   ounces (170 g) cooked crabmeat

3   cups (390 g) cooked long-grain white rice

Salt and pepper

1. Heat oil in a 4- to 5-quart (3.8- to 5-liter) pan over medium-high heat. Add onion, mushrooms, and thyme; cook, stirring often, until vegetables begin to brown (about 8 minutes). Add broccoli and bell pepper; cook, stirring often, until broccoli turns bright green and begins to soften (about 4 minutes).

2. Stir in broth, milk, and corn; cook just until heated through (5 to 7 minutes); do not boil. Stir in crab and rice and cook just until heated through (2 to 3 minutes). Season with salt and pepper.
Makes 6 servings

NUTRIENTS

Per serving: 318 calories (14% calories from fat), 5 g total fat, 1 g saturated fat, 35 mg cholesterol, 578 mg sodium, 54 g carbohydrates, 4 g fiber, 16 g protein, 170 mg calcium, 3 mg iron

FISH & PEA SOUP

Preparation time: **About 15 minutes**
Cooking time: **About 20 minutes**

Ladle chunks of lean white fish and tarragon-scented broth into wide bowls, then serve with a crusty baguette.

3   large leeks (about 1¾ lbs./795 g total)

2   tablespoons (30 ml) vegetable oil

1   clove garlic, minced or pressed

1   large carrot (about 4 oz./115 g), finely chopped

1   cup (240 ml) dry white wine or fat-free reduced-sodium chicken broth

6   cups (1.4 liters) fat-free reduced-sodium chicken broth

1   dried bay leaf

1   teaspoon dried tarragon

1½ to 2 pounds (680 to 905 g) skinless rockfish or lingcod fillets

1   package (about 10 oz./285 g) frozen tiny peas, broken apart

    Salt and pepper

1. Cut off and discard root ends and green tops of leeks; discard coarse outer leaves. Split leeks lengthwise and rinse well; thinly slice crosswise.

2. Heat oil in a 5- to 6-quart (5 to 6-liter) pan over medium heat. Add leeks, garlic, and carrot; cook, stirring occasionally, until leeks are soft but not browned (6 to 8 minutes). Add wine, broth, bay leaf, and tarragon. Bring to a boil; then reduce heat to medium-low and cook for 5 minutes.

3. Meanwhile, rinse fish, pat dry, and cut into 1-inch (2.5-cm) chunks. To pan, add fish and peas. Cover and cook until fish is just opaque but still moist in thickest part; cut to test (about 6 minutes). Season to taste with salt and pepper.

Makes 6 servings

NUTRIENTS

Per serving: 285 calories (24% calories from fat), 7 g total fat, 1 g saturated fat, 46 mg cholesterol, 808 mg sodium, 17 g carbohydrates, 3 g fiber, 32 g protein, 68 mg calcium, 3 mg iron

SALSA FISH SOUP

Preparation time: **About 5 minutes**
Cooking time: **About 20 minutes**

This simple soup makes a hearty starter before a salad main course, or it can be a meal in itself when you want dinner *fast*. The results are delicious, cleanup is minimal, and you can be out of the kitchen in under half an hour—or in less than 15 minutes, if you use quick-cooking rice.

6   cups (1.4 liters) fat-free reduced-sodium chicken broth

⅔   cup (124 g) regular or quick-cooking rice

2   cups (330 g) frozen corn kernels

1   pound (455 g) skinned, boned mild-flavored white-fleshed fish (such as rockfish or lingcod), cut into 1-inch/2.5-cm chunks

1   cup (240 ml) refrigerated or canned tomato-based chunk-style salsa; or 1 cup (240 ml) canned Mexican-style stewed tomatoes

    Lime wedges

1. In a 5- to 6-quart (5- to 6-liter) pan, combine broth and rice. Bring to a boil over high heat. Reduce heat, cover, and simmer until rice is tender to bite (about 15 minutes; about 5 minutes for quick-cooking rice).

2. Add corn, fish, and salsa to pan. Cover and simmer soup until fish is just opaque in thickest part; cut to test (about 5 minutes). Offer lime wedges to squeeze into soup to taste.

Makes 4 servings

NUTRIENTS

Per serving: 338 calories (7% calories from fat), 3 g total fat, 0.6g saturated fat, 40 mg cholesterol, 1,679 mg sodium, 48 g carbohydrates, 2 g fiber, 31 g protein, 22 mg calcium, 2 mg iron

ASPARAGUS, SHRIMP & WATERCRESS SOUP

Preparation time: **About 20 minutes**
Cooking time: **About 10 minutes**

There's more than a hint of spring in this light but satisfying soup. Each bowlful brings together vivid green watercress, blushing pink shrimp, and delicate strands of pasta. Serve with seeded breadsticks and a crisp white wine, such as Pinot Grigio.

12 ounces (340 g) asparagus

7 cups (1.7 liters) fat-free reduced-sodium chicken broth

1 teaspoon grated lemon peel

1 teaspoon dried tarragon

⅛ teaspoon ground white pepper

1 ounce (30 g) dried capellini

12 ounces (340 g) medium-size raw shrimp (40 to 45 per lb.), shelled and deveined

2 cups (70 g) lightly packed watercress sprigs, rinsed and drained

3 tablespoons (45 ml) lemon juice

1. Snap off and discard tough ends of asparagus, then cut spears into ½-inch-thick (1-cm-thick) diagonal slices. Set aside.

2. In a 4- to 5-quart (3.8- to 5-liter) pan, combine broth, lemon peel, tarragon, and white pepper; bring to a boil over high heat. Add capellini; when broth returns to a boil, reduce heat and boil gently for 4 minutes. Add shrimp and asparagus. Continue to cook just until shrimp are opaque in center; cut to test (about 3 minutes). Stir in watercress, then lemon juice. Serve immediately (greens will lose their bright color as soup stands).

Makes 4 to 6 servings

NUTRIENTS

Per serving: 121 calories (9% calories from fat), 1 g total fat, 0.2 g saturated fat, 84 mg cholesterol, 996 mg sodium, 9 g carbohydrates, 1 g fiber, 19 g protein, 71 mg calcium, 2 mg iron

GINGERED SHRIMP & CAPELLINI SOUP

Preparation time: **About 30 minutes**
Cooking time: **About 10 minutes**

Steeping—cooking food in hot liquid off the heat—helps preserve delicate textures and flavors. In this easy Asian-inspired soup, shrimp are quickly steeped in a ginger-infused broth. Keep fresh ginger in the freezer and just use what you need.

6 cups (1.4 liters) fat free reduced-sodium chicken broth

2 tablespoons minced fresh ginger

12 ounces (340 g) extra-large shrimp (26 to 30 per lb.), shelled and deveined

2 ounces (55 g) dried capellini, broken into 2-inch (5-cm) pieces

1 package (about 10 oz./285 g) frozen tiny peas, thawed

½ cup (50 g) thinly sliced green onions

Fish sauce (*nam pla or nuoc mam*), oyster sauce, or reduced-sodium soy sauce

1. Combine broth and ginger in a 4- to 5-quart (3.8- to 5-liter) pan. Cover and bring to a boil over high heat. Stir in shrimp and pasta; cover, immediately remove pan from heat, and let stand for 4 minutes (do not uncover). Check shrimp for doneness (shrimp should be opaque but moist-looking in center of thickest part; cut to test). If shrimp are still translucent, cover and let stand until done, checking at 2-minute intervals.

2. Add peas, cover, and let stand until heated through (about 3 minutes).

3. Stir in onions and ladle soup into bowls. Offer fish sauce to add to taste.

Makes 4 to 6 servings

NUTRIENTS

Per serving: 172 calories (20% calories from fat), 4 g total fat, 1 g saturated fat, 84 mg cholesterol, 299 mg sodium, 18 g carbohydrates, 3 g fiber, 19 g protein, 68 mg calcium, 3 mg iron

SHRIMP & WHITE BEAN SOUP

Preparation time: **About 15 minutes**
Cooking time: **About 30 minutes**

No one needs to know that this elegant soup is made with canned beans! The pretty garnish of tiny pink shrimp and the appealing flavor will attract all the attention.

1 tablespoon (15 ml) vegetable oil

2 large onions, chopped

1 cup (120 g) thinly sliced celery

3 cloves garlic, minced or pressed

2 cans (about 15 oz./425 g each) white kidney beans (cannellini), drained and rinsed

4 cups (950 ml) fat-free reduced-sodium chicken broth

¼ cup (60 ml) catsup

⅓ pound (150 g) small cooked shrimp

¼ cup (15 g) chopped parsley

Salt and pepper

1. Heat oil in a 4- to 5-quart (3.8- to 5-liter) pan over medium-high heat. Add onions, celery, and garlic; cook, stirring often, until all vegetables are browned (about 20 minutes).

2. Transfer vegetable mixture to a food processor or blender; add half the beans and 2 cups (470 ml) of the broth. Whirl until smoothly puréed, then return to pan. Purée remaining beans with remaining 2 cups (470 ml) broth; add to pan. Stir in catsup. (At this point, you may cover and refrigerate until next day.)

3. To serve, stir soup over medium heat until hot. Ladle soup into 4 bowls; top equally with shrimp and parsley. Season to taste with salt and pepper.

Makes 4 servings

NUTRIENTS

Per serving: 297 calories (22% calories from fat), 7 g total fat, 0.7 g saturated fat, 73 mg cholesterol, 1,172 mg sodium, 38 g carbohydrates, 8 g fiber, 21 g protein, 103 mg calcium, 4 mg iron

TURKEY ALBÓNDIGAS SOUP

Preparation time: About 30 minutes
Cooking time: About 15 minutes

This flavorful and nutritious meal-in-a-bowl is the perfect choice for a warming autumn supper. It features turkey meatballs, tomatoes, carrots, and spinach in a light broth. If you like, you can make the meatballs a day ahead. Offer homemade corn muffins or Warm Tortillas (page 160) alongside.

- 1 pound (455 g) lean ground turkey
- ½ cup (73 g) cooked brown or white rice
- ¼ cup (30 g) all-purpose flour
- ¼ cup (60 ml) water
- 1 teaspoon ground cumin
- 1 can (about 14½ oz./415 g) pear-shaped (Roma-style) tomatoes
- 6 cups (1.4 liters) fat-free reduced-sodium chicken broth
- 4 cups (950 ml) beef broth
- 2 cups (340 g) chopped onions
- 6 medium-size carrots (about 1½ lbs./680 g total), thinly sliced
- 1 teaspoon dried oregano
- 2 teaspoons chili powder
- 12 ounces (340 g) stemmed spinach leaves, rinsed well and drained (about 3 cups lightly packed)
- ⅓ cup (15 g) chopped cilantro
- 1 or 2 limes, cut into wedges

1. To prepare turkey meatballs, in a bowl, mix the turkey, rice, flour, water, and cumin. Shape mixture into 1- to 1½-inch (2.5- to 3.5-cm) balls and place, slightly apart, in a 10- by 15-inch (25- by 38-cm) rimmed baking pan. Bake in a 450°F (230°C) oven until well browned (about 15 minutes). Pour off fat; set aside. (At this point, you may make ahead, let cool; then cover and refrigerate until next day.)

2. Pour tomatoes and their liquid into an 8- to 10-quart (8- to 10-liter) pan; break tomatoes up with a spoon. Add chicken broth, beef broth, onions, carrots, oregano, and chili powder.

3. Bring to a boil over high heat; then reduce heat to low. Add meatballs and simmer for 10 minutes. Stir in spinach and cilantro and cook until greens are wilted (about 3 more minutes).

4. To serve, ladle soup into bowls; serve with lime wedges to squeeze into soup to taste.

Makes 6 to 8 servings

NUTRIENTS

Per serving: 235 calories (27% calories from fat), 8 g total fat, 2 g saturated fat, 47 mg cholesterol, 341 mg sodium, 28 g carbohydrates, 6 g fiber, 19 g protein, 137 mg calcium, 4 mg iron

CHICKEN NOODLE SOUP

Preparation time: **About 20 minutes**
Cooking time: **About 25 minutes**

Fresh zucchini and tomato enliven not only the appearance but also the flavor of this traditional chicken noodle soup. The recipe calls for packaged dried wide egg noodles, but you can substitute 6 ounces (170 g) of freshly made pasta noodles if you prefer. Should you want to make the pasta noodles yourself, you can freeze them for up to 2 months. Don't thaw the frozen noodles before adding them to the soup, however.

 1 teaspoon vegetable oil
 1 large onion, chopped
 8 cups (1.9 liters) fat-free reduced-sodium chicken broth
 3 cloves garlic, minced or pressed
 ½ teaspoon dried thyme
 ¼ teaspoon pepper
 2 large carrots (about 8 oz./230 g total), thinly sliced
 ½ cup (60 g) chopped celery
 5 ounces (140 g) dried wide egg noodles
 3 cups (420 g) shredded cooked chicken
 1 small zucchini (about 3 oz./85 g), chopped
 1 medium-size tomato (about 5 oz./140 g), peeled, seeded, and chopped
 2 tablespoons chopped parsley

1. Heat oil in a 5- to 6-quart (5- to 6-liter) pan over medium-high heat. Add onion and cook, stirring often, until onion is soft (about 5 minutes); if pan appears dry or onion sticks to pan bottom, stir in water, 1 tablespoon (15 ml) at a time.

2. Add broth, garlic, thyme, and pepper; bring to a boil. Stir in carrots, celery, and noodles; reduce heat, cover, and boil gently just until carrots are barely tender to bite (about 10 minutes).

3. Stir in chicken, zucchini, and tomato; heat until steaming. Garnish with parsley.

Makes 6 servings

NUTRIENTS

Per serving: 276 calories (23% calories from fat), 7 g total fat, 2 g saturated fat, 91 mg cholesterol, 955 mg sodium, 24 g carbohydrates, 3 g fiber, 29 g protein, 48 mg calcium, 2 mg iron

MARITATA SOUP

Preparation time: **About 10 minutes**
Cooking time: **About 15 minutes**

If you're sodium sensitive, then you might want to use reduced-sodium beef broth in this recipe and slightly reduce the amount of Parmesan cheese.

12 cups (2.8 liters) beef broth
 8 ounces (230 g) dried vermicelli, broken into short lengths
 ½ cup (40 g) freshly grated Parmesan cheese
 ⅓ cup (80 g) Neufchâtel or nonfat cream cheese
 3 large egg whites

1. Bring broth to a boil in a 5- to 6-quart (5- to 6-liter) pan over high heat. Stir in pasta; reduce heat, cover, and simmer just until pasta is tender to bite (8 to 10 minutes).

2. Meanwhile, beat Parmesan cheese, Neufchâtel cheese, and egg whites with an electric mixer or in a blender until well combined.

3. Slowly pour about 1 cup of the simmering broth into cheese mixture, mixing to combine. Then return cheese-broth mixture to pan, stirring constantly until hot (2 to 3 minutes).

Makes 8 servings

NUTRIENTS

Per serving: 188 calories (26% calories from fat), 5 g total fat, 2 g saturated fat, 11 mg cholesterol, 2,613 mg sodium, 22 g carbohydrates, 0.7 g fiber, 9 g protein, 82 mg calcium, 2 mg iron

Black Bean Soup

Preparation time: **About 10 minutes**
Cooking time: **About 30 minutes**

To make this filling soup, you can use home-cooked dried beans, if you like, but we suggest that you speed up preparation with the canned or instant refried variety.

Soup:

2 teaspoons vegetable oil

1 large onion, chopped

1¾ or 2¾ cups (420 or 650 ml) fat-free reduced-sodium chicken broth

1 large can (about 28 oz./795 g) tomatoes

3 cans (about 15 oz./425 g each) black beans, drained, rinsed, and puréed; or 1 package (about 7 oz./200 g) instant refried black bean mix

1 fresh jalapeño chile, seeded and minced

2 teaspoons cumin seeds

Condiments:

Cheddar cheese

Plain nonfat yogurt

Cilantro leaves

Lime wedges

Water-Crisped Tortilla Chips (page 25)

1. In a 5- to 6-quart (5- to 6-liter) pan, combine oil and onion. Cook over medium heat, stirring often, until onion is deep golden (about 20 minutes). Add 1¾ cups (420 ml) broth (or 2¾ cups/650 ml if using instant beans).

2. Add tomatoes and their liquid to pan; break tomatoes up with a spoon. Stir in beans, chile, and cumin seeds. Bring to a boil; then reduce heat and simmer, uncovered, until soup is thick and flavors are blended (7 to 10 minutes).

3. To serve, ladle soup into bowls. Add condiments to taste.   *Makes 4 servings*

NUTRIENTS

Per serving: 327 calories (17% calories from fat), 6 g total fat, 1 g saturated fat, 0 mg cholesterol, 795 mg sodium, 51 g carbohydrates, 15 g fiber, 21 g protein, 154 mg calcium, 5 mg iron

20 MINUTES OR LESS

2 cans (about 15 oz./425 g each) pickled beets

About 4 cups (950 ml) plain nonfat yogurt

1 cup (240 ml) vegetable broth

Dill sprigs

Pepper

Creamy Beet Borscht

1. Drain beets, reserving 1½ cups (360 ml) of the liquid. In a large bowl, combine beets, reserved liquid, 4 cups (950 ml) of the yogurt, and broth. In a food processor or blender, whirl beet mixture, about a third at a time, until smoothly puréed. (At this point, you may cover and refrigerate until next day.)

2. Serve borscht cool or cold. To serve, ladle into wide soup bowls. Add additional yogurt to taste and garnish with dill sprigs. Season to taste with pepper.   *Makes 6 to 8 servings*

Per serving: 113 calories (4% calories from fat), 0.5 g total fat, 0.2 g saturated fat, 3 mg cholesterol, 582 mg sodium, 19 g carbohydrates, 1 g fiber, 8 g protein, 276 mg calcium, 1 mg iron

SWEET POTATO SOUP

Preparation time: **About 20 minutes**
Cooking time: **About 25 minutes**

Despite their rich flavor, sweet potatoes contain no more calories by weight than thin-skinned potatoes or russets. This smooth sweet potato purée, accented with curry and sherry, makes a sophisticated starter for a special meal.

- 4 medium-large sweet potatoes (about 3 lbs./1.35 kg total), peeled and diced

  About 6 cups (1.4 liters) fat-free reduced-sodium chicken broth

- 1½ tablespoons curry powder

- ¼ cup (65 g) tomato paste

- 2 tablespoons (30 ml) lemon juice

- ¼ cup (60 ml) dry sherry

  Salt and pepper

  Cilantro leaves

1. In a 4- to 5-quart (3.8- to 5-liter) pan, combine potatoes and 6 cups (1.4 liters) of the broth. Bring to a boil over medium-high heat; reduce heat, cover, and boil gently until potatoes are soft enough to mash readily (about 20 minutes). With a slotted spoon, transfer potatoes to a food processor or blender; add curry powder and about ½ cup (120 ml) of the cooking broth. Whirl until puréed.

2. Return sweet potato purée to pan; stir in tomato paste, lemon juice, and sherry. (At this point, you may cover and refrigerate for up to a day.)

3. To serve, reheat soup over medium heat, stirring often, until hot. If soup is too thick, thin with a little more broth. Season to taste with salt and pepper. Garnish with cilantro.

Makes 8 to 10 servings

NUTRIENTS

Per serving: 146 calories (3% calories from fat), 0.5 g total fat, 0.1 g saturated fat, 0 mg cholesterol, 503 mg sodium, 30 g carbohydrates, 4 g fiber, 5 g protein, 32 mg calcium, 1 mg iron

SPRING VEGETABLE SOUP WITH SHELLS

Preparation time: **About 25 minutes**
Cooking time: **About 15 minutes**

Fresh and light, this quick-to-make springtime soup takes advantage of crunchy, sweet asparagus. Each bowlful is enriched with a generous helping of seasoned tiny shrimp.

- 8 cups (1.9 liters) fat-free reduced-sodium chicken broth

- 2 cups (220 g) diced carrots

- 4 ounces/115 g (about 1 cup) dried small shell-shaped pasta

- 2 cups (270 g) thinly sliced asparagus

- 1 package (about 10 oz./285 g) frozen tiny peas

- 1¼ to 1½ pounds (565 to 680 g) tiny cooked shrimp

- ½ cup (50 g) thinly sliced green onions

- ¼ cup (15 g) minced parsley

  Parsley sprigs (optional)

  Salt and pepper

1. Bring broth to a boil in a 5- to 6-quart (5- to 6-liter) pan over high heat. Stir in carrots and pasta; reduce heat, cover, and boil gently just until carrots and pasta are tender to bite (8 to 10 minutes; or according to package directions).

2. Add asparagus and peas; cook until heated through (about 2 minutes). Remove from heat and keep warm.

3. Combine shrimp, onions, and minced parsley in a small bowl. Ladle soup into bowls and spoon in shrimp mixture. Garnish with parsley sprigs, if desired. Offer salt and pepper to add to taste.

Makes 8 to 10 servings

NUTRIENTS

Per serving: 178 calories (16% calories from fat), 3 g total fat, 1 g saturated fat, 136 mg cholesterol, 312 mg sodium, 18 g carbohydrates, 3 g fiber, 22 g protein, 69 mg calcium, 4 mg iron

TORTELLINI & ESCAROLE SOUP

Preparation time: **About 20 minutes**
Cooking time: **About 25 minutes**

Once hard to find, filled pasta is now readily available in many supermarkets, as well as in pasta shops and some delicatessens. In this recipe, fresh cheese or meat tortellini float in chicken broth along with shredded escarole and other vegetables. Nutmeg and lemon enhance the soup's flavors. Grate the nutmeg, if you have the time; it has a much stronger flavor than the preground variety.

1 tablespoon (15 ml) olive oil

1 large onion, chopped

2 large carrots (about 8 oz./230 g total), chopped

1 strip lemon zest, about ¼ inch by 4 inches (6 mm by 10 cm)

10 cups (2.4 liters) fat-free reduced-sodium chicken broth

1 package (about 9 oz./255 g) fresh cheese or meat tortellini or ravioli

1 package (about 10 oz./285 g) frozen tiny peas, thawed

8 ounces/230 g (about 6 cups) shredded escarole

Freshly grated or ground nutmeg

Lemon wedges

Salt

1. Heat oil in a 5- to 6-quart (5- to 6-liter) pan over medium-high heat. Add onion, carrots, and lemon zest. Cook, stirring, until onion is soft (5 to 8 minutes).

2. Add broth and bring to a boil over high heat. Add pasta; reduce heat and boil gently, stirring occasionally, just until pasta is tender to bite (4 to 6 minutes; or according to package directions).

3. Stir in peas and escarole; cook just until escarole is wilted (1 to 2 minutes). Remove and discard zest.

4. Ladle soup into bowls. Dust generously with nutmeg. Offer lemon and salt to add to taste.

Makes 8 servings

NUTRIENTS

Per serving: 193 calories (30% calories from fat), 7 g total fat, 2 g saturated fat, 13 mg cholesterol, 316 mg sodium, 27 g carbohydrates, 4 g fiber, 11 g protein, 92 mg calcium, 1 mg iron

SALADS

RED & YELLOW PEPPER SALAD

Preparation time: **About 25 minutes**

Show off the season's best bell peppers in this nutritious salad. Since you use the peppers as edible individual bowls—choose bright, glossy ones that are firm and well shaped, and that will make a pretty presentation.

- 5 large yellow bell peppers (about 2½ lbs./1.15 kg total)
- 1 large red bell pepper (about 8 oz./230 g), seeded and diced
- ⅔ cup (76 g) peeled, minced jicama
- 2 tablespoons minced cilantro
- 1½ tablespoons (23 ml) distilled white vinegar
- 1 teaspoon honey

  About ⅛ teaspoon ground red pepper (cayenne), or to taste

1. Set 4 of the yellow bell peppers upright, then cut off the top quarter of each. Remove and discard seeds from pepper shells; set shells aside. Cut out and discard stems from top pieces of peppers; then dice these pieces and transfer to a large nonmetal bowl.

2. Seed and dice remaining yellow bell pepper and add to bowl. Then add red bell pepper, jicama, cilantro, vinegar, honey, and ground red pepper; mix gently.

3. Spoon pepper mixture equally into pepper shells. (At this point, you may cover and refrigerate salad for up to 4 hours.)

Makes 4 servings

NUTRIENTS

Per serving: 90 calories (5% calories from fat), 0.6 g total fat, 0.1 g saturated fat, 0 mg cholesterol, 7 mg sodium, 21 g carbohydrates, 5 g fiber, 3 g protein, 29 mg calcium, 1 mg iron

WARM CHINESE CHICKEN SALAD

Preparation time: **About 20 minutes**
Cooking time: **About 5 minutes**

Offer this stir-fried Asian-style salad winter or summer. The cooking time is so brief that you won't heat up your kitchen preparing it. For the best results, serve this salad at once, just as soon as the greens are wilted from the heat of the topping.

- ⅓ cup (80 ml) seasoned rice vinegar (or ⅓ cup/80 ml distilled white vinegar plus 2 teaspoons sugar)
- 1 tablespoon (15 ml) reduced-sodium soy sauce
- 1½ teaspoons sugar
- 1½ teaspoons Oriental sesame oil
- 7 cups (about 7 oz./200g) finely shredded iceberg lettuce
- 3 cups (about 3 oz./85 g) bite-size pieces of radicchio
- ⅓ cup (15 g) lightly packed cilantro leaves
- ¼ cup (25 g) sliced green onions
- 1 pound (455 g) skinless, boneless chicken breast, cut into thin strips
- 2 cloves garlic, minced or pressed

  Cilantro sprigs

1. In a small bowl, stir together vinegar, 1 tablespoon (15 ml) water, soy sauce, sugar, and oil; set aside.

2. In a large serving bowl, combine lettuce, radicchio, cilantro leaves, and onions; cover and set aside.

3. In a wide nonstick frying pan or wok, combine chicken, 1 tablespoon (15 ml) water, and garlic. Stir-fry over medium-high heat until chicken is no longer pink in center; cut to test (3 to 4 minutes). Add water, 1 tablespoon (15 ml) at a time, if pan appears dry. Add vinegar mixture to pan and bring to a boil. Quickly pour chicken and sauce over greens, then mix gently but thoroughly. Garnish with cilantro sprigs and serve immediately.

Makes 4 servings

NUTRIENTS

Per serving: 185 calories (17% calories from fat), 3 g total fat, 0.6 g saturated fat, 66 mg cholesterol, 626 mg sodium, 10 g carbohydrates, 1 g fiber, 28 g protein, 84 mg calcium, 2 mg iron

MELON, PAPAYA & CUCUMBER SALAD

Pictured on page 51
Preparation time: **About 25 minutes**

Cool off a hot day or a spicy meal with this refreshing salad. The mouth-watering blend of melon, papaya, and cool cucumber is delicious with fish, grilled meats, or tamale pie.

3   small cantaloupes (about 4 lbs./1.8 kg total)

1   medium-size firm-ripe papaya (about 1 lb./455 g), peeled, seeded, and diced

1   medium-size cucumber (about 8 oz./230 g), peeled, seeded, and diced

About 2 tablespoons minced fresh mint or 1 teaspoon dried mint, or to taste

3   tablespoons (45 ml) lime juice

1   tablespoon (15 ml) honey

Mint sprigs

1. Cut 2 of the melons in half lengthwise. Scoop out and discard seeds. If a melon half does not sit steadily, cut a very thin slice from the base so the melon half does sit steadily. Set melon halves aside.

2. Peel, seed, and dice remaining melon. Transfer to a large nonmetal bowl. Add papaya, cucumber, minced mint, lime juice, and honey. Mix gently to combine.

3. Set a melon half in each of 4 bowls (or on each of 4 dinner plates). Spoon a fourth of the fruit mixture into each melon half. (At this point, you may cover and refrigerate for up to 4 hours.) Just before serving, garnish each melon half with mint sprigs.

Makes 4 servings

NUTRIENTS

Per serving: 135 calories (5% calories from fat), 0.8 g total fat, 0 g saturated fat, 0 mg cholesterol, 28 mg sodium, 33 g carbohydrates, 3 g fiber, 3 g protein, 54 mg calcium, 0.8 mg iron

20 MINUTES OR LESS

2 large firm-ripe nectarines (about 12 oz./340 g total), pitted and diced

2 large firm-ripe plums (about 6 oz./170 g total), pitted and diced

¼ cup (10 g) firmly packed fresh basil leaves (minced) or about 1 tablespoon dried basil, or to taste

1½ tablespoons (23 ml) red wine vinegar

1 tablespoon (15 ml) honey

4 to 8 large butter lettuce leaves, rinsed and crisped

NECTARINE, PLUM & BASIL SALAD-SALSA

1. In a large nonmetal bowl, mix nectarines, plums, basil, vinegar, and honey. (At this point, you may cover and refrigerate for up to 4 hours.)

2. To serve, place 1 or 2 lettuce leaves on each of 4 dinner plates. Spoon a fourth of the fruit mixture onto each plate.

Makes 4 servings

Per serving: 83 calories (7% calories from fat), 0.7 g total fat, 0 g saturated fat, 0 mg cholesterol, 2 mg sodium, 20 g carbohydrates, 2 g fiber, 1 g protein, 41 mg calcium, 0.9 mg iron

WARM SPINACH, PEAR & SAUSAGE SALAD

Preparation time: **About 15 minutes**
Cooking time: **About 15 minutes**

Either Bartlett or Comice pears, which are particularly sweet varieties, would do nicely in this salad. You should use firm-ripe pears for best results.

3   green onions

8   ounces (230 g) spinach, stems removed, leaves rinsed and crisped

1   large yellow or red bell pepper (about 8 oz./230 g), seeded and cut lengthwise into thin strips

5   medium-size firm-ripe pears (1¾ to 2 lbs./795 to 905 g total)

1   teaspoon olive oil or vegetable oil

8   to 10 ounces (230 to 285 g) mild or hot turkey Italian sausages, casings removed

⅓   cup (80 ml) balsamic vinegar

¾   teaspoon fennel seeds

1. Trim and discard ends of onions. Cut onions into 2-inch (5-cm) lengths; then cut each piece lengthwise into slivers. Tear spinach into bite-size pieces. Place onions, spinach, and bell pepper in a large serving bowl, cover, and set aside.

2. Peel and core pears; slice thinly. Heat oil in a wide nonstick frying pan or wok over medium-high heat. When oil is hot, add pears and stir-fry until almost tender to bite (about 5 minutes). Lift pears from pan with a slotted spoon; transfer to a bowl and keep warm.

3. Crumble sausage into pan and stir-fry over medium-high heat until browned (5 to 7 minutes); add water, 1 tablespoon (15 ml) at a time, if pan appears dry. Add pears, vinegar, and fennel seeds to pan. Stir gently to mix, scraping browned bits free from pan bottom. Immediately pour hot

pear mixture over spinach mixture; toss gently but thoroughly until spinach is slightly wilted.

Makes 4 servings

NUTRIENTS

Per serving: 155 calories (11% calories from fat), 2 g total fat, 0.2 g saturated fat, 0 mg cholesterol, 36 mg sodium, 36 g carbohydrates, 7 g fiber, 3 g protein, 79 mg calcium, 2 mg iron

STIR-FRIED PORK & ESCAROLE SALAD

Preparation time: **About 25 minutes**
Cooking time: **About 5 minutes**

Because pork loin is very lean, it is important to slice it paper thin so it cooks very quickly and doesn't toughen.

3   quarts (about 12 oz./340 g) lightly packed rinsed, crisped escarole or spinach leaves

⅔   cup (160 ml) cider vinegar

3   tablespoons (45 ml) honey

2   large Red Delicious apples (about 1 lb./455 g total), cored and thinly sliced

4   teaspoons cornstarch

1   cup (240 ml) fat-free reduced-sodium chicken broth

2   teaspoons Dijon mustard

½   teaspoon dried thyme

2   teaspoons olive oil

2   large shallots, chopped

1   pound (455 g) lean boneless pork loin, loin end, or leg, trimmed of fat and cut into paper-thin ½- by 3-inch (1- by 8-cm) slices

1   cup (145 g) raisins

1. Place escarole on a wide serving platter. In a medium-size bowl, stir together vinegar, honey, and apples. Then remove apples with a slotted spoon and scatter over escarole. Add cornstarch, broth, mustard, and thyme to vinegar mixture in bowl; stir well and set aside.

2. Heat oil in a wide nonstick frying pan or wok over medium-high heat. When oil is hot, add shallots and pork and stir-fry until meat is lightly browned (about 3 minutes). Push meat to one side of pan. Stir vinegar mixture well, pour into pan, and stir just until boiling (about 1 minute). Stir meat into sauce; then quickly spoon meat mixture over escarole and sprinkle with raisins.

Makes 4 servings

NUTRIENTS

Per serving: 443 calories (18% calories from fat), 9 g total fat, 3 g saturated fat, 67 mg cholesterol, 305 mg sodium, 67 g carbohydrates, 6 g fiber, 28 g protein, 98 mg calcium, 3 mg iron

LitcHi, Penne & CHicken Salad

Preparation time: **About 20 minutes**
Cooking time: **About 20 minutes**

Sweet litchis bring refreshing flavor to this chicken and pasta salad, which is tossed with a lemony yogurt dressing. Look for litchis in Asian markets or in the Asian section of your supermarket.

  5 ounces/140 g (about 1½ cups) dried penne

  1 can (about 11 oz./310 g) litchis

  ¾ cup (180 ml) plain low-fat yogurt

  ¾ teaspoon grated lemon peel

  4 teaspoons (20 ml) lemon juice

1½ teaspoons dried thyme

  2 cups (280 g) bite-size pieces cooked chicken

  ½ cup (60 g) finely diced celery

  8 large butter lettuce leaves, rinsed and crisped

  ⅓ cup (35 g) chopped green onions

     Salt and pepper

1. Bring 8 cups (1.9 liters) water to a boil in a 4- to 5-quart (3.8- to 5-liter) pan over medium-high heat. Stir in pasta and cook just until tender to bite (8 to 10 minutes); or cook according to package directions. Drain, rinse with cold water until cool, and drain well.

2. Drain litchis, reserving ⅓ cup (80 ml) of the syrup; set fruit aside. In a large nonmetal bowl, mix reserved ⅓ cup (80 ml) litchi syrup, yogurt, lemon peel, lemon juice, and thyme. Add pasta, chicken, and celery. Mix thoroughly but gently. (At this point, you may cover pasta mixture and fruit separately and refrigerate for up to 4 hours; stir pasta occasionally.)

3. Arrange lettuce on individual plates. Top with pasta mixture and litchis. Sprinkle with onions. Offer salt and pepper to add to taste.

Makes 4 servings

NUTRIENTS

Per serving: 358 calories (17% calories from fat), 7 g total fat, 2 g saturated fat, 65 mg cholesterol, 136 mg sodium, 47 g carbohydrates, 2 g fiber, 28 g protein, 120 mg calcium, 4 mg iron

KIDNEY COBB SALAD

Preparation time: **About 25 minutes**

This hearty main dish resembles the classic Cobb salad because its ingredients are arranged spoke-fashion on the serving platter—but that's where the similarity ends. We've replaced the traditional chicken, bacon, avocado, and blue cheese with beans, green peas, bell pepper, and tangy feta. Serve it with chilled mineral water or iced tea, if you like.

DRESSING:

- ⅓ cup (80 ml) nonfat mayonnaise
- ⅓ cup (80 ml) nonfat sour cream
- 2 tablespoons (30 ml) balsamic vinegar
- 2 tablespoons (30 ml) smooth unsweetened applesauce
- 1 tablespoon (15 ml) olive oil
- 1 tablespoon (15 ml) Dijon mustard
- 1 tablespoon chopped fresh dill or 1 teaspoon dried dill weed
- 1 teaspoon sugar, or to taste
  Dill sprigs (optional)

SALAD:

- 2 cans (about 15 oz./425 g each) red kidney beans
- 1 large yellow or red bell pepper (about 8 oz./230 g)
- 6 ounces (170 g) feta cheese
- 1 very small red onion (about 4 oz./ 115 g)
- 1 large head red leaf lettuce (1½ lbs./680 g), separated into leaves, rinsed, and crisped
- 1 package (about 10 oz./285 g) frozen tiny peas, thawed and drained

1. For dressing, in a small bowl, combine mayonnaise, sour cream, vinegar, applesauce, oil, mustard, chopped dill, and sugar. Beat until smoothly blended. If a thinner dressing is desired, add water,

1 tablespoon (15 ml) at a time, until dressing has the desired consistency. Spoon into a small serving bowl; garnish with dill sprigs, if desired. Cover lightly and refrigerate while you prepare salad.

2. Drain beans and rinse well. Seed and finely chop bell pepper. Crumble cheese. Thinly slice onion; separate slices into rings.

3. To assemble salad, line a rimmed platter or a wide salad bowl with large lettuce leaves, then break remaining leaves into bite-size pieces and arrange atop whole leaves. Mound peas, beans, bell pepper, and cheese separately on lettuce; place onion in center. Offer dressing to add to taste.

Makes 6 servings

NUTRIENTS

Per serving: 256 calories (26% calories from fat), 7 g total fat, 4 g saturated fat, 25 mg cholesterol, 718 mg sodium, 32 g carbohydrates, 9 g fiber, 16 g protein, 279 mg calcium, 4 mg iron

ROASTED BELL PEPPER & BLACK BEAN SALAD

Preparation time: **About 15 minutes**
Cooking time: **About 8 minutes**

Authentic Mexican ingredients, carefully chosen for their contrasting textures and flavors, distinguish this cold bean dish. You combine nutty-tasting black beans with roasted red peppers, cilantro, and a little onion, then enliven the mixture with a tart-sweet vinegar dressing.

- 2 large red bell peppers (about 1 lb./ 455 g total)
- ½ cup (120 ml) seasoned rice vinegar; or ½ cup (120 ml) distilled white vinegar plus 1 tablespoon sugar
- 1 tablespoon (15 ml) olive oil
- 1 tablespoon (15 ml) honey
- ½ teaspoon chili oil

3 cans (about 15 oz./425 g each) black
   beans, drained and rinsed; or 6 cups
   cooked (about 3 cups/600 g dried)
   black beans, drained and rinsed

¼ cup (10 g) minced cilantro

2 tablespoons thinly sliced green onion

   Salt

   Cilantro sprigs

1. Cut peppers in half lengthwise. Set pepper halves, cut side down, in a 10- by 15-inch (25- by 38-cm) rimmed baking pan. Broil 4 to 6 inches (10 to 15 cm) below heat until charred all over (about 8 minutes). Cover with foil and let cool in pan. Then remove and discard skins, stems, and seeds; cut peppers into strips or chunks.

2. In a bowl, mix vinegar, 1 tablespoon (15 ml) water, olive oil, honey, and chili oil. Add beans and roasted peppers; mix gently but thoroughly. (At this point, you may cover and refrigerate until next day.)

3. To serve, stir minced cilantro and green onion into bean mixture. Season to taste with salt and garnish with some cilantro sprigs.

Makes 6 servings

NUTRIENTS

Per serving: 295 calories (11% calories from fat), 4 g total fat, 0.6 g saturated fat, 0 mg cholesterol, 400 mg sodium, 52 g carbohydrates, 5 g fiber, 16 g protein, 54 mg calcium, 4 mg iron

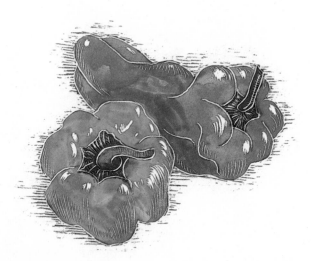

STRAWBERRY TARRAGON DRESSING

Preparation time: **About 15 minutes**
Cooking time: **About 3 minutes**

A fruit-based dressing such as this one would be good on chicken salad, or try it instead of the dressing in the Kidney Cobb Salad (facing page).

1½ cups (224 g) strawberries, hulled

   About ¼ cup (60 ml) lemon juice

1 tablespoon sugar

1 tablespoon finely chopped shallot

1 teaspoon chopped fresh tarragon or
   ½ teaspoon dried tarragon

½ teaspoon cornstarch

2 tablespoons (30 ml) orange juice

1. Whirl strawberries in a blender or food processor until puréed. Rub through a fine wire strainer into a 2-cup (470 ml) glass measure. Add ¼ cup (60 ml) of the lemon juice and enough water to make 1 cup (240 ml). Transfer to a small pan and add sugar, shallot, and tarragon.

2. Smoothly mix cornstarch and orange juice; stir into strawberry mixture. Bring to a boil over high heat, stirring constantly. Set pan in a bowl of ice water to chill mixture quickly; then taste and add more lemon juice, if needed. (At this point, you may cover and refrigerate for up to a day.)

Makes about 1 cup (240 ml)

NUTRIENTS

Per tablespoon: 10 calories (5% calories from fat), 0.1 g total fat, 0.1 g saturated fat, 0 mg cholesterol, 1 mg sodium, 2 g carbohydrates, 0.4 g fiber, 0.1 g protein, 3 mg calcium, 0.1 mg iron

FRUITED QUINOA SALAD

Preparation time: **About 15 minutes**
Cooking time: **About 30 minutes**

Often called the "super grain," thanks to its high protein content, quinoa is the base for this simple yet elegant fruited salad. You'll find quinoa in well-stocked supermarkets and natural-foods stores; be sure to rinse it well before cooking to remove the slightly bitter coating.

2   tablespoons pine nuts or slivered almonds

1¼ cups (213 g) dried apricots

1½ cups (255 g) quinoa or 1 cup (175 g) bulgur

2   teaspoons olive oil or vegetable oil

2   or 3 cups (470 or 710 ml) fat-free reduced-sodium chicken broth

2   teaspoons grated lemon peel

2   tablespoons (30 ml) lemon juice

1   cup (150 g) dried currants
    Salt

1. Toast pine nuts in a small frying pan over medium heat until golden brown (3 to 5 minutes), stirring often. Transfer nuts to a bowl; set aside. Coarsely chop ½ cup (85 g) of the apricots; set aside.

2. Place quinoa in a fine strainer; rinse thoroughly with water (bulgur needs no rinsing). Heat oil in a 3- to 4-quart (2.8- to 3.8-liter) pan over medium heat. Add quinoa or bulgur; cook, stirring often, until grain turns a slightly darker brown (8 to 10 minutes).

3. To pan, add broth (3 cups/710 ml for quinoa, 2 cups/470 ml for bulgur), lemon peel, and lemon juice. Bring to a boil over high heat. Reduce heat, cover, and simmer until grain is just tender to bite (10 to 15 minutes). Drain and discard any liquid from grain. Stir chopped apricots and ½ cup

(75 g) of the currants into grain. Let stand until warm; or let cool, then cover and refrigerate until next day.

4. To serve, season quinoa mixture to taste with salt. Mound mixture in center of a serving dish or large rimmed serving platter. Garnish with remaining ¾ cup (130 g) apricots, remaining ½ cup (75 g) currants, and pine nuts.

Makes 6 servings

NUTRIENTS

Per serving: 349 calories (16% calories from fat), 7 g total fat, 1 g saturated fat, 0 mg cholesterol, 81 mg sodium, 70 g carbohydrates, 10 g fiber, 10 g protein, 70 mg calcium, 7 mg iron

Wilted Spinach Salad with Oranges

Preparation time: **About 15 minutes**
Cooking time: **6 to 8 minutes**

A little heat can heighten flavors. Here, onion rings warmed in a blend of balsamic vinegar, tarragon, and fresh orange peel enliven a green-and-gold combination of spinach and orange segments. Be sure to serve the salad as soon as possible after preparing it, so that the spinach leaves stay crisp.

2 medium-size oranges (about 1 lb./ 455 g total)

2 quarts (1.9 liters) lightly packed spinach leaves, rinsed and crisped

1 large onion, thinly sliced and separated into rings

¼ cup (60 ml) balsamic or red wine vinegar

2 teaspoons vegetable oil

1 teaspoon dried tarragon

1. Grate 1 teaspoon peel (colored part only) from one of the oranges; set aside. With a sharp knife, cut remaining peel and all white membrane from both oranges. Holding fruit over a bowl to catch juice, cut between membranes to free segments; place segments in bowl with juice and set aside. Place spinach in a large salad bowl.

2. In a wide frying pan, combine onion, vinegar, oil, tarragon, and grated orange peel. Place over medium-low heat, cover, and cook until onions are tender-crisp when pierced (6 to 8 minutes). Gently stir in orange segments and juice. Pour orange mixture over spinach. Mix lightly, then serve at once. *Makes 4 servings*

NUTRIENTS

Per serving: 103 calories (22% calories from fat), 3 g total fat, 0.4 g saturated fat, 0 mg cholesterol, 70 mg sodium, 18 g carbohydrates, 5 g fiber, 4 g protein, 137 mg calcium, 3 mg iron

20 MINUTES OR LESS

1 can (about 15 oz./425 g) black beans, drained and rinsed; or 2 cups cooked (about 1 cup/200 g dried) black beans, drained and rinsed

1 cup (115 g) peeled, finely chopped jicama

¼ cup (33 g) crumbled panela or feta cheese

3 tablespoons (45 ml) lime juice

⅓ cup (15 g) minced cilantro

2 tablespoons thinly sliced green onion

2 teaspoons honey

¼ teaspoon crushed red pepper flakes

4 to 8 butter lettuce leaves, rinsed and crisped

Black Bean & Jicama Salad

1. In a bowl, combine beans, jicama, cheese, lime juice, cilantro, onion, honey, and red pepper flakes. Mix well. (At this point, you may cover and refrigerate for up to 4 hours.)

2. To serve, spoon bean mixture into lettuce leaves.
Makes 4 servings

Per serving: 164 calories (13% calories from fat), 2 g total fat, 1 g saturated fat, 8 mg cholesterol, 100 mg sodium, 28 g carbohydrates, 3 g fiber, 9 g protein, 75 mg calcium, 2 mg iron

SHRIMP & SPINACH SLAW

Preparation time: **About 25 minutes**

For your next barbecue, forget the familiar and prepare a new version of coleslaw. Here fresh spinach, tiny shrimp, and shredded are cabbage tossed in a lemon dressing.

- 4 cups finely shredded green cabbage (about 1 lb./455 g)
- 3 cups thinly sliced spinach leaves (about 4 oz./115 g)
- 1 medium-size cucumber (8 to 10 oz./230 to 285 g), peeled and sliced
- 2 medium-size celery stalks, sliced
- ⅔ cup (45 ml) plain nonfat yogurt
- 3 tablespoons (45 ml) reduced-calorie mayonnaise
- ½ cup (50 g) thinly sliced green onions
- 1 teaspoon grated lemon peel
- 2 tablespoons (30 ml) lemon juice
- 1 tablespoon sugar

  About 12 large spinach leaves, rinsed and crisped (optional)
- ¾ to 1 pound (340 to 455 g) small cooked shrimp

  Lemon wedges

  Salt and pepper

1. To prepare salad, in a large bowl, combine cabbage, sliced spinach leaves, cucumber, and celery.

2. To prepare yogurt-lemon dressing, in a small bowl, combine yogurt, mayonnaise, onions, lemon peel, lemon juice, and sugar. (At this point, you may cover and refrigerate the salad and dressing separately until next day.)

3. Add dressing to salad and mix well. If using large spinach leaves, use them to garnish salad in bowl; or arrange them around rim of a large

20 MINUTES OR LESS

12 ounces (340 g) fennel

⅔ pound (300 g) mizuna, bare stems trimmed, leaves rinsed and crisped

⅔ cup (160 ml) plain nonfat yogurt

¼ cup (60 ml) reduced-fat sour cream

2 tablespoons (30 ml) lemon juice

1 tablespoon (15 ml) Dijon mustard

1 teaspoon dried tarragon

½ teaspoon sugar

1½ pounds (680 g) cooked crabmeat

MIZUNA, FENNEL & CRAB SALAD

1. Cut feathery tops from fennel; chop tops and set aside for dressing. Cut root ends and any bruised spots from fennel head; then thinly slice (you should have 2 cups/195 g) and place in a large bowl.

2. Reserve ¾ cup (20 g) of the mizuna for dressing. Cut remaining mizuna into 2- to 3-inch (5- to 8-cm) long pieces; add to bowl with fennel.

3. To prepare dressing, in a blender or food processor, combine the ¾ cup (20 g) reserved mizuna, yogurt, sour cream, lemon juice, mustard, 1 tablespoon of the reserved chopped fennel tops, tarragon, and sugar. Whirl until puréed; set aside.

4. Mound crab on mizuna mixture, placing the most attractive crab pieces on top. At the table, add dressing to salad; mix gently.

Makes 6 servings

Per serving: 172 calories (19% calories from fat), 4 g total fat, 1 g saturated fat, 117 mg cholesterol, 460 mg sodium, 7 g carbohydrates, 0.7 g fiber, 27 g protein, 243 mg calcium, 2 mg iron

platter and mound salad in center. Sprinkle shrimp over salad. Offer lemon wedges to squeeze over salad to taste; season to taste with salt and pepper.

Makes 8 servings

NUTRIENTS

Per serving: 107 calories (22% calories from fat), 3 g total fat, 0.5 g saturated fat, 100 mg cholesterol, 189 mg sodium, 9 g carbohydrates, 3 g fiber, 13 g protein, 112 mg calcium, 3 mg iron

WARM CIOPPINO SALAD

Preparation time: **About 20 minutes**
Cooking time: **About 10 minutes**

In season, you can substitute 1½ cups (235 g) of chopped fresh tomatoes for the canned variety called for in this recipe.

¼ cup (60 ml) lemon juice

1 teaspoon dried basil

1 teaspoon dried oregano

2 cloves garlic, minced or pressed

3 quarts (about 12 oz./340 g) lightly packed rinsed, crisped spinach leaves, torn into bite-size pieces

1 tablespoon (15 ml) olive oil

8 ounces (230 g) extra-large raw shrimp (26 to 30 per lb.), shelled and deveined

2 cups (170 g) thinly sliced mushrooms

2 cups (340 g) thinly sliced zucchini

1 can (about 14½ oz./415 g) tomatoes, drained and chopped

12 pitted ripe olives

8 ounces (230 g) cooked crabmeat

1. To prepare lemon dressing, in a small bowl, stir together lemon juice, basil, oregano, and garlic; set aside.

2. Place spinach in a wide serving bowl, cover, and set aside.

3. Heat oil in a wide nonstick frying pan or wok over medium-high heat. When oil is hot, add shrimp and stir-fry until just opaque in center; cut to test (3 to 4 minutes). Remove from pan with tongs or a slotted spoon and set aside.

4. Add mushrooms and zucchini to pan; stir-fry until zucchini is just tender to bite (about 3 minutes). Return shrimp to pan; add tomatoes, olives, and lemon dressing. Stir until mixture is heated through. Pour shrimp mixture over spinach, top with crab, and mix gently but thoroughly.

Makes 6 servings

NUTRIENTS

Per serving: 149 calories (28% calories from fat), 5 g total fat, 0.7 g saturated fat, 85 mg cholesterol, 380 mg sodium, 10 g carbohydrates, 3 g fiber, 18 g protein, 159 mg calcium, 4 mg iron

SHALLOT DRESSING

Preparation time: **About 5 minutes**
Cooking time: **About 2 minutes**

Try this dressing on the Warm Cioppino Salad (this page). You can make the dressing up to a day before you need it.

⅔ cup (160 ml) water

1 teaspoon arrowroot

1 tablespoon (15 ml) Dijon mustard

¼ cup (40 g) finely slivered shallots

¼ cup (60 ml) sherry vinegar

1. In a small pan, blend water and arrowroot. Bring to a boil over high heat, stirring constantly. Set pan in a bowl of ice water to chill quickly; then stir in mustard, shallots, and vinegar.

Makes about 1 cup (240 ml)

NUTRIENTS

Per tablespoon: 6 calories (0% calories from fat), 0 g total fat, 0 g saturated fat, 0 mg cholesterol, 23 mg sodium, 0.6 g carbohydrates, 0 g fiber, 0.1 g protein, 1 mg calcium, 0 mg iron

Shrimp & Orzo with Pesto Dressing

Preparation time: **About 25 minutes**
Cooking time: **About 10 minutes**

Fresh basil and cilantro lend flavor and color to the creamy dressing for this pasta and shrimp salad, nestled in a bed of crisp shredded lettuce. You can buy precooked shrimp or prepare the shrimp in advance, if you have the time.

½ cup (20 g) chopped fresh basil

½ cup (20 g) chopped cilantro

1 cup (240 ml) plain nonfat yogurt

1 tablespoon (15 ml) white wine vinegar

6 cups (1.4 liters) fat-free reduced-sodium chicken broth

8 ounces/230 g (about 1⅓ cups) dried orzo or other rice-shaped pasta

1 pound (455 g) tiny cooked shrimp

1 cup (100 g) chopped green onions

1 tablespoon grated lemon peel

½ cup (120 ml) lemon juice

1 small head iceberg lettuce (about 1 lb./455 g), rinsed and crisped

3 cups (425 g) tiny cherry tomatoes

1. To prepare pesto dressing, in a blender or food processor, combine basil, cilantro, yogurt, and vinegar. Whirl until smooth. (At this point, you may cover and refrigerate for up to 4 hours.)

2. Bring broth to a boil in a 4- to 5-quart (3.8- to 5-liter) pan over medium-high heat. Stir in pasta and cook just until barely tender to bite (about 5 minutes). Drain well, reserving liquid for other uses. Let cool completely.

3. Transfer pasta to a large bowl. Add shrimp, onions, lemon peel, and lemon juice. Mix thoroughly but gently.

4. Shred lettuce and place in a shallow serving bowl. Spoon pasta mixture into bowl. Arrange tomatoes around edge of bowl. Stir dressing well and offer dressing to add to taste.

Makes 6 servings

Per serving without dressing: 274 calories (13% calories from fat), 4 g total fat, 1 g saturated fat, 148 mg cholesterol, 305 mg sodium, 38 g carbohydrates, 3 g fiber, 26 g protein, 122 mg calcium, 5 mg iron

Per tablespoon dressing: 8 calories (3% from fat), 0 g total fat, 0 g saturated fat, 0 mg cholesterol, 9 mg sodium, 1 g carbohydrates, 0 g fiber, 1 g protein, 32 mg calcium, 0 mg iron

Basil Oil

Preparation time: **About 10 minutes**
Cooking time: **About 10 minutes**

This basil-flavored oil not only makes a great addition to salad dressings, but is also excellent for sautéing. Add some to the dressing for the Shrimp & Orzo salad (this page) or use it instead of olive oil in the Halibut Piccata with Lemon Linguine recipe (page 60). And remember that while flavored oils get almost all their calories from fat, if used sparingly, they still have a place in a low-fat diet.

½ cup (20 g) firmly packed fresh basil leaves

1 cup (240 ml) vegetable oil or olive oil

1. In a 4- to 5-quart (3.8- to 5-liter) pan, bring 8 cups (1.9 liters) water to a boil over high heat. Drop basil into boiling water and cook just until bright green (about 3 seconds); immediately drain, then plunge into ice water until cool. Drain basil well again; blot dry.

2. In a blender or food processor, combine basil and ¼ cup (60 ml) of the oil. Whirl until well blended. Add remaining ¾ cup (180 ml) oil and whirl until smoothly puréed. Transfer oil mixture to a small pan and heat over medium heat, stirring occasionally, just until warm (not hot or boiling). Remove from heat and let cool slightly.

3. Carefully pour oil into a clean, dry glass bottle or jar, leaving basil sediment behind; discard sediment. (Or strain oil, if desired.) Cover airtight and store for up to 6 months.

Makes about 1 cup (240 ml)

NUTRIENTS

Per tablespoon: 121 calories (99% calories from fat), 14 g total fat, 2 g saturated fat, 0 mg cholesterol, 0.2 mg sodium, 0.3 g carbohydrates, 0 g fiber, 0.1 g protein, 12 mg calcium, 0.3 mg iron

WATERCRESS, BUTTER LETTUCE & SHRIMP SALAD

Pictured on page 50
Preparation time: **About 20 minutes**
Baking time: **12 to 15 minutes**

Oven-browned croutons provide a crisp accent for a piquant first-course salad lightly dressed with balsamic vinegar, Dijon mustard, and whole mustard seeds.

- 1 tablespoon mustard seeds
- ¼ cup (60 ml) boiling water
  Olive oil cooking spray
- 2½ cups (75 g) ½-inch (1-cm) cubes sourdough French bread
- ¼ cup (60 ml) balsamic or red wine vinegar
- 2 teaspoons Dijon mustard
- 1 tablespoon (15 ml) olive oil
- 2½ quarts (550 g) torn butter lettuce leaves, rinsed and crisped
- 2½ quarts (360 g) lightly packed watercress sprigs, rinsed and crisped
- 8 ounces (230 g) small cooked shrimp

1. Place mustard seeds in a small bowl; pour boiling water over them. Let stand for at least 10 minutes or up to 8 hours; drain well.

2. Spray a shallow rimmed baking pan with cooking spray. Spread bread cubes in pan; spray with cooking spray. Bake in a 350°F (175C°) oven until crisp and golden brown (12 to 15 minutes). Let cool in pan on a rack. (At this point, you may store airtight at room temperature for up to 2 days.)

3. In a small bowl, stir together mustard seeds, vinegar, mustard, and oil. Arrange lettuce, watercress, and shrimp in a large salad bowl; add mustard seed dressing and mix lightly until greens are coated. Top salad with croutons.

Makes 6 servings

NUTRIENTS

Per serving: 123 calories (28% calories from fat), 4 g total fat, 0.5 g saturated fat, 74 mg cholesterol, 229 mg sodium, 10 g carbohydrates, 3 g fiber, 12 g protein, 102 mg calcium, 2 mg iron

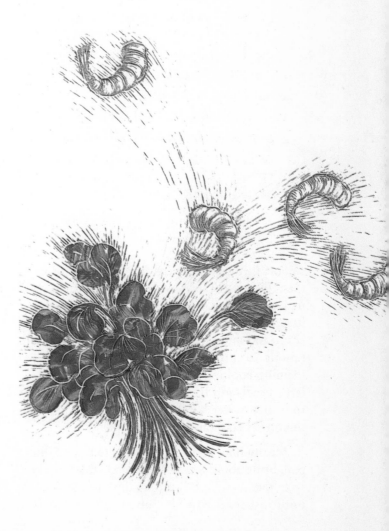

Split Pea & Green Pea Salad

Pictured on facing page
Preparation time: **About 15 minutes**
Cooking time: **About 30 minutes**

Dotted with sweet green peas and split peas, this simple orzo salad is seasoned with fresh mint and lemon. Don't thaw the green peas before you stir them into the salad.

1   cup (200 g) green split peas

2   cups (470 ml) vegetable broth

½   teaspoon dried thyme

1   package (about 10 oz./285 g) frozen tiny peas (do not thaw)

4   ounces/115 g (about 10 tablespoons) dried orzo or other rice-shaped pasta

¼   cup (25 g) thinly sliced green onions

¼   cup (10 g) chopped fresh mint

¼   cup (60 ml) vegetable oil

1   teaspoon finely shredded lemon peel

2   tablespoons (30 ml) lemon juice
    About 24 large butter lettuce leaves, rinsed and crisped
    Mint sprigs
    Thyme sprigs
    Salt and pepper

1. Sort through split peas, discarding any debris; then rinse and drain peas. In a 1½- to 2-quart (1.4- to 1.9-liter) pan, bring broth to a boil over high heat. Add split peas and dried thyme. Reduce heat, cover, and simmer until split peas are tender to bite (about 25 minutes); drain and discard any remaining cooking liquid. Transfer split peas to a large bowl, add frozen peas, and mix gently but thoroughly. Let stand, stirring occasionally, until mixture is cool (about 3 minutes).

2. Meanwhile, in a 4- to 5-quart (3.8- to 5-liter) pan, bring about 8 cups (1.9 liters) water to a boil over medium-high heat; stir in pasta and cook until just tender to bite, about 5 minutes. (Or cook pasta according to package directions.) Drain, rinse with cold water, and drain well again. Transfer pasta to bowl with peas. Add onions and chopped mint; mix gently. In a small bowl, beat oil, lemon peel, and lemon juice until blended. Add to pea mixture; mix gently but thoroughly.

3. To serve, line 4 individual plates with lettuce leaves; top each plate equally with pea mixture. Garnish salads with mint and thyme sprigs. Season to taste with salt and pepper.

Makes 4 servings

NUTRIENTS

Per serving: 458 calories (30% calories from fat), 15 g total fat, 2 g saturated fat, 0 mg cholesterol, 607 mg sodium, 62 g carbohydrates, 6 g fiber, 19 g protein, 56 mg calcium, 2 mg iron

Thyme Oil

Preparation time: **About 5 minutes**
Cooking time: **About 5 minutes**

Thyme oil is a fine option to plain vegetable oil in many dressings. Try it in the Split Pea & Green Pea Salad (at left).

¼   cup (10 g) chopped fresh thyme

1   cup (240 ml) vegetable oil or olive oil

1. In a small pan, whisk together thyme and ¼ cup (60 ml) of the oil until well blended. Gradually whisk in remaining ¾ cup (180 ml) oil. Heat over medium heat, stirring often, just until warm (not hot or boiling). Remove from heat and let cool slightly.

2. Carefully pour oil into a clean, dry glass bottle or jar, leaving thyme sediment behind; discard sediment. (Or strain oil, if desired.) Cover airtight and store for up to 6 months.

Makes about 1 cup (240 ml)

NUTRIENTS

Per tablespoon: 120 calories (99% calories from fat), 14 g total fat, 2 g saturated fat, 0 mg cholesterol, 0.1 mg sodium, 0.2 g carbohydrates, 0 g fiber, 0 g protein, 5 mg calcium, 0.4 mg iron

Split Pea & Green Pea Salad (recipe on facing page)

Watercress, Butter Lettuce & Shrimp Salad (recipe on page 47)

MELON, PAPAYA & CUCUMBER SALAD (RECIPE ON PAGE 37)

Orange-Onion Salad with Red Chile Dressing (recipes on facing page)

ORANGE-ONION SALAD WITH RED CHILE DRESSING

Pictured on facing page
Preparation time: **About 25 minutes**

Here, red onion rings and a chile dressing enliven a colorful combination of oranges, avocado, cucumber, and shrimp.

Red Chile Dressing (at right)

4   quarts (about 1 lb./455 g) rinsed and crisped leaf lettuce, torn into in bite-size pieces

⅓   pound (150 g) tiny cooked shrimp

½   cup (60 g) thinly sliced red onion

1   large cucumber (10 to 12 oz./285 to 340 g), peeled (if desired) and thinly sliced

3   small oranges (about 1 lb./455 g total)

1   medium-size firm-ripe avocado

1   tablespoon (15 ml) lemon juice

1. Prepare Red Chile Dressing; set aside.

2. Place lettuce in a large salad bowl or on a rimmed platter. Arrange shrimp, onion, and cucumber on lettuce.

3. With a sharp knife, cut peel and all white membrane from oranges; then cut oranges crosswise into ¼-inch-thick (6-mm-thick) slices and arrange on salad.

4. Pit and peel avocado; thinly slice lengthwise. Coat slices with lemon juice; then arrange on salad. Pour dressing over salad and mix gently.

Makes 8 servings

NUTRIENTS

Per serving: 106 calories (26% calories from fat), 3 g total fat, 0.6 g saturated fat, 37 mg cholesterol, 52 mg sodium, 16 g carbohydrates, 2 g fiber, 6 g protein, 79 mg calcium, 2 mg iron

RED CHILE DRESSING

Pictured on facing page
Preparation time: **About 15 minutes**

Dried red New Mexico or California chiles lend body, color, and heat to this oil-free dressing. Sandia is one of the hottest New Mexican varieties; Anaheim (grown in New Mexico as well as California) is a milder type. Experiment with the number of chiles to satisfy your taste.

3   large dried red New Mexico or California chiles (about ¾ oz./23 g total)

¾   cup (180 ml) water

6   tablespoons (90 ml) cider vinegar

2   tablespoons sugar

1   tablespoon chopped fresh ginger

1. Remove and discard stems and most of seeds from chiles. Rinse chiles and cut into ½-inch (1-cm) strips with scissors. In a 1- to 1½-quart (950-ml to 1.4-liter) pan, combine chiles and water. Bring to a boil. Remove pan from heat; let chiles soak until slightly softened (about 5 minutes).

2. In a blender or food processor, combine chile mixture, vinegar, sugar, and ginger; whirl until smoothly puréed. (At this point, you may cool; then cover and refrigerate for up to 1 week.)

Makes about 1 cup (240 ml)

NUTRIENTS

Per tablespoon: 11 calories (15% calories from fat), 0.2 g total fat, 0 g saturated fat, 0 mg cholesterol, 0.5 mg sodium, 3 g carbohydrates, 0 g fiber, 0.2 g protein, 2 mg calcium, 0.1 mg iron

ORIENTAL SALAD

Preparation time: **About 15 minutes**
Cooking time: **About 25 minutes**

This warm, crunchy stir-fried offering is most welcome on blustery winter days. Be sure to use dark Oriental sesame oil, which has a stronger flavor and fragrance than the lighter type.

- 6 cups (about 6 oz./170 g) lightly packed rinsed, crisped spinach leaves
- ¼ cup (60 ml) unseasoned rice vinegar or white wine vinegar
- 2 tablespoons (30 ml) reduced-sodium soy sauce
- 2 teaspoons honey
- 1 teaspoon Oriental sesame oil
- 2 teaspoons sesame seeds
- 2 teaspoons vegetable oil
- 5 cups (355 g) broccoli flowerets
- 1 pound (455 g) carrots, cut into ¼-inch (6-mm) diagonal slices
- 1½ cups (180 g) thinly sliced celery
- 1 medium-size onion, thinly sliced

1. Arrange spinach leaves on a large platter; cover and set aside. In a small bowl, stir together vinegar, soy sauce, honey, and sesame oil; set aside.

2. In a wide nonstick frying pan or wok, stir sesame seeds over medium heat until golden (about 3 minutes). Pour out of pan and set aside. Heat 1 teaspoon of the vegetable oil in pan over medium-high heat. When oil is hot, add half of the broccoli, carrots, celery, and onion. Stir-fry until vegetables are hot and bright in color (about 3 minutes). Add ⅓ cup (80 ml) water to pan, cover, and cook until vegetables are just tender to bite (about 3 minutes). Uncover and continue to cook, stirring, until liquid has evaporated (1 to 2 more minutes). Remove vegetables from pan and set aside. Repeat to cook remaining broccoli, carrots, celery, and onion, using remaining 1 teaspoon vegetable oil and adding ⅓ cup (80 ml) water after the first 3 minutes of cooking.

3. Return all cooked vegetables to pan and stir in vinegar mixture. Spoon vegetables onto spinach-lined platter and sprinkle with sesame seeds.

Makes 6 servings

NUTRIENTS

Per serving: 118 calories (22% calories from fat), 3 g total fat, 0.4 g saturated fat, 0 mg cholesterol, 297 mg sodium, 20 g carbohydrates, 7 g fiber, 6 g protein, 114 mg calcium, 2 mg iron

GARLIC OIL

Preparation time: **About 10 minutes**
Cooking time: **About 15 minutes**

Garlic oil is fine in salad dressings and for sautéing. Substitute it for the vegetable oil in the Oriental Salad (at left).

- 1 medium-size head garlic (about 3 oz./85 g)
- About 1 cup (240 ml) vegetable oil or olive oil

1. Separate garlic into cloves; then peel and thinly slice garlic cloves. Heat ⅓ cup (80 ml) of the oil in a wide nonstick frying pan or wok over medium-low heat. Add garlic and stir-fry until tinged with gold (about 10 minutes; do not scorch). If pan appears dry or garlic sticks to pan, add more oil, 1 tablespoon (15 ml) at a time.

2. Add ⅔ cup (160 ml) more oil to pan. Increase heat to medium and stir often just until oil is warm (not hot or boiling). Remove from heat and let cool slightly.

3. With a clean, dry slotted spoon, lift garlic from pan; discard garlic (garlic left in oil may spoil). Then carefully pour oil into a clean, dry glass bottle or jar. (Or strain oil, if desired.) Cover airtight and store for up to 6 months.

Makes about 1 cup (240 ml)

NUTRIENTS

Per tablespoon: 122 calories (98% calories from fat), 14 g total fat, 2 g saturated fat, 0 mg cholesterol, 0.3 mg sodium, 0.6 g carbohydrates, 0 g fiber, 0.1 g protein, 3 mg calcium, 0.1 mg iron

CURRY OIL

Preparation time: **About 5 minutes**
Cooking time: **About 5 minutes**

Curry oil would make a delicious addition to chicken, beef, or seafood salad dressings. It's also good for sautéing and stir-frying. Like all oils, curry oil gets almost all its calories from fat. So use it sparingly.

¼ cup (15 g) curry powder

1 cup (240 ml) vegetable oil or olive oil

1 to 3 cinnamon sticks (each about 3 inches/8 cm long)

1. In a small pan, whisk together curry powder and ¼ cup (60 ml) of the oil until well blended. Gradually whisk in remaining ¾ cup (180 ml) oil. Add cinnamon stick(s). Heat over medium heat, stirring often, just until warm (not hot or boiling). Remove from heat and let cool slightly.

2. With a clean, dry slotted spoon, lift out cinnamon stick(s); set aside. Carefully pour oil into a clean, dry glass bottle or jar, leaving curry sediment behind; discard sediment. (Or strain oil, if desired.) Add cinnamon stick(s) to bottle; cover airtight and store for up to 6 months.

Makes about 1 cup (240 ml)

NUTRIENTS

Per tablespoon: 125 calories (96% calories from fat), 14 g total fat, 2 g saturated fat, 0 mg cholesterol, 0.8 mg sodium, 1 g carbohydrates, 0.5 g fiber, 0.2 g protein, 8 mg calcium, 0.5 mg iron

HOT CHILE OIL

Preparation time: **About 5 minutes**
Cooking time: **About 5 minutes**

Dried chiles are usually sold in cellophane packets or strung on long *ristras*, or strands. Stored in a cool, dry place, they will keep for several months.

6 to 12 small dried hot red chiles (use the greater number of chiles for more heat)

1 cup (240 ml) vegetable oil or olive oil

1. Place 3 whole chiles in a small pan; add oil. Split each of the remaining 3 to 9 chiles in half; add to pan. Heat over medium heat, stirring gently, just until warm (not hot or boiling). Remove from heat and let cool slightly.

2. With a slotted spoon, remove split chiles and seeds from oil; discard. Remove whole chiles; set aside. Carefully (watch that you don't splatter) pour oil into a clean, dry glass bottle or jar. (Or strain oil, if desired.) Add whole chiles to bottle; cover airtight and store for up to 6 months.

Makes about 1 cup (240 ml)

NUTRIENTS

Per tablespoon: 121 calories (99% calories from fat), 14 g total fat, 2 g saturated fat, 0 mg cholesterol, 0.2 mg sodium, 0.4 g carbohydrates, 0 g fiber, 0.1 g protein, 1 mg calcium, 0.1 mg iron

Green Chile Dressing

Preparation time: **About 10 minutes**

Fresh lime juice and two kinds of chiles go into this tart, oil-free dressing, which is great with simply cooked vegetables.

- 1 small can (about 4 oz./115 g) diced green chiles
- ⅓ cup (80 ml) lime juice
- ¼ cup (60 ml) water
- ¼ cup (10 g) chopped cilantro
- 1 clove garlic, peeled
- 1 or 2 fresh jalapeño chiles, seeded and chopped
- 1½ teaspoons sugar

1. In a blender or food processor, combine green chiles, lime juice, water, cilantro, garlic, jalapeño chiles, and sugar; whirl until smoothly puréed. (At this point, you may cover and refrigerate dressing for up to 4 hours.)

Makes about 1 cup (240 ml)

NUTRIENTS

Per tablespoon: 5 calories (2% calories from fat), 0.01 g total fat, 0 g saturated fat, 0 mg cholesterol, 44 mg sodium, 1 g carbohydrates, 0.1 g fiber, 0.1 g protein, 2 mg calcium, 0.1 mg iron

Ginger Oil

Preparation time: **About 5 minutes**
Cooking time: **About 5 minutes**

Ginger oil adds a pungent flavor to dressings for fruit and meat salads. You can also use it for sautéing meats, poultry, and vegetables for curry dishes.

- ¼ cup (15 g) ground ginger
- 1 cup (240 ml) vegetable oil or olive oil

1. In a small pan, whisk together ginger and ¼ cup (60 ml) of the oil until well blended. Gradually whisk in remaining ¾ cup (180 ml) oil. Heat over medium heat, stirring often, just until warm (not hot or boiling). Remove from heat and let cool slightly.

2. Carefully pour oil into a clean, dry glass bottle or jar, leaving ginger sediment behind; discard sediment. (Or strain oil, if desired.) Cover airtight and store for up to 6 months.

Makes about 1 cup (240 ml)

NUTRIENTS

Per tablespoon: 124 calories (97% calories from fat), 14 g total fat, 2 g saturated fat, 0 mg cholesterol, 0.4 mg sodium, 1 g carbohydrates, 0 g fiber, 0.1 g protein, 2 mg calcium, 0.2 mg iron

SEAFOOD

Poached Fish with Horseradish Sauce

Preparation time: **About 25 minutes**
Cooking time: **About 20 minutes**

Tiny boiled potatoes and slivered green onions garnish a savory supper dish that's delicious prepared with any of a variety of fish. The simple sauce, based on the poaching liquid, gets a flavor boost from horseradish. When kept in the refrigerator too long, horseradish can lose it's punch. Be sure to check your bottle for freshness before preparing this recipe.

1½ pounds (680 g) skinless, boneless lingcod, halibut, rockfish, or sole fillets or steaks (fillets no thicker than 1 inch/2.5 cm, steaks about 1 inch/ 2.5 cm thick)

  About ⅔ cup (160 ml) fat-free reduced-sodium chicken broth

1 tablespoon cornstarch

1 tablespoon (15 ml) prepared horseradish

8 to 12 hot boiled tiny potatoes (each about 1 inch/2.5 cm in diameter)

3 green onions, cut into 2-inch (5-cm) lengths and slivered

1. Rinse fish and pat dry; fold any thin fillets in half. Arrange fish in a shallow 8-inch (20-cm) baking dish. Pour ⅔ cup (160 ml) of the broth over fish. Cover and bake in a 400°F (205°C) oven until fish is just opaque but still moist in thickest part; cut to test (about 15 minutes). With a slotted spatula, lift fish to a warm platter; keep warm.

2. Drain cooking liquid from baking dish into a measuring cup; you should have about 1 cup (240 ml). If necessary, boil to reduce to 1 cup (240 ml) or add more broth to make 1 cup (240 ml). In a 1½- to 2-quart (1.4- to 1.9-liter) pan, smoothly blend cornstarch, horseradish, and cooking liquid. Bring to a boil over high heat, stirring.

3. Spoon sauce evenly over fish. Arrange potatoes on platter around fish; sprinkle with onions.

Makes 4 servings

NUTRIENTS

Per serving: 206 calories (9% calories from fat), 2 g total fat, 0.3 g saturated fat, 89 mg cholesterol, 218 mg sodium, 13 g carbohydrates, 1 g fiber, 32 g protein, 34 mg calcium, 1 mg iron

Whole Tilapia with Onion & Lemon

Preparation time: **About 15 minutes**
Baking time: **20 to 25 minutes**

Farmed in both Mexico and the United States, tilapia is a perchlike fish with a clean, delicate flavor similar to that of petrale sole. It's appealingly lean, but remains moist and tender after cooking. In this recipe, which makes a special dinner for two, a whole dressed tilapia is baked on a bed of ginger-spiked onion and lemon slices.

1¼ pounds (565 g) red onions, cut into ⅛-inch-thick (3-mm-thick) slices

3 tablespoons (45 ml) lemon juice

1 tablespoon minced fresh ginger

1 whole tilapia (about 1½ lbs./680 g), dressed (gutted, with head and tail attached)

1 tablespoon (15 ml) extra-virgin olive oil

2 large lemons

3 tablespoons minced cilantro

  Salt and pepper

1. In a large bowl, mix onions, lemon juice, and ginger. Reserve a couple of onion slices; arrange remaining slices over bottom of a 9- by 13-inch (23- by 33-cm) or shallow 4- to 5-quart (3.8- to 4.8-liter) baking dish.

2. Rinse fish and pat dry. Brush both sides of fish with oil; then place fish on top of onion mixture.

3. Cut a ½-inch (1-cm) slice from each end of each lemon; stuff fish cavity with lemon ends, reserved onion slices, and half the cilantro. Thinly slice remaining piece of each lemon; tuck slices around fish. Sprinkle remaining cilantro over onion and lemon in baking dish. Bake in a 400°F (205°C) oven until a meat thermometer inserted in thickest part of fish registers 135°F (57°C) and flesh is just opaque but still moist; cut to test (20 to 25 minutes).

4. To serve, gently pull skin from fish; then spoon fish, onions, and lemon slices onto 2 dinner plates. Season to taste with salt and pepper.

Makes 2 servings

NUTRIENTS

Per serving: 359 calories (22% calories from fat), 10 g total fat, 2 g saturated fat, 82 mg cholesterol, 177 mg sodium, 40 g carbohydrates, 5 g fiber, 38 g protein, 184 mg calcium, 3 mg iron

SEA BASS WITH GREEN BEANS & SESAME-ORANGE SAUCE

Preparation time: **About 20 minutes**
Cooking time: **About 15 minutes**

Mild, rich-tasting Chilean sea bass, red onion, and slender green beans combine in this simple dish. Sea bass is often sold in 1-inch-thick (2.5-cm-thick) fillets; if necessary, cut the pieces horizontally to make them ½ inch (1 cm) thick. This will ensure that they cook quickly.

¾ teaspoon grated orange peel

¼ cup (60 ml) orange juice

2 tablespoons (30 ml) reduced-sodium soy sauce

1 clove garlic, minced or pressed

1½ teaspoons honey

1 teaspoon minced fresh ginger

½ teaspoon Oriental sesame oil

1 teaspoon sesame seeds

8 ounces (230 g) slender green beans (ends removed), cut diagonally into 1-inch (2.5-cm) lengths

½ cup (60 g) sliced red onion

1 teaspoon vegetable oil or olive oil

1 pound (455 g) Chilean sea bass, halibut, or orange roughy fillets (about ½ inch/1 cm thick), cut into 1-inch (2.5-cm) pieces

1. To prepare sesame-orange sauce, in a small bowl, stir together orange peel, orange juice, soy sauce, garlic, honey, ginger, and sesame oil; set aside.

2. In a wide nonstick frying pan or wok, stir sesame seeds over medium heat until golden (about 3 minutes). Pour out of pan and set aside.

3. In pan, combine beans, onion, and ⅓ cup (80 ml) water. Increase heat to medium-high; cover and cook until beans are almost tender to bite (about 3 minutes). Uncover and stir-fry until liquid has evaporated. Transfer bean mixture to a rimmed platter and keep warm.

4. Heat oil in pan. When oil is hot, add fish and stir-fry gently until just opaque but still moist in thickest part; cut to test (3 to 4 minutes). Remove fish from pan with a slotted spoon; add to bean mixture and mix gently but thoroughly. Sprinkle with sesame seeds. Stir sesame-orange sauce; offer sauce to add to individual servings.

Makes 4 servings

NUTRIENTS

Per serving: 177 calories (23% calories from fat), 4 g total fat, 0.9 g saturated fat, 47 mg cholesterol, 383 mg sodium, 11 g carbohydrates, 1 g fiber, 23 g protein, 51 mg calcium, 1 mg iron

HALIBUT PICCATA WITH LEMON LINGUINE

Preparation time: **About 15 minutes**
Cooking time: **About 25 minutes**

Succulent halibut fillets are very quickly broiled and then served with lemony linguine and a lemon sauce.

1 teaspoon olive oil
2 cloves garlic, minced or pressed
⅔ cup (160 ml) dry white wine
⅓ cup (80 ml) lemon juice

2 tablespoons drained capers
8 ounces (230 g) dried linguine
1½ pounds (680 g) Pacific halibut fillets (each ¾ to 1 inch/2 to 2.5 cm thick)
 Pepper
¼ cup (20 g) freshly grated Parmesan cheese
½ cup (120 ml) fat-free reduced-sodium chicken broth
½ teaspoon grated lemon peel
2 teaspoons honey
1 teaspoon Dijon mustard
2 ounces (55 g) Neufchâtel or nonfat cream cheese
¼ cup (15 g) minced parsley

1. Heat oil in a small nonstick frying pan over medium-high heat. Add garlic and cook, stirring,

20 MINUTES OR LESS

2 tablespoons (30 ml) olive oil

1½ tablespoons (23 ml) lime juice

1 tablespoon drained capers

4 small pear-shaped (Roma-type) tomatoes (about 8 oz./230 g total), at room temperature, seeded and chopped

2 cloves garlic, minced or pressed

¼ teaspoon ground red pepper (cayenne)

⅓ cup (15 g) cilantro leaves

1¼ to 1½ pounds (565 to 680 g) halibut steaks or other white-fleshed fish steaks such as sea bass (about ¾ inch/2 cm thick)

Salt and black pepper

Olive oil cooking spray

1 package (10 oz./255 or 285 g) fresh linguine

HALIBUT WITH TOMATO & CILANTRO LINGUINE

1. In a large bowl, stir together oil, lime juice, capers, tomatoes, garlic, red pepper, and cilantro; set aside. Remove and discard any skin from fish, then rinse fish and pat dry. Cut fish into 4 serving-size pieces; season to taste with salt and black pepper.

2. Spray a wide nonstick frying pan with cooking spray; place over medium-high heat. Add fish and cook, turning once, until lightly browned on outside and just opaque but still moist in thickest part; cut to test (6 to 8 minutes).

3. Meanwhile, in a 5- to 6-quart (5- to 6-liter) pan, cook linguine in 3 quarts (2.8 liters) boiling water just until tender to bite (1 to 2 minutes); or cook according to package directions. Drain pasta well. Set 2 tablespoons (30 ml) of the tomato mixture aside; lightly mix remaining mixture with hot pasta.

4. Divide pasta among 4 warm plates; top each serving with a piece of fish, then top fish evenly with reserved tomato mixture.

Makes 4 servings

Per serving: 420 calories (25% calories from fat), 12 g total fat, 2 g saturated fat, 92 mg cholesterol, 148 mg sodium, 42 g carbohydrates, 2 g fiber, 35 g protein, 78 mg calcium, 4 mg iron

until fragrant and hot; do not scorch. Add ½ cup (120 ml) of the wine, 3 tablespoons (45 ml) of the lemon juice, and capers. Bring to a boil and cook until reduced to about ½ cup/120 ml (about 4 minutes). Remove from heat and keep warm.

2. Bring 8 cups (1.9 liters) water to a boil in a 4- to 5-quart (3.8- to 5-liter) pan over medium-high heat. Stir in pasta and cook just until tender to bite (8 to 10 minutes); or cook according to package directions. Drain well and keep warm.

3. Cut fish into 4 equal portions and sprinkle with pepper. Place in a single layer in a lightly oiled broiler pan without a rack. Broil about 3 inches (8 cm) below heat for 3 minutes. Turn, sprinkle with Parmesan cheese, and continue to broil until opaque but still moist in center of thickest part; cut to test (about 3 more minutes). Keep warm.

4. Combine broth, lemon peel, remaining lemon juice, honey, and mustard in a 3- to 4-quart (2.8- to 3.8-liter) pan. Bring to a boil over high heat. Remove from heat; whisk in Neufchâtel just until melted. Add pasta, remaining wine, and parsley; lift with 2 forks to mix. Mound on individual plates. Arrange fish alongside; drizzle with sauce.

Makes 4 servings

NUTRIENTS

Per serving: 522 calories (21% calories from fat), 11 g total fat, 4 g saturated fat, 70 mg cholesterol, 428 mg sodium, 48 g carbohydrates, 2 g fiber, 47 g protein, 201 mg calcium, 4 mg iron

SWORDFISH WITH MANGO RELISH

Preparation time: **About 10 minutes**
Soaking time: **30 minutes**
Cooking time: **About 5 minutes**

The bright colors and bold flavors of this delicious fruit relish will please both the eye and the palate. The relish is served over thin strips of swordfish, quickly stir-fried to stay moist.

¼ cup (45 g) minced white onion
1½ cups (250 g) diced ripe mango
¾ cup (115 g) diced red bell pepper
¼ cup (10 g) chopped cilantro
1 tablespoon minced fresh ginger
2 tablespoons (30 ml) lemon juice
2 teaspoons vegetable oil
1½ pounds (680 g) swordfish, cut into ½- by 2-inch (1- by 5-cm) strips
½ cup (20 g) lightly packed cilantro sprigs

1. To prepare mango relish, place onion in a fine strainer; rinse with cold water. Place in a bowl, cover with ice water, and let stand for 30 minutes. Drain. Return onion to bowl; stir in mango, bell pepper, chopped cilantro, ginger, and lemon juice; set aside.

2. Heat oil in a wide nonstick frying pan or wok over medium-high heat. When oil is hot, add swordfish and stir-fry gently (flipping with a spatula, if needed) until just opaque but still moist in thickest part; cut to test (about 4 minutes). Spoon swordfish onto a platter; top with mango relish and garnish with cilantro sprigs.

Makes 6 servings

NUTRIENTS

Per serving: 186 calories (30% calories from fat), 6 g total fat, 1 g saturated fat, 44 mg cholesterol, 106 mg sodium, 9 g carbohydrates, 0.8 g fiber, 23 g protein, 14 mg calcium, 1 mg iron

2 cloves garlic, minced or pressed

1 teaspoon sugar

1 teaspoon Oriental sesame oil

⅛ teaspoon crushed red pepper flakes

1 pound (455 g) red snapper fillets
   (about ½ inch/1 cm thick), cut into
   1-inch (2.5-cm) pieces

1 medium-size pineapple (3 to
   3½ lbs./1.35 to 1.6 kg)

1 teaspoon vegetable oil

1½ cups (115 g) fresh Chinese pea pods
    (also called snow or sugar peas) or
    sugar snap peas, ends and strings
    removed; or 1 package (about
    6 oz./170 g) frozen Chinese pea pods,
    thawed and drained

1 tablespoon cornstarch blended with
   1 tablespoon (15 ml) cold water

½ cup (50 g) thinly sliced green onions

ORIENTAL-STYLE
RED SNAPPER
STIR-FRY

Preparation time: **About 20 minutes**
Cooking time: **About 10 minutes**

Here's an interesting combination of both sweet and savory flavors. Crunchy pea pods and chunks of mild red snapper—cloaked in a sauce laced with ginger and garlic—are served over juicy fresh pineapple rings. Red snapper is available fresh year round and is a great choice for a healthy meal because its firm-textured flesh contains very little fat. Serve the snapper and vegetables over white or brown rice or with a bulgur pilaf.

1 tablespoon finely minced fresh
   ginger

2 tablespoons (30 ml) reduced-
   sodium soy sauce

2 tablespoons (30 ml) unsweetened
   pineapple juice

1. In a large bowl, stir together ginger, soy sauce, pineapple juice, garlic, sugar, sesame oil, and red pepper flakes. Add fish and stir to coat. Set aside; stir occasionally.

2. Peel and core pineapple, then cut crosswise into thin slices. Arrange slices on a rimmed platter; cover and set aside.

3. Heat vegetable oil in a wide nonstick frying pan or wok over medium-high heat. When oil is hot, add fish mixture and stir-fry gently until fish is just opaque but still moist in thickest part; cut to test (2 to 3 minutes). Remove fish from pan with a slotted spoon; keep warm.

4. Add pea pods to pan and stir-fry for 30 seconds (15 seconds if using frozen pea pods). Stir cornstarch mixture well, then pour into pan. Cook, stirring constantly, until sauce boils and thickens slightly (1 to 2 minutes). Return fish to pan and add onions; mix gently but thoroughly, just until fish is hot and coated with sauce. To serve, spoon fish mixture over pineapple slices.

Makes 4 servings

NUTRIENTS

Per serving: 278 calories (15% calories from fat), 5 g total fat, 0.7 g saturated fat, 42 mg cholesterol, 379 mg sodium, 34 g carbohydrates, 4 g fiber, 26 g protein, 88 mg calcium, 2 mg iron

SALMON WITH CREAMY TOMATILLO SAUCE

Preparation time: **About 20 minutes**
Cooking time: **About 15 minutes**

Rich pink salmon served on a creamy, pale green tomatillo sauce makes a lovely entrée. Before using fresh tomatillos, remove the parchmentlike husks and rinse the fruit well to remove the sticky coating. You can store fresh tomatillos refrigerated for up to a month.

4 medium-size tomatillos (about 4 oz./115 g total), husked, rinsed, and chopped

1 tablespoon sliced green onion

1 clove garlic, peeled

¼ teaspoon grated lime peel

1 tablespoon (15 ml) lime juice

About ¾ teaspoon sugar, or to taste

⅛ teaspoon salt

½ cup (120 ml) plain low-fat yogurt (do not use nonfat yogurt) blended with 2 teaspoons cornstarch

8 low-fat flour tortillas (each 7 to 9 inches/18 to 23 cm in diameter)

1 tablespoon butter or margarine

1 pound (455 g) salmon fillets (about ½ inch/1 cm thick), skinned and cut into ¾-inch (2-cm) pieces

1 medium-size tomato (about 6 oz./ 170 g), chopped and drained well

2 tablespoons cilantro leaves

Lime wedges

Ground white pepper.

1. In a blender or food processor, combine tomatillos, onion, garlic, lime peel, lime juice, sugar, and salt. Whirl until smooth. By hand, stir in yogurt mixture just until combined; do not over beat or sauce will separate. Set aside.

2. Brush tortillas lightly with hot water; then stack, wrap in foil, and heat in a 350°F (175°C) oven until warm (10 to 12 minutes).

3. Meanwhile, melt butter in a wide nonstick frying pan or wok over medium-high heat. Add fish and stir-fry gently until just opaque but still moist in thickest part; cut to test (about 4 minutes). Remove from pan and keep warm. Wipe pan clean (be careful; pan is hot).

4. Add yogurt-tomatillo sauce to pan. Reduce heat to medium-low and simmer gently, stirring constantly, until sauce is slightly thickened (2 to 3 minutes); do not boil.

5. Divide sauce among 4 individual rimmed plates; spread sauce out evenly, then top equally with fish. Sprinkle with tomato and cilantro leaves, garnish with lime wedges, and season to taste with white pepper. Serve with tortillas.

Makes 4 servings

NUTRIENTS

Per serving: 370 calories (27% calories from fat), 12 g total fat, 3 g saturated fat, 72 mg cholesterol, 533 mg sodium, 44 g carbohydrates, 9 g fiber, 29 g protein, 195 mg calcium, 3 mg iron

5. Transfer salmon to a warm platter; drizzle with any cooking juices. Surround with potatoes. Sprinkle salmon and potatoes with minced mint; garnish with mint sprigs and lemon slices.

Makes 4 servings

N U T R I E N T S

Per serving: 332 calories (26% calories from fat), 9 g total fat, 1 g saturated fat, 71 mg cholesterol, 68 mg sodium, 33 g carbohydrates, 2 g fiber, 28 g protein, 21 mg calcium, 2 mg iron

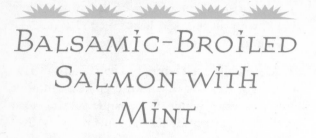

BALSAMIC-BROILED SALMON WITH MINT

Preparation time: **About 15 minutes**
Cooking time: **About 25 minutes**

In this recipe, salmon fillets are broiled with a drizzle of balsamic vinegar, honey, and oil. Balsamic vinegar, which is made from grape juice rather than wine, is uniquely sweet and mild and provides just the right note for this sweet-sour entrée. A sprinkling of fresh mint is a nice counterpoint.

1¼ pounds (565 g) small red thin-skinned potatoes (each 1½ to 2 inches/3.5 to 5 cm in diameter), scrubbed

3 tablespoons (45 ml) balsamic or raspberry vinegar

1½ tablespoons (23 ml) honey

¾ teaspoon vegetable oil

1 to 1¼ pounds (455 to 565 g) salmon fillets (¾ inch/2 cm thick)

½ cup (20 g) fresh mint leaves, minced

Mint sprigs

Lemon slices

1. Peel a 1-inch-wide (2.5-cm-wide) strip around center of each potato. Steam potatoes, covered, on a rack above about 1 inch (2.5 cm) of boiling water until tender when pierced (about 25 minutes).

2. Meanwhile, in a small bowl, stir together vinegar, honey, and oil.

3. Remove and discard any skin from salmon; rinse salmon and pat dry. Cut salmon into 4 serving-size pieces; place, skinned sides down, in a lightly greased shallow rimmed baking pan. Drizzle salmon with half the vinegar mixture.

4. Broil about 6 inches (15 cm) below heat, brushing several times with remaining vinegar mixture, until just opaque but still moist in thickest part; cut to test (8 to 10 minutes).

SALMON SAUTÉ WITH CITRUS SAUCE

Pictured on page 71
Preparation time: **About 30 minutes**
Cooking time: **About 10 minutes**

A beautiful choice for a company meal, this stir-fry combines silky salmon with a trio of citrus fruits. Fresh orange, grapefruit, and lime segments, lightly warmed in a marmalade-sweetened sauce, mingle with the moist strips of fish. Complete the menu with steamed green beans and a loaf of crusty bread for soaking up the sauce.

3 or 4 medium-size oranges (1½ to 2 lbs./680 to 905 g total)

1 large pink grapefruit (about 12 oz./340 g)

1 large lime (about 4 oz./115 g)

3 green onions

1 tablespoon butter or margarine

1 pound (455 g) salmon fillets (about ½ inch/1 cm thick), skinned and cut into 1- by 2-inch (2.5- by 5-cm) strips

¼ cup (60 ml) dry vermouth

⅓ cup (100 g) orange marmalade

1 tablespoon chopped fresh mint

Mint sprigs (optional)

Salt and pepper

1. Shred enough peel (colored part only) from oranges, grapefruit, and lime to make ½ teaspoon of each kind of peel. Combine peels in a small bowl; cover and set aside.

2. Cut off and discard remaining peel and all white membrane from grapefruit, lime, and 2 of the oranges. Holding fruit over a bowl to catch juice, cut between membranes to release segments; set segments aside. Pour juice from bowl into a glass measure. Squeeze juice from remaining oranges; add enough of this orange juice to juice in glass measure to make ½ cup/120 ml (reserve remaining orange juice for other uses). Set juice aside.

3. Trim and discard ends of onions. Cut onions into 2-inch (5-cm) lengths, then cut each piece lengthwise into slivers; set aside.

4. Melt butter in a wide nonstick frying pan or wok over medium-high heat. Add fish. Stir-fry gently (flipping with a spatula, if needed) until fish is just opaque but still moist in thickest part; cut to test (about 4 minutes). With a slotted spoon, transfer fish to a large bowl; keep warm.

5. Add citrus juices and vermouth to pan. Bring to a boil; then boil, stirring often, until reduced to ⅓ cup/80 ml (about 3 minutes). Reduce heat to low, add marmalade, and stir until melted. Add onions and citrus segments; stir gently just until heated through. Remove from heat and stir in chopped mint.

6. Spoon fruit sauce over fish; mix gently. Divide fish mixture among 4 individual rimmed plates; garnish with citrus peels and mint sprigs, if desired. Season to taste with salt and pepper.

Makes 4 servings

NUTRIENTS

Per serving: 352 calories (27% calories from fat), 10 g total fat, 3 g saturated fat, 70 mg cholesterol, 98 mg sodium, 39 g carbohydrates, 3 g fiber, 24 g protein, 89 mg calcium, 1 mg iron

TUNA & CHERRY TOMATO SALSA

Preparation time: **About 20 minutes**
Grilling time: **About 3 minutes**

Fresh flavors and fast cooking characterize this easy-to-prepare entrée. If you prefer a milder salsa, eliminate one jalapeño.

1 pound (455 g) red or yellow cherry tomatoes (about 3 cups), chopped

½ cup (20 g) lightly packed cilantro leaves, coarsely chopped

2 fresh jalapeño chiles, seeded and coarsely chopped

1 clove garlic, minced or pressed

3 green onions, thinly sliced

5 tablespoons (75 ml) lime juice

1 teaspoon olive oil

4 skinless, boneless tuna steaks (about 4 oz./115 g each), ¾ to 1 inch (2 to 2.5 cm) thick

2 medium-size cucumbers, thinly sliced

Freshly ground pepper

1. In a medium-size bowl, mix tomatoes, cilantro, chiles, garlic, onions, and 2 tablespoons (30 ml) of the lime juice. Cover and set aside.

2. Mix remaining 3 tablespoons (45 ml) lime juice with oil. Rinse tuna and pat dry; then brush both sides of each steak with oil mixture. Place tuna on a greased grill 4 to 6 inches (10 to 15 cm) above a solid bed of hot coals. Cook, turning once, until browned on outside but still pale pink in the center; cut to test (about 3 minutes).

3. Transfer tuna to a warm platter; surround with cucumber slices. Evenly top tuna with tomato salsa; season to taste with pepper.

Makes 4 servings

NUTRIENTS

Per serving: 225 calories (29% calories from fat), 7 g total fat, 2 g saturated fat, 43 mg cholesterol, 64 mg sodium, 12 g carbohydrates, 3 g fiber, 29 g protein, 40 mg calcium, 2 mg iron

Tuna with Tomato-Orange Relish

Preparation time: **About 10 minutes**
Cooking time: **About 30 minutes**

The pungent crimson relish that accompanies these garlicky grilled tuna steaks also goes very well with other barbecued fish and chicken recipes.

1 small orange (about 6 oz./170g)

2 medium-size tomatoes (about 12 oz./340 g total), coarsely chopped

1 tablespoon tomato paste

1 tablespoon (15 ml) cider vinegar

Vegetable oil cooking spray

1 small dried hot red chile

½ teaspoon mustard seeds

½ teaspoon cumin seeds

¼ teaspoon ground allspice

2 tablespoons firmly packed brown sugar

¼ cup (35 g) raisins

1 teaspoon olive oil

2 cloves garlic, minced or pressed

2 tablespoons (30 ml) lemon juice

6 skinless, boneless tuna steaks (about 6 oz./170 g each), ¾ to 1 inch (2 to 2.5 cm) thick

Freshly ground pepper

Italian parsley sprigs

Orange slices

1. To prepare tomato-orange relish, grate ½ teaspoon peel (colored part only) from orange; set grated peel aside. Cut remaining peel and all white membrane from orange; cut fruit into chunks.

2. In a food processor or blender, combine chopped orange, tomatoes, tomato paste, and vinegar. Whirl until coarsely puréed; set aside.

3. Spray a 1½- to 2-quart (1.4- to 1.9-liter) pan with cooking spray. Add chile, mustard seeds, and cumin seeds; stir over medium-high heat until seeds begin to pop (about 2 minutes). Mix in allspice, brown sugar, raisins, tomato mixture, and grated orange peel. Cook, stirring, until sugar is dissolved. Reduce heat so mixture cooks at a gentle boil; cook, stirring often, until consistency is jamlike (20 to 25 minutes). Remove chile, if desired. (Relish can be served hot or at room temperature.)

4. Mix oil, garlic, and lemon juice. Rinse tuna steaks, pat dry, and brush all over with oil mixture. Place tuna steaks on a greased grill 4 to 6 inches (10 to 15 cm) above a solid bed of hot coals. Cook, turning once, until browned on outside but still pale pink in center; cut to test (3 to 5 minutes).

5. Transfer tuna steaks to a warm platter; season to taste with pepper. Spoon a dollop of tomato-orange relish over each piece of tuna; serve with remaining relish to add to taste. Garnish with parsley sprigs and orange slices.

Makes 6 servings

NUTRIENTS

Per serving: 317 calories (28% calories from fat), 10 g total fat, 2 g saturated fat, 65 mg cholesterol, 97 mg sodium, 16 g carbohydrates, 2 g fiber, 41 g protein, 26 mg calcium, 2 mg iron

STIR-FRIED TUNA ON SPINACH

Preparation time: About 30 minutes
Cooking time: About 8 minutes

Here's an eye-catching entrée: hot, gingery fresh tuna served over cool, crisp spinach leaves. The recipe calls for *mirin* (sometimes referred to as rice wine), a low-alcohol, sweet golden wine made from glutinous rice. Mirin is available at Japanese markets and in the gourmet section of some supermarkets. If you can't find it, use cream sherry instead, or a mix of white wine or sake and a little sugar.

¼ cup (60 ml) mirin or cream sherry

6 tablespoons (85 ml) unseasoned rice vinegar or cider vinegar

2 tablespoons (30 ml) reduced-sodium soy sauce

1 teaspoon prepared horseradish

3 quarts (about 12 oz./340 g) lightly packed rinsed, crisped spinach leaves

1 tablespoon sesame seeds

1 teaspoon vegetable oil

2 tablespoons finely minced fresh ginger

12 ounces (340 g) fresh tuna, cut into ½- by 2-inch (1- by 5-cm) strips

½ cup (50 g) thinly sliced green onions

1 cup (115 g) thinly sliced red radishes

Whole green onions (ends trimmed)

1. To prepare soy dressing, in a small bowl, stir together mirin, vinegar, soy sauce, and horseradish; set aside.

2. Arrange spinach on a large platter, cover, and set aside.

3. In a wide nonstick frying pan or wok, stir sesame seeds over medium heat until golden (about 3 minutes). Pour out of pan and set aside.

4. Heat oil in pan over medium-high heat. When oil is hot, add ginger and stir-fry just until light brown (about 30 seconds; do not scorch). Add tuna and stir-fry gently (flipping with a spatula, if needed) until just opaque but still moist and pink in thickest part; cut to test (about 3 minutes). Stir soy dressing and pour into pan; stir to mix, then remove pan from heat.

5. Spoon tuna mixture over spinach on platter. Sprinkle with sliced green onions, radishes, and sesame seeds. Garnish with whole green onions.
Makes 4 servings

NUTRIENTS

Per serving: 220 calories (30% calories from fat), 7 g total fat, 1 g saturated fat, 32 mg cholesterol, 411 mg sodium, 12 g carbohydrates, 3 g fiber, 24 g protein, 125 mg calcium, 4 mg iron

CRAB WITH EMERALD SAUCE

Pictured on facing page
Preparation time: **About 20 minutes**
Cooking time: **About 8 minutes**

A bright green sauce puréed from fresh basil and cilantro sets off delicate pasta and chunks of fresh crab.

  8 ounces (230 g) basil sprigs

  4 ounces (115 g) cilantro sprigs

  8 ounces (230 g) dried capellini

  ¼ cup (60 ml) seasoned rice vinegar; or
     ¼ cup (60 ml) rice vinegar and
     1 teaspoon sugar

  1 tablespoon minced lemon peel

  1 tablespoon (15 ml) Oriental sesame oil

  ¾ cup (180 ml) fat-free reduced-sodium
     chicken broth

  2 tablespoons (30 ml) vegetable oil

  ⅓ to ½ pound (150 to 230 g) cooked
     crabmeat

1. Reserve 4 of the basil sprigs and cilantro sprigs for garnish. Bring 8 cups (1.9 liters) water to a boil in a 4- to 5-quart (3.8- to 5-liter) pan over medium-high heat. Gather half the remaining fresh basil into a bunch. Holding stem ends with tongs, dip leaves into boiling water just until bright green (about 3 seconds). At once plunge into ice water. Repeat with cilantro and remaining basil.

2. Stir pasta into water and cook just until tender to bite (about 4 minutes); or cook according to package directions. Drain well. Place in a bowl. Add vinegar, lemon peel, and sesame oil; lift with 2 forks to mix. Keep warm.

3. Drain basil and cilantro; blot dry. Cut leaves from stems, discarding stems. Place leaves in a blender or food processor with broth and vegetable oil. Whirl until smooth. Spread on individual plates. Top with pasta and crab. Garnish with reserved basil and cilantro sprigs.

Makes 4 servings

NUTRIENTS

Per serving: 382 calories (30% calories from fat), 13 g total fat, 2 g saturated fat, 43 mg cholesterol, 485 mg sodium, 49 g carbohydrates, 4 g fiber, 19 g protein, 172 mg calcium, 5 mg iron

CRACKED CRAB WITH ONION

Preparation time: **About 15 minutes**
Cooking time: **About 10 minutes**

D ungeness crab, a Pacific Coast delicacy, is particularly sweet and succulent. Look for crabs about 2 pounds apiece.

  ⅓ cup (80 ml) dry sherry

  ⅓ cup (80 ml) water

  ¼ cup (60 ml) oyster sauce

  2 teaspoons cornstarch

 14 green onions

  1 tablespoon (15 ml) vegetable oil

  3 tablespoons minced fresh ginger

  3 cooked Dungeness crabs (about 6 lbs. /
     2.7 kg total), cleaned and cracked

1. In a small bowl, stir together sherry, ⅓ cup water, oyster sauce, and cornstarch until blended; set aside. Cut onions into 2-inch (5-cm) lengths, keeping white and green parts separate.

2. Heat oil in a wide nonstick frying pan or wok over medium-high heat. Add ginger and white parts of onions; stir-fry until onions just begin to brown (about 2 minutes). Stir sherry mixture and pour into pan; stir until sauce boils and thickens slightly (about 1 minute). Add crab and green parts of onions; stir to coat with sauce. Reduce heat to low, cover, and cook, stirring occasionally, until crab is heated through (5 to 8 minutes).

Makes 6 servings

NUTRIENTS

Per serving: 163 calories (21% calories from fat), 3 g total fat, 0.4 g saturated fat, 64 mg cholesterol, 805 mg sodium, 8 g carbohydrates, 0.8 g fiber, 21 g protein, 80 mg calcium, 1 mg iron

CRAB WITH EMERALD SAUCE (RECIPE ON FACING PAGE)

LEMON SHRIMP OVER CAPER COUSCOUS (RECIPE ON PAGE 78)

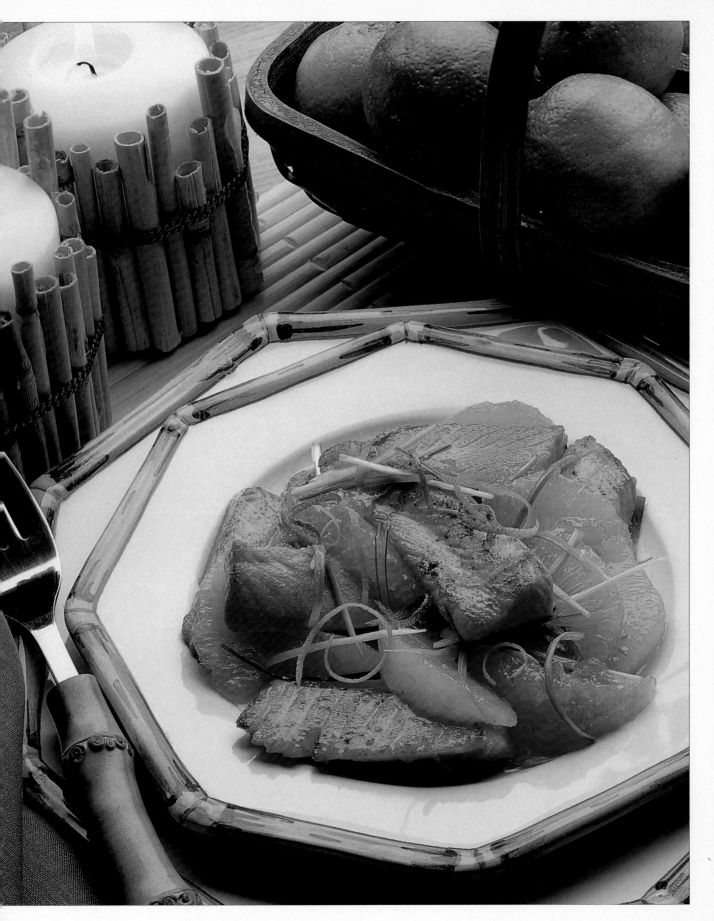

SALMON SAUTÉ WITH CITRUS SAUCE (RECIPE ON PAGE 64)

Soft Crab Tacos with Tomatillo & Lime Salsa (recipe on facing page)

SOFT CRAB TACOS WITH TOMATILLO & LIME SALSA

Pictured on facing page
Preparation time: **About 20 minutes**
Cooking time: **About 15 minutes**

For this speedy meal, warm tortillas are topped with a blend of sweet crab, chiles, and tomatoes, then further topped with sour cream and a tart salsa.

TOMATILLO & LIME SALSA:

8 medium-size tomatillos (about 8 oz./230 g total), husked, rinsed, and finely chopped

2 tablespoons sliced green onion

¼ teaspoon grated lime peel

2 tablespoons (30 ml) lime juice

1 teaspoon sugar, or to taste

⅛ teaspoon salt, or to taste

SOFT CRAB TACOS:

6 to 12 corn tortillas (each about 6 inches/15 cm in diameter) or 6 to 12 low-fat flour tortillas (each 7 to 9 inches/18 to 23 cm in diameter)

2 tablespoons (30 ml) olive oil

1 clove garlic, minced or pressed

1 small red onion, finely chopped

1 can (about 4 oz./115 g) diced green chiles

2 large firm-ripe tomatoes (about 1 lb./455 g total), chopped

1 pound (455 g) cooked crabmeat

3 to 6 cups (3 to 6 oz./85 to 170 g) finely shredded lettuce

¼ cup (10 g) lightly packed cilantro leaves

½ cup (120 ml) nonfat sour cream

GARNISH:

Lime wedges

1. To prepare tomatillo & lime salsa, in a medium-size bowl, combine tomatillos, green onion, lime peel, lime juice, sugar, and salt; set aside. (At this point, the salsa can be covered and refrigerated for up to 4 hours; stir before serving.)

2. Brush tortillas lightly with hot water; stack, wrap in foil, and heat in a 350°F (175°C) oven until warm (10 to 12 minutes.)

3. Meanwhile, heat oil in a wide nonstick frying pan or wok over medium-high heat. When oil is hot add garlic and red onion; stir-fry until onion begins to brown (about 5 minutes). Add chiles and half the tomatoes; stir-fry until tomatoes are soft (about 4 minutes). Remove from heat and gently stir in crab.

4. Divide lettuce among tortillas; then top tortillas equally with crab mixture, remaining tomatoes, and cilantro. Top with tomatillo & lime salsa and sour cream. Garnish with lime wedges.

Makes 6 servings

NUTRIENTS

Per serving: 263 calories (25% calories from fat), 7 g total fat, 0.9 g saturated fat, 76 mg cholesterol, 460 mg sodium, 29 g carbohydrates, 4 g fiber, 21 g protein, 216 mg calcium, 2 mg iron

GRILLED SCALLOPS WITH PEAR-GINGER COULIS

Preparation time: **About 15 minutes**
Cooking time: **About 20 minutes**

A gingery purée of fresh pears makes a saucy dip for sea scallops cooked on the barbecue. Instead of skewering the scallops, you can place them on a grill topper (see page 10 for more information on this handy tool), which will keep the scallops from falling into the fire.

4　teaspoons (20 ml) olive oil

1　small onion, chopped

2　tablespoons chopped fresh ginger

3　medium-size firm-ripe pears (1¼ to 1½ lbs./565 g to 680 g total), peeled, cored, and diced

¼　cup (60 ml) rice vinegar or white wine vinegar

1　pound (455 g) sea scallops, rinsed and patted dry

1. Heat 1 tablespoon (15 ml) of the oil in a 2-quart (1.9 liter) pan over medium-high heat. Add onion and cook, stirring often, until soft but not browned (3 to 5 minutes). Add ginger, pears, and vinegar. Cook, stirring occasionally, until pears are tender when pierced (12 to 15 minutes). Transfer mixture to a food processor or blender; whirl until smoothly puréed. Return to pan and keep warm over lowest heat.

2. Meanwhile, cut scallops in half horizontally, if necessary, to make ½-inch-thick (1-cm-thick) discs. Lightly mix scallops and remaining 1 teaspoon oil. Thread a fourth of the scallops on each of 4 metal skewers, piercing scallops horizontally (through diameter) so they lie flat.

3. Place skewers on a greased grill 4 to 6 inches above a solid bed of hot coals. Cook, turning once, until scallops are opaque in center; cut to test

(5 to 7 minutes). Spoon the warm pear mixture onto 4 dinner plates; lay a skewer alongside.

Makes 4 servings

NUTRIENTS

Per serving: 240 calories (22% calories from fat), 6 g total fat, 0.7 g saturated fat, 37 mg cholesterol, 184 mg sodium, 28 g carbohydrates, 4 g fiber, 20 g protein, 49 mg calcium, 0.8 mg iron

SCALLOP & PEA POD STIR-FRY WITH PAPAYA

Preparation time: **About 15 minutes**
Cooking time: **About 8 minutes**

Colorful, fragrant, and just plain delicious, this dish is a winner. Be prepared—it's likely to disappear instantly.

2　teaspoons cornstarch

1　tablespoon (15 ml) honey

1　tablespoon (15 ml) lemon juice

½　teaspoon ground ginger

½　teaspoon Chinese five-spice (or ⅛ teaspoon each anise seeds, ground allspice, ground cinnamon, and ground cloves)

2　medium-size papayas (about 1 lb./455 g each)

1　pound (455 g) sea scallops

1　tablespoon butter or margarine

1½　cups (115 g) fresh Chinese pea pods (also called snow or sugar peas) or sugar snap peas, ends and strings removed; or 1 package (about 6 oz./170 g) frozen Chinese pea pods, thawed and drained

1. To prepare ginger sauce, in a small bowl, stir together cornstarch and ¼ cup (60 ml) water until blended. Stir in honey, lemon juice, ginger, and five-spice; set aside.

2. Cut unpeeled papayas lengthwise into halves; remove and discard seeds. Set papaya halves, cut side up, on a platter; cover and set aside.

3. Rinse scallops and pat dry; cut into bite-size pieces, if desired. Melt butter in a wide nonstick frying pan or wok over medium-high heat. Add scallops and fresh pea pods (if using frozen pea pods, add later, as directed below). Stir-fry until scallops are just opaque in center; cut to test (3 to 4 minutes).

4. Stir ginger sauce well, then pour into pan. Stir in frozen pea pods, if using. Cook, stirring, until sauce boils and thickens slightly (1 to 2 minutes). Spoon scallop mixture equally into papaya halves.

Makes 4 servings

NUTRIENTS

Per serving: 220 calories (16% calories from fat), 4 g total fat, 2 g saturated fat, 45 mg cholesterol, 219 mg sodium, 26 g carbohydrates, 2 g fiber, 21 g protein, 78 mg calcium, 1 mg iron

SCALLOP SCAMPI

Preparation time: **About 15 minutes**
Cooking time: **About 15 minutes**

In Italy, *scampi* means "shrimp." In America, though, the word usually refers to shrimp prepared a certain way: sautéed with plenty of oil, butter, and garlic. In making this scampi-inspired scallop dish, we've been generous with the garlic—there are three cloves in the stir-fry, another in the crisp crumb topping—but we've cut the fat to about a tablespoon. The result? A great-tasting dish that's lean, too.

1 slice (about 1 oz./30 g) sourdough sandwich bread, torn into pieces

2 teaspoons olive oil

4 cloves garlic, minced or pressed

1 tablespoon chopped parsley

2 tablespoons (30 ml) dry white wine

1 teaspoon lemon juice

½ teaspoon honey

1 bunch watercress (about 5 oz./140 g), coarse stems removed, sprigs rinsed and crisped

1 pound (455 g) sea scallops

1½ teaspoons butter or margarine

   Lemon wedges

1. To prepare stir-fried crumbs, whirl bread in a blender or food processor to make fine crumbs. In a wide nonstick frying pan or wok, combine crumbs, 1½ teaspoons water, ½ teaspoon of the olive oil, and a fourth of the garlic. Stir-fry over medium heat until crumbs are crisp and golden (about 5 minutes); remove from pan and set aside. (At this point, the crumbs can be cooled, covered in an airtight container, and stored at room temperature until next day.)

2. Let crumbs cool slightly. Stir parsley into crumbs and set aside.

3. In a small bowl, stir together wine, lemon juice, and honey; set aside. Arrange watercress on a large rimmed platter; cover and set aside.

4. Rinse scallops and pat dry; cut into bite-size pieces, if desired. Melt butter in remaining 1½ teaspoons oil in a wide nonstick frying pan or wok over medium-high heat. When butter mixture is hot, add remaining garlic, 1 tablespoon (15 ml) water, and the scallops. Stir-fry until scallops are just opaque in center; cut to test (3 to 4 minutes).

5. Stir wine mixture well and pour into pan; bring just to a boil. With a slotted spoon, lift scallops from pan; arrange over watercress. Pour pan juices into a small pitcher. Sprinkle scallops with stir-fried crumbs and garnish with lemon wedges. Offer pan juices to add to taste.

Makes 4 servings

NUTRIENTS

Per serving: 168 calories (27% calories from fat), 5 g total fat, 1 g saturated fat, 41 mg cholesterol, 257 mg sodium, 9 g carbohydrates, 1 g fiber, 21 g protein, 83 mg calcium, 0.7 mg iron

SAUTÉED SCALLOPS WITH SPINACH & FARFALLE

Preparation time: **About 20 minutes**
Cooking time: **About 15 minutes**

Whimsical pasta "butterflies" are a perfect foil for stir-fried scallops seasoned with sage. Add shredded spinach and chopped tomato for a light supper.

8 ounces (230 g) dried farfalle or other pasta shapes (about 1½-inch/3.5-cm size)

1 pound (455 g) sea scallops

2 tablespoons (30 g) butter or margarine

2 cloves garlic, minced or pressed

About ¾ teaspoon chopped fresh sage or ¼ teaspoon dried rubbed sage, or to taste

1 large tomato (about 8 oz./230 g), chopped and drained well

¼ cup (60 ml) dry white wine

½ to ¾ cup (15 to 23 g) finely shredded spinach

About ⅓ cup (30 g) freshly grated Parmesan cheese

Sage sprigs

Pepper

1. In a 4- to 5-quart (3.8- to 5-liter) pan, cook pasta in about 8 cups (1.9 liters) boiling water until just tender to bite (8 to 10 minutes); or cook according to package directions. Drain well, transfer to a warm rimmed platter, and keep warm.

2. While pasta is cooking, rinse scallops and pat dry; cut into bite-size pieces, if desired. Melt butter in a wide nonstick frying pan or wok over medium-high heat. Add scallops and stir-fry until just opaque in center; cut to test (3 to 4 minutes). Remove scallops from pan with a slotted spoon; keep warm.

3. Add garlic and chopped sage to pan; stir-fry just until garlic is fragrant (about 30 seconds; do not scorch). Stir in tomato and wine; bring to a boil. Remove from heat, add scallops and spinach, and mix gently but thoroughly. Spoon scallop mixture over pasta; sprinkle with cheese and garnish with sage sprigs. Season to taste with pepper.

Makes 4 servings

NUTRIENTS

Per serving: 417 calories (22% calories from fat), 10 g total fat, 5 g saturated fat, 58 mg cholesterol, 381 mg sodium, 49 g carbohydrates, 2 g fiber, 30 g protein, 146 mg calcium, 3 mg iron

SCALLOPS WITH BROCCOLI & BELL PEPPER

Preparation time: **About 15 minutes**
Cooking time: **About 10 minutes**

Saucy and bright—that describes this combination of green broccoli, red bell pepper, and white sea scallops. Serve it with fresh Chinese noodles or hot, fluffy rice.

2 tablespoons (30 ml) reduced-sodium soy sauce

4 teaspoons cornstarch

¾ cup (180 ml) fat-free reduced-sodium chicken broth

2 tablespoons (30 ml) dry sherry

2 teaspoons finely minced fresh ginger

1½ teaspoons sugar

1 pound (455 g) sea scallops

2 cups (145 g) broccoli flowerets

1 medium-size red or green bell pepper (about 6 oz./170 g), seeded and cut into thin strips

1 small onion, thinly sliced

2 teaspoons vegetable oil

1 or 2 cloves garlic, minced or pressed

1. To prepare sauce, in a small bowl, stir together soy sauce and cornstarch until blended. Stir in broth, sherry, ginger, and sugar; set aside.

2. Rinse scallops and pat dry; cut into bite-size pieces, if desired. Set aside.

3. In a wide nonstick frying pan or wok, combine broccoli, bell pepper, onion, and ⅓ cup (80 ml) water. Cover and cook over medium-high heat just until vegetables are tender to bite (about 4 minutes). Uncover and stir-fry until liquid has evaporated.

4. Stir sauce well and pour into pan. Cook, stirring, until sauce boils and thickens slightly (1 to 2 minutes). Transfer vegetable mixture to a serving bowl and keep warm. Wipe pan clean.

5. Heat oil in pan over medium-high heat. When oil is hot, add garlic and 1 tablespoon (15 ml) water to pan. Stir-fry just until garlic is fragrant (about 30 seconds). Add scallops. Stir-fry until scallops are just opaque in center; cut to test (3 to 4 minutes). Pour scallops and any pan juices over vegetable mixture; mix gently but thoroughly.

Makes 4 servings

NUTRIENTS

Per serving: 196 calories (16% calories from fat), 3 g total fat, 0.4 g saturated fat, 37 mg cholesterol, 591 mg sodium, 17 g carbohydrates, 3 g fiber, 23 g protein, 68 mg calcium, 1 mg iron

LEMON SHRIMP OVER CAPER COUSCOUS

Pictured on page 70
Preparation time: **About 20 minutes**
Cooking time: **About 15 minutes**

Add plenty of tangy flavor, and you won't miss the fat! That's the rule we've followed in this recipe. Shrimp are seasoned with lemon peel and garlic, then served with asparagus on a bed of lemony couscous dotted with pungent capers. Offer lemon wedges to squeeze over the shrimp.

1   pound (455 g) large raw shrimp (31 to 35 per lb.), shelled and deveined

2   cloves garlic, minced or pressed (optional)

¾   teaspoon chopped fresh oregano or ¼ teaspoon dried oregano

½   teaspoon grated lemon peel

⅛   teaspoon pepper

2   tablespoons (30 ml) dry sherry

1   tablespoon cornstarch

2   cups (470 ml) fat-free reduced-sodium chicken broth

8   ounces (230 g) asparagus

1   medium-size red bell pepper (about 6 oz./170 g)

1   cup (185 g) couscous

2   tablespoons (30 ml) seasoned rice vinegar (or 2 tablespoons/30 ml distilled white vinegar plus 1 teaspoon sugar)

1   to 2 tablespoons drained capers

1   tablespoon (15 ml) olive oil

    Lemon wedges and oregano sprigs

1. In a large bowl, mix shrimp, garlic (if used) chopped oregano, ¼ teaspoon of the lemon peel, and pepper. Set aside; stir occasionally.

2. To prepare sauce, in a small bowl, combine sherry and cornstarch; stir until blended. Stir in ½ cup (120 ml) of the broth; set aside.

3. Snap off and discard tough ends of asparagus; cut spears into ½-inch (1-cm) diagonal slices and set aside. Seed bell pepper, cut into thin strips, and set aside.

4. In a 3- to 4-quart (2.8- to 3.8-liter) pan, combine remaining 1½ cups broth and remaining ¼ teaspoon lemon peel. Bring to a boil over high heat; stir in couscous. Cover, remove from heat, and let stand until liquid has been absorbed (about 5 minutes). Stir in vinegar and capers. Keep couscous warm; fluff occasionally with a fork.

5. In a wide nonstick frying pan or wok, combine asparagus, bell pepper, and ⅓ cup (80 ml) water. Cover and cook over medium-high heat until asparagus is almost tender to bite (about 3 minutes). Uncover and stir-fry until liquid has evaporated. Remove vegetables from pan and set aside.

6. Heat oil in pan. When oil is hot, add shrimp mixture and stir-fry for 2 minutes. Stir sauce well and pour into pan; then return asparagus and bell pepper to pan. Cook, stirring, until sauce boils and thickens slightly and shrimp are just opaque in center; cut to test (1 to 2 more minutes). Remove from heat.

7. To serve, spoon couscous onto a rimmed platter; top with shrimp mixture. Offer lemon wedges to squeeze to taste; garnish with oregano sprigs.
Makes 4 servings

NUTRIENTS

Per serving: 355 calories (14% calories from fat), 5 g total fat, 0.8 g saturated fat, 140 mg cholesterol, 696 mg sodium, 46 g carbohydrates, 2 g fiber, 28 g protein, 71 mg calcium, 3 mg iron

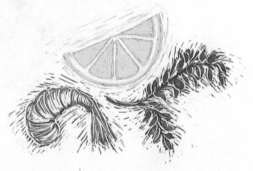

SHRIMP SAUTÉ

Preparation time: **About 15 minutes**
Cooking time: **About 25 minutes**

Large shrimp in a simple vegetable-wine sauce are perfect for family meals or casual company gatherings. Accompany the shrimp with steamed broccoli or asparagus and a crusty loaf of French bread.

- 2 teaspoons butter or margarine
- ½ cup (60 g) finely chopped celery
- ⅓ cup (40 g) finely chopped shallots
- 2 cloves garlic, minced or pressed
- 1 medium-size red bell pepper (about 6 oz./170 g), seeded and finely chopped
- 1¼ cups (300 ml) fat-free reduced-sodium chicken broth
- 1 pound (455 g) large raw shrimp (31 to 35 per lb.), shelled and deveined
- ⅔ cup (160 ml) fruity white wine, such as Johannisberg Riesling

1. Melt butter in a wide nonstick frying pan or wok over medium-high heat. Add celery, shallots, garlic, bell pepper, and broth. Cook, stirring often, until liquid evaporates (about 10 minutes).

2. Add shrimp to pan and stir-fry until just opaque in center; cut to test (3 to 4 minutes). Remove shrimp from pan with tongs or a slotted spoon; place in a serving bowl and keep warm. Add wine to pan and bring to a boil; then boil, stirring often, until liquid is reduced by about two-thirds (about 7 minutes). Spoon sauce over shrimp.

Makes 4 servings

NUTRIENTS

Per serving: 140 calories (23% calories from fat), 4 g total fat, 1 g saturated fat, 145 mg cholesterol, 374 mg sodium, 6 g carbohydrates, 0.7 g fiber, 20 g protein, 67 mg calcium, 3 mg iron

LEMONY SHRIMP TOSTADAS

Preparation time: **About 15 minutes**
Chilling time: **At least 20 minutes**

Served cold, this light tostada features a mixture of shrimp and jicama in a lemon-honey marinade. It's ideal for a hot-weather lunch or supper.

- 1 pound (455 g) tiny cooked shrimp
- 1 cup (115 g) peeled, minced jicama
- 3 tablespoons sliced green onions
- 1 teaspoon grated lemon peel
- 3 tablespoons (45 ml) lemon juice
- 2 teaspoons honey
   White pepper
   About 1½ cups (360 ml) Cherry Tomato Salsa (page 22) or other salsa of your choice
- 6 crisp corn taco shells or Warm Tortillas (page 160)
- 3 cups (85 g) shredded lettuce
- 1 medium-size firm-ripe tomato (about 6 oz./170 g), finely chopped

1. In a nonmetal bowl, mix shrimp, jicama, onions, lemon peel, lemon juice, and honey; season to taste with white pepper. Cover and refrigerate for at least 20 minutes or up to 3 hours.

2. Meanwhile, prepare Cherry Tomato Salsa and refrigerate.

3. To serve, place a taco shell on each of 6 dinner plates; top equally with lettuce. Scoop out shrimp mixture with a slotted spoon, drain, and divide equally among taco shells. Top equally with tomato. Add Cherry Tomato Salsa to taste.

Makes 6 servings

NUTRIENTS

Per serving: 156 calories (9% calories from fat), 2 g total fat, 0.3 g saturated fat, 148 mg cholesterol, 217 mg sodium, 18 g carbohydrates, 2 g fiber, 18 g protein, 94 mg calcium, 3 mg iron

SHRIMP CUSTARD

Preparation time: **About 15 minutes**
Cooking time: **About 30 minutes**

If you decide to cook the shrimp yourself rather than purchasing precooked shrimp (often the latter are expensive), then you'll need about a pound of uncooked shrimp to yield 8 ounces cooked. Raw shrimp should smell of the sea, with no hint of ammonia. In general, small shrimp do not need deveining, except for cosmetic purposes.

8   ounces (230 g) small cooked shrimp

1   cup (240 ml) nonfat milk

1   large egg

2   large egg whites

4   teaspoons (20 ml) dry sherry

2   teaspoons finely chopped fresh ginger

2   teaspoons reduced-sodium soy sauce

1   clove garlic, minced or pressed

⅛   teaspoon Oriental sesame oil

⅛   teaspoon ground white pepper

1   teaspoon sesame seeds

1. Divide half the shrimp evenly among four ¾-cup (180-ml) custard cups or ovenproof bowls; cover and refrigerate remaining shrimp. Set custard cups in a large baking pan at least 2 inches (5 cm) deep.

2. In a medium-size bowl, combine milk, egg, egg whites, sherry, ginger, soy sauce, garlic, oil, and white pepper; beat lightly just until blended. Pour egg mixture evenly over shrimp in custard cups.

3. Set pan on center rack of a 325°F (165°C) oven. Pour boiling water into pan around cups up to level of custard. Bake until custard jiggles only slightly in center when cups are gently shaken (about 25 minutes). Lift cups from pan. Let stand for about 5 minutes before serving. (At this point, you may let cool; then cover and refrigerate until next day and serve cold.)

4. Meanwhile, toast sesame seeds in a small frying pan over medium heat, stirring often, until golden (about 3 minutes). Remove from pan and set aside. Just before serving, top custards with remaining shrimp; then sprinkle with sesame seeds.

Makes 4 servings

NUTRIENTS

Per serving: 120 calories (20% calories from fat), 2 g total fat, 1 g saturated fat, 165 mg cholesterol, 303 mg sodium, 4 g carbohydrates, 0 g fiber, 18 g protein, 115 mg calcium, 2 mg iron

20 MINUTES OR LESS

2 teaspoons butter or margarine

2 teaspoons olive oil

3 cloves garlic, minced or pressed

1 pound (455 g) large shrimp (about 25 per lb.), shelled and deveined

About 4 cups (520 g) hot cooked rice

3 tablespoons chopped parsley

Salt and pepper

Lemon wedges

GARLIC SHRIMP WITH RICE

1. Melt butter in a wide nonstick frying pan over medium-high heat. Add oil, garlic, 3 tablespoons (45 ml) water, and shrimp. Cook, stirring, until shrimp are just opaque but still moist in center; cut to test (3 to 4 minutes).

2. To serve, spoon rice onto a platter or 4 dinner plates; spoon shrimp and pan juices over rice. Sprinkle with parsley. Season to taste with salt and pepper, then serve with lemon wedges.

Makes 4 servings

Per serving: 403 calories (15% calories from fat), 6 g total fat, 2 g saturated fat, 145 mg cholesterol, 161 mg sodium, 59 g carbohydrates, 0.9 g fiber, 24 g protein, 79 mg calcium, 5 mg iron

SHRIMP & AVOCADO TOSTADAS WITH PAPAYA SALSA

Preparation time: **About 35 minutes**
Cooking time: **About 8 minutes**

This recipe calls for avocados and papayas, delicious in combination. When buying avocados, you will discover that most are sold unripe. To speed the ripening process, place the avocados in a paper bag and set the bag aside at room temperature for 2 to 4 days. When choosing papayas, select fruits that are at least partially yellow, then leave them at room temperature, away from direct sunlight, until they are firm-ripe.

CRISP TACO SHELLS:

- 4 corn tortillas (each about 6 inches/ 15 cm in diameter)

   Salt (optional)

PAPAYA SALSA:

- 1 medium-size firm-ripe papaya (about 1 lb./455 g), peeled, seeded, and diced
- 1 small cucumber (about 8 oz./230 g), peeled, seeded, and diced
- 1 tablespoon chopped fresh mint, or to taste
- 2 tablespoons (30 ml) lime juice
- 1 tablespoon (15 ml) honey

AVOCADO & SHRIMP TOPPING:

- 1 teaspoon grated lemon peel
- 2 tablespoons (30 ml) lemon juice
- 1 medium-size soft-ripe avocado
- 1 cup (240 ml) low-fat (2%) cottage cheese
- 2 or 3 cloves garlic, peeled
- 1/8 teaspoon salt
- 2 tablespoons finely chopped cilantro

- 1 small fresh jalapeño or serrano chile, seeded and finely chopped
- 1 tablespoon thinly sliced green onion
- 1 large tomato (about 8 oz./230 g), finely chopped and drained well
- 4 cups (about 4 oz./115 g) shredded lettuce
- 6 ounces (170 g) small cooked shrimp

1. To prepare taco shells, dip tortillas, one at a time, in hot water; drain briefly. Season to taste with salt, if desired. Arrange tortillas, not overlapping, in a single layer on a large baking sheet. Bake in a 500°F (260°C) oven for 6 minutes. With a metal spatula, turn tortillas over; continue to bake until crisp and tinged with brown, about 2 more minutes. (At this point, you may let cool completely; then store airtight at room temperature until next day.)

2. To prepare papaya salsa, in a medium-size bowl, stir together papaya, cucumber, mint, lime juice, and honey; set aside. (At this point, you may cover and refrigerate for up to 4 hours.)

3. To prepare topping, place lemon peel and lemon juice in a blender or food processor. Halve and pit avocado; scoop flesh from peel into blender. Add cottage cheese, garlic, and salt. Whirl until smoothly puréed. With a spoon, gently stir in cilantro, chile, onion, and half the tomato.

4. To serve, place one taco shell on each of 4 individual plates. Evenly top taco shells with avocado mixture; then top shells equally with lettuce, shrimp, and remaining chopped tomato. Offer papaya salsa on the side to add to taste.

Makes 4 servings

NUTRIENTS

Per serving: 308 calories (29% calories from fat), 10 g total fat, 2 g saturated fat, 87 mg cholesterol, 387 mg sodium, 37 g carbohydrates, 4 g fiber, 21 g protein, 179 mg calcium, 4 mg iron

CHILI SHRIMP

Preparation time: **About 20 minutes**
Cooking time: **About 25 minutes**

East meets West in this spicy-sweet entrée, which makes a fine hot-day meal. The sauce will remind you of basic barbecue, but it's accented with ginger, soy sauce, and sesame oil.

- 1 cup (185 g) long-grain white rice
- 1 tablespoon sugar
- 3 tablespoons (45 ml) catsup
- 1 tablespoon (15 ml) cider vinegar
- 1 tablespoon (15 ml) reduced-sodium soy sauce
- ½ to 1 teaspoon crushed red pepper flakes
- 1 tablespoon (15 ml) vegetable oil
- 1 pound (455 g) large raw shrimp (31 to 35 per lb.), shelled (leave tails attached) and deveined
- 1 tablespoon minced fresh ginger
- 3 cloves garlic, minced or pressed
- ½ teaspoon Oriental sesame oil
  About ¼ cup (25 g) sliced green onions, or to taste

1. In a 3- to 4-quart (2.8- to 3.8-liter) pan, bring 2 cups (470 ml) water to a boil over high heat; stir in rice. Reduce heat, cover, and simmer until liquid has been absorbed and rice is tender to bite (about 20 minutes).

2. Meanwhile, in a small bowl, stir together sugar, catsup, vinegar, soy sauce, and red pepper flakes until sugar is dissolved; set aside.

3. Heat vegetable oil in a wide nonstick frying pan or wok over medium-high heat. When oil is hot, add shrimp. Stir-fry until just opaque in center; cut to test (3 to 4 minutes). Remove shrimp from pan with tongs or a slotted spoon; keep warm.

4. To pan, add ginger and garlic; stir-fry just until garlic is fragrant (about 30 seconds; do not scorch). Stir catsup mixture and pour into pan; bring to a boil, stirring. Remove pan from heat and add shrimp and sesame oil; stir the mixture gently but thoroughly.

5. Spoon rice onto a rimmed platter; spoon shrimp mixture over rice and sprinkle with onions.

Makes 4 servings

NUTRIENTS

Per serving: 336 calories (16% calories from fat), 6 g total fat, 0.9 g saturated fat, 140 mg cholesterol, 423 mg sodium, 46 g carbohydrates, 0.8 g fiber, 23 g protein, 73 mg calcium, 5 mg iron

THAI PIZZA WITH SHRIMP

Preparation time: **About 20 minutes**
Cooking time: **About 15 minutes**

Reduced-fat peanut butter combines with hoisin sauce, vinegar, and Oriental sesame oil to make an interesting Thai-style topping for these mini pizzas. Precede the pizzas with soup or salad for a light lunch.

- 6 small Italian bread shells (each about 5½ inches/13.5 cm in diameter and about 4 oz./115 g); or 6 pita breads (each about 5 inches/12.5 cm in diameter); or 6 English muffins, split
- ½ cup (120 ml) reduced-fat creamy peanut butter
- 3 tablespoons (45 ml) hoisin sauce
- 2 tablespoons (30 ml) seasoned rice vinegar (or 2 tablespoons/30 ml distilled white vinegar plus 1 teaspoon sugar)
- 1 teaspoon Oriental sesame oil
- 1 cup (170 g) bean sprouts
- 1 cup (about 4 oz./115 g) shredded reduced-fat jack cheese
- 5 to 6 ounces (140 to 170 g) small cooked shrimp
- ¼ cup (25 g) thinly sliced green onions
  Crushed red pepper flakes

1. Place bread shells, pita breads, or muffin halves (cut side up) on two 12- by 15-inch (30- by 38-cm) baking sheets.

2. In a bowl, combine peanut butter, hoisin sauce, vinegar, and sesame oil. Beat until smoothly blended; if necessary, add a little water so sauce is easy to spread. Spread equally over cupped area of bread shells or top of pita breads (or spread to edge of muffin halves). Scatter bean sprouts equally over sauce; sprinkle with cheese.

3. Bake in a 350°F (175°C) oven until cheese is melted and beginning to brown (12 to 15 minutes; if using one oven, switch positions of baking sheets after 7 minutes). Place each pizza on an individual plate; top pizzas equally with shrimp and onions. Season to taste with red pepper flakes.

Makes 6 servings

NUTRIENTS

Per serving: 410 calories (29% calories from fat), 13 g total fat, 4 g saturated fat, 62 mg cholesterol, 876 mg sodium, 50 g carbohydrates, 2 g fiber, 23 g protein, 233 mg calcium, 3 mg iron

SHRIMP WITH PARSLEY PESTO & LINGUINE

Preparation time: **About 10 minutes**
Cooking time: **About 25 minutes**

Ideal for any time of year, this pretty pasta entrée features plump pink shrimp and a refreshing pesto based on parsley and toasted almonds. It's great with any pasta you prefer.

¼ cup (35 g) whole unblanched almonds

2 cups (120 g) lightly packed parsley sprigs

¼ cup (60 ml) plus 1 teaspoon olive oil

3 tablespoons (45 ml) white wine vinegar

1 clove garlic, peeled

1 tablespoon drained capers

¼ teaspoon crushed red pepper flakes

1 pound (455 g) dried linguine

1 pound (455 g) large raw shrimp (31 to 35 per lb.), shelled and deveined

1. In a wide nonstick frying pan or wok, stir almonds over medium heat until golden beneath skins (about 8 minutes). Pour almonds into a food processor or blender; let cool. Then add parsley, ¼ cup (60 ml) of the oil, vinegar, garlic, capers, and red pepper flakes to processor. Whirl until pesto is smooth. Set aside.

2. In a 6- to 8-quart (6- to 8-liter) pan, cook linguine in about 4 quarts (3.8 liters) boiling water until just tender to bite (8 to 10 minutes); or cook according to package directions. Drain well, transfer to a warm wide bowl, and keep warm.

3. While pasta is cooking, heat remaining 1 teaspoon oil in frying pan or wok over medium-high heat. When oil is hot, add shrimp and stir-fry until just opaque in center; cut to test (3 to 4 minutes).

4. Spoon shrimp and pesto over pasta; mix gently but thoroughly to combine.

Makes 6 servings

NUTRIENTS

Per serving: 474 calories (28% calories from fat), 15 g total fat, 2 g saturated fat, 93 mg cholesterol, 143 mg sodium, 60 g carbohydrates, 4 g fiber, 24 g protein, 93 mg calcium, 6 mg iron

CORIANDER-CURRY SHRIMP

Preparation time: **About 15 minutes**
Cooking time: **About 15 minutes**

Shrimp and coconut taste delicious together—and the flavor gets even better when you add pineapple and curry. Serve this mildly spicy stir-fry over vermicelli, perhaps with a selection of tropical fruits on the side.

12 ounces to 1 pound (340 to 455 g) dried vermicelli or spaghetti

⅔ cup (160 ml) pineapple-coconut juice (or ⅔ cup/160 ml unsweetened pineapple juice plus ¼ cup/20 g sweetened shredded coconut)

2 teaspoons cornstarch

1 teaspoon vegetable oil

1 large onion, thinly sliced

1 clove garlic, minced or pressed

1 tablespoon curry powder

1 tablespoon ground coriander

⅛ teaspoon ground red pepper (cayenne)

1½ pounds (680 g) large raw shrimp (31 to 35 per lb.), shelled and deveined

2 tablespoons finely chopped parsley

Lime wedges

Salt

1. In a 6- to 8-quart (6- to 8-liter) pan, cook vermicelli in about 4 quarts (3.8 liters) boiling water until just tender to bite (8 to 10 minutes); or cook according to package directions. Drain well, transfer to a warm rimmed platter, and keep warm.

2. While pasta is cooking, in a small bowl, stir together pineapple-coconut juice and cornstarch until blended; set aside. Heat oil in a wide nonstick frying pan or wok over medium-high heat. When oil is hot, add onion, garlic, and 2 tablespoons (30 ml) water. Stir-fry until liquid has evaporated and onion is soft and beginning to brown (about 5 minutes).

3. Add curry powder, coriander, and red pepper to pan; stir to blend. Immediately add shrimp and stir-fry for 2 minutes. Stir cornstarch mixture well; pour into pan. Stir until sauce is bubbly and shrimp are just opaque in center; cut to test (1 to 2 more minutes). Add parsley and mix gently but thoroughly. Spoon shrimp mixture over pasta; garnish with lime wedges. Season with salt.

Makes 6 servings

NUTRIENTS

Per serving: 402 calories (10% calories from fat), 5 g total fat, 1 g saturated fat, 140 mg cholesterol, 152 mg sodium, 60 g carbohydrates, 3 g fiber, 28 g protein, 81 mg calcium, 5 mg iron

POULTRY

LEMON CHICKEN

Preparation time: **About 20 minutes**
Cooking time: **About 10 minutes**

Batter-dipped, deep-fried chicken topped with a sweet lemon sauce is a popular choice at many Chinese restaurants. Our stir-fried interpretation of the dish features strips of boneless chicken breast in a thin, golden crust; the light lemon sauce is delightfully tart-sweet. For a pretty presentation, serve the chicken on a bed of lemon slices. You'll find that the best way to prepare this recipe is to heat the oil just before you drain the batter-dipped chicken. Then, you can transfer the chicken directly from the batter to the hot pan or wok, with no need to set it aside.

5   or 6 large lemons (about 2 lbs./905 g)

¾   cup (96 g) plus 1 tablespoon cornstarch

⅓   cup (80 ml) fat-free reduced-sodium chicken broth

¼   cup (50 g) sugar

2   tablespoons (30 ml) light corn syrup

2   tablespoons (30 ml) distilled white vinegar

1   tablespoon (15 ml) plus 1 teaspoon vegetable oil

½   teaspoon salt (optional)

2   cloves garlic, minced or pressed

2   large egg whites

¼   cup (30 g) all-purpose flour

1   teaspoon baking powder

1   teaspoon finely minced fresh ginger

⅛   teaspoon ground white pepper

1   pound (455 g) skinless, boneless chicken breast, cut into ½- by 3-inch (1- by 8-cm) strips

Finely shredded lemon peel

Cilantro sprigs

1. To prepare sauce, finely shred enough peel (colored part only) from 1 or 2 of the lemons to make ½ teaspoon; set aside. Squeeze enough juice to measure 3 tablespoons (45 ml). In a small bowl, stir together lemon juice and 1 tablespoon of the cornstarch until blended. Stir in lemon peel, broth, sugar, corn syrup, vinegar, 1 tablespoon (15 ml) water, 1 teaspoon of the oil, ¼ teaspoon of the salt (if using), and garlic. Set sauce aside.

2. Thinly slice the remaining lemons and place slices on a rimmed platter, overlapping them, if necessary; cover and set aside.

3. In a large bowl, beat egg whites and ½ cup (120 ml) water to blend. Add remaining ¾ cup (96 g) cornstarch, flour, baking powder, ginger, remaining ¼ teaspoon salt (if using), and white pepper; stir until smoothly blended.

4. Heat remaining 1 tablespoon (15 ml) oil in a wide nonstick frying pan or wok over medium-high heat. Meanwhile, dip chicken pieces in egg-white batter. Lift out and drain briefly to let excess batter drip off; discard remaining batter.

5. When oil is hot, add chicken and stir-fry gently, separating pieces, until meat is lightly browned on outside and no longer pink in center; cut to test (5 to 7 minutes; if any pieces brown too much, remove them from pan and keep warm). Arrange chicken over lemon slices on platter; keep warm.

6. Wipe pan clean (be careful; pan is hot). Stir reserved lemon sauce well; pour into pan. Stir over medium-high heat until sauce boils and thickens slightly (1 to 2 minutes). Pour sauce over chicken and sprinkle with additional shredded lemon peel. Garnish with cilantro sprigs.

Makes 4 servings

NUTRIENTS

Per serving: 368 calories (14% calories from fat), 6 g total fat, 1 g saturated fat, 66 mg cholesterol, 245 mg sodium, 56 g carbohydrates, 0.3 g fiber, 30 g protein, 136 mg calcium, 2 mg iron

PEANUT CHICKEN WITH RICE

Preparation time: **About 15 minutes**
Cooking time: **About 25 minutes**

What goes into a grade-school lunch box—and into a savory stir-fry sauce? Peanut butter and jam! Just a few tablespoons of each give this dish a rich, slightly sweet peanut taste that both children and adults will enjoy.

1 cup (185 g) long-grain white rice

1 package (about 10 oz./285 g) frozen tiny peas, thawed and drained

3 tablespoons (45 g) crunchy or smooth peanut butter

3 tablespoons plum jam or grape jelly

1½ teaspoons lemon juice

1½ teaspoons reduced-sodium soy sauce

1 teaspoon Oriental sesame oil

2 teaspoons Ginger Oil (page 56); or 2 teaspoons vegetable oil mixed with ¼ teaspoon ground ginger

1 pound (455 g) skinless, boneless chicken breast, cut into ¾-inch (2-cm) pieces

2 tablespoons sliced green onion

Lemon wedges

1. In a 3- to 4-quart (2.8- to 3.8-liter) pan, bring 2 cups (470 ml) water to a boil over high heat; stir in rice. Reduce heat, cover, and simmer until liquid has been absorbed and rice is tender to bite (about 20 minutes). Stir peas into rice; remove from heat and keep warm. Fluff occasionally with a fork.

2. While rice is cooking, prepare sauce. In a small bowl, stir together peanut butter, jam, 2 tablespoons (30 ml) water, lemon juice, soy sauce, and sesame oil. Set aside.

3. Heat ginger oil in a wide nonstick frying pan or wok over medium-high heat. When oil is hot, add chicken and stir-fry until no longer pink in center; cut to test (4 to 6 minutes). Remove chicken from pan with a slotted spoon and keep warm. Discard drippings from pan and wipe pan clean (be careful; pan is hot).

4. Stir sauce well and pour into pan. Stir over medium heat just until smoothly blended and heated through. Add chicken and onion; remove pan from heat and stir to coat chicken and onion with sauce.

5. Spoon rice mixture onto a rimmed platter and top with chicken mixture. Offer lemon wedges to squeeze over stir-fry to taste.

Makes 4 servings

NUTRIENTS

Per serving: 481 calories (21% calories from fat), 11 g total fat, 2 g saturated fat, 66 mg cholesterol, 312 mg sodium, 58 g carbohydrates, 4 g fiber, 36 g protein, 49 mg calcium, 4 mg iron

Jalapeño Chicken with Mole Poblano

Pictured on facing page
Preparation time: **About 25 minutes**
Cooking time: **About 20 minutes**

The single word *mole* denotes a whole category of Mexican sauces. One popular member of the group is mellow, slightly sweet *mole poblano*, well known for its inclusion of bitter chocolate. Traditional moles are made with chiles, fruits, nuts, spices, thickeners, and—often—volumes of lard. Our streamlined mole poblano eliminates much of the fat and replaces the chocolate with unsweetened cocoa, yet its flavor is still as temptingly complex as that of the original.

1 tablespoon sesame seeds

1 large onion, chopped

4 cloves garlic, minced or pressed

1 small very ripe banana (about 3 oz./85 g), chopped

¼ cup (45 g) chopped pitted prunes

2 tablespoons raisins

1 tablespoon creamy peanut butter

5 tablespoons (27 g) unsweetened cocoa powder

3 tablespoons chili powder

2 teaspoons sugar

½ teaspoon ground cinnamon

⅛ teaspoon ground coriander

⅛ teaspoon ground cumin

⅛ teaspoon ground cloves

⅛ teaspoon anise seeds, crushed

2 cups (470 ml) fat-free reduced-sodium chicken broth

1 small can (about 6 oz./170 g) tomato paste

8 skinless, boneless chicken breast halves (about 6 oz./170 g each)

2 tablespoons (36 g) mild jalapeño jelly, melted; or 2 tablespoons (36 g) apple jelly, melted and mixed with a small pinch ground red pepper (cayenne)

Salt

Lime wedges

1. Toast sesame seeds in a wide nonstick frying pan over medium heat until golden (about 4 minutes), stirring often. Transfer to a bowl; set aside.

2. To pan, add onion, garlic, banana, prunes, raisins, peanut butter, and 3 tablespoons (45 ml) water. Cook over medium heat, stirring often, until mixture is richly browned (10 to 15 minutes); if pan appears dry, add more water, 1 tablespoon (15 ml) at a time. Stir in cocoa, chili powder, sugar, cinnamon, coriander, cumin, cloves, anise seeds, and ¾ cup (180 ml) of the broth. Bring mixture to a boil over medium-high heat.

3. Transfer hot onion mixture to a food processor or blender and add tomato paste, 2 teaspoons of the sesame seeds, and a little of the remaining broth. Whirl until smoothly puréed; then stir in remaining broth. Cover and keep warm. (At this point, you may let cool; then cover and refrigerate for up to 3 days; freeze for longer storage. Reheat before continuing.)

4. While onion mixture is browning, rinse chicken and pat dry. Place jelly in a bowl and stir to soften; add chicken and mix to coat. Then place chicken in a lightly oiled 10- by 15-inch (25- by 38-cm) rimmed baking pan. Bake in a 450°F (230°C) oven until meat in thickest part is no longer pink; cut to test (12 to 15 minutes).

5. To serve, spoon some of the warm mole sauce onto dinner plates; top with chicken, then more mole sauce. Sprinkle with remaining 1 teaspoon sesame seeds. Season to taste with salt; serve with lime wedges to squeeze over chicken to taste.

Makes 8 servings

NUTRIENTS

Per serving: 264 calories (18% calories from fat), 6 g total fat, 1 g saturated fat, 74 mg cholesterol, 322 mg sodium, 23 g carbohydrates, 4 g fiber, 34 g protein, 65 mg calcium, 3 mg iron

Jalapeño Chicken with Mole Poblano (recipe on facing page)

SESAME CHICKEN WITH STIR-FRIED VEGETABLES (RECIPE ON PAGE 94)

Raspberry-Glazed Turkey Sauté (recipe on page 98)

Chicken Curry in Pita Bread (recipe on facing page)

CHICKEN CURRY IN PITA BREAD

Pictured on facing page
Preparation time: **About 20 minutes**
Cooking time: **About 20 minutes**

Pita bread stuffed with chicken and veg-etables is a satisfying choice for lunch or supper. The filling gets its appealing tangy-sweet flavor from yogurt, raisins, and apricot jam. When you add the yogurt, be sure to reduce the heat and stir gently and constantly; if the mixture is allowed to boil, it will curdle.

½ cup (75 g) raisins or dried currants

1 cup (240 ml) plain nonfat yogurt

2 tablespoons cornstarch

2 teaspoons olive oil

12 ounces (340 g) skinless, boneless chicken breast, cut into ½-inch (1-cm) pieces

1 medium-size onion, chopped

2 cloves garlic, minced or pressed

2 teaspoons curry powder

½ cup (160 g) apricot jam or preserves
    Salt and pepper

1 medium-size cucumber (about 8 oz./230 g), very thinly sliced

4 pita breads (each about 6 inches/ 15 cm in diameter), cut crosswise into halves

1. In a small bowl, combine raisins and ¼ cup (60 ml) water; let stand until raisins are softened (about 10 minutes), stirring occasionally. Mean-while, in another small bowl, stir together yogurt and cornstarch until smoothly blended; set aside.

2. Heat oil in a wide nonstick frying pan or wok over medium-high heat. When oil is hot, add chicken and 1 tablespoon (15 ml) water. Stir-fry until meat is no longer pink in center; cut to test (3 to 4 minutes). Remove chicken from pan with a slotted spoon and keep warm. Discard drip-pings from pan.

3. Add onion, garlic, curry powder, and ¼ cup (60 ml) water to pan; stir-fry until onion is soft (about 4 minutes; do not scorch). Add water, 1 ta-blespoon (15 ml) at a time, if pan appears dry. Add raisins (and soaking water) and jam. Bring to a boil; then boil, stirring, until almost all liquid has evaporated (5 to 7 minutes). Reduce heat to medi-um-low; stir in chicken and yogurt mixture. Sim-mer gently, stirring constantly, until sauce is slightly thickened (do not boil). Season to taste with salt and pepper.

4. To serve, divide cucumber slices equally among pita halves; fill pitas equally with chicken mixture.
Makes 4 servings

NUTRIENTS

Per serving: 506 calories (8% calories from fat), 5 g total fat, 0.8 g saturated fat, 51 mg cholesterol, 442 mg sodium, 88 g carbohy-drates, 4 g fiber, 30 g protein, 215 mg calcium, 3 mg iron

Sesame Chicken with Stir-Fried Vegetables

Pictured on page 90
Preparation time: **About 20 minutes**
Cooking time: **12 to 15 minutes**

A bed of stir-fried red cabbage and emerald snow peas provides a crisp, colorful contrast to these grilled chicken breasts sprinkled with sesame seeds.

- 4 chicken breast halves (about 2 lbs./905 g total), skinned and boned
- 1 teaspoon sesame seeds
  Vegetable oil cooking spray
- 4 teaspoons (20 ml) rice vinegar
- 4 teaspoons (20 ml) reduced-sodium soy sauce
- 1½ teaspoons Oriental sesame oil
- 1 tablespoon grated fresh ginger
- 2 cloves garlic, minced or pressed
- ½ teaspoon sugar
- 1 tablespoon (15 ml) vegetable oil
- 8 ounces (230 g) mushrooms, sliced
- 4 cups (280 g) thinly sliced red cabbage
- 4 ounces (115 g) Chinese pea pods (also called snow peas), ends and strings removed
- 2 cups (260 g) hot cooked rice

1. Rinse chicken, pat dry, and sprinkle with sesame seeds. Spray a ridged cooktop grill pan with cooking spray. Place over medium heat and preheat until a drop of water dances on surface. Then place chicken on grill and cook, turning once, until well browned on outside and no longer pink in thickest part; cut to test (12 to 15 minutes).

2. Meanwhile, in a small bowl, stir together vinegar, soy sauce, sesame oil, ginger, garlic, and sugar; set aside. Then heat vegetable oil in a wide nonstick frying pan or wok over medium-high heat.

Add mushrooms and cook, stirring often, for about 3 minutes. Add cabbage and cook, stirring often, until it begins to soften (about 2 minutes). Add pea pods and cook, stirring, just until they turn bright green (1 to 2 minutes). Add vinegar mixture and stir for 1 more minute.

3. Divide vegetables among 4 warm dinner plates. Cut each chicken piece diagonally across the grain into ½-inch-wide (1-cm-wide) strips. Arrange chicken over vegetables; serve with rice.

Makes 4 servings

NUTRIENTS

Per serving: 400 calories (19% calories from fat), 8 g total fat, 1 g saturated fat, 86 mg cholesterol, 310 mg sodium, 40 g carbohydrates, 3 g fiber, 40 g protein, 90 mg calcium, 4 mg iron

Chicken Breasts Calvados

Preparation time: **About 10 minutes**
Baking & broiling time: **About 34 minutes**

T opped with a golden cheese crust and served on applesauce spiked with apple brandy, these tender chicken breasts make a substantial meal for two.

- 1 large Golden Delicious apple (about 8 oz./230 g), peeled, cored, and thinly sliced
- ¼ cup (60 ml) apple brandy, brandy, or apple juice
- ¼ teaspoon ground nutmeg
- 2 skinless, boneless chicken breast halves (about 6 oz./170 g each)
- 2 slices Havarti cheese (about 1 oz./30 g each)
  Chopped parsley

1. Divide apple slices between 2 shallow ovenproof 1½- to 2-cup (360- to 470-ml) ramekins. Pour 2 tablespoons (30 ml) of the brandy into each ramekin, then sprinkle ⅛ teaspoon of the nutmeg evenly over apples. Cover ramekins tightly with foil and bake in a 400°F (205°C) oven until apples are tender when pierced (about 20 minutes).

2. Rinse chicken and pat dry. Place one piece in each ramekin; baste with cooking juices, then sprinkle evenly with remaining ⅛ teaspoon nutmeg. Bake, uncovered, until meat in thickest part is no longer pink; cut to test (about 12 minutes).

3. Top each chicken piece with a cheese slice. Broil 6 inches (15 cm) below heat until cheese is bubbly (about 2 minutes). Sprinkle with parsley.

Makes 2 servings

NUTRIENTS

Per serving: 413 calories (27% calories from fat), 10 g total fat, 5 g saturated fat, 128 mg cholesterol, 324 mg sodium, 15 g carbohydrates, 2 g fiber, 46 g protein, 222 mg calcium, 1 mg iron

SALSA CHICKEN

Preparation time: **About 20 minutes**
Cooking time: **About 10 minutes**

A main-dish salad? A tostada without the crisp-fried tortilla? You could describe this dish either way. Cornmeal-crusted chicken chunks, topped with warm homemade salsa and sour cream, are served on a cool, crunchy bed of shredded lettuce. On the side, you might offer Water-Crisped Tortilla Chips (page 25) and an orange-and-onion salad.

   2 medium-size tomatoes (about
       12 oz./340 g total), chopped and
       drained well
  ¼ cup (25 g) thinly sliced green onions
  ¼ cup (60 ml) lime juice
   1 small fresh jalapeño chile, seeded and
       finely chopped
   1 tablespoon chopped cilantro
   1 clove garlic, minced or pressed
       About 8 cups (about 8 oz./230 g)
       finely shredded iceberg lettuce

   2 large egg whites
  ½ cup (69 g) yellow cornmeal
  1½ teaspoons chili powder
  ½ teaspoon ground cumin
   1 pound (455 g) skinless, boneless
       chicken breast, cut into 1-inch
       (2.5-cm) pieces
   2 teaspoons olive oil or vegetable oil
  ½ cup (120 ml) nonfat sour cream
       Cilantro sprigs

1. To prepare tomato salsa, in a large bowl, combine tomatoes, onions, lime juice, jalapeño, chopped cilantro, and garlic; set aside. (At this point, you may cover and refrigerate for up to 3 hours.) Divide lettuce among 4 individual plates; cover and set aside.

2. In a shallow bowl, beat egg whites to blend; set aside. In a large bowl, combine cornmeal, chili powder, and cumin. Add chicken and turn to coat. Then lift chicken from bowl, shaking off excess coating. Dip chicken into egg whites, then coat again with remaining cornmeal mixture.

3. Heat oil in a wide nonstick frying pan or wok over medium-high heat. When oil is hot, add chicken and stir-fry gently until no longer pink in center; cut to test (5 to 7 minutes). Remove from pan and keep warm. Pour reserved salsa into pan; reduce heat to medium and cook, stirring, until salsa is heated through and slightly thickened (1 to 2 minutes).

4. Arrange chicken over lettuce; top with salsa and sour cream. Garnish with cilantro sprigs.

Makes 4 servings

NUTRIENTS

Per serving: 284 calories (15% calories from fat), 5 g total fat, 0.8 g saturated fat, 66 mg cholesterol, 152 mg sodium, 26 g carbohydrates, 4 g fiber, 34 g protein, 146 mg calcium, 4 mg iron

CHICKEN & APPLE STIR-FRY

Preparation time: About 20 minutes
Cooking time: About 15 minutes

To balance the sweetness of this unusual stir-fry's creamy sherry sauce, choose crisp, tart apples, such as Granny Smith, Newtown Pippin, or Idared.

4 teaspoons butter or margarine

2 large tart apples (about 1 lb./455 g total), peeled, cored, and cut into ¼-inch-thick (6-mm-thick) slices

1 pound (455 g) skinless, boneless chicken breast, cut into ½- by 2-inch (1- by 5-cm) strips

1 large onion, finely chopped

⅔ cup (160 ml) dry sherry or apple juice

⅓ cup (80 ml) half-and-half

1. Melt 1 tablespoon of the butter in a wide non-stick frying pan or wok over medium heat. Add apples and stir-fry just until tender to bite (about 2 minutes). Remove apples from pan with a slotted spoon and keep warm.

2. Increase heat to medium-high and melt remaining 1 teaspoon butter in pan. Add chicken and stir-fry until no longer pink in center; cut to test (3 to 4 minutes). Remove chicken from pan with a slotted spoon and keep warm.

3. Add onion and 2 tablespoons (30 ml) of the sherry to pan; stir-fry until onion is soft (about 3 minutes). Add remaining sherry and bring to a boil; boil, stirring, for 1 minute. Add half-and-half and boil, stirring, until sauce is slightly thickened (about 2 minutes). Return apples and chicken to pan and mix gently but thoroughly.

Makes 4 servings

NUTRIENTS

Per serving: 309 calories (26% calories from fat), 8 g total fat, 4 g saturated fat, 84 mg cholesterol, 126 mg sodium, 21 g carbohydrates, 2 g fiber, 28 g protein, 52 mg calcium, 1 mg iron

20 MINUTES OR LESS

⅔ cup (160 ml) Major Grey chutney, large pieces chopped

1½ tablespoons (23 ml) lemon juice

1 tablespoon (15 ml) Dijon mustard

¾ pound (340 g) ground chicken

¼ cup (25 g) sliced green onion

½ teaspoon ground cumin

8 slices (each ½ in./1 cm thick, 3 by 6 in./8 by 15 cm) sourdough French bread

4 thin slices red onion

20 prewashed spinach leaves (each about 4 in./10 cm long)

CHICKEN CHUTNEY BURGERS

1. Combine chutney, lemon juice, and mustard; set two-thirds of mixture aside. Combine remaining chutney mixture with chicken, green onion, and cumin. Shape into 4 patties, each about 4 inches (10 cm) wide, and place on a rack in a broiler pan. Broil 3 inches (8 cm) below heat until well browned on both sides, turning as needed (6 to 7 minutes).

2. Meanwhile, brown bread in a toaster, then spread one side of each slice with reserved chutney mixture.

3. Separate red onion into rings and place between bread with burgers and spinach. *Makes 4 servings*

Per serving: 387 calories (10% calories from fat), 4 g total fat, 1 g saturated fat, 60 mg cholesterol, 948 mg sodium, 61 g carbohydrates, 2 g fiber, 23 g protein, 73 mg calcium, 3 mg iron

Spicy Chicken Tortas

Preparation time: **About 15 minutes**
Cooking time: **15 to 20 minutes**

Succulent chicken, steeped in a spicy-sweet broth, makes a lively tasting filling for French rolls. If you can get fresh Mexican *semitas*, use them instead of the rolls.

Tortas:

1 pound (455 g) skinless, boneless chicken thighs

2 cups (470 ml) fat-free reduced-sodium chicken broth

¼ cup (30 g) chili powder

¼ cup (55 g) firmly packed brown sugar

2 teaspoons dried oregano

1 teaspoon anise seeds

About 1 tablespoon (15 ml) red wine vinegar, or to taste

2 tablespoons chopped cilantro

2 tablespoons thinly sliced green onion

4 French rolls (each about 6 inches/15 cm long)

8 to 12 butter lettuce leaves, rinsed and crisped

Condiments:

Pickled Vegetables (page 247)

Avocado slices

Asadero or string cheese

1. Rinse chicken and pat dry; set aside. In a 4- to 5-quart (3.8- to 5-liter) pan with a tight-fitting lid, combine 4 cups (950 ml) water, broth, chili powder, sugar, oregano, and anise seeds. Bring to a rolling boil over high heat. Remove pan from heat and immediately add chicken. Cover pan and let stand until meat in thickest part is no longer pink; cut to test (15 to 20 minutes; *do not uncover* until ready to test). If chicken is not done, return it to hot water, cover, and let steep for 2 to 3 more minutes.

2. Drain chicken, reserving 2 cups (470 ml) of the cooking liquid. Return reserved liquid to pan. Bring to a boil over high heat; boil until reduced to ½ cup (120 ml), watching closely to prevent scorching.

3. Serve chicken and sauce warm or cold. To serve, stir vinegar, cilantro, and onion into sauce. Cut chicken diagonally across the grain into thin slices; set aside. Cut rolls in half lengthwise and moisten cut surfaces evenly with sauce. Fill rolls with chicken and lettuce. Offer additional sauce and condiments to add to taste.

Makes 4 servings

NUTRIENTS

Per serving: 464 calories (14% calories from fat), 7 g total fat, 1 g saturated fat, 94 mg cholesterol, 1,819 mg sodium, 68 g carbohydrates, 4 g fiber, 33 g protein, 71 mg calcium, 6 mg iron

CHICKEN & MUSHROOMS WITH COUSCOUS

Preparation time: **About 20 minutes**
Cooking time: **About 20 minutes**

Mild, creamy, quick-cooking couscous is the perfect foil for tender stir-fried chicken in a cayenne-sparked sauce. Offer the freshest asparagus spears alongside.

　1　pound (455 g) skinless, boneless chicken thighs, trimmed of fat
　1　tablespoon margarine
　1　large onion, finely chopped
　12　ounces (340 g) mushrooms, sliced
　2　teaspoons cornstarch
　1　cup (240 ml) fat-free reduced-sodium chicken broth
　3　tablespoons (45 ml) dry sherry
　2　tablespoons (30 ml) soy sauce
　⅛　teaspoon ground red pepper (cayenne)
　2　cups (470 ml) low-fat (2%) milk
　1½　cups (275 g) couscous
　　　Vegetable oil cooking spray
　　　Cilantro sprigs

1. Rinse chicken; pat dry. Place pieces between sheets of plastic wrap and pound with a flat-surfaced mallet until about ¼ inch (6 mm) thick; then cut chicken into ½-inch-wide (1-cm-wide) strips. Set aside.

2. Melt margarine in a wide nonstick frying pan over medium-high heat. Add onion and mushrooms; cook, stirring often, until liquid has evaporated and onion is golden and sweet tasting (10 to 12 minutes).

3. Meanwhile, in a bowl, blend cornstarch and ¼ cup (60 ml) of the broth; stir in sherry, soy sauce, and red pepper. Set aside. In a 2-quart (1.9-liter) pan, bring milk and remaining ¾ cup

(180 ml) broth to a boil. Stir in couscous; cover, remove from heat, and let stand for 10 minutes.

4. Remove onion mixture from frying pan and set aside. Spray pan with cooking spray and place over high heat. Add chicken and cook, lifting and stirring, until meat is tinged with brown and is no longer pink in center; cut to test (4 to 5 minutes). Return onion mixture to pan; add cornstarch mixture and cook, stirring constantly, until sauce is bubbly (about 1 minute). Fluff couscous with a fork, then mound on a warm platter; spoon chicken beside couscous. Garnish with cilantro sprigs.

Makes 4 to 6 servings

NUTRIENTS

Per serving: 446 calories (18% calories from fat), 9 g total fat, 3 g saturated fat, 83 mg cholesterol, 705 mg sodium, 57 g carbohydrates, 3 g fiber, 31 g protein, 157 mg calcium, 3 mg iron

RASPBERRY-GLAZED TURKEY SAUTÉ

Pictured on page 91
Preparation time: **About 20 minutes**
Cooking time: **About 15 minutes**

Poultry and fruit are classic partners: witness the traditional pairing of roast turkey with cranberry sauce. Here, turkey tenderloin is complemented by sweet red raspberries. You toss thin strips of meat with a sauce of raspberry vinegar and jam, then top the dish with whole berries. (If raspberries are unavailable, use 1 cup of orange segments instead.)

　3　green onions
　⅓　cup (100 g) seedless red raspberry jam or jelly
　3　tablespoons (45 ml) raspberry or red wine vinegar
　1　tablespoon (15 ml) Dijon mustard
　½　teaspoon grated orange peel
　¾　teaspoon chopped fresh tarragon or ¼ teaspoon dried tarragon

8 ounces (230 g) dried eggless spinach fettuccine or plain fettuccine

1 teaspoon olive oil or vegetable oil

2 turkey breast tenderloins (about 1 lb./455 g total), cut into ¼- by 2-inch (6-mm by 5-cm) strips

About 1 cup (123 g) fresh raspberries

Tarragon sprigs

1. Trim and discard ends of onions. Cut onions into 2-inch (5-cm) lengths; then cut each piece lengthwise into slivers. Set aside. In a small bowl, stir together jam, vinegar, mustard, orange peel, and chopped tarragon; set aside.

2. In a 4- to 5-quart (3.8- to 5-liter) pan, cook fettuccine in about 8 cups (1.9 liters) boiling water until just tender to bite (8 to 10 minutes); or cook according to package directions.

3. Meanwhile, heat oil in a wide nonstick frying pan or wok over medium-high heat. When oil is hot, add turkey and 1 tablespoon (15 ml) water.

Stir-fry just until turkey is no longer pink in center; cut to test (about 2 minutes). Add water, 1 tablespoon (15 ml) at a time, if pan appears dry. Remove turkey from pan with a slotted spoon and keep warm. Discard drippings from pan; wipe pan clean (be careful; pan is hot).

4. Add jam mixture to pan and bring to a boil over medium-high heat; then boil, stirring, just until jam is melted and sauce is smooth (about 1 minute). Remove from heat and stir in turkey and onions.

5. Drain pasta well and divide among 4 warm individual rimmed plates or shallow bowls; top with turkey mixture. Sprinkle each with raspberries and garnish with tarragon sprigs.

Makes 4 servings

NUTRIENTS

Per serving: 435 calories (6% calories from fat), 3 g total fat, 0.5 g saturated fat, 70 mg cholesterol, 178 mg sodium, 64 g carbohydrates, 8 g fiber, 36 g protein, 66 mg calcium, 3 mg iron

20 MINUTES OR LESS

1 pound (455 g) thinly sliced turkey breast

2 teaspoons finely chopped fresh sage or 1 teaspoon dried sage

2 teaspoons olive oil

½ cup (55 g) finely shredded provolone or part-skim mozzarella cheese

Pepper

Sage sprigs

Lemon wedges

Salt

SAUTÉED TURKEY WITH PROVOLONE & SAGE

1. Rinse turkey and pat dry. Sprinkle one side of each slice with chopped sage; set aside.

2. Heat 1 teaspoon of the oil in a wide nonstick frying pan over medium-high heat. Add half the turkey, sage-coated side down, and cook until golden on bottom (about 1½ minutes). Then turn pieces over and continue to cook until no longer pink in center; cut to test (30 to 60 more seconds). Transfer cooked turkey to a platter and sprinkle with half the cheese. Cover loosely with foil and keep warm.

3. Repeat to cook remaining turkey; using remaining 1 teaspoon oil; add water, 1 tablespoon (15 ml) at a time, if pan appears dry. Transfer turkey to platter; sprinkle with remaining cheese.

4. Sprinkle turkey with pepper; garnish with sage sprigs. Season to taste with lemon and salt. *Makes 4 servings*

Per serving: 184 calories (30% calories from fat), 6 g total fat, 2 g saturated fat, 78 mg cholesterol, 149 mg sodium, 0.3 g carbohydrates, 0 g fiber, 31 g protein, 94 mg calcium, 1 mg iron

CURRIED TURKEY & COCONUT RICE

Preparation time: **About 20 minutes**
Cooking time: **About 25 minutes**

Rice cooked in low-fat milk and sweetened with a little coconut makes a superb foil for this golden curry.

1   cup (240 ml) low-fat (1%) milk

1   cup (185 g) long-grain white rice

¼   cup (20 g) sweetened shredded coconut

2   tablespoons (30 ml) lemon juice

1   clove garlic, minced or pressed

½   teaspoon ground cumin

¼   teaspoon chili powder

2   turkey breast tenderloins (about 1 lb./455 g total), cut into 1-inch (2.5-cm) pieces

½   cup (75 g) golden raisins

¼   cup (60 ml) dry white wine

2   medium-size carrots (about 6 oz./ 170 g total), cut into ¼-inch (6-mm) slanting slices

1   large onion, thinly sliced

2   teaspoons olive oil or vegetable oil

2 to 3 teaspoons curry powder

1 to 2 tablespoons chopped fresh mint

2   tablespoons salted roasted cashews, chopped

    Mint or parsley sprigs

1. To prepare coconut rice, in a 3- to 4-quart (2.8- to 3.8-liter) pan, combine 1 cup (240 ml) water and milk. Bring just to a boil over medium-high heat. Stir in rice. Reduce heat, cover, and simmer until liquid has been absorbed and rice is tender to bite (about 20 minutes). Stir in coconut. Keep warm until ready to serve, fluffing occasionally with a fork.

2. Meanwhile, in a large bowl, combine 1 tablespoon (15 ml) water, lemon juice, garlic, cumin,

and chili powder. Add turkey and stir to coat. Set aside; stir occasionally. In a small bowl, combine raisins and wine; let stand until raisins are softened (about 10 minutes), stirring occasionally.

3. In a wide nonstick frying pan or wok, combine carrots, onion, and ¼ cup (60 ml) water. Cover and cook over medium-high heat until carrots are tender-crisp to bite (about 5 minutes). Uncover and stir-fry until liquid has evaporated. Remove vegetables from pan with a slotted spoon and keep warm.

4. Heat oil in pan. When oil is hot, add turkey mixture. Stir-fry just until meat is no longer pink in center; cut to test (3 to 4 minutes). Add water, 1 tablespoon (15 ml) at a time, if pan appears dry. Add curry powder and stir-fry just until fragrant (about 30 seconds; do not scorch).

5. Add raisins (and soaking liquid) to pan; return vegetables to pan. Bring to a boil; boil, stirring, until liquid has evaporated (about 2 minutes). Remove from heat; stir in chopped mint and cashews. Spoon coconut rice into 4 wide bowls; top with turkey mixture and garnish with mint sprigs.

Makes 4 servings

NUTRIENTS

Per serving: 506 calories (14% calories from fat), 8 g total fat, 3 g saturated fat, 73 mg cholesterol, 156 mg sodium, 70 g carbohydrates, 5 g fiber, 36 g protein, 151 mg calcium, 5 mg iron

TURKEY FAJITAS

Preparation time: **About 10 minutes**
Cooking time: **About 15 minutes**

A marinade of lime juice and balsamic vinegar imparts a wonderful flavor to this lean stir-fry.

¼   cup (60 ml) lime juice

1   tablespoon (15 ml) balsamic vinegar or red wine vinegar

1   clove garlic, minced or pressed

½   teaspoon ground coriander

½ teaspoon ground cumin

½ teaspoon honey

2 turkey breast tenderloins (about
1 lb./455 g total, cut into ½- by 2-inch
(1- by 5-cm) strips

4 reduced-fat flour tortillas (each 7 to
9 inches/18 to 23 cm in diameter)

1 tablespoon (15 ml) olive oil

1 large green bell pepper (about
8 oz./230 g), seeded and cut into thin
strips

1 large red onion, thinly sliced

Lime wedges

1. In a large bowl, stir together lime juice, vinegar, garlic, coriander, cumin, and honey. Add turkey and stir to coat. Set aside to marinate, stirring occasionally.

2. Brush tortillas lightly with hot water; then stack tortillas, wrap in foil, and heat in a 350°F (175°C) oven until warm (10 to 12 minutes).

3. Meanwhile, heat 2 teaspoons of the oil in a wide nonstick frying pan or wok over medium-high heat. When oil is hot, add bell pepper and onion and stir-fry until vegetables are lightly browned (2 to 3 minutes). Remove vegetables from pan with a slotted spoon and keep warm.

4. Heat remaining 1 teaspoon oil in pan. When oil is hot, lift turkey from marinade and drain briefly (reserve marinade). Add turkey to pan and stir-fry until no longer pink in center; cut to test (2 to 3 minutes). Add marinade and bring to a boil; return vegetables to pan and mix gently. Spoon mixture onto a platter.

5. Offer tortillas and lime wedges alongside turkey mixture. Fill tortillas with turkey mixture; add a squeeze of lime, roll up, and eat out of hand.

Makes 4 servings

NUTRIENTS

Per serving: 280 calories (21% calories from fat), 6 g total fat, 0.7 g saturated fat, 70 mg cholesterol, 356 mg sodium, 23 g carbohydrates, 3 g fiber, 31 g protein, 138 mg calcium, 2 mg iron

TURKEY & MUSHROOM BURGERS

Preparation time: **About 15 minutes**
Cooking time: **8 to 10 minutes**

Feel free to lavish these lean turkey-breast burgers with such favorite trimmings as tomato slices, mustard, lettuce, and dill pickles—none will add much fat.

1 egg white

¼ cup (60 ml) dry white wine

⅓ cup (15 g) soft French bread crumbs

¼ teaspoon salt

⅛ teaspoon pepper

¼ cup (40 g) finely chopped shallots

1 pound (455 g) lean ground turkey
breast

4 ounces (115 g) mushrooms, finely
chopped

Olive oil cooking spray

6 onion hamburger rolls, split and
warmed

1. In a medium-size bowl, beat egg white and wine until blended. Stir in bread crumbs, salt, pepper, and shallots; then lightly mix in turkey and mushrooms. Shape turkey mixture into 6 patties, each about ½ inch (1 cm) thick.

2. Spray a wide nonstick frying pan with cooking spray. Place over medium-high heat; add turkey patties. Cook, turning once, until patties are lightly browned on both sides and juices run clear when a knife is inserted in center (8 to 10 minutes). Serve on warm rolls.

Makes 6 servings

NUTRIENTS

Per serving: 235 calories (12% calories from fat), 3 g total fat, 0.7 g saturated fat, 47 mg cholesterol, 394 mg sodium, 25 g carbohydrates, 1 g fiber, 24 g protein, 75 mg calcium, 3 mg iron

MEDITERRANEAN TURKEY WITH COUSCOUS

Preparation time: **About 15 minutes**
Cooking time: **About 10 minutes**

Oregano, lemon, and pungent Greek olives give this dish its Mediterranean flavor. Start by cooking the couscous, then prepare a garlicky stir-fry of turkey and red bell pepper strips to serve alongside.

2 turkey breast tenderloins (about 1 lb./455 g total), cut into ½-inch (1-cm) pieces

2 cloves garlic, minced or pressed

1 teaspoon paprika

½ teaspoon grated lemon peel

⅛ teaspoon salt (optional)

⅛ teaspoon pepper

2 teaspoons cornstarch

2 tablespoons (30 ml) balsamic vinegar

1½ cups (360 ml) fat-free reduced-sodium chicken broth

⅔ cup (160 ml) low-fat (1%) milk

1½ teaspoons chopped fresh oregano or ½ teaspoon dried oregano

1 cup (185 g) couscous

1 medium-size red bell pepper (about 6 oz./170 g), seeded and cut into thin strips

2 teaspoons olive oil

⅓ to ½ cup (45 to 70 g) chopped pitted calamata olives

¼ cup (15 g) finely chopped parsley

Oregano sprigs

1. In a large bowl, mix turkey, garlic, paprika, ¼ teaspoon of the lemon peel, salt (if used), and pepper; set aside.

2. To prepare sauce, in a bowl, smoothly blend cornstarch and vinegar. Stir in ½ cup (120 ml) of the broth. Set aside.

3. In a 3- to 4-quart (2.8- to 3.8-liter) pan, combine remaining 1 cup (240 ml) broth, milk, chopped oregano, and remaining ¼ teaspoon lemon peel. Bring just to a boil over medium-high heat; stir in couscous. Cover, remove from heat, and let stand until liquid has been absorbed (about 5 minutes). Transfer to a rimmed platter and keep warm; fluff occasionally with a fork.

4. While couscous is standing, in a wide nonstick frying pan or wok, combine bell pepper and 2 tablespoons (30 ml) water. Stir-fry over medium-high heat until pepper is just tender-crisp to bite (about 2 minutes); add water, 1 tablespoon (15 ml) at a time, if pan appears dry. Remove from pan with a slotted spoon and keep warm.

5. Heat oil in pan. When oil is hot, add turkey mixture and stir-fry just until meat is no longer pink in center; cut to test (2 to 3 minutes). Stir reserved sauce well; pour into pan. Then add bell pepper and olives; cook, stirring, until sauce boils and thickens slightly (1 to 2 minutes). Pour turkey mixture over couscous. Sprinkle with parsley and garnish with oregano sprigs.

Makes 4 servings

NUTRIENTS

Per serving: 415 calories (20% calories from fat), 9 g total fat, 1 g saturated fat, 72 mg cholesterol, 823 mg sodium, 44 g carbohydrates, 2 g fiber, 37 g protein, 101 mg calcium, 3 mg iron

MEATS

PORK TENDERLOIN WITH BULGUR

Preparation time: **About 10 minutes**
Cooking time: **About 30 minutes**

By taking advantage of quick-cooking pork tenderloin, you can have a complete meal on the table in little more than half an hour. The asparagus is an appetizing addition.

3   cups (710 ml) beef broth

1   cup (175 g) bulgur (cracked wheat)

½   cup (50 g) sliced green onions

1½   pounds (680 g) pork tenderloin (about 2 tenderloins), trimmed of fat

2   teaspoons sugar

1   tablespoon (15 ml) vegetable oil

1   tablespoon mustard seeds

1   tablespoon (15 ml) balsamic vinegar

2   teaspoons minced fresh oregano or 1 teaspoon dried oregano

½   cup (120 ml) dry red wine

2   teaspoons cornstarch mixed with 2 teaspoons cold water

1   pound (455 g) asparagus, tough ends broken off

     Salt and pepper

1. In a 2- to 3-quart (1.9- to 2.8-liter) pan, bring 2 cups (470 ml) of the broth to a boil; stir in bulgur. Cover, remove from heat, and let stand until bulgur is tender to bite (about 30 minutes). Stir in onions.

2. While bulgur is standing, sprinkle pork with sugar. Heat oil in a wide frying pan over medium-high heat; add pork and cook, turning as needed, until browned on all sides (about 4 minutes). Add ⅔ cup (160 ml) of the broth, mustard seeds, vinegar, and oregano. Cover, reduce heat to medium-low, and simmer just until meat is no longer pink in center; cut to test (about 12 minutes).

3. Lift pork to a warm platter and keep warm. To pan, add wine and remaining ⅓ cup (80 ml) broth.

Bring to a boil over high heat; then boil until reduced to ¾ cup/180 ml (about 2 minutes). Stir in cornstarch mixture; return to a boil, stirring.

4. While sauce is boiling, bring ½ inch (1 cm) of water to a boil in another wide frying pan over high heat. Add asparagus and cook, uncovered, just until barely tender when pierced (about 4 minutes). Drain.

5. Slice pork; mound bulgur mixture alongside, then top with asparagus. Spoon sauce over meat. Season to taste with salt and pepper.

Makes 4 servings

NUTRIENTS

Per serving: 442 calories (24% calories from fat), 11 g total fat, 3 g saturated fat, 111 mg cholesterol, 1,327 mg sodium, 36 g carbohydrates, 8 g fiber, 45 g protein, 73 mg calcium, 5 mg iron

HERBED PORK CHOPS WITH APPLES

Preparation time: **About 10 minutes**
Cooking time: **About 30 minutes**

Sweet apple jelly and tart cider vinegar combine in a tempting sauce for quickly cooked pork chops. To complete the dish, poach sliced Golden Delicious apples in the pan juices, then spoon them alongside the meat. Apples are the perfect complement to pork.

6   center-cut loin pork chops (about 2 lbs./905 g total), trimmed of fat

     Pepper

¼   cup (72 g) apple jelly

1   tablespoon (15 ml) Dijon mustard

½   teaspoon ground cumin

3   large Golden Delicious apples (about 1½ lbs./680 g total)

¼   cup (60 ml) cider vinegar

1. Sprinkle pork chops with pepper; then cook in a wide nonstick frying pan over medium-high heat, turning once, until well browned on both sides (about 14 minutes).

2. In a small bowl, mix jelly, mustard, 1 table-spoon (15 ml) water, and cumin. Spoon evenly over pork chops. Reduce heat to low, cover, and cook until pork chops look faintly pink to white in center; cut to test (about 10 minutes; meat should still be moist). With a slotted spoon or a fork, transfer pork chops to a platter; keep warm.

3. Peel, core, and thinly slice apples. Add apples and vinegar to pan; stir to coat apples with pan juices, scraping browned bits free. Cover and cook over medium heat until apples are barely tender when pierced (about 5 minutes).

4. With a slotted spoon, transfer apples to warm platter with pork chops. Offer hot pan juices to pour over pork chops and apples.

Makes 6 servings

NUTRIENTS

Per serving: 236 calories (21% calories from fat), 5 g total fat, 2 g saturated fat, 64 mg cholesterol, 132 mg sodium, 24 g carbohydrates, 2 g fiber, 23 g protein, 28 mg calcium, 1 mg iron

SMOKED PORK CHOPS WITH RUOTE

Preparation time: **About 10 minutes**
Cooking time: **About 25 minutes**

For this filling main dish, ruote (wheel-shaped pasta) is enveloped in a mustard-sparked cheese sauce and served with pan-browned smoked pork chops.

4   smoked pork loin chops (about 1¼ lbs./565 g total), each about ¾ inch (2 cm) thick, trimmed of fat

8   ounces/230 g (about 4 cups) dried ruote or other medium-size pasta

1   tablespoon butter or margarine

1   large onion (about 8 oz./230 g), chopped

1   tablespoon (15 ml) all-purpose flour

1½   cups (360 ml) nonfat milk

1   tablespoon (15 ml) Dijon mustard

¼   teaspoon pepper

1   package (about 10 oz./285 g) frozen tiny peas

1   cup (about 4 oz./115 g) shredded Emmenthaler or Swiss cheese

1. Place pork chops in a wide nonstick frying pan and cook over medium-high heat, turning as needed, until browned on both sides (about 10 minutes). Transfer to a platter and keep warm. Discard any pan drippings.

2. Bring 8 cups (1.9 liters) water to a boil in a 4- to 5-quart (3.8- to 5-liter) pan over medium-high heat. Stir in pasta and cook just until tender to bite (8 to 10 minutes); or cook according to package directions. Meanwhile, melt butter in frying pan over medium-high heat. Add onion and cook, stirring often, until soft (about 5 minutes). Stir in flour and remove from heat. Add milk, mustard, and pepper; mix until blended.

3. Stir peas into pasta and water; drain and set aside. Return sauce to medium-high heat and cook, stirring, until mixture comes to a boil. Add cheese and stir until melted. Remove from heat and add pasta mixture. Mix thoroughly but gently. Spoon alongside pork chops.

Makes 4 servings

NUTRIENTS

Per serving: 593 calories (27% calories from fat), 17 g total fat, 9 g saturated fat, 86 mg cholesterol, 1,867 mg sodium, 63 g carbohydrates, 5 g fiber, 43 g protein, 429 mg calcium, 4 mg iron

SWEET & SOUR PORK

Preparation time: **About 25 minutes**
Cooking time: **About 15 minutes**

All of the classic ingredients are here—tender pork, crisp bell pepper and onion, juicy pineapple chunks, and a tart-sweet sauce—but this rendition of sweet-and-sour pork is far lower in fat than most traditional recipes. To streamline this long-time favorite dish, we use lean pork tenderloin (be sure it's trimmed), then stir-fry the meat in a light batter, using a minimum of oil.

⅓ cup (45 g) plus 4 teaspoons cornstarch

¼ cup (60 ml) white wine vinegar or distilled white vinegar

¼ cup (50 g) sugar

1 tablespoon (15 ml) catsup

1 tablespoon (15 ml) reduced-sodium soy sauce

⅛ teaspoon Hot Chile Oil (page 55) or purchased hot chili oil, or to taste

1 large egg white

1 pound (455 g) pork tenderloin, trimmed of fat and cut into 1-inch (2.5-cm) chunks

1 tablespoon (15 ml) vegetable oil

1 large onion, cut into thin wedges

1 large green bell pepper (about 8 oz./230 g), seeded and cut into 1-inch (2.5-cm) squares

1 or 2 cloves garlic, minced or pressed

1 large tomato (about 8 oz./230 g), cut into wedges

1½ cups (235 g) fresh or canned pineapple chunks, drained

1. For sweet-sour sauce, in a medium-size bowl, stir together 4 teaspoons of the cornstarch and the vinegar until blended. Stir in ¾ cup (180 ml) water, sugar, catsup, soy sauce and Hot Chile Oil. Set aside.

2. In a medium-size bowl, beat egg white to blend well. Place remaining ⅓ cup (45 g) cornstarch in another medium-size bowl. Dip pork chunks, a portion at a time, in egg white; then coat lightly with cornstarch and shake off excess.

3. Heat vegetable oil in a wide nonstick frying pan or wok over medium-high heat. When oil is hot, add meat and stir-fry gently until golden brown on outside and no longer pink in center; cut to test (about 8 minutes). Add water, 1 tablespoon (15 ml) at a time, if pan appears dry. Remove meat from pan with a slotted spoon; keep warm.

4. Add onion, bell pepper, garlic, and 1 tablespoon (15 ml) water to pan; stir-fry for 1 minute. Add more water, 1 tablespoon (15 ml) at a time, if pan appears dry. Stir reserved sweet-sour sauce well and pour into pan. Cook, stirring, until sauce boils and thickens slightly (2 to 3 minutes).

5. Add tomato, pineapple, and meat to pan. Cook, stirring gently but thoroughly, just until heated through (1 to 2 minutes). Serve immediately.

Makes 4 servings

NUTRIENTS

Per serving: 355 calories (20% calories from fat), 8 g total fat, 2 g saturated fat, 74 mg cholesterol, 275 mg sodium, 45 g carbohydrates, 3 g fiber, 27 g protein, 32 mg calcium, 2 mg iron

ISLAND PORK WITH COCONUT COUSCOUS

Preparation time: **About 25 minutes**
Cooking time: **About 15 minutes**

To make couscous and rice seem richer, try cooking them in low-fat milk—or in a combination of broth and milk, as we do here. The creamy-tasting couscous, sweetened with a little shredded coconut, accompanies luscious sliced mangoes and a ginger-seasoned stir-fry of pork tenderloin and bright bell pepper.

2   or 3 large mangoes (1½ to 2¼ lbs./680 g to 1.02 kg total)

1   to 2 tablespoons (15 to 30 ml) lime juice

1   tablespoon cornstarch

¾   cup (180 ml) mango or pear nectar

1½   teaspoons Oriental sesame oil

¼   teaspoon salt

1   cup (240 ml) fat-free reduced-sodium chicken broth

⅔   cup (160 ml) low-fat (2%) milk

1   cup (185 g) couscous

¼   cup (20 g) sweetened shredded coconut

2   teaspoons olive oil

1   tablespoon minced fresh ginger

2   cloves garlic, minced or pressed

1   pound (455 g) pork tenderloin, trimmed of fat and cut into 1-inch (2.5-cm) chunks

1   large red or green bell pepper (about 8 oz./230 g), seeded and cut into thin strips

¼   cup (25 g) thinly sliced green onions

Lime wedges

1. Peel mangoes; cut fruit from pits into thin slices and place in a large bowl. Add lime juice (use 2 tablespoons/30 ml juice if using 3 mangoes) and mix gently to coat. Arrange mangoes attractively on 4 individual plates; cover and set aside.

2. For sauce, place cornstarch in a small bowl. Gradually add nectar, stirring until cornstarch is smoothly dissolved. Stir in sesame oil and salt. Set aside.

3. In a 3- to 4-quart (2.8- to 3.8-liter) pan, bring broth and milk just to a boil over medium-high heat; stir in couscous. Cover, remove from heat, and let stand until liquid has been absorbed (about 5 minutes). Stir in coconut. Keep warm; fluff occasionally with a fork.

4. Heat olive oil in a wide nonstick frying pan or wok over medium-high heat. When oil is hot, add ginger and garlic; stir-fry just until fragrant (about 30 seconds; do not scorch). Add pork and stir-fry until lightly browned on outside and no longer pink in center; cut to test (about 8 minutes). Add water, 1 tablespoon (15 ml) at a time, if pan appears dry. Remove meat from pan with a slotted spoon; keep warm.

5. Add bell pepper and 2 tablespoons (30 ml) water to pan. Stir-fry until bell pepper is just tender-crisp to bite (about 2 minutes); add water, 1 tablespoon (15 ml) at a time, if pan appears dry.

6. Stir sauce well and pour into pan. Cook, stirring, until sauce boils and thickens slightly (1 to 2 minutes). Remove pan from heat and add meat and onions; mix gently but thoroughly.

7. Spoon couscous alongside mango slices; spoon meat mixture alongside couscous. Serve with lime wedges to squeeze over pork and couscous.

Makes 4 servings

NUTRIENTS

Per serving: 541 calories (18% calories from fat), 11 g total fat, 4 g saturated fat, 77 mg cholesterol, 398 mg sodium, 79 g carbohydrates, 5 g fiber, 33 g protein, 98 mg calcium, 3 mg iron

TRIPLE CORN STEW

Preparation time: **About 5 minutes**
Cooking time: **25 to 30 minutes**

Spicy chorizo seasons a hearty stew containing corn in three forms: hominy, creamed corn, and the whole kernels. Top each bowlful with a peppery garnish of crisp radish slices.

- 8 ounces (230 g) chorizo sausages, casings removed
- 1 can (about 14 oz./400 g) yellow hominy, drained
- 1 can (about 17 oz./480 g) cream-style corn
- 2 cups (300 g) fresh-cut yellow or white corn kernels (from 2 large ears corn); or 1 package (about 10 oz./285 g) frozen corn kernels, thawed; or 1 can (about 1 lb./455 g) corn kernels, drained
- 1 teaspoon cornstarch
- ½ cup (120 ml) fat-free reduced-sodium chicken broth

  Thinly sliced red radishes

1. Coarsely chop or crumble sausage; place in a 4- to 5-quart (3.8- to 5-liter) pan. Cook over medium heat, stirring, until well browned (15 to 20 minutes). Discard fat.

2. Add hominy, cream-style corn, and corn kernels to pan. Cook, stirring occasionally, until heated through (about 5 minutes).

3. In a small bowl, mix cornstarch and broth; stir into corn mixture and cook, stirring, until stew comes to a boil. Ladle stew into wide serving bowls; garnish with radishes.

Makes 4 servings

NUTRIENTS

Per serving: 347 calories (27% calories from fat), 11 g total fat, 3 g saturated fat, 32 mg cholesterol, 752 mg sodium, 54 g carbohydrates, 5 g fiber, 14 g protein, 30 mg calcium, 2 mg iron

GINGERED PORK WITH ASIAN PEARS

Preparation time: **About 15 minutes**
Cooking time: **About 20 minutes**

Round, crisp Asian pears—sometimes called "apple pears"—make a mild, slightly sweet foil for stir-fried pork chunks. If you can't find Asian pears, use your favorite regular variety; Bartlett and Anjou are both good choices.

- 3 large firm-ripe Asian or regular pears (about 1½ lbs./680 g total), peeled, cored, and thinly sliced
- 3 tablespoons (45 ml) cider vinegar
- 1 teaspoon vegetable oil
- 1 pound (455 g) pork tenderloin, trimmed of fat and cut into 1-inch (2.5-cm) chunks
- 2 tablespoons firmly packed brown sugar
- ⅔ cup (160 ml) dry white wine
- ⅔ cup (160 ml) fat-free reduced-sodium chicken broth
- 2 teaspoons minced fresh ginger

4 teaspoons cornstarch blended with
4 teaspoons cold water

½ to ¾ cup (15 to 23 g) finely shredded
spinach

1. In a large bowl, gently mix pears and 1 table-spoon (15 ml) of the vinegar. Set aside.

2. Heat oil in a wide nonstick frying pan or wok over medium-high heat. When oil is hot, add pork and stir-fry until lightly browned on outside and no longer pink in center; cut to test (about 8 minutes). Add water, 1 tablespoon (15 ml) at a time, if pan appears dry. Remove meat from pan with a slotted spoon; keep warm.

3. Add sugar and remaining 2 tablespoons (30 ml) vinegar to pan. Bring to a boil; then boil, stirring, for 1 minute. Add wine, broth, and ginger; return to a boil. Boil, stirring, for 3 minutes. Add pears and cook, gently turning pears often, until pears are heated through (about 3 minutes). Stir cornstarch mixture well and pour into pan. Cook, stirring, until sauce boils and thickens slightly (1 to 2 minutes).

4. Remove pan from heat; return meat to pan and mix gently but thoroughly. Gently stir in spinach.

Makes 4 servings

NUTRIENTS

Per serving: 309 calories (18% calories from fat), 6 g total fat, 2 g saturated fat, 74 mg cholesterol, 177 mg sodium, 34 g carbohydrates, 4 g fiber, 25 g protein, 42 mg calcium, 2 mg iron

PORK & APPLE
STIR-FRY

Preparation time: **About 20 minutes**
Marinating time: **At least 15 minutes**
Cooking time: **About 6 minutes**

Have the rice ready—this meal cooks in minutes! Make your own teriyaki sauce with ginger, mint, and orange juice; marinate the pork while the rice simmers.

½ cup (120 ml) orange juice

¼ cup (10 g) minced fresh mint

2 tablespoons (30 ml) reduced-sodium soy sauce

1 tablespoon minced fresh ginger

1 clove garlic, minced or pressed

1 pound (455 g) boned pork loin or shoulder (butt), trimmed of fat

2 medium-size red-skinned apples such as Red Gravenstein or Red Delicious (about 12 oz./340 g total), cored and chopped

2 tablespoons (30 ml) lemon juice

1 tablespoon (15 ml) vegetable oil

1 small onion, cut into thin wedges

3 cups (390 g) hot cooked rice

1 or 2 medium-size oranges (peeled, if desired), sliced crosswise

Mint sprigs (optional)

1. To prepare teriyaki sauce, in a medium-size bowl, mix orange juice, minced mint, soy sauce, ginger, and garlic; set aside.

2. Slice pork across the grain into ⅛-inch-thick (3-mm-thick) strips about 2 inches (5 cm) long. Add pork to teriyaki sauce in bowl; cover and refrigerate for at least 15 minutes or until next day. Mix apples with lemon juice; set aside.

3. Heat oil in a wok or wide frying pan over high heat. Add onion; cook, stirring, until soft (about 2 minutes). Add apples; cook, stirring, until hot (about 1 minute). Spoon mixture into a bowl and set aside.

4. With a slotted spoon, transfer pork to pan; reserve teriyaki sauce in bowl. Cook, stirring, until meat is lightly browned (about 2 minutes). Return apple mixture to pan, then add any remaining teriyaki sauce and bring to a boil, stirring.

5. Mound rice on a platter. Pour pork mixture over rice; garnish with orange slices and, if desired, mint sprigs. *Makes 4 servings*

NUTRIENTS

Per serving: 497 calories (20% calories from fat), 11 g total fat, 3 g saturated fat, 67 mg cholesterol, 365 mg sodium, 69 g carbohydrates, 4 g fiber, 30 g protein, 81 mg calcium, 3 mg iron

LAMB CHOPS WITH CHERRIES & ORECCHIETTE

Preparation time: **About 15 minutes**
Cooking time: **About 15 minutes**

When cherries are in season, use them to make a delicious tart-sweet sauce for lamb rib chops.

8   lamb rib chops (about 2 lbs./905 g total), each about ¾ inch (2.5 cm) thick, trimmed of fat

12 ounces/340 g (about 3½ cups) dried orecchiette or other medium-size pasta shape

⅓   cup (80 ml) seasoned rice vinegar

1   tablespoon chopped cilantro

1   tablespoon chopped parsley

1   to 2 cloves garlic, minced or pressed

½   teaspoon ground coriander

¾   cup (225 g) currant jelly

½   cup (120 ml) raspberry vinegar

¼   cup (60 ml) orange juice

1   tablespoon chopped fresh tarragon or ¾ teaspoon dried tarragon

1½ cups (220 g) pitted dark sweet cherries

1. Place chops on lightly oiled rack of a broiler pan. Broil about 6 inches (15 cm) below heat, turning once, until done to your liking; cut to test (8 to 10 minutes). Meanwhile, bring 12 cups (2.8 liters) water to a boil in a 5- to 6-quart (5- to 6-liter) pan over medium-high heat. Stir in pasta and cook just until tender to bite (8 to 10 minutes); or cook according to package directions. Drain well. Transfer to a large nonmetal bowl and add rice vinegar, cilantro, parsley, garlic, and coriander; mix thoroughly but gently. Keep warm.

2. Combine jelly, raspberry vinegar, orange juice, and tarragon in a 1½- to 2-quart (1.4- to 1.9-liter) pan. Cook over medium heat, whisking, until

smoothly blended. Add cherries and cook, stirring gently, just until warm. Remove from heat.

3. Spoon pasta onto individual plates. Arrange lamb chops alongside and top with fruit sauce.

Makes 4 servings

NUTRIENTS

Per serving: 709 calories (14% calories from fat), 11 g total fat, 4 g saturated fat, 66 mg cholesterol, 481 mg sodium, 120 g carbohydrates, 3 g fiber, 32 g protein, 48 mg calcium, 5 mg iron

SAUTÉED LAMB WITH APPLES

Preparation time: **About 20 minutes**
Cooking time: **About 10 minutes**

Stir-fried Golden Delicious apples, sauced with a blend of apple jelly and cider vinegar, are the perfect partner for lamb.

4   to 8 large radicchio leaves, rinsed and crisped

1   pound (455 g) lean boneless leg of lamb, trimmed of fat and cut into ¾-inch (2-cm) chunks

¼   teaspoon salt

⅛   teaspoon pepper

⅓   cup (100 g) apple jelly

⅓   cup (80 ml) cider vinegar

1   tablespoon cornstarch blended with 1 tablespoon (15 ml) cold water

1   teaspoon Dijon mustard

¾   teaspoon chopped fresh thyme or ¼ teaspoon dried thyme

⅓   cup (50 g) dried currants or raisins

3   large Golden Delicious apples (about 1½ lbs./680 g total), peeled, cored, and sliced ½ inch (1 cm) thick

2   teaspoons vegetable oil

1   to 2 tablespoons chopped parsley

Thyme sprigs

1. Arrange 1 or 2 radicchio leaves on each of 4 individual plates; cover and set aside.

2. In a large bowl, mix lamb, salt, and pepper; set aside. In a small bowl, stir together jelly, 3 tablespoons (45 ml) of the vinegar, cornstarch mixture, mustard, and chopped thyme until well blended. Stir in currants and set aside. In a medium-size bowl, gently mix apples with remaining vinegar.

3. Heat 1 teaspoon of the oil in a wide nonstick frying pan or wok over medium-high heat. When oil is hot, add apples and stir-fry gently until almost tender when pierced (about 4 minutes). Add water, 1 tablespoon (15 ml) at a time, if pan appears dry. Stir jelly mixture well; pour into pan and cook, stirring, just until sauce boils and thickens slightly (1 to 2 minutes). Remove apple mixture from pan and keep warm. Wipe pan clean.

4. Heat remaining 1 teaspoon oil in pan over medium-high heat. When oil is hot, add meat and stir-fry just until done to your liking; cut to test (about 3 minutes for medium-rare). Remove from heat and stir in parsley.

5. Spoon meat into radicchio leaves; spoon apple mixture alongside. Garnish with thyme sprigs.

Makes 4 servings

NUTRIENTS

Per serving: 367 calories (19% calories from fat), 8 g total fat, 2 g saturated fat, 73 mg cholesterol, 114 mg sodium, 52 g carbohydrates, 4 g fiber, 25 g protein, 49 mg calcium, 3 mg iron

STIR-FRIED BEEF & ASPARAGUS

Preparation time: **About 15 minutes**
Cooking time: **About 10 minutes**

This elegant-looking dish, which combines lean sirloin with fresh asparagus, is an ideal springtime main course. Buy the asparagus the same day you plan to use it; look for apple-green spears with tightly furled tips.

½ cup (120 ml) dry red wine

¼ cup (60 ml) orange juice

2 tablespoons (30 ml) raspberry or red wine vinegar

¼ cup (40 g) finely chopped shallots

2 teaspoons chopped fresh tarragon or ½ teaspoon dried tarragon

1 pound (455 g) lean boneless top sirloin steak (about 1 inch/2.5 cm thick), trimmed of fat and cut across the grain into ⅛- by 2-inch (3-mm by 5-cm) strips

1½ pounds (680 g) asparagus

1 teaspoon olive oil

About ½ cup (60 g) fresh raspberries

1. In a large bowl, stir together wine, orange juice, vinegar, shallots, and tarragon. Add steak and stir to coat. Set aside; stir occasionally.

2. Snap off and discard tough ends of asparagus; then cut spears into 3-inch (8-cm) lengths. Place asparagus and ½ cup (120 ml) water in a wide nonstick frying pan or wok. Cover; cook over medium-high heat, stirring occasionally, until asparagus is tender-crisp to bite (4 to 5 minutes). Drain asparagus, transfer to a platter, and keep warm. Wipe pan dry (be careful; pan is hot).

3. Heat oil in pan over medium-high heat. When oil is hot, lift meat from marinade and drain; reserve ¼ cup (60 ml) of the marinade. Add meat to pan and stir-fry until done to your liking; cut to test (2 to 3 minutes for rare). Add the reserved ¼ cup (60 ml) marinade and bring to a boil. Spoon meat mixture over asparagus; top with raspberries.

Makes 4 servings

NUTRIENTS

Per serving: 213 calories (29% calories from fat), 6 g total fat, 2 g saturated fat, 69 mg cholesterol, 70 mg sodium, 8 g carbohydrates, 2 g fiber, 27 g protein, 39 mg calcium, 4 mg iron

⅛ teaspoon crushed red pepper flakes

1 pound (455 g) lean boneless top sirloin steak (about 1 inch/2.5 cm thick), trimmed of fat and cut across the grain into ⅛- by 2-inch (3-mm by 5-cm) strips

3 green onions

1 teaspoon vegetable oil

1 teaspoon cornstarch blended with 1 teaspoon cold water

5 to 6 cups (5 to 6 oz./140 to 170 g) mixed salad greens, rinsed and crisped

4 pita breads (each about 6 inches/ 15 cm in diameter), cut crosswise into halves

1. Prepare Cool Yogurt Sauce and set aside.

2. In a large bowl, stir together garlic, soy sauce, sugar, and red pepper flakes. Add steak and stir to coat. Set aside; stir occasionally. Trim and discard ends of onions; then cut onions into 1-inch (2.5-cm) lengths and sliver each piece lengthwise. Set aside.

3. Heat oil in a wide nonstick frying pan or wok over medium-high heat. When oil is hot, lift meat from marinade and drain briefly (reserve marinade). Add meat to pan and stir-fry until done to your liking; cut to test (2 to 3 minutes for rare). With a slotted spoon, transfer meat to a bowl; keep warm.

4. Stir cornstarch mixture well; pour into pan along with reserved marinade and any meat juices that have accumulated in bowl. Cook, stirring, until sauce boils and thickens slightly (1 to 2 minutes). Remove pan from heat and stir in meat and onions.

5. To serve, divide salad greens equally among pita bread halves; then spoon in meat mixture. Drizzle Cool Yogurt Sauce over meat.

Makes 4 servings

GARLIC BEEF IN PITA BREAD WITH COOL YOGURT SAUCE

Preparation time: **About 15 minutes**
Cooking time: **About 15 minutes**

Stir-fries make great hot fillings for pita breads. These sandwiches are stuffed with mixed greens and garlicky strips of sirloin; a minted yogurt sauce adds a cool, refreshing accent.

Cool Yogurt Sauce (facing page)

4 to 6 cloves garlic, minced or pressed

3 tablespoons (45 ml) reduced-sodium soy sauce

1½ teaspoons sugar

NUTRIENTS

Per serving: 386 calories (17% calories from fat), 7 g total fat, 2 g saturated fat, 70 mg cholesterol, 886 mg sodium, 44 g carbohydrates, 2 g fiber, 34 g protein, 207 mg calcium, 6 mg iron

Cool Yogurt Sauce

Preparation time: **About 5 minutes**

This low-fat sauce, a variation on Indian *raita*, will temper the heat in spicy dishes. Try it with any dish that includes chiles.

1 cup (240 ml) plain nonfat yogurt
1 tablespoon chopped fresh mint
1 tablespoon chopped fresh cilantro
Salt
Fresh mint and cilantro leaves (optional)

1. In a small bowl, stir together yogurt, chopped mint, and chopped cilantro. Season to taste with salt. (At this point, you may cover and refrigerate for up to 4 hours; stir before serving.) Sprinkle with mint and cilantro leaves just before serving, if desired.

Makes about 1 cup (240 ml)

NUTRIENTS

Per tablespoon: 8 calories (2% calories from fat), 0.02 g total fat, 0 g saturated fat, 0.3 mg cholesterol, 11 mg sodium, 1 g carbohydrates, 0 g fiber, 0.8 g protein, 28 mg calcium, 0 mg iron

20 MINUTES OR LESS

Marsala Beef & Couscous

1 pound (455 g) lean boneless top sirloin steak (about 1 in./2.5 cm thick), trimmed of fat and cut across grain into ⅛- by 2-inch (3-mm by 5-cm) strips

¼ cup (60 ml) marsala

3 green onions

2½ cups (590 ml) canned beef broth

⅛ teaspoon saffron threads, or to taste

1 can (about 14 oz./400 g) artichoke hearts in water, drained

1 cup (100 g) pitted bite-size dried prunes

1 cup (100 g) dried apricots

1 package (about 10 oz./285 g) dried couscous

1 tablespoon (15 ml) olive oil

2 teaspoons cornstarch blended with 1 tablespoon (15 ml) cold water

Salt and pepper

1. In a large bowl, combine steak and marsala; set aside. Cut onions into 1-inch (2.5-cm) lengths and sliver lengthwise; set aside.

2. In a 4- to 5-quart (3.8- to 5-liter) pan, bring broth, saffron, artichokes, prunes, and apricots to a boil over high heat. Stir in couscous. Cover pan, remove from heat, and let stand until liquid has been absorbed (about 5 minutes).

3. While couscous stands, heat oil in a wide nonstick frying pan over medium-high heat. When oil is hot, lift meat from marinade and drain briefly (reserve marinade). Add meat to pan and cook, stirring, until done to your liking, cut to test (2 to 3 minutes for rare). With a slotted spoon, transfer meat to a bowl; keep warm.

4. Stir cornstarch mixture well; pour into pan along with reserved marinade and any meat juices in bowl. Cook, stirring, until sauce boils and thickens slightly (about 1 minute). Remove pan from heat and stir in meat and onions. Transfer couscous to a platter, fluffing with a fork; top with meat mixture. Add salt and pepper to taste.

Makes 6 servings

Per serving: 456 calories (13% calories from fat), 6 g total fat, 2 g saturated fat, 46 mg cholesterol, 737 mg sodium, 72 g carbohydrates, 6 g fiber, 25 g protein, 56 mg calcium, 5 mg iron

CHILE BEEF BURRITOS

Preparation time: **About 15 minutes**
Cooking time: **About 15 minutes**

Don't let the cayenne-and-jalapeño marinade frighten you away; this dish has just the right amount of heat. If you have the time, you can marinate the beef in the refrigerator up to a day in advance. Otherwise, mix it with the seasonings just before cooking.

BURRITOS:

1 fresh jalapeño or other small fresh hot chile, seeded and minced

2 cloves garlic, minced or pressed

¼ to ½ teaspoon ground red pepper (cayenne)

1 tablespoon (15 ml) reduced-sodium soy sauce

½ teaspoon sugar

1 pound (455 g) lean boneless top sirloin steak (about 1 inch/2.5 cm thick), trimmed of fat and cut across the grain into ⅛- by 2-inch (3-mm by 5-cm) strips

4 to 8 low-fat flour tortillas (each 7 to 9 inches/18 to 23 cm in diameter)

1 large onion, thinly sliced

1 teaspoon olive oil

CONDIMENTS:

Tomatillo & Lime Salsa (page 73) or purchased salsa

Shredded lettuce

Chopped tomatoes

Nonfat sour cream

Cilantro leaves

Lime wedges

1. In a large bowl, stir together chile, garlic, red pepper, soy sauce, and sugar. Add steak and stir to coat. Set aside.

---

20 MINUTES OR LESS

¾ pound (340 g) top sirloin steak (about 1 in./2.5 cm thick), fat trimmed

1 tablespoon Cajun or blackening spice blend

½ cup (120 ml) salsa

½ cup (120ml) nonfat sour cream

2 tablespoons (30 ml) lime juice

¾ pound (340 g) prewashed spinach leaves

1 can (about 15 oz/425 g) black beans, rinsed and drained

1 jar (about 7.25 oz./208 g) peeled roasted red peppers, drained and cut into thin strips

Pepper

BLACKENED STEAK WITH BEANS & GREENS

1. Pat steak with spice blend to coat both sides evenly. Heat a wide frying pan over medium-high heat. When pan is very hot, add steak. Cook, turning occasionally, until meat is well browned on the outside and done to your liking (cut to test; about 14 minutes for medium-rare).

2. Meanwhile, in a blender or food processor, whirl salsa, sour cream, and lime juice until smooth. Arrange spinach, beans, and peppers decoratively on a large platter.

3. When meat is done, cut it into thin bite-size slices; add to platter. At the table, toss with salsa mixture. Add pepper to taste.

Makes 4 servings

Per serving: 247 calories (18% calories from fat), 5 g total fat, 1 g saturated fat, 52 mg cholesterol, 1,370 mg sodium, 22 g carbohydrates, 5 g fiber, 27 g protein, 150 mg calcium, 6 mg iron

2. Brush tortillas lightly with hot water; then stack, wrap in foil, and heat in a 350°F (175°C) oven until warm (10 to 12 minutes).

3. Meanwhile, in a wide nonstick frying pan or wok, combine onion and ¼ cup (60 ml) water. Stir-fry over medium-high heat until onion is soft and liquid has evaporated (4 to 5 minutes). Add oil; then stir in meat and its marinade. Stir-fry until meat is done to your liking; cut to test (2 to 3 minutes for rare).

4. To serve, spoon meat mixture into tortillas. Offer a choice of condiments to add to taste.

Makes 4 servings

NUTRIENTS

Per serving: 293 calories (20% calories from fat), 7 g total fat, 2 g saturated fat, 69 mg cholesterol, 488 mg sodium, 34 g carbohydrates, 7 g fiber, 28 g protein, 114 mg calcium, 5 mg iron

STIR-FRIED VEAL PICCATA

Preparation time: **About 15 minutes**
Cooking time: **About 10 minutes**

Thin, tender strips of veal and a piquant lemon-caper sauce give this lean stir-fry the taste of a classic veal piccata. You might serve it with steamed asparagus and a basket of crusty French rolls.

½ cup (120 ml) dry white wine

2 tablespoons (30 ml) lemon juice

1½ teaspoons honey

1 pound (455 g) veal scaloppine, cut into ¼- by 2-inch (6-mm by 5-cm) strips

½ teaspoon paprika

¼ teaspoon grated lemon peel

⅛ teaspoon salt

1 teaspoon butter or margarine

1 teaspoon olive oil

½ teaspoon cornstarch blended with 1 teaspoon cold water

2 tablespoons drained capers, or to taste

Chopped parsley and lemon wedges

Pepper

1. For the sauce, in a small bowl, stir together wine, lemon juice, and honey; set aside.

2. In a large bowl, combine veal, paprika, lemon peel, and salt. Melt butter in oil in a wide nonstick frying pan or wok over medium-high heat. When butter mixture is hot, add meat mixture; stir-fry just until meat is no longer pink on outside (1 to 2 minutes). With a slotted spoon, transfer meat to a rimmed platter; keep warm.

3. Stir reserved sauce well; pour into pan. Bring to a boil; then boil, stirring constantly, for 3 minutes. Stir cornstarch mixture well; add to pan along with capers. Cook, stirring, until sauce boils and thickens slightly (about 1 minute). Spoon sauce over meat; garnish with parsley and lemon wedges. Season to taste with pepper.

Makes 4 servings

NUTRIENTS

Per serving: 172 calories (25% calories from fat), 4 g total fat, 1 g saturated fat, 91 mg cholesterol, 265 mg sodium, 3 g carbohydrates, 0.1 g fiber, 24 g protein, 13 mg calcium, 1 mg iron

VEAL WITH MUSHROOMS

Preparation time: **About 20 minutes**
Cooking time: **About 15 minutes**

Marsala flavors a mild stir-fry of veal and sliced mushrooms, spooned over hot linguine. Italy's most famous fortified wine, marsala ranges from sweet to dry. You can use whichever you prefer in this recipe.

- 1 pound (455 g) veal scaloppine, cut into ¼- by 2-inch (6-mm by 5-cm) strips
- ⅛ teaspoon salt
- ⅛ teaspoon pepper
- 8 ounces (230 g) dried linguine
- 1 tablespoon butter or margarine
- 2 cloves garlic, minced or pressed
- 2 cups (170 g) sliced mushrooms
- ½ cup (120 ml) marsala or cream sherry
- 3 tablespoons chopped parsley
- 1 large tomato (about 8 oz./230 g), chopped and drained well
- ¼ cup (35 g) pitted ripe olives, chopped

1. In a large bowl, mix veal, salt, and pepper; set aside.

2. In a 4- to 5-quart (3.8- to 5-liter) pan, cook linguine in about 8 cups (1.9 liters) boiling water until just tender to bite (8 to 10 minutes); or cook according to package directions. Drain well, transfer to a warm rimmed platter, and keep warm.

3. While pasta is cooking, melt butter in a wide nonstick frying pan or wok over medium-high heat. Add meat and garlic; stir-fry just until meat is no longer pink on outside (1 to 2 minutes). Add water, 1 tablespoon (15 ml) at a time, if pan appears dry. Remove meat from pan with a slotted spoon; keep warm.

4. Add mushrooms and 3 tablespoons (45 ml) water to pan. Stir-fry until mushrooms are soft (about 3 minutes), gently scraping any browned bits free from pan. Add marsala and bring to a boil; then boil, stirring, until sauce is slightly thickened (about 3 minutes). Remove pan from heat and stir in meat and parsley.

5. To serve, spoon meat mixture over pasta; sprinkle with chopped tomato and olives.

Makes 4 servings

NUTRIENTS

Per serving: 440 calories (16% calories from fat), 7 g total fat, 3 g saturated fat, 96 mg cholesterol, 191 mg sodium, 52 g carbohydrates, 3 g fiber, 33 g protein, 39 mg calcium, 4 mg iron

Pasta

ARTICHOKE PESTO PASTA

Preparation time: **About 15 minutes**
Cooking time: **About 15 minutes**

Artichoke hearts, rather than basil, star in the nontraditional pesto for this pasta dish. You could use frozen artichoke hearts instead of canned, but you'll need to cook them before adding them to the recipe.

¼ cup (35 g) pine nuts

1 can (about 10 oz./285 g) artichoke hearts in water, drained

½ cup (40 g) freshly grated Parmesan cheese

3 ounces (85 g) Neufchâtel or nonfat cream cheese

¼ cup (45 g) diced onion

1 tablespoon (15 ml) Dijon mustard

1 clove garlic, minced or pressed

⅛ teaspoon ground nutmeg

¾ cup (180 ml) vegetable broth

1 pound (455 g) dried fettuccine

¼ cup (15 g) minced parsley

¼ teaspoon crushed red pepper flakes

1. Toast pine nuts in a small frying pan over medium heat, shaking pan often, until golden (about 3 minutes). Remove from pan and set aside.

2. Combine artichokes, Parmesan, Neufchâtel, onion, mustard, garlic, nutmeg, and ½ cup (120 ml) of the broth in a food processor or blender. Whirl until blended. Set aside.

3. Bring 16 cups (3.8 liters) water to a boil in a 6- to 8-quart (6- to 8-liter) pan over medium-high heat. Stir in pasta and cook just until tender to bite (8 to 10 minutes); or cook according to package directions. Drain well and return to pan. Reduce heat to medium, add remaining ¼ cup (60 ml) broth, and cook, lifting pasta with 2 forks, until broth is hot (about 30 seconds).

4. Transfer to a large serving bowl. Quickly add artichoke mixture, parsley, red pepper flakes, and nuts; lift with 2 forks to mix.

Makes 8 servings

NUTRIENTS

Per serving: 307 calories (26% calories from fat), 9 g total fat, 3 g saturated fat, 66 mg cholesterol, 309 mg sodium, 44 g carbohydrates, 3 g fiber, 13 g protein, 105 mg calcium, 3 mg iron

ITALIAN GARDEN PASTA

Preparation time: **About 25 minutes**
Cooking time: **About 15 minutes**

Roma tomatoes, mushrooms, and plenty of leafy chard go into this fresh and hearty supper dish. For the pasta, choose the whimsical little corkscrews called rotini, or opt for elbow macaroni or another favorite pasta shape. You can use any type of mushrooms.

12 ounces (340 g) Swiss chard

1 pound (455 g) dried rotini or elbow macaroni

3 tablespoons (45 ml) olive oil or vegetable oil

1 pound (455 g) mushrooms, sliced

1 medium-size onion, chopped

3 cloves garlic, minced or pressed

½ cup (120 ml) canned vegetable broth

½ cup (43 g) grated Parmesan cheese

1½ pounds (680 g) pear-shaped (Roma-type) tomatoes, chopped and drained well

1. Trim and discard discolored stem ends from chard; then rinse and drain chard. Cut stems from leaves; finely chop stems and leaves, keeping them in separate piles.

2. In a 6- to 8-quart (6- to 8-liter) pan, cook pasta in about 4 quarts (3.8 liters) boiling water until just tender to bite (8 to 10 minutes); or cook according to package directions. Drain well, transfer to a warm wide bowl, and keep warm.

3. While pasta is cooking, heat oil in a wide nonstick frying pan or wok over medium-high heat. When oil is hot, add chard stems, mushrooms, onion, and garlic. Cover and cook until mushrooms release their liquid and onion is soft (about 6 minutes). Then uncover and stir-fry until liquid has evaporated and mushrooms are tinged with brown. Add broth and chard leaves; stir until chard is just wilted (1 to 2 more minutes).

4. Pour chard-mushroom mixture over pasta, sprinkle with half the cheese, and top with tomatoes. Mix gently but thoroughly. Sprinkle with remaining Parmesan cheese.

Makes 4 to 6 servings

NUTRIENTS

Per serving: 531 calories (22% calories from fat), 13 g total fat, 3 g saturated fat, 8 mg cholesterol, 402 mg sodium, 84 g carbohydrates, 7 g fiber, 21 g protein, 203 mg calcium, 7 mg iron

Farfalle with Chard, Garlic & Ricotta

Preparation time: **About 15 minutes**
Cooking time: **About 10 minutes**

For a hearty meal in a hurry, choose this fresh-tasting and quick-to-fix entrée. Alongside, you might serve sliced tomatoes, whole grain bread, and a fruity, light red Italian wine.

1 bunch chard (about 1¼ lbs./570 g), rinsed and drained

10 ounces (285 g) dried farfalle (pasta bow ties)

2 tablespoons (30 ml) olive oil

1 medium-size onion, finely chopped

4 cloves garlic, minced or pressed

1½ cups (345 g) part-skim ricotta cheese, at room temperature

Salt and coarsely ground pepper

Freshly ground nutmeg

Grated Parmesan cheese (optional)

1. Trim off and discard ends of chard stems; then cut off remainder of stems at base of each leaf. Thinly slice stems and leaves crosswise, keeping them in separate piles. Set aside.

2. In a 5- to 6-quart (5- to 6 liter) pan, cook pasta in 3 quarts boiling water just until tender to bite (8 to 10 minutes); or cook according to package directions.

3. Meanwhile, heat oil in a wide (at least 12-inch/30 cm) frying pan over medium-high heat. Add onion and chard stems; cook, stirring often, until onion is soft but not browned (3 to 5 minutes). Add garlic and chard leaves and cook, stirring often, until leaves are bright green (about 3 more minutes). Add ¾ cup (180 ml) water and bring to a boil. Remove from heat and blend in ricotta cheese; season to taste with salt, pepper, and nutmeg.

4. Drain pasta well and place in a warm wide serving bowl. Add ricotta mixture; mix lightly but thoroughly, using 2 forks to combine. If desired, serve with Parmesan cheese to add to taste.

Makes 4 servings

NUTRIENTS

Per serving: 495 calories (28% calories from fat), 15 g total fat, 6 g saturated fat, 29 mg cholesterol, 400 mg sodium, 67 g carbohydrates, 5 g fiber, 23 g protein, 344 mg calcium, 6 mg iron

RAVIOLI WITH GORGONZOLA

Preparation time: **About 15 minutes**
Cooking time: **About 25 minutes**

Gorgonzola cheese and a hint of sherry give this creamy ravioli dish its rather sprightly character.

2 packages (about 9 oz./255 g each) fresh low-fat cheese-filled ravioli

¼ cup (45 g) finely chopped onion

2 cloves garlic, minced or pressed

4 teaspoons cornstarch

1 cup (240 ml) nonfat milk

½ cup (120 ml) half-and-half

½ cup (120 ml) vegetable broth

2 ounces (55 g) Gorgonzola or other blue-veined cheese, crumbled

¼ teaspoon dried thyme

¼ teaspoon dried marjoram

¼ teaspoon rubbed sage

⅛ teaspoon ground nutmeg

1 teaspoon dry sherry, or to taste
 Finely shredded lemon peel
 Salt and pepper

1. In a 6- to 8-quart (6- to 8-liter) pan, bring about 4 quarts (3.8 liters) water to a boil over medium-high heat. Stir in ravioli, separating any that are stuck together; reduce heat and boil gently, stirring occasionally, until pasta is just tender to bite, 4 to 6 minutes. (Or cook pasta according to package directions.) Drain well, return to pan, and keep warm.

2. While pasta is cooking, combine onion, garlic, and 1 tablespoon (15 ml) water in a wide nonstick frying pan. Cook over medium-high heat, stirring often, until onion is soft (3 to 4 minutes); add water, 1 tablespoon (15 ml) at a time, if pan appears dry. Remove from heat.

20 MINUTES OR LESS

8 ounces (230 g) dried linguine

1 jar (about 6 oz./170 g) marinated artichoke hearts

2 cloves garlic, minced or pressed

1 tablespoon anchovy paste

1 can (about 2¼ oz./65 g) sliced ripe olives, drained

½ cup (30 g) chopped parsley

¼ cup (20 g) grated Parmesan cheese

Parsley sprigs

Pepper

PASTA WITH ARTICHOKES & ANCHOVIES

1. In a 4- to 5-quart (3.8- to 5-liter) pan, cook linguine in about 8 cups (1.9 liters) boiling water until just tender to bite (8 to 10 minutes); or cook according to package directions. Drain well, transfer to a warm wide bowl, and keep warm.

2. While pasta is cooking, carefully drain marinade from artichokes into a wide nonstick frying pan or wok. Cut artichokes into bite-size pieces and set aside. Heat marinade over medium heat; add garlic and stir-fry until pale gold (about 3 minutes). Add anchovy paste, olives, and artichokes; stir-fry until heated through (about 2 minutes).

3. Pour artichoke mixture over pasta. Add chopped parsley and cheese; mix gently but thoroughly. Garnish with parsley sprigs; season to taste with pepper. *Makes 4 to 6 servings*

Per serving: 245 calories (23% calories from fat), 6 g total fat, 1 g saturated fat, 5 mg cholesterol, 499 mg sodium, 38 g carbohydrates, 3 g fiber, 10 g protein, 100 mg calcium, 3 mg iron

3. Smoothly blend cornstarch with 2 tablespoons (30 ml) of the milk. Add cornstarch mixture, remaining milk, half-and-half, and broth to pan. Return to medium-high heat and bring to a boil, stirring. Reduce heat to low and add cheese, thyme, marjoram, sage, and nutmeg; stir until cheese is melted. Remove pan from heat and stir in sherry.

4. Spoon sauce over pasta; mix gently. Spoon pasta onto individual plates; sprinkle with lemon peel. Season to taste with salt and pepper.

Makes 6 servings

NUTRIENTS

Per serving: 315 calories (29% calories from fat), 10 g total fat, 6 g saturated fat, 69 mg cholesterol, 545 mg sodium, 40 g carbohydrates, 2 g fiber, 15 g protein, 270 mg calcium, 2 mg iron

PASTA PIE

Preparation time: **About 15 minutes**
Cooking time: **About 30 minutes**

Pasta lovers will enjoy this light and savory pie, made from cooked spaghetti, eggs, and two kinds of cheese. A creamy tomato sauce enhances the dish.

PASTA PIE:

½ cup (120 ml) nonfat milk

1 teaspoon cornstarch

2 large eggs

6 large egg whites

¾ cup (85 g) shredded part-skim mozzarella cheese

¼ cup (20 g) grated Parmesan cheese

2 tablespoons chopped fresh oregano or 1½ teaspoons dried oregano

2 cloves garlic, minced or pressed

¼ teaspoon salt

⅛ teaspoon crushed red pepper flakes

3 cups (390 g) cold cooked spaghetti

1 teaspoon vegetable oil

TOMATO CREAM SAUCE:

1 large can (about 28 oz./795 g) diced tomatoes

½ cup (120 ml) reduced-fat sour cream

2 or 3 cloves garlic, peeled

2 teaspoons chopped fresh thyme or ½ teaspoon dried thyme

1 teaspoon sugar, or to taste

Salt and pepper

GARNISH:

Oregano sprigs and fresh oregano leaves

1. In a large bowl, combine milk and cornstarch; beat until smoothly blended. Add eggs and egg whites and beat well. Stir in mozzarella cheese, Parmesan cheese, chopped oregano, minced garlic, the ¼ teaspoon salt, and red pepper flakes. Add pasta to egg mixture; lift with 2 forks to mix well. Set aside.

2. Place a 9-inch-round (23-cm-round) baking pan (do not use a nonstick pan) in oven while it heats to 500°F (260°C). When pan is hot (after about 5 minutes), carefully remove it from oven and pour in oil, tilting pan to coat. Mix pasta mixture again; then transfer to pan. Bake on lowest rack of oven until top of pie is golden and center is firm when lightly pressed (about 25 minutes).

3. Meanwhile, to prepare tomato cream sauce, pour tomatoes and their liquid into a food processor or blender. Add sour cream, peeled garlic, thyme, and sugar; whirl until smoothly puréed. Season to taste with salt and pepper; set aside. Use at room temperature.

4. When pie is done, spread about ¾ cup (180 ml) of the sauce on each of 4 individual plates. Cut pie into 4 wedges; place one wedge atop sauce on each plate. Garnish with oregano sprigs and leaves. Offer remaining sauce to drizzle over pie.

Makes 4 servings

NUTRIENTS

Per serving: 411 calories (30% calories from fat), 14 g total fat, 6 g saturated fat, 133 mg cholesterol, 782 mg sodium, 47 g carbohydrates, 3 g fiber, 26 g protein, 340 mg calcium, 4 mg iron

1. Trim off and discard bare stem ends and any yellow or bruised leaves from mizuna; then chop leaves coarsely and set aside.

2. In a 5- to 6-quart (5- to 6-liter) pan, cook pasta in 3 quarts (2.8 liters) boiling water just until tender to bite (10 to 12 minutes); or cook according to package directions. When pasta is almost done, heat oil in a 4- to 5-quart (3.8- to 5-liter) pan over high heat. Add mizuna and stir until leaves are wilted (2 to 4 minutes).

3. Drain pasta and place in a warm serving bowl. Add mizuna; mix lightly, using 2 forks. Sprinkle with red pepper flakes and cheese; mix again.

Makes 4 servings

NUTRIENTS

Per serving: 449 calories (23% calories from fat), 11 g total fat, 3 g saturated fat, 8 mg cholesterol, 219 mg sodium, 69 g carbohydrates, 3 g fiber, 18 g protein, 262 mg calcium, 5 mg iron

SAUTÉED MIZUNA & SHELLS

Preparation time: **About 10 minutes**
Cooking time: **About 15 minutes**

A feathery-leaved member of the mustard family, mildly tart mizuna is becoming increasingly available in well-stocked supermarkets and gourmet stores. Delicious raw in salads, the tender-firm leaves are distinctive in cooked dishes, too—as here, where the gently wilted greens combine beautifully with hot pasta and Parmesan cheese.

1 pound (455 g) mizuna, rinsed and drained

12 ounces (340 g) medium-size dried pasta shells

2 tablespoons (30 ml) olive oil

¼ teaspoon crushed red pepper flakes

½ cup (40 g) grated Parmesan cheese

GOAT CHEESE & SPINACH PASTA

Preparation time: **About 20 minutes**
Cooking time: **About 15 minutes**

Made from pure white goat's milk, goat cheese (often marketed under its French name, *chèvre*) is distinguished by its unique tart flavor. In this recipe, it's melted into a smooth sauce to serve over pasta and spinach.

12 ounces (340 g) dried spinach fettuccine

3 quarts (about 12 oz./340 g) lightly packed rinsed, drained fresh spinach leaves, cut or torn into 2-inch (5-cm) pieces

⅔ cup (160 ml) vegetable broth

8 ounces (230 g) unsweetened soft fresh goat cheese (plain or flavored), broken into chunks, if possible (some types may be too soft to break)

2 cups (285 g) ripe cherry tomatoes (at room temperature), cut into ⅓-inch (1-cm) slices

Salt and pepper

1. In a 5- to 6-quart (5- to 6-liter) pan, bring about 3 quarts water to a boil over medium-high heat; stir in pasta and cook until just tender to bite, 8 to 10 minutes. (Or cook pasta according to package directions.) Stir spinach into boiling water with pasta; continue to boil until spinach is wilted (30 to 45 more seconds). Drain pasta-spinach mixture well and return to pan.

2. While pasta is cooking, bring broth to a boil in a 1- to 2-quart (950-ml to 1.9-liter) pan over medium-high heat. Add cheese and stir until melted; remove from heat.

3. Spoon cheese mixture over pasta and spinach; mix gently. Spoon onto a platter; scatter tomatoes over top. Season to taste with salt and pepper.

Makes 4 servings

NUTRIENTS

Per serving: 537 calories (28% calories from fat), 17 g total fat, 9 g saturated fat, 107 mg cholesterol, 617 mg sodium, 70 g carbohydrates, 12 g fiber, 30 g protein, 351 mg calcium, 11 mg iron

Southwestern Fettuccine

Pictured on page 126
Preparation time: **About 15 minutes**
Cooking time: **About 20 minutes**

This satisfying Tex-Mex pasta sauce is based on bell pepper, corn kernels, and nippy jalapeño jack cheese. To thicken it, we've used rich-tasting cream-style corn, puréed in a blender or food processor until smooth.

12 ounces (340 g) dried fettuccine

1 can (about 15 oz./425 g) cream-style corn

⅔ cup (160 ml) nonfat milk

1 teaspoon vegetable oil

½ teaspoon cumin seeds

1 small onion, chopped

1 large red or yellow bell pepper (about 8 oz./230 g), seeded and cut into thin strips

1 package (about 10 oz./285 g) frozen corn kernels, thawed and drained

1 cup (about 4 oz./115 g) shredded jalapeño jack cheese

¼ cup (10 g) cilantro leaves

1½ to 2 cups (210 to 285 g) yellow or red cherry tomatoes, cut into halves

Cilantro sprigs

Lime wedges

Salt

1. In a 5- to 6-quart (5- to 6-liter) pan, bring about 3 quarts (2.8 liters) water to boil over medium-high heat; stir in pasta and cook until just tender to bite, 8 to 10 minutes. (Or cook pasta according to package directions.) Drain pasta well and return to pan; keep warm. While pasta is cooking, whirl cream-style corn and milk in a blender or food processor until smoothly puréed; set aside.

2. Heat oil in a wide nonstick frying pan over medium-high heat. Add cumin seeds, onion, and bell pepper. Cook, stirring often, until onion is soft (about 5 minutes); add water, 1 tablespoon (15 ml) at a time, if pan appears dry. Stir in cream-style corn mixture, corn kernels, and cheese. Reduce heat to medium and cook, stirring, just until cheese is melted.

3. Pour corn-cheese sauce over pasta. Add cilantro leaves; mix gently but thoroughly. Divide pasta among 4 shallow individual bowls; sprinkle with tomatoes. Garnish with cilantro sprigs. Season to taste with lime and salt.

Makes 4 servings

NUTRIENTS

Per serving: 627 calories (21% calories from fat), 15 g total fat, 6 g saturated fat, 112 mg cholesterol, 540 mg sodium, 104 g carbohydrates, 7 g fiber, 25 g protein, 298 mg calcium, 5 mg iron

Capellini with Cilantro Pesto & White Beans

Pictured on facing page
Preparation time: **About 20 minutes**
Cooking time: **About 15 minutes**

To make this attractive layered dish, spread a vivid cilantro pesto on each plate, then top with angel hair pasta and a sauce of mild cannellini beans and diced tomatoes. Because the pesto is based on water rather than oil, it may weep a bit on standing—so be sure to stir it well before using it.

3 cups (120 g) firmly packed cilantro leaves

1 cup (about 3 oz./85 g) grated Parmesan cheese

1 tablespoon grated lemon peel

1 tablespoon (15 ml) Oriental sesame oil

3 cloves garlic, peeled

2 teaspoons honey

8 ounces (230 g) dried capellini

2 tablespoons (30 ml) seasoned rice vinegar (or 2 tablespoons/30 ml distilled white vinegar plus ¾ teaspoon sugar)

1 medium-size red onion, cut into thin slivers

1 tablespoon (15 ml) balsamic vinegar

1 can (about 15 oz./430 g) cannellini (white kidney beans), drained and rinsed

7 medium-size firm-ripe pear-shaped (Roma-type) tomatoes (about 1 lb./455 g total), chopped

1½ teaspoons chopped fresh thyme or ½ teaspoon dried thyme

Thyme and cilantro sprigs

Pepper

1. To prepare cilantro pesto, in a blender or food processor, combine cilantro leaves, Parmesan, ½ cup (120 ml) water, lemon peel, sesame oil, garlic, and honey. Whirl until smoothly puréed. If pesto is too thick, add a little more water; set aside. (At this point, you may cover and refrigerate for up to 3 hours; bring to room temperature before using.)

2. In a 4- to 5-quart (3.8- to 5-liter) pan, cook pasta in about 8 cups (1.9 liters) boiling water until just tender to bite (about 3 minutes); or cook according to package directions. Drain well, rinse with hot water, and drain well again. Quickly return pasta to pan; add rice vinegar and lift with 2 forks to mix. Keep warm.

3. While pasta is cooking, combine onion and ⅓ cup (80 ml) water in a wide nonstick frying pan or wok. Cover and cook over medium-high heat until onion is almost soft (about 3 minutes). Uncover, add balsamic vinegar, and stir-fry until liquid has evaporated. Add beans, tomatoes, and chopped thyme to pan; stir-fry gently until beans are heated through and tomatoes are soft (about 3 minutes). Remove pan from heat.

4. Stir cilantro pesto well; spread evenly on 4 individual plates. Top with pasta, then with bean mixture. Garnish with thyme and cilantro sprigs; serve immediately. Season to taste with pepper.

Makes 4 servings

NUTRIENT

Per serving: 473 calories (21% calories from fat), 11 g total fat, 4 g saturated fat, 16 mg cholesterol, 786 mg sodium, 73 g carbohydrates, 9 g fiber, 20 g protein, 340 mg calcium, 4 mg iron

Capellini with Cilantro Pesto & White Beans (recipe on facing page)

SOUTHWESTERN FETTUCCINE (RECIPE ON PAGE 123)

Penne with Turkey Sausage (recipe on page 136)

BOW-TIE PASTA WITH BROCCOLI PESTO (RECIPE ON FACING PAGE)

Bow-Tie Pasta with Broccoli Pesto

Pictured on facing page
Preparation time: **About 15 minutes**
Cooking time: **About 20 minutes**

Classic pesto sauce is made with fresh basil, but this version is based on bright broccoli flowerets instead. Accented with sesame oil and rice vinegar, the smooth green sauce is delicious over any kind of pasta; we use bow ties here.

1 pound (455 g) broccoli flowerets (about 7 cups)

2 or 3 cloves garlic, minced or pressed

½ cup (40 g) grated Parmesan cheese

3 tablespoons (45 ml) olive oil

1½ teaspoons Oriental sesame oil

½ teaspoon salt

12 ounces (340 g) dried pasta bow ties (farfalle)

1 to 2 tablespoons (15 to 30 ml) seasoned rice vinegar (or 1 to 2 tablespoons/15 to 30 ml distilled white vinegar plus ½ to 1 teaspoon sugar)

1 small tomato (about 4 oz./115 g), chopped

1. In a 4- to 5-quart (3.8- to 5-liter) pan, bring 8 cups (1.9 liters) water to a boil over medium-high heat. Stir in broccoli and cook until just tender to bite (about 7 minutes). Immediately drain broccoli, immerse in ice water until cool, and drain again.

2. In a food processor or blender, combine a third of the broccoli with garlic, cheese, olive oil, sesame oil, salt, and 3 tablespoons (45 ml) water. Whirl until smooth. Scrape down sides of container, add half the remaining broccoli, and whirl until smooth again. Add remaining broccoli; whirl until smooth. Set aside.

3. In a 5- to 6-quart (5- to 6-liter) pan, bring about 3 quarts (2.8 liters) water to a boil over medium-high heat; stir in pasta and cook until just tender to bite, 8 to 10 minutes. (Or cook pasta according to package directions.)

4. Drain pasta well. Transfer to a large serving bowl and stir in vinegar. Add pesto and mix gently but thoroughly. Garnish with tomato and serve immediately. *Makes 4 servings*

NUTRIENTS

Per serving: 510 calories (29% calories from fat), 17 g total fat, 4 g saturated fat, 8 mg cholesterol, 604 mg sodium, 73 g carbohydrates, 6 g fiber, 19 g protein, 204 mg calcium, 4 mg iron

THAI TOFU & TAGLIATELLE

Preparation time: **About 15 minutes**
Cooking time: **20 to 25 minutes**

Offer this spicy entrée with a refreshing cucumber salad, or serve it with Cool Yogurt Sauce (page 113).

1 cup (240 ml) vegetable broth

1 cup (200 g) sugar

¼ cup (60 ml) reduced-sodium soy sauce

2 tablespoons cider vinegar

1 tablespoon cornstarch

2 teaspoons paprika

1 teaspoon crushed red pepper flakes

1 teaspoon vegetable oil

⅓ cup (50 g) minced garlic

8 to 10 ounces (230 to 285 g) dried tagliatelle or fettuccine

1 pound (455 g) regular tofu, rinsed and drained, cut into ½-inch (1-cm) cubes

1 large red bell pepper (about 8 oz./ 230 g), cut into ½-inch (1-cm) pieces

1 package (about 10 oz./285 g) frozen tiny peas, thawed

1. Combine broth, sugar, soy sauce, vinegar, cornstarch, paprika, and red pepper flakes in a small bowl; mix until well blended. Set aside.

2. Heat oil in a wide nonstick frying pan over medium-high heat. Add garlic and cook, stirring often, until tinged with gold (about 4 minutes; do not scorch); if pan appears dry, stir in water, 1 tablespoon (15 ml) at a time.

3. Add broth mixture. Cook, stirring often, until sauce comes to a boil. Continue to cook until reduced to about 1¼ cups/300 ml (10 to 15 minutes). Meanwhile, bring 12 cups (2.8 liters) water to a boil in a 5- to 6-quart (5- to 6-liter) pan over medium-high heat. Stir in pasta and cook just until

---

☀ 20 MINUTES OR LESS ☀

12 ounces/340 g (about 5 cups) dried rotini or other corkscrew-shaped pasta

2 tablespoons (30 ml) olive oil

5 green onions, thinly sliced

1 pound (455 g) broccoli flowerets, cut into bite-size pieces

1½ cups (345 g) part-skim ricotta cheese

Freshly grated Parmesan cheese

Coarsely ground pepper

ROTINI WITH BROCCOLI & RICOTTA

1. Bring 12 cups (2.8 liters) water to a boil in a 5- to 6-quart (5- to 6-liter) pan over medium-high heat. Stir in pasta and cook just until tender to bite (8 to 10 minutes); or cook according to package directions. Meanwhile, heat oil in a wide nonstick frying pan over medium-high heat. Add onions and cook, stirring, for 1 minute. Add broccoli and continue to cook, stirring, until bright green (about 3 minutes). Pour in ¼ cup (60 ml) water and bring to a boil; reduce heat, cover, and simmer until broccoli is tender-crisp (about 5 minutes).

2. Drain pasta well, reserving ¼ cup (60 ml) of the water. Place in a serving bowl. Add vegetables and ricotta. Mix thoroughly but gently; if too dry, stir in enough of the reserved water to moisten. Offer Parmesan and pepper to add to taste.   *Makes 4 servings*

Per serving: 540 calories (26% calories from fat), 16 g total fat, 6 g saturated fat, 29 mg cholesterol, 149 mg sodium, 75 g carbohydrates, 6 g fiber, 25 g protein, 324 mg calcium, 5 mg iron

tender to bite (8 to 10 minutes); or cook according to package directions. Drain well and transfer
to a wide, shallow serving bowl.

4. Combine tofu, bell pepper, peas, and half the
sauce in a large bowl. Mix well but gently. Spoon
over pasta. Offer remaining sauce to add to taste.

Makes 4 servings

NUTRIENTS

Per serving: 634 calories (12% calories from fat), 8 g total fat, 1 g
saturated fat, 0 mg cholesterol, 987 mg sodium, 121 g carbohydrates, 6 g fiber, 23 g protein, 178 mg calcium, 11 mg iron

PEANUT PASTA & TOFU

Preparation time: **About 20 minutes**
Cooking time: **About 20 minutes**

Asian-style peanut sauce is great with all
sorts of foods, from pork and beef to
chicken and noodles. Here, it's tossed
with chunky pasta tubes and marinated tofu.

¼ cup (60 ml) seasoned rice vinegar (or
   ¼ cup/60 ml distilled white vinegar
   plus 2 teaspoons sugar)

3 tablespoons (45 ml) Oriental
   sesame oil

1 tablespoon (15 ml) reduced-sodium
   soy sauce

1 teaspoon sugar

1 package (about 14 oz./400 g) regular
   tofu, rinsed, drained, and cut into
   ½-inch (1-cm) cubes

12 ounces (340 g) dried penne

2 cups (170 g) Chinese pea pods (also
   called snow or sugar peas), ends and
   strings removed

2 cloves garlic, minced

½ cup (144 g) plum jam

¼ cup (65 g) crunchy peanut butter

⅛ teaspoon ground ginger

⅓ cup (15 g) cilantro leaves

¼ cup (25 g) sliced green onions
   Cilantro sprigs
   Crushed red pepper flakes

1. In a shallow bowl, beat vinegar, 1 tablespoon
(15 ml) of the oil, soy sauce, and sugar until blended. Add tofu and mix gently. Set aside; stir occasionally.

2. In a 5- to 6-quart (5- to 6-liter) pan, bring about
3 quarts (2.8 liters) water to a boil over medium-
high heat; stir in pasta and cook until almost tender to bite, 7 to 9 minutes. (Or cook pasta
according to package directions, cooking for a little less than the recommended time.) Add pea
pods to boiling water with pasta and cook for 1
more minute. Drain pasta mixture, rinse with hot
water, and drain well again; keep warm.

3. With a slotted spoon, transfer tofu to a large,
shallow serving bowl; reserve marinade from tofu.

4. In pan used to cook pasta, heat remaining
2 tablespoons (30 ml) oil over medium heat. Add
garlic and cook, stirring, just until fragrant (about
30 seconds; do not scorch). Add jam, peanut butter, marinade from tofu, and ginger. Cook, whisking, just until sauce is smooth and well blended.

5. Remove pan from heat and add pasta mixture,
cilantro leaves, and onions. Mix gently but thoroughly. Transfer pasta to bowl with tofu and mix
very gently. Garnish with cilantro sprigs. Serve at
once; season to taste with red pepper flakes.

Makes 4 servings

NUTRIENTS

Per serving: 714 calories (30% calories from fat), 25 g total fat, 4 g
saturated fat, 0 mg cholesterol, 558 mg sodium, 103 g carbohydrates, 6 g fiber, 25 g protein, 162 mg calcium, 10 mg iron

ORECCHIETTE WITH LENTILS & GOAT CHEESE

Preparation time: About 10 minutes
Cooking time: About 35 minutes

Tangy goat cheese transforms a savory pasta-lentil mixture into a sprightly main-course offering.

2 cups (470 ml) vegetable broth

6 ounces/170 g (about 1 cup) lentils, rinsed and drained

1 tablespoon chopped fresh thyme or 1 teaspoon dried thyme

8 ounces/230 g (about 2⅓ cups) dried orecchiette or other medium-size pasta shape

⅓ cup (80 ml) white wine vinegar

3 tablespoons chopped parsley

2 tablespoons (30 ml) olive oil

1 teaspoon honey, or to taste

1 clove garlic, minced or pressed

½ cup (65 g) crumbled goat or feta cheese

Thyme sprigs

Salt and pepper

1. Bring broth to a boil in a 1½- to 2-quart (1.4- to 1.9-liter) pan over high heat. Add lentils and chopped thyme; reduce heat, cover, and simmer until lentils are tender to bite (20 to 30 minutes).

2. Meanwhile, bring 8 cups (1.9 liters) water to a boil in a 4- to 5-quart (3.8- to 5-liter) pan over medium-high heat. Stir in pasta and cook just until tender to bite (8 to 10 minutes); or cook according to package directions. Drain pasta and, if necessary, lentils well. Transfer pasta and lentils to a large serving bowl; keep warm.

3. Combine vinegar, parsley, oil, honey, and garlic in a small bowl. Beat until blended. Add to pasta mixture and mix thoroughly but gently. Sprinkle with cheese. Garnish with thyme sprigs. Offer salt and pepper to add to taste.

Makes 4 servings

NUTRIENTS

Per serving: 514 calories (24% calories from fat), 14 g total fat, 5 g saturated fat, 13 mg cholesterol, 648 mg sodium, 75 g carbohydrates, 7 g fiber, 25 g protein, 91 mg calcium, 7 mg iron

BUCATINI & BLACK BEANS

Preparation time: **About 15 minutes**
Cooking time: **About 20 minutes**

Offer this piquant pasta dish with chunks of crusty Italian bread to dunk into any leftover sauce.

10 ounces (285 g) dried bucatini, perciatelli, or spaghetti

⅔ cup (160 ml) seasoned rice vinegar (or ⅔ cup/160 ml distilled white vinegar and 2 tablespoons sugar)

2 tablespoons (30 ml) honey

1 tablespoon (15 ml) olive oil

½ teaspoon chili oil

2 cans (about 15 oz./425 g each) black beans, drained and rinsed

4 large pear-shaped tomatoes (about 12 oz./340 g total), diced

⅓ cup (20 g) finely chopped parsley

¼ cup (25 g) thinly sliced green onions

¾ cup (100 g) crumbled feta cheese

Parsley sprigs

1. Bring 12 cups (2.8 liters) water to a boil in a 5- to 6-quart (5- to 6-liter) pan over medium-high heat. Stir in pasta and cook just until tender to bite (10 to 12 minutes); or cook according to package directions. Drain well and keep warm.

2. Combine vinegar, honey, olive oil, and chili oil in pan. Bring just to a boil over medium-high heat. Add pasta, beans, and tomatoes. Cook, stirring, until hot. Remove from heat; stir in chopped parsley and onions.

3. Spoon pasta mixture into bowls. Sprinkle with cheese. Garnish with parsley sprigs.

Makes 4 servings

NUTRIENTS

Per serving: 564 calories (18% calories from fat), 11 g total fat, 5 g saturated fat, 23 mg cholesterol, 1,095 mg sodium, 96 g carbohydrates, 5 g fiber, 21 g protein, 176 mg calcium, 6 mg iron

20 MINUTES OR LESS

1 pound (455 g) dried linguine

2 tablespoons (30 ml) olive oil

1 clove garlic, minced or pressed

¼ teaspoon crushed red pepper flakes

1 large onion, finely chopped

3 cups red cherry tomatoes (about 1 lb./455 g), cut into halves lengthwise

3 cups yellow cherry tomatoes (about 1 lb./455 g), cut into halves lengthwise

2 cups (80 g) firmly packed fresh basil leaves or ¼ cup dried basil

Salt and pepper

¼ to ½ cup (20 to 40 g) grated Parmesan cheese

LINGUINE WITH RED & YELLOW TOMATOES

1. In a 6- to 8-quart (6- to 8-liter) pan, cook pasta in 4 quarts (3.8 liters) boiling water just until tender to bite (7 to 9 minutes); or cook according to package directions.

2. Meanwhile, heat oil in a wide frying pan over high heat. Add garlic, red pepper flakes, and onion; cook, stirring often, until onion is lightly browned (3 to 5 minutes). Add tomatoes and basil; cook, stirring gently, just until tomatoes are hot (about 2 minutes).

3. Drain pasta well and place in a warm wide serving bowl. Pour tomato mixture over pasta; mix lightly, using 2 forks. Season pasta to taste with salt and pepper; serve with cheese to add to taste.

Makes 4 to 6 servings

Per serving: 478 calories (18% calories from fat), 9 g total fat, 2 g saturated fat, 5 mg cholesterol, 139 mg sodium, 83 g carbohydrates, 5 g fiber, 17 g protein, 195 mg calcium, 6 mg iron

COUSCOUS PAELLA

Preparation time: **About 15 minutes**
Cooking time: **20 to 25 minutes**

Although traditionally based on rice, this paella is made with quick-cooking couscous (it cooks in about 5 minutes).

4   ounces (115 g) chorizo sausages, casings removed

1   large onion, chopped

1   bottle (about 8 oz./240 ml) clam juice

1¼ cups (300 ml) fat-free reduced-sodium chicken broth

2   teaspoons cumin seeds

9¼ ounces/260 g (about 1½ cups) dried couscous

1   medium-size red bell pepper (about 6 oz./170 g), seeded and chopped

8   ounces (230 g) tiny cooked shrimp

Lime or lemon wedges

1. Crumble chorizo into a wide nonstick frying pan; add onion. Cook over medium heat, stirring often, until well browned (15 to 20 minutes); if pan appears dry or mixture sticks to pan bottom, add water, 1 tablespoon (15 ml) at a time.

2. Add clam juice, broth, and cumin seeds. Increase heat to medium-high and bring to a boil. Stir in couscous; cover, remove from heat, and let stand until liquid is absorbed (about 5 minutes). Transfer to a wide serving bowl.

3. Stir in bell pepper and top with shrimp. Offer lime wedges to squeeze to taste.

Makes 4 to 6 servings

NUTRIENTS

Per serving: 377 calories (25% calories from fat), 10 g total fat, 4 g saturated fat, 106 mg cholesterol, 242 mg sodium, 47 g carbohydrates, 3 g fiber, 24 g protein, 60 mg calcium, 3 mg iron

SAUSAGE, BASIL & PORT FETTUCCINE

Preparation time: **About 20 minutes**
Cooking time: **About 25 minutes**

Red and green onions simmered in port make a superb base for a rich sausage-tomato sauce, which is marvelous served over tender fettuccine.

1   pound (455 g) mild or hot pork Italian sausages (casings removed), crumbled into ½-inch (1-cm) pieces

2   cloves garlic, minced or pressed

1½ cups (150 g) sliced green onions

3   cups (345 g) thinly sliced red onions

1½ cups (240 ml) port

3   medium-size tomatoes (about 1¼ lbs./565 g total), chopped

2   tablespoons (30 ml) balsamic vinegar

¾   cup (30 g) chopped fresh basil

1   pound (455 g) dried fettuccine

Basil sprigs

1. In a wide nonstick frying pan or wok, stir-fry sausage over medium-high heat until browned (7 to 10 minutes). Remove from pan with a slotted spoon; keep warm. Pour off and discard all but 1 teaspoon fat from pan.

2. Add garlic, green onions, and red onions to pan and stir-fry until soft (5 to 7 minutes). Add water, 1 tablespoon (15 ml) at a time, if pan appears dry. Add port and bring to a boil. Then boil, stirring often, until liquid is reduced by half (5 to 6 minutes). Add tomatoes, vinegar, and sausage; reduce heat and simmer for 2 minutes. Stir in chopped basil.

3. While sauce is cooking, in a 6- to 8-quart (6- to 8-liter) pan, cook fettuccine in about 4 quarts (3.8 liters) boiling water until just tender to bite (8 to 10 minutes); or cook according to package directions.

4. Drain pasta well and transfer to a warm bowl; top with sausage sauce. Garnish with basil sprigs.

Makes 8 servings

Per serving: 473 calories (29% calories from fat), 14 g total fat, 4 g saturated fat, 87 mg cholesterol, 417 mg sodium, 58 g carbohydrates, 4 g fiber, 18 g protein, 102 mg calcium, 5 mg iron

ZiTi WiTH TURKEY, FETA & SUN-DRiED TOMATOES

Preparation time: **About 15 minutes**
Cooking time: **About 15 minutes**

If you're eating light but can't do without cheese, choose the sharper, tangier types—the stronger the flavor, the less you'll need to use. Here, just a half cup of feta adds zest to a hearty turkey-and-pasta dish.

2 to 4 tablespoons (15 to 30 g) sun-dried tomatoes in olive oil

½ cup (120 ml) fat-free reduced-sodium chicken broth

2 tablespoons (30 ml) dry white wine

1 teaspoon cornstarch

1 small onion

8 ounces (230 g) dried ziti or penne

2 turkey breast tenderloins (about 1 lb./455 g total), cut into ½-inch (1-cm) pieces

1½ teaspoons chopped fresh oregano or ½ teaspoon dried oregano

1 large tomato (about 8 oz./230 g), chopped and drained well

2 tablespoons drained capers

½ cup (65 g) crumbled feta cheese

Oregano sprigs

1. Drain sun-dried tomatoes well (reserve oil) and pat dry with paper towels. Then chop tomatoes and set aside.

2. To prepare sauce, in a small bowl, stir together broth, wine, and cornstarch until blended; set aside.

3. Cut onion in half lengthwise; then cut each half crosswise into thin slices. Set aside.

4. In a 4- to 5-quart (3.8- to 5-liter) pan, cook pasta in about 8 cups (1.9 liters) boiling water until just tender to bite (8 to 10 minutes); or cook according to package directions. Drain pasta well and transfer to a warm large bowl; keep warm.

5. While pasta is cooking, measure 2 teaspoons of the oil from sun-dried tomatoes. Heat oil in a wide nonstick frying pan or wok over medium-high heat. When oil is hot, add turkey and chopped oregano. Stir-fry just until meat is no longer pink in center; cut to test (2 to 3 minutes). Add water, 1 tablespoon (15 ml) at a time, if pan appears to be dry. Remove turkey with a slotted spoon; transfer to bowl with pasta and keep warm.

6. Add sun-dried tomatoes and onion to pan; stir-fry until onion is soft (about 4 minutes). Add water, 1 tablespoon (15 ml) at a time, if pan appears to be dry.

7. Stir reserved sauce well and pour into pan. Cook, stirring, until sauce boils and thickens slightly (1 to 2 minutes). Remove from heat and stir in fresh tomato and capers. Spoon tomato mixture over pasta and turkey; mix gently but thoroughly.

8. Divide turkey mixture among 4 warm individual rimmed plates or shallow bowls. Sprinkle with cheese and garnish with oregano sprigs.

Makes 4 servings

Per serving: 489 calories (24% calories from fat), 13 g total fat, 4 g saturated fat, 83 mg cholesterol, 464 mg sodium, 52 g carbohydrates, 3 g fiber, 39 g protein, 108 mg calcium, 4 mg iron

Vermicelli with Turkey

Preparation time: **About 15 minutes**
Cooking time: **About 15 minutes**

This quick and colorful stir-fry is practically a whole meal in itself. Offer whole wheat baguette and a crisp white wine, such as a Zinfandel, as accompaniments.

8   ounces (230 g) dried vermicelli

⅓   cup (40 g) sun-dried tomatoes packed in oil, drained (reserve oil) and slivered

2   cloves garlic, minced or pressed

1   medium-size onion, chopped

1   large yellow or red bell pepper (about 8 oz./ 230 g), chopped

3   medium-size zucchini (about 12 oz./340 g total), thinly sliced

1   cup (240 ml) fat-free reduced-sodium chicken broth

2   cups (280 g) shredded cooked turkey breast

½   cup (20 g) chopped fresh basil or 3 tablespoons dried basil

Freshly grated Parmesan cheese

1. Bring 8 cups (1.9 liters) water to a boil in a 4- to 5-quart (3.8- to 5-liter) pan over medium-high heat. Stir in pasta and cook just until tender to bite (8 to 10 minutes); or cook according to package directions.

2. Meanwhile, heat 1 tablespoon (15 ml) of the reserved oil from tomatoes in a wide nonstick frying pan over medium-high heat. Add tomatoes, garlic, onion, bell pepper, and zucchini. Cook, stirring often, until vegetables begin to brown (about 8 minutes).

3. Pour broth over vegetables and bring to a boil. Drain pasta well and add to vegetables with turkey and basil. Lift with 2 forks to mix. Transfer to a platter. Offer cheese to add to taste.

Makes 4 servings

NUTRIENTS

Per serving: 500 calories (28% calories from fat), 16 g total fat, 2 g saturated fat, 59 mg cholesterol, 85 mg sodium, 59 g carbohydrates, 5 g fiber, 33 g protein, 130 mg calcium, 6 mg iron

Penne with Turkey Sausage

Pictured on page 127
Preparation time: **About 15 minutes**
Cooking time: **About 20 minutes**

For a nutritious dinner that you can prepare in just over half an hour, toss spinach, bell pepper, and pasta with a tangy fennel-accented sausage sauce.

12   ounces (340 g) spinach, coarse stems removed, rinsed and drained

1   large red or yellow bell pepper (about 8 oz./ 230 g), seeded

3   green onions

8   ounces/230 g (about 2½ cups) dried penne

8   to 12 ounces (230 to 340 g) mild or hot turkey Italian sausages, casings removed

½   cup (120 ml) balsamic vinegar (or ½ cup/120 ml red wine vinegar and 5 teaspoons sugar)

½   to ¾ teaspoon fennel seeds

Salt and pepper

1. Tear spinach into pieces. Cut bell pepper lengthwise into thin strips. Cut onions into 3-inch (8-cm) lengths and sliver lengthwise. Place vegetables in a large serving bowl and set aside.

2. Bring 8 cups (1.9 liters) water to a boil in a 4- to 5-quart (3.8- to 5-liter) pan over medium-high heat. Stir in pasta and cook just until tender to bite (8 to 10 minutes); or cook according to package directions. Drain well and keep warm.

3. Chop or crumble sausages. Cook in a wide nonstick frying pan or wok over medium-high heat, stirring often, until browned (about 10 minutes). Add vinegar and fennel seeds, stirring to loosen browned bits.

4. Add pasta to vegetables and immediately pour on sausage mixture; toss gently but well until spinach is slightly wilted. Serve immediately. Offer salt and pepper to add to taste.

Makes 6 servings

NUTRIENTS

Per serving: 238 calories (22% calories from fat), 6 g total fat, 2 g saturated fat, 36 mg cholesterol, 327 mg sodium, 32 g carbohydrates, 2 g fiber, 15 g protein, 57 mg calcium, 3 mg iron

LOW-FAT LO MEIN

Preparation time: **About 15 minutes**
Cooking time: **About 15 minutes**

If you're planning a banquet of Asian-inspired offerings, don't leave out this colorful medley of noodles, vegetables, and browned ground turkey. The combination of textures and tastes—soft with crisp, sweet with salty—makes the dish memorable. Be sure to use reduced-sodium chicken broth and soy sauce.

- 12 ounces (340 g) fresh Chinese noodles or linguine
- 1 teaspoon Oriental sesame oil
- 1 tablespoon (15 ml) vegetable oil
- 1 small onion, thinly sliced lengthwise
- 2 tablespoons (30 ml) oyster sauce
- 8 ounces (230 g) ground turkey
- 1 pound (455 g) napa cabbage, thinly sliced crosswise
- 4 ounces (115 g) oyster mushrooms, thinly sliced
- 2 medium-size carrots (about 6 oz./ 170 g total), cut into matchstick strips
- ½ cup (120 ml) fat-free reduced-sodium chicken broth
- 2 tablespoons (30 ml) reduced-sodium soy sauce

1. In a 5- to 6-quart (5- to 6-liter) pan, cook noodles in about 3 quarts (2.8 liters) boiling water until just tender to bite (3 to 5 minutes); or cook according to package directions. Drain well, toss with sesame oil, and keep warm.

2. Heat vegetable in a wide nonstick frying pan or wok over medium-high heat. When oil is hot, add onion and oyster sauce; then crumble in turkey. Stir-fry until onion is soft and turkey is no longer pink (about 3 minutes). Add cabbage, mushrooms, carrots, and broth; cover and cook until carrots are just tender to bite (about 3 minutes). Uncover and continue to cook until liquid has evaporated (1 to 2 more minutes). Stir in soy sauce; add noodles and stir-fry until heated.

Makes 6 servings

NUTRIENTS

Per serving: 295 calories (23% calories from fat), 7 g total fat, 1 g saturated fat, 69 mg cholesterol, 563 mg sodium, 41 g carbohydrates, 4 g fiber, 16 g protein, 89 mg calcium, 3 mg iron

1. In a small bowl, stir together broth, mustard, lemon juice, and basil. Set aside.

2. In a 4- to 5-quart (3.8- to 5-liter) pan, cook spaghetti in about 8 cups (1.9 liters) boiling water until just tender to bite (8 to 10 minutes); or cook according to package directions.

3. Meanwhile, heat oil in a wide nonstick frying pan or wok over medium heat. When oil is hot, add onions, garlic, and prosciutto; stir-fry until prosciutto is lightly browned (about 3 minutes). Increase heat to medium-high. Add chicken and stir-fry until no longer pink in center; cut to test (3 to 4 minutes). Add broth mixture to pan and bring to a boil. Remove from heat.

4. Drain pasta well and place in a warm wide bowl; spoon chicken mixture over pasta.

Makes 4 servings

NUTRIENTS

Per serving: 399 calories (13% calories from fat), 6 g total fat, 1 g saturated fat, 72 mg cholesterol, 670 mg sodium, 45 g carbohydrates, 6 g fiber, 37 g protein, 68 mg calcium, 3 mg iron

PASTA WITH CHICKEN & PROSCIUTTO

Preparation time: **About 10 minutes**
Cooking time: **About 15 minutes**

The flavors of Dijon mustard, basil, and prosciutto combine beautifully in this hearty stir-fry, served over spinach pasta.

½ cup (120 ml) fat-free reduced-sodium chicken broth or dry white wine

¼ cup (60 ml) Dijon mustard

2 tablespoons (30 ml) lemon juice

1 teaspoon dried basil

8 ounces (230 g) dried spinach spaghetti

2 teaspoons olive oil

4 green onions, thinly sliced

2 cloves garlic, minced or pressed

1 ounce (30 g) prosciutto, cut into thin strips

1 pound (455 g) skinless, boneless chicken breast, cut into ½- by 2-inch (1- by 5-cm) strips

FARFALLE WITH SMOKED SALMON & VODKA

Preparation time: **About 15 minutes**
Cooking time: **About 25 minutes**

A vodka-infused "cream" sauce enhances bow-tie shaped pasta tossed with silken smoked salmon.

12 ounces/340 g (about 6 cups) dried farfalle (about 1½-inch/3.5-cm size)

1 teaspoon olive oil

1 small shallot, thinly sliced

4 small pear-shaped (Roma-type) tomatoes (about 6 oz./170 g total), peeled, seeded, and chopped

⅔ cup (160 ml) half-and-half

3 tablespoons (45 ml) vodka

2 tablespoons chopped fresh dill or
  ½ teaspoon dried dill weed, or to taste

  Pinch of ground nutmeg

4 to 6 ounces (115 to 170 g) sliced
  smoked salmon or lox, cut into
  bite-size strips

  Dill sprigs

  Ground white pepper

1. Bring 12 cups (2.8 liters) water to a boil in a 5- to 6-quart (5- to 6-liter) pan over medium-high heat. Stir in pasta and cook just until tender to bite (8 to 10 minutes); or cook according to package directions. Drain well and keep warm.

2. Heat oil in a wide nonstick frying pan over medium-low heat. Add shallot and cook, stirring often, until soft but not browned (about 3 minutes). Stir in tomatoes; cover and simmer for 5 minutes. Add half-and-half, vodka, chopped dill, and nutmeg. Increase heat to medium-high and bring to a boil. Cook, stirring often, for 1 minute.

3. Add pasta and mix thoroughly but gently. Remove from heat and stir in salmon. Transfer to a serving platter. Garnish with dill sprigs. Offer white pepper to add to taste.

Makes 5 servings

NUTRIENTS

Per serving: 385 calories (24% calories from fat), 10 g total fat, 4 g saturated fat, 28 mg cholesterol, 243 mg sodium, 54 g carbohydrates, 2 g fiber, 15 g protein, 50 mg calcium, 3 mg iron

ROTINI WITH SCALLOPS

Preparation time: **About 10 minutes**
Cooking time: **About 20 minutes**

There's a hint of heat coming from the paprika, dry mustard, and white pepper in this quickly prepared entrée. If you can't find rotini, use any corkscrew-shaped pasta.

1 pound/455 g (about 7 cups) dried
  rotini or other corkscrew-shaped pasta

1½ pounds (680 g) bay scallops, rinsed
  and drained

1 teaspoon paprika

½ teaspoon dried basil

½ teaspoon dried thyme

½ teaspoon dry mustard

½ teaspoon ground white pepper

2 teaspoons vegetable oil

1 cup (240 ml) fat-free reduced-sodium
  chicken broth

1½ tablespoons cornstarch blended with
  ⅓ cup (80 ml) water

½ cup (120 ml) reduced-fat or regular
  sour cream

1. Bring 16 cups (3.8 liters) water to a boil in a 6- to 8-quart (6- to 8-liter) pan over medium-high heat. Stir in pasta and cook just until tender to bite (8 to 10 minutes); or cook according to package directions.

2. Meanwhile, place scallops in a large bowl. Add paprika, basil, thyme, mustard, and white pepper. Mix until scallops are well coated.

3. Heat oil in a wide nonstick frying pan over medium-high heat. Add scallops and cook, stirring often, just until opaque in center; cut to test (about 3 minutes). Lift out and set aside, reserving juices in pan.

4. Drain pasta well. Transfer to a serving platter and keep warm.

5. Increase heat to high and cook reserved juices until reduced to about ¼ cup (60 ml). Add broth and bring to a boil. Stir cornstarch mixture well and add to broth. Bring to a boil again, stirring constantly. Remove from heat and stir in sour cream and scallops. Spoon over pasta.

Makes 6 servings

NUTRIENTS

Per serving: 442 calories (14% calories from fat), 7 g total fat, 2 g saturated fat, 44 mg cholesterol, 218 mg sodium, 63 g carbohydrates, 2 g fiber, 31 g protein, 50 mg calcium, 4 mg iron

Pasta with Shrimp & Shiitakes

Preparation time: **About 20 minutes**
Cooking time: **About 15 minutes**

This festive pasta calls for dried shiitake mushrooms. These meaty-tasting mushrooms are sold in many supermarkets.

2 cups (about 2 oz./55 g) dried shiitake mushrooms

8 ounces (230 g) dried capellini

2 teaspoons Oriental sesame oil

6 tablespoons (90 ml) oyster sauce or reduced-sodium soy sauce

1 tablespoon (15 ml) vegetable oil

12 ounces (340 g) medium-size raw shrimp (31 to 35 per lb.), shelled and deveined

1 tablespoon finely chopped fresh ginger

3 green onions, thinly sliced

1. Place mushrooms in a medium-size bowl and add enough boiling water to cover; let stand until mushrooms are softened (about 10 minutes). Squeeze mushrooms dry. Cut off and discard stems. Slice caps into strips about ¼ inch (6 mm) thick.

2. In a 4- to 5-quart (3.8- to 5-liter) pan, bring about 8 cups (1.9 liters) water to a boil over medium-high heat; stir in pasta and cook until just tender to bite, about 3 minutes. (Or cook according to package directions.) Drain pasta, rinse with hot water, and drain well again. Then return to pan, add sesame oil and 3 tablespoons (45 ml) of the oyster sauce; lift with 2 forks to mix well. Keep pasta mixture warm.

20 MINUTES OR LESS

8 ounces (230 g) dried spinach fettuccine or 1 package (9 oz./ 255 g) fresh spinach fettuccine

2 tablespoons pine nuts

2 tablespoons (30 ml) olive oil

1 pound (455 g) bay scallops, rinsed and patted dry

2 cloves garlic, minced or pressed

1 large tomato (about 8 oz./230 g), seeded and chopped

¼ cup (60 ml) dry white wine

¼ cup (15 g) chopped Italian parsley

Salt and freshly ground pepper

Spinach Pasta & Scallops

1. In a 5- to 6-quart (5- to 6-liter) pan, cook fettuccine in 3 quarts (2.8 liters) boiling water just until tender to bite (8 to 10 minutes for dry pasta, 3 to 4 minutes for fresh); or cook according to package directions. Drain well.

2. While pasta is cooking, toast pine nuts in a wide nonstick frying pan over medium-low heat until lightly browned (about 3 minutes), stirring often. Remove nuts from pan and set aside. Then heat oil in pan over medium-high heat. Add scallops and cook, turning often with a wide spatula, until opaque in center; cut to test (2 to 3 minutes). Lift from pan, place on a warm plate, and keep warm.

3. Add garlic to pan; cook, stirring, just until it begins to brown (1 to 2 minutes). Stir in tomato, then wine; bring to a full boil. Remove pan from heat and add pasta, scallops and any accumulated liquid, and parsley; mix lightly, using 2 spoons. Season to taste with salt and pepper. Sprinkle with pine nuts. *Makes 4 servings*

Per serving: 425 calories (27% calories from fat), 13 g total fat, 2 g saturated fat, 91 mg cholesterol, 231 mg sodium, 47 g carbohydrates, 5 g fiber, 29 g protein, 72 mg calcium, 4 mg iron

3. Heat vegetable oil in a wide nonstick frying pan over medium-high heat. Add mushrooms, shrimp, and ginger. Cook, stirring often, until shrimp are just opaque in center; cut to test (about 5 minutes). Add onions and remaining 3 tablespoons (45 ml) oyster sauce; mix thoroughly. Pour noodles into a wide bowl; pour shrimp mixture over noodles.

Makes 4 servings

NUTRIENTS

Per serving: 409 calories (17% calories from fat), 8 g total fat, 1 g saturated fat, 105 mg cholesterol, 1,181 mg sodium, 64 g carbohydrates, 2 g fiber, 25 g protein, 59 mg calcium, 5 mg iron

2. Melt butter in a wide nonstick frying pan over medium-high heat. Add mushrooms and cook, stirring often, until browned (about 8 minutes). Add half-and-half, cheese, and broth. Reduce heat to medium and cook, stirring, until cheese is melted (about 2 minutes); do not boil.

3. Add shrimp and pasta quickly. Lift with 2 forks until most of the liquid is absorbed. Transfer to a platter. Sprinkle with parsley.

Makes 6 servings

NUTRIENTS

Per serving: 372 calories (29% calories from fat), 12 g total fat, 6 g saturated fat, 153 mg cholesterol, 366 mg sodium, 44 g carbohydrates, 5 g fiber, 22 g protein, 160 mg calcium, 4 mg iron

Fettuccine with Shrimp & Gorgonzola

Preparation time: **About 10 minutes**
Cooking time: **About 15 minutes**

Just a little Gorgonzola packs a big punch in this entrée. You can use half spinach and half regular fettuccine for a jazzier look.

12	ounces (340 g) dried spinach fettuccine or regular fettuccine
2	teaspoons butter or margarine
12	ounces (340 g) mushrooms, sliced
¾	cup (180 ml) half-and-half
3	ounces/85 g (about ⅔ cup) Gorgonzola cheese, crumbled
¾	cup (180 ml) fat-free reduced-sodium chicken broth
8	ounces (230 g) tiny cooked shrimp
2	tablespoons minced parsley

1. Bring 12 cups (2.8 liters) water to a boil in a 5- to 6-quart (5- to 6-liter) pan over medium-high heat. Stir in pasta and cook just until tender to bite (8 to 10 minutes); or cook according to package directions. Drain well and keep warm.

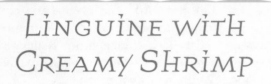

LINGUINE WITH CREAMY SHRIMP

Preparation time: About 15 minutes
Cooking time: About 20 minutes

For an impressive main course, cook shrimp in a creamy sauce of sun-dried tomatoes and serve over hot linguine.

3 tablespoons sun-dried tomatoes packed in oil, drained (reserve oil) and chopped

1 clove garlic, minced or pressed

1 pound (455 g) large shrimp (31 to 35 per lb.), shelled and deveined

10 ounces (285 g) dried linguine

⅔ cup (160 ml) light cream

¼ cup (25 g) thinly sliced green onions

2 tablespoons chopped fresh basil or 1 teaspoon dried basil

⅛ teaspoon ground white pepper

2 teaspoons cornstarch blended with ¾ cup (180 ml) nonfat milk

3 tablespoons (45 ml) dry vermouth, or to taste

Freshly grated Parmesan cheese

Salt

1. Heat 1 teaspoon of the reserved oil from tomatoes in a wide nonstick frying pan over medium-high heat. Add garlic and shrimp. Cook, stirring often, just until shrimp are opaque in center; cut to test (about 6 minutes). Lift out and set aside, reserving any juices in pan.

2. Bring 12 cups (2.8 liters) water to a boil in a 5- to 6-quart (5- to 6-liter) pan over medium-high heat. Stir in pasta and cook just until tender to bite (8 to 10 minutes); or cook according to package directions.

3. Meanwhile, combine cream, onions, basil, tomatoes, and white pepper with juices in frying pan. Bring to a boil over medium-high heat and cook, stirring, for 1 minute. Stir cornstarch mixture and add to pan. Return mixture to a boil and cook, stirring, just until slightly thickened. Remove from heat; stir in vermouth and shrimp.

4. Drain pasta well and arrange on 4 individual plates. Top with shrimp mixture. Offer Parmesan cheese and salt to add to taste.

Makes 4 servings

NUTRIENTS

Per serving: 546 calories (29% calories from fat), 17 g total fat, 6 g saturated fat, 167 mg cholesterol, 188 mg sodium, 62 g carbohydrates, 3 g fiber, 31 g protein, 175 mg calcium, 6 mg iron

Meatless Dishes

COUSCOUS BEAN PAELLA

Preparation time: **About 15 minutes**
Cooking time: **About 15 minutes**

Like traditional paellas, this meatless version calls for sweet peppers, green peas, artichokes, and saffron—but it's made with quick-cooking couscous, not rice, and the protein comes from black beans rather than chicken and shellfish.

2 teaspoons olive oil

1 large onion, chopped

1 medium-size red bell pepper (about 6 oz./170 g), seeded and cut into ½-inch (1-cm) squares

2¼ cups (590 ml) canned vegetable broth

⅛ teaspoon saffron threads, or to taste

1 package (about 9 oz./255 g) frozen artichoke hearts, thawed and drained

1 cup (145 g) frozen peas, thawed and drained

1½ cups (275 g) couscous

1 can (about 15 oz./430 g) black beans, drained and rinsed

Lime or lemon wedges

1. Heat oil in a wide nonstick frying pan or wok over medium-high heat. When oil is hot, add onion, bell pepper, and ¼ cup (60 ml) water. Stir-fry until onion is soft (about 5 minutes); add water, 1 tablespoon (15 ml) at a time, if pan appears dry.

2. Add broth, saffron, artichokes, and peas to pan. Bring to a rolling boil. Stir in couscous. Cover pan, remove from heat, and let stand until liquid has been absorbed (about 5 minutes). Gently stir in beans; cover and let stand for 2 to 3 minutes to heat beans. Serve with lime wedges.

Makes 4 servings

NUTRIENTS

Per serving: 435 calories (9% calories from fat), 4 g total fat, 0.5 g saturated fat, 0 mg cholesterol, 816 mg sodium, 82 g carbohydrates, 11 g fiber, 17 g protein, 73 mg calcium, 4 mg iron

PEANUT STEW WITH BANANA COUSCOUS

Preparation time: **About 20 minutes**
Cooking time: **About 20 minutes**

Pineapple, ripe banana, and a hearty helping of peanut butter give this fruit-and-vegetable stew its rich, slightly sweet flavor. Serve the dish over creamy couscous simmered in a fragrant blend of low-fat milk and banana nectar. For a change of pace, offer the stew with Golden Curried Couscous (page 172).

1 can (about 12 oz./360 ml) banana nectar

About 1¼ cups (300 ml) low-fat (2%) milk

1 medium-size red onion (about 8 oz./230 g), finely chopped

1 can (about 20 oz./570 g) crushed pineapple packed in its own juice

1 medium-size very ripe banana (about 6 oz./170 g), mashed

1 package (about 10 oz./285 g) frozen chopped spinach, thawed and squeezed dry

½ cup (130 g) crunchy peanut butter

About ⅛ teaspoon crushed red pepper flakes

1 package (about 10 oz./285 g) couscous

¼ cup (10 g) coarsely chopped fresh mint

¼ cup (10 g) coarsely chopped cilantro

Lime wedges

1. Pour banana nectar into a 4-cup (950-ml) glass measure. Add enough milk to make 2¾ cups (650 ml); set aside.

2. In a wide nonstick frying pan, combine onion and ¼ cup (60 ml) water. Cook over medium-high heat, stirring often, until onion is soft (about 5 minutes); add water, 1 tablespoon (15 ml) at a time, if pan appears dry.

3. Add undrained pineapple and mashed banana to onion mixture; bring to a boil. Stir in spinach; then reduce heat, cover, and simmer for 5 minutes. Add peanut butter and red pepper flakes. Simmer, uncovered, for 5 minutes, stirring until peanut butter is melted and smoothly blended into sauce.

4. Meanwhile, pour milk mixture into a 2- to 3-quart (1.9- to 2.8-liter) pan and bring just to a boil over medium-high heat. Stir in couscous. Cover, remove from heat, and let stand until liquid has been absorbed (5 to 6 minutes).

5. Spoon couscous into 4 wide individual bowls and top with spinach mixture. Sprinkle with mint and cilantro; garnish with lime wedges.

Makes 4 servings

NUTRIENTS

Per serving: 696 calories (23% calories from fat), 19 g total fat, 4 g saturated fat, 6 mg cholesterol, 271 mg sodium, 115 g carbohydrates, 8 g fiber, 23 g protein, 243 mg calcium, 4 mg iron

COUSCOUS WITH RATATOUILLE & FETA CHEESE

Preparation time: **About 20 minutes**
Cooking time: **About 15 minutes**

Flavored with basil and thyme, this garden-fresh specialty features ratatouille—a Provençal vegetable stew of eggplant, zucchini, and bell peppers. Tangy feta cheese is added to the couscous and also sprinkled on top of the finished dish.

RATATOUILLE:

1 small onion, cut into thin slivers

1 small red bell pepper (about 4 oz./ 115 g), seeded and thinly sliced

1 small eggplant (about 1 lb./455 g), peeled and cut into ½-inch (1-cm) cubes

1 tablespoon chopped fresh basil or ¾ teaspoon dried basil, or to taste

1½ teaspoons chopped fresh thyme or ½ teaspoon dried thyme, or to taste

¼ teaspoon salt, or to taste

¼ teaspoon pepper, or to taste

1 small zucchini (about 4 oz./115 g), cut into ¼-inch (6-mm) slices

1 can (about 15 oz./425 g) garbanzo beans, drained and rinsed

1 large tomato (about 8 oz./230 g), coarsely chopped

COUSCOUS:

2¼ cups (530 ml) low-fat (1%) milk

1 package (about 10 oz./285 g) couscous

1 cup (about 4½ oz./133 g) crumbled feta cheese

GARNISH:

Basil or thyme sprigs

1. In a wide nonstick frying pan, combine onion, bell pepper, eggplant, chopped basil, chopped thyme, salt, pepper, and ½ cup (120 ml) water. Cover and cook over medium-high heat until vegetables are almost tender when pierced (about 5 minutes). Uncover and add zucchini. Cook, stirring gently, until almost all liquid has evaporated. Add beans and tomato; stir gently just until heated through (about 3 minutes).

2. Meanwhile, in a 2½- to 3-quart (2.4- to 2.8-liter) pan, bring milk just to a boil (do not scald) over medium-high heat. Stir in couscous and ¾ cup (100 g) of the feta cheese; cover, remove from heat, and let stand until liquid has been absorbed (about 5 minutes).

3. To serve, divide couscous equally among 4 shallow individual bowls. Top with vegetable mixture and sprinkle with remaining ¼ cup (33 g) feta cheese. Garnish with basil sprigs.

Makes 4 servings

NUTRIENTS

Per serving: 537 calories (19% calories from fat), 11 g total fat, 6 g saturated fat, 36 mg cholesterol, 714 mg sodium, 85 g carbohydrates, 8 g fiber, 24 g protein, 430 mg calcium, 4 mg iron

3. Ladle into bowls. Offer yogurt, salt, and red pepper flakes to add to taste.

Makes 4 to 6 servings

NUTRIENTS

Per serving: 399 calories (7% calories from fat), 3 g total fat, 0.3 g saturated fat, 0.5 mg cholesterol, 1,637 mg sodium, 77 g carbohydrates, 14 g fiber, 18 g protein, 163 mg calcium, 6 mg iron

SPICY CHILI-MAC

Preparation time: **About 15 minutes**
Cooking time: **About 25 minutes**

This pasta and bean stew is sure to become a favorite for cool-weather meals. Instead of using plain nonfat yogurt as a topping, try Cool Yogurt Sauce (page 113).

2   large carrots (about 8 oz./230 g total), chopped

1   large onion, coarsely chopped

    About 3½ cups (830 ml) vegetable broth

1   can (about 15 oz./425 g) tomatoes

1   can (about 15 oz./425 g) pinto beans; or 2 cups cooked (about 1 cup/190 g dried) pinto beans

1   can (about 15 oz./425 g) kidney beans; or 2 cups cooked (about 1 cup/185 g dried) kidney beans

3   tablespoons chili powder

8   ounces/230 g (about 2 cups) dried elbow macaroni

    About ½ cup (120 ml) plain nonfat yogurt

    Salt

    Crushed red pepper flakes

1. Combine carrots, onion, and ¼ cup (60 ml) water in a 4- to 5-quart (3.8- to 5-liter) pan. Cook over medium-high heat, stirring often, until liquid has evaporated and vegetables begin to brown (about 10 minutes).

2. Add 3½ cups (830 ml) of the broth and tomatoes and their liquid; break up tomatoes with a spoon. Stir in pinto and kidney beans and their liquid (if using home-cooked beans, add 1 cup/ 240 ml more broth smoothly blended with 1 teaspoon cornstarch). Add chili powder, stirring to loosen browned bits. Bring to a boil. Stir in pasta and boil gently just until pasta is tender to bite (8 to 10 minutes). If mixture is too thick, add broth; if too thin, continue to simmer until mixture is of desired consistency.

ALL-VEGETABLE CHILI

Preparation time: **About 15 minutes**
Cooking time: **About 30 minutes**

While this substantial dish is every bit as hearty as traditional chili—it is made entirely without meat.

2   medium-size carrots (about 6 oz./ 170 g total), chopped

1   large onion, coarsely chopped

1   can (about 14½ oz./415 g) tomatoes

1   can (about 15 oz./425 g) pinto beans; or 2 cups cooked (about 1 cup/190 g dried) pinto beans

1   can (about 15 oz./425 g) red kidney beans; or 2 cups cooked (about 1 cup/185 g dried) red kidney beans

2   tablespoons chili powder

    About ½ cup (120 ml) plain nonfat yogurt

    Salt

    Crushed red pepper flakes

1. In a 4- to 5-quart (3.8- to 5-liter) pan, combine carrots, onion, and ¼ cup (60 ml) water. Cook over high heat, stirring, until liquid evaporates and vegetables start to brown and stick to pan (about 10 minutes).

2. Add tomatoes and their liquid to pan; break tomatoes up with a spoon. Stir in all beans and their liquid (if using home-cooked beans, add 1 cup/240 ml canned vegetable broth blended with

1 teaspoon cornstarch). Add chili powder; stir to scrape browned bits free. Bring to a boil; then reduce heat and simmer, uncovered, until flavors are blended (about 15 minutes). If chili is too thick, add a little water; if it's too thin, continue to simmer until it's as thick as you like.

3. Ladle chili into 4 individual bowls. Add yogurt, salt, and red pepper flakes to taste.

Makes 4 servings

NUTRIENTS

Per serving: 260 calories (6% calories from fat), 2 g total fat, 0.2 g saturated fat, 0.6 mg cholesterol, 1,057 mg sodium, 50 g carbohydrates, 16 g fiber, 15 g protein, 187 mg calcium, 5 mg iron

VEGETABLE-BEAN CHILI

Preparation time: **About 15 minutes**
Cooking time: **About 15 minutes**

This meatless chili is quite mild in flavor. If you prefer more heat, use more chili powder and red pepper flakes. We call for Worcestershire sauce as a seasoning, but since it's made with anchovies (or other fish), strict vegetarians can substitute soy sauce instead.

  3 tablespoons (45 ml) molasses

1½ teaspoons dry mustard

1½ teaspoons Worcestershire sauce or reduced-sodium soy sauce

  1 teaspoon olive oil or vegetable oil

  2 cloves garlic, minced or pressed

  2 medium-size carrots (about 6 oz./ 170 g total), cut diagonally into ¼-inch (6-mm) slices

  1 large onion, chopped

  1 tablespoon chili powder, or to taste

  2 or 3 large tomatoes (1 to 1½ lbs./ 455 to 680 g total), chopped

  1 can (about 15 oz./430 g) pinto beans, drained and rinsed

  1 can (about 15 oz./430 g) red kidney beans, drained and rinsed

About ½ cup (120 ml) plain nonfat yogurt

Crushed red pepper flakes

1. In a small bowl, stir together molasses, mustard, and Worcestershire. Set aside.

2. Heat oil in a wide nonstick frying pan or wok over medium-high heat. When oil is hot, add garlic and stir-fry just until fragrant (about 30 seconds; do not scorch). Add carrots, onion, chili powder, and ¼ cup (60 ml) water. Cover and cook until carrots are almost tender to bite (about 4 minutes). Uncover and stir-fry until liquid has evaporated.

3. Stir molasses mixture and pour into pan; then add tomatoes and beans. Stir-fry gently until beans are heated through and tomatoes are soft (3 to 5 minutes). Ladle chili into bowls and top with yogurt. Season to taste with red pepper flakes.

Makes 4 servings

NUTRIENTS

Per serving: 290 calories (10% calories from fat), 3 g total fat, 0.4 g saturated fat, 0.6 mg cholesterol, 405 mg sodium, 54 g carbohydrates, 12 g fiber, 14 g protein, 176 mg calcium, 4 mg iron

VEGETABLE BURRITOS

Preparation time: About 15 minutes
Chilling time: At least 20 minutes

Meatless but surprisingly filling, these burritos are stuffed with fresh corn, cucumber, and beans. Marinating the vegetables for 4 hours gives them a richer, more intense lime flavor.

  1 teaspoon grated lime peel

 ⅓ cup (80 ml) lime juice

  2 tablespoons (60 ml) distilled white vinegar

  1 tablespoon (15 ml) honey

  2 teaspoons Dijon mustard

  1 teaspoon ground cumin

  2 cloves garlic, minced or pressed

  1 fresh jalapeño chile, seeded and minced

1½ cups (300 g) fresh-cut yellow or white corn kernels (from 2 medium-size ears corn); or 1 package (about 10 oz./285 g) frozen corn kernels, thawed

  1 can (about 15 oz./425 g) red kidney beans, drained and rinsed; or 2 cups cooked (about 1 cup/185 g dried) red kidney beans, drained and rinsed

  1 medium-size cucumber (about 8 oz./230 g), peeled, seeded, and finely chopped

 ½ cup (50 g) sliced green onions

  2 tablespoons minced cilantro

  8 Warm Tortillas (page 160)

1. To prepare lime marinade, in a nonmetal bowl, stir together lime peel, lime juice, vinegar, honey, mustard, cumin, garlic, and chile. Pour into a large (1-gallon/3.8-liter) heavy-duty resealable plastic bag or large nonmetal bowl. Add corn, beans, cucumber, onions, and cilantro. Seal bag; rotate to mix vegetables (or mix vegetables in bowl, then cover airtight). Refrigerate for at least 20 minutes or up to 4 hours; rotate bag (or stir vegetables in bowl) occasionally.

---

20 MINUTES OR LESS

1 can (about 15 oz./425 g) black beans, drained and rinsed well

¼ cup (60 ml) nonfat mayonnaise

2 teaspoons wine vinegar

1 teaspoon chili powder

4 nonfat flour tortillas (each about 7 inches/18 cm in diameter)

1 cup (about 4 oz./115 g) shredded reduced-fat jack or sharp Cheddar cheese

2 small firm-ripe pear-shaped (Roma-type) tomatoes (about 4 oz./115 g total), chopped

½ cup (85 g) chopped red onion

⅓ cup (15 g) cilantro leaves

½ cup (120 ml) purchased or homemade green tomatillo salsa

BAKED QUESADILLAS

1. In a medium-size bowl, coarsely mash beans. Add mayonnaise, vinegar, and chili powder; stir until well blended.

2. Lightly brush both sides of each tortilla with water. Spoon a fourth of the bean mixture over half of each tortilla; evenly sprinkle a fourth each of the cheese, tomatoes, onion, and cilantro over bean mixture on each tortilla. Fold plain half of tortilla over to cover filling.

3. Set quesadillas slightly apart on a lightly greased 12- by 15-inch (30- by 38-cm) baking sheet. Bake in a 500°F (260°C) oven until crisp and golden (about 7 minutes). Serve with salsa.

Makes 4 servings

Per serving: 323 calories (29% calories from fat), 8 g total fat, 4 g saturated fat, 20 mg cholesterol, 998 mg sodium, 30 g carbohydrates, 5 g fiber, 16 g protein, 381 mg calcium, 2 mg iron

2. Scoop out corn mixture with a slotted spoon; drain (discard marinade), then divide equally among tortillas. Roll up tortillas to enclose filling.

Makes 8 servings

NUTRIENTS

Per serving: 189 calories (15% calories from fat), 3 g total fat, 0.4 g saturated fat, 0 mg cholesterol, 256 mg sodium, 34 g carbohydrates, 4 g fiber, 7 g protein, 68 mg calcium, 2 mg iron

Swiss Chard with Garbanzos & Parmesan

Preparation time: **About 20 minutes**
Cooking time: **About 20 minutes**

Swiss chard, a variety of beet grown for its tops, tastes something like spinach—and like spinach, it is leafy, deep green, and rich in vitamin A and iron. Here, the slivered leaves are sautéed with onions and a little lemon peel, then topped with nutty garbanzo beans and tomatoes for an appealing supper dish. Serve the chard with best-quality Parmesan, a crusty whole wheat loaf, and a fresh fruit salad.

3 tablespoons (45 ml) molasses

1½ teaspoons dry mustard

1½ teaspoons Worcestershire sauce or reduced-sodium soy sauce

¾ teaspoon chopped fresh oregano or ¼ teaspoon dried oregano

1 pound (455 g) Swiss chard

1 teaspoon olive oil

2 large onions, thinly sliced

½ teaspoon grated lemon peel
   Salt

2 large tomatoes (about 1 lb./455 g total), chopped

1 can (about 15 oz./430 g) garbanzo beans, drained and rinsed

1 teaspoon cornstarch blended with 1 teaspoon cold water

½ cup (43 g) shredded Parmesan cheese
   Oregano sprigs

1. In a small bowl, stir together molasses, mustard, Worcestershire, and chopped oregano. Set aside.

2. Trim and discard discolored stem ends from chard; then rinse chard, drain, and cut crosswise into ½-inch (1-cm) strips. Set aside.

3. Heat oil in a wide nonstick frying pan or wok over medium-high heat. When oil is hot, add onions, lemon peel, and 2 tablespoons (30 ml) water. Stir-fry until onions are soft (about 7 minutes). Add water, 1 tablespoon (15 ml) at a time, if pan appears dry. Add half the chard and 1 tablespoon (15 ml) more water to pan; stir-fry until chard just begins to wilt. Then add remaining chard and 1 tablespoon (15 ml) more water; stir-fry until all chard is wilted and bright green (3 to 4 more minutes). Season to taste with salt. Spoon chard mixture around edge of a rimmed platter and keep warm.

4. Stir molasses mixture and pour into pan; add tomatoes and beans. Stir-fry gently until beans are heated through and tomatoes are soft (about 3 minutes). Stir cornstarch mixture well and pour into pan. Cook, stirring gently, until mixture boils and thickens slightly (1 to 2 minutes).

5. Spoon bean mixture into center of platter; sprinkle Parmesan cheese over chard and beans. Garnish with oregano sprigs.

Makes 4 servings

NUTRIENTS

Per serving: 264 calories (22% calories from fat), 7 g total fat, 2 g saturated fat, 8 mg cholesterol, 566 mg sodium, 42 g carbohydrates, 8 g fiber, 12 g protein, 275 mg calcium, 5 mg iron

WHITE BEAN TAGINE

Preparation time: **About 15 minutes**
Cooking time: **About 20 minutes**

Fresh, juicy apricots add a tart and surprising accent to this vegetarian version of a sweet-spiced Moroccan-style stew.

- 1 teaspoon sesame seeds
- 1 large onion, chopped
- 1½ cups (360 ml) low-fat (2%) milk
- 1 package (about 10 oz./285 g) couscous
- 2 cans (about 15 oz./425 g each) cannellini, drained and rinsed
- ½ cup (120 ml) vegetable broth
- 3 tablespoons (45 ml) honey
- ¼ teaspoon ground ginger
- ¼ teaspoon ground cinnamon
- ⅛ teaspoon ground saffron or a large pinch of saffron threads
- ⅛ teaspoon ground white pepper
- 6 apricots (about 12 oz./340 g total), pitted and quartered
- ⅓ cup (15 g) cilantro leaves
  Salt

1. Toast sesame seeds in a wide nonstick frying pan over medium heat, stirring often, until golden (about 3 minutes). Remove from pan; set aside.

2. In same pan, combine onion and ¼ cup (60 ml) water. Cook over medium-high heat, stirring often, until onion is soft (about 5 minutes); add water, 1 tablespoon (15 ml) at a time, if pan appears dry. Remove from heat.

3. In a 2- to 3-quart (1.9- to 2.8-liter) pan, bring milk and 1 cup (240 ml) water just to a boil over medium-high heat. Stir in couscous; cover, remove from heat, and let stand until liquid has been absorbed (about 5 minutes). Keep warm; fluff occasionally with a fork.

4. Meanwhile, to onion mixture, add beans, broth, honey, ginger, cinnamon, saffron, and white pepper. Bring to a boil over medium-high heat. Then reduce heat so mixture boils gently; cook, stirring occasionally, for 5 minutes. Add apricots; cook, stirring gently, just until heated through (about 3 minutes).

5. To serve, spoon couscous onto a rimmed platter; top with bean mixture. Sprinkle with cilantro and sesame seeds; season to taste with salt.

Makes 4 servings

NUTRIENTS

Per serving: 578 calories (7% calories from fat), 4 g total fat, 1 g saturated fat, 7 mg cholesterol, 445 mg sodium, 111 g carbohydrates, 13 g fiber, 25 g protein, 210 mg calcium, 4 mg iron

PINTO BEAN CAKES WITH SALSA

Pictured on page 162
Preparation time: **About 15 minutes**
Cooking time: **About 15 minutes**

Serve a favorite prepared salsa—or your own fresh, homemade sauce—with these cumin-seasoned bean cakes.

- 1½ tablespoons (23 ml) vegetable oil
- 1 small onion, finely chopped
- ¼ cup (38 g) finely chopped red bell pepper
- 2 cloves garlic, minced or pressed
- 1 medium-size fresh jalapeño chile, seeded and finely chopped
- 2 cans (about 15 oz./425 g each) pinto beans, drained and rinsed
- ⅛ teaspoon liquid smoke
- ¼ cup (10 g) chopped cilantro
- ½ teaspoon ground cumin
- ¼ teaspoon pepper
- ⅓ cup (45 g) yellow cornmeal

Vegetable oil cooking spray, if needed

½ to 1 cup (120 to 240 ml) purchased or homemade salsa

1. Heat 1½ teaspoons of the oil in a wide nonstick frying pan over medium heat. Add onion, bell pepper, garlic, and chile; cook, stirring often, until onion is soft but not browned (about 5 minutes). Meanwhile, place beans in a large bowl and mash coarsely with a potato masher (mashed beans should stick together). Stir in onion mixture; then add liquid smoke, cilantro, cumin, and pepper. Mix well. If necessary, refrigerate until cool.

2. Spread cornmeal on a sheet of wax paper. Divide bean mixture into 8 equal portions; shape each into a ½-inch-thick (1-cm-thick) cake. Coat cakes with cornmeal.

3. In pan used to cook onion, heat remaining 1 tablespoon (15 ml) oil over medium-high heat. Add bean cakes and cook, turning once, until golden brown on both sides (8 to 10 minutes); if necessary, spray pan with cooking spray to prevent sticking. Serve with salsa to add to taste.

Makes 4 servings (2 cakes each)

NUTRIENTS

Per serving: 232 calories (25% calories from fat), 6 g total fat, 0.8 g saturated fat, 0 mg cholesterol, 666 mg sodium, 34 g carbohydrates, 7 g fiber, 9 g protein, 56 mg calcium, 3 mg iron

Bean Burritos

Preparation time: **About 20 minutes**
Cooking time: **About 15 minutes**

Jalapeño jack cheese adds just the right amount of heat to burritos filled with a quick sauté of pinto beans and corn.

½ teaspoon cornstarch blended with 1 teaspoon cold water

½ teaspoon grated lime peel

2 tablespoons (30 ml) lime juice

1 teaspoon honey

½ teaspoon ground coriander

¼ teaspoon ground cumin

8 low-fat flour tortillas (each 7 to 9 inches/18 to 23 cm in diameter)

1 teaspoon vegetable oil

1 large onion, chopped

1 medium-size red or green bell pepper (about 6 oz./170 g), seeded and diced

1 can (about 15 oz./430 g) pinto or kidney beans, drained and rinsed

About 1½ cups (250 g) cooked fresh corn kernels (from 2 small ears yellow or white corn); or 1 package (about 10 oz./285 g) frozen corn kernels, thawed and drained

1 cup (about 4 oz./115 g) shredded jalapeño or regular jack cheese

½ cup (20 g) cilantro leaves

¾ cup (180 ml) nonfat sour cream

1. To prepare sauce, in a small bowl, stir cornstarch mixture to recombine. Stir in lime peel, lime juice, honey, coriander, and cumin. Set aside.

2. Brush tortillas lightly with hot water; then stack, wrap in foil, and heat in a 350°F (175°C) oven until warm (10 to 12 minutes).

3. Meanwhile, heat oil in a wide nonstick frying pan or wok over medium-high heat. When oil is hot, add onion, bell pepper, and 2 tablespoons (30 ml) water; stir-fry until onion is softened (about 5 minutes). Add more water, 1 tablespoon (15 ml) at a time, if pan appears dry. Add beans and corn; stir-fry gently until heated through (about 3 minutes).

4. Stir sauce well and pour into pan. Cook, stirring gently, until sauce boils and thickens slightly (1 to 2 minutes).

5. Top tortillas equally with bean mixture. Sprinkle with jack cheese and cilantro, top with sour cream, and roll to enclose filling.

Makes 4 servings

NUTRIENTS

Per serving: 456 calories (23% calories from fat), 13 g total fat, 5 g saturated fat, 30 mg cholesterol, 766 mg sodium, 75 g carbohydrates, 15 g fiber, 21 g protein, 419 mg calcium, 4 mg iron

Quick Fruit & Ricotta Pizza

Preparation time: **About 20 minutes**
Baking time: **15 to 20 minutes**

Take advantage of refrigerated dough for this quick main dish, which is perfect for a weekend brunch.

1 package (about 10 oz./285 g) refrigerated pizza crust dough

1 cup (about 8 oz./230 g) part-skim ricotta cheese

2 teaspoons grated lemon peel

2 cups (about 8 oz./230 g) shredded part-skim mozzarella cheese

2 medium-size nectarines (about 8 oz./230 g total), thinly sliced

4 ounces (115 g) dried peaches, sliced

¾ cup (130 g) halved red seedless grapes

2 tablespoons sugar

¼ teaspoon ground cinnamon

3 tablespoons sliced almonds

1. Unroll dough, place on a 12- by 15-inch (30- by 38-cm) nonstick baking sheet, and press with your fingers to make a 10- by 15-inch (25- by 38-cm) rectangle. Bake on lowest rack of a 425°F (220°C) oven until browned (about 8 minutes).

2. In a small bowl, stir together ricotta cheese and lemon peel; spread over crust. Sprinkle with mozzarella cheese. Arrange nectarines, peaches, and grapes over cheese. In another small bowl, mix sugar and cinnamon. Sprinkle sugar mixture and almonds evenly over fruit. Return to oven and bake until fruit is hot to the touch and mozzarella cheese is melted (5 to 10 minutes).

Makes 8 servings

NUTRIENTS

Per serving: 287 calories (29% calories from fat), 9 g total fat, 5 g saturated fat, 25 mg cholesterol, 364 mg sodium, 36 g carbohydrates, 2 g fiber, 14 g protein, 274 mg calcium, 2 mg iron

Fruit & Cheese Quesadillas

Preparation time: **About 15 minutes**
Baking time: **7 to 9 minutes**

Even when you don't have much time to put together a meal, try to keep good nutrition in mind. These slightly sweet quesadillas, easy to assemble in just a few minutes, make a filling, low-fat breakfast or lunch.

½ cup (70 g) chopped dried apricots

1 teaspoon grated orange peel

6 tablespoons (90 ml) orange juice

About 2 cups (460 g) part-skim ricotta cheese

About 6 tablespoons (90 ml) honey, or to taste

1 teaspoon ground coriander

12 flour tortillas (7- to 9-inch/18- to 23-cm diameter)

3 cups (470 g) chopped fresh or canned pineapple, drained well

Mint sprigs (optional)

1. In a bowl, combine apricots, orange peel, and orange juice; let stand until apricots are softened (about 10 minutes).

2. In a food processor or blender, combine apricot-juice mixture, ricotta cheese, honey, and coriander; whirl until smoothly puréed. (At this point, you may cover and refrigerate for up to 2 days.)

3. Arrange 6 tortillas in a single layer on 2 or 3 lightly oiled large baking sheets. Spread tortillas evenly with cheese mixture, covering tortillas to within ½ inch (1 cm) of edges. Evenly cover cheese mixture with pineapple, then top each tortilla with one of the remaining tortillas; press lightly.

4. Bake in a 450°F (230°C) oven until tortillas are lightly browned (7 to 9 minutes), switching positions of baking sheets halfway through baking.

5. Slide quesadillas onto a board; cut each into 4 to 6 wedges. Arrange on a platter and garnish with mint sprigs, if desired.

Makes 8 to 10 servings

NUTRIENTS

Per serving: 312 calories (21% calories from fat), 8 g total fat, 3 g saturated fat, 16 mg cholesterol, 288 mg sodium, 52 g carbohydrates, 3 g fiber, 10 g protein, 205 mg calcium, 2 mg iron

GREEN POTATOES WITH BLUE CHEESE SAUCE

Pictured on page 163
Preparation time: **About 25 minutes**
Cooking time: **About 15 minutes**

Here sautéed sliced potatoes are tossed with slivered fresh spinach and cilantro, then topped with a cool, zesty sauce of tofu and blue cheese. When you prepare the spinach, reserve the best-looking leaves for lining the platter; use the torn ones for shredding.

4 ounces (115 g) soft tofu, rinsed and drained

⅓ cup (80 ml) low-fat buttermilk

1 tablespoon (15 ml) white wine vinegar

1 tablespoon (15 ml) honey

1 teaspoon Dijon mustard

1 or 2 cloves garlic, peeled

½ cup (70 g) crumbled blue-veined cheese

Salt and pepper

3 to 4 cups (3 to 4 oz./85 to 115 g) lightly packed, rinsed, crisped spinach leaves

1 tablespoon butter or margarine

1¼ pounds (565 g) small red thin-skinned potatoes, scrubbed and cut crosswise into ¼-inch (6-mm) slices

1 medium-size red bell pepper (about 6 oz./170 g), seeded and cut into thin strips

1 medium-size onion, cut into thin slivers

1 tablespoon ground cumin

1 teaspoon ground coriander

⅛ teaspoon ground red pepper (cayenne)

½ to ¾ cup (20 to 30 g) lightly packed cilantro leaves

Cilantro sprigs (optional)

1 tablespoon thinly sliced green onion

1. To prepare blue cheese sauce, in a blender or food processor, combine tofu, buttermilk, vinegar, honey, mustard, and garlic. Whirl until smoothly puréed. Gently mix in cheese and season to taste with salt and black pepper. Set aside. (At this point you may cover and refrigerate for up to 3 hours.)

2. Cut 1 to 1½ cups (30 to 43 g) of the spinach into thin shreds about 2 inches (5 cm) long. Cover and set aside. Line a rimmed platter with remaining spinach leaves; cover and set aside.

3. Melt butter in a wide nonstick frying pan or wok over medium-high heat. Add potatoes, bell pepper, onion, cumin, coriander, ¼ teaspoon salt, ground red pepper, and ¼ cup (60 ml) water. Stir-fry gently until potatoes are tinged with brown and tender when pierced (about 15 minutes; do not scorch). Add water, 1 tablespoon (15 ml) at a time, if pan appears dry.

4. Remove pan from heat. Sprinkle potato mixture with shredded spinach; mix gently but thoroughly. Then spoon potato mixture over spinach leaves on platter. Sprinkle with cilantro leaves; garnish with cilantro sprigs, if desired.

5. Just before serving, stir onion into blue cheese sauce. Offer blue cheese sauce to add to taste.

Makes 4 servings

NUTRIENTS

Per serving: 279 calories (30% calories from fat), 9 g total fat, 5 g saturated fat, 21 mg cholesterol, 436 mg sodium, 39 g carbohydrates, 5 g fiber, 11 g protein, 192 mg calcium, 4 mg iron

SCRAMBLED EGGS & BULGUR

Preparation time: **About 10 minutes**
Standing time: **About 10 minutes**
Cooking time: **About 15 minutes**

Serve this hearty entrée as you would any other egg dish, at brunch or for a light lunch or dinner.

2 cups (470 ml) vegetable broth

1 cup (175 g) bulgur

2 teaspoons butter or margarine

1 medium-size onion, thinly sliced

1 medium-size red bell pepper (about 6 oz./170 g), seeded and thinly sliced

2 large eggs

4 large egg whites

¼ cup (20 g) grated Parmesan cheese

1. In a 1- to 1½-quart (950-ml to 1.4-liter) pan, bring broth to a boil over high heat. Stir in bulgur; cover, remove from heat, and let stand until liquid has been absorbed (about 10 minutes).

2. Meanwhile, melt 1 teaspoon of the butter in a wide nonstick frying pan over medium heat. Add onion and bell pepper; cook, stirring often, until onion is lightly browned (about 10 minutes). Add water, 1 tablespoon (15 ml) at a time, if pan appears dry. Meanwhile, in a small bowl, beat eggs, egg whites, and ¼ cup (60 ml) water until blended.

3. Add remaining 1 teaspoon butter to onion mixture in pan and reduce heat to medium-low. Add egg mixture; cook until eggs are softly set, gently lifting cooked portion with a wide spatula to allow uncooked eggs to flow underneath. Divide bulgur and egg mixture equally among 4 individual plates. Sprinkle with Parmesan cheese.

Makes 4 servings

NUTRIENTS

Per serving: 254 calories (25% calories from fat), 7 g total fat, 3 g saturated fat, 116 mg cholesterol, 726 mg sodium, 35 g carbohydrates, 8 g fiber, 14 g protein, 123 mg calcium, 2 mg iron

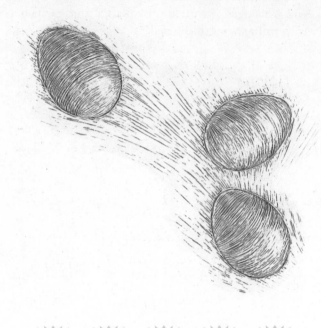

DROWNED EGGS

Preparation time: **About 10 minutes**
Cooking time: **About 25 minutes**

Eggs poached in a tomato sauce enriched with fiery serrano chiles, onions, and spices make a great one-pan meal.

1 can (about 14½ oz./415 g) tomatoes

2 cloves garlic, peeled

¾ cup (180 ml) water

2 teaspoons chili powder

1½ teaspoons dried oregano

1½ teaspoons sugar

4 large eggs

¼ cup (25 g) thinly sliced green onions

4 fresh serrano chiles, halved and seeded

2 tablespoons cilantro leaves
Salt and pepper

8 Warm Tortillas (page 160)

1. Pour tomatoes and their liquid into a blender or food processor. Add garlic, then whirl until smoothly puréed.

2. Transfer tomato purée to a wide frying pan. Stir in water, chili powder, oregano, and sugar; bring to a boil over medium-high heat. Reduce heat so sauce is simmering. Carefully crack eggs, one at a time, into sauce. Distribute onions and chile halves over sauce, disturbing eggs as little as possible. Cook, carefully basting eggs occasionally with sauce, until yolks are set to your liking (about 20 minutes for firm but moist yolks).

3. Divide eggs, onions, chile halves, and sauce equally among 4 shallow (about 1½-cup/360-ml) casseroles. Sprinkle with cilantro; season to taste with salt and pepper. Serve with tortillas.

Makes 4 servings

NUTRIENTS

Per serving: 225 calories (26% calories from fat), 7 g total fat, 2 g saturated fat, 213 mg cholesterol, 326 mg sodium, 33 g carbohydrates, 4 g fiber, 11 protein, 160 mg calcium, 3 mg iron

ROASTED CHILES WITH EGGS

Preparation time: **About 20 minutes**
Cooking time: **About 10 minutes**

For a leaner twist on a classic favorite, these chiles are roasted, not battered and fried—and they're stuffed with thyme-accented eggs and egg whites instead of cheese. If you have the time, you can prepare the Lime Salsa early in the day.

4 fresh green poblano or Anaheim chiles

1 cup (240 ml) Lime Salsa (page 21)

2 large eggs

4 large egg whites

½ cup (120 g) nonfat cottage cheese

½ cup (15 g) finely chopped spinach

About 1 tablespoon thinly sliced green onion

2 teaspoons cornstarch blended with 1 tablespoon (15 ml) cold water

1½ teaspoons fresh thyme leaves or ¼ teaspoon dried thyme

⅛ teaspoon salt

⅛ teaspoon white pepper

1 teaspoon vegetable oil

Sliced fresh hot red chiles (seeded, if desired)

Thyme sprigs

About ¾ cup (180 ml) plain nonfat yogurt

1. To roast chiles, place chiles on a 12- by 15-inch (30- by 38-cm) baking sheet. Broil 4 to 6 inches below heat, turning often, until charred all over (5 to 8 minutes). Cover with foil and let cool on baking sheet; then remove and discard skins. Cut a slit down one side of each chile, but do not cut all the way to stem end and tip; be careful not to puncture opposite side of chile. Remove and discard seeds and veins from chiles; set aside.

2. Prepare Lime Salsa; refrigerate.

3. In a food processor, whirl eggs, egg whites, cottage cheese, spinach, 1 tablespoon of the onion, cornstarch mixture, thyme leaves, salt, and white pepper until smoothly puréed. Set aside.

4. Heat oil in a medium-size nonstick frying pan over medium heat. Add egg mixture to pan; stir to combine. Cook until mixture is softly set and looks like scrambled eggs (3 to 5 minutes).

5. Spoon hot egg mixture equally into chiles. Place filled chiles on a platter and garnish with red chile slices and thyme sprigs. Add yogurt, additional thinly sliced onion, and Lime Salsa to taste.

Makes 4 servings

NUTRIENTS

Per serving: 138 calories (26% calories from fat), 4 g total fat, 1 g saturated fat, 110 mg cholesterol, 298 mg sodium, 11 g carbohydrates, 0.7 g fiber, 14 g protein, 132 mg calcium, 1 mg iron

EAST-WEST HASH

Preparation time: **About 25 minutes**
Cooking time: **About 20 minutes**

Seasoned with jalapeño chiles and Oriental sesame oil, this wholesome hash draws its flavors from both East and West. Serve it with warm flour tortillas and your favorite salsa.

> 2 *large russet potatoes (about 1¼ lbs./565 g total), peeled and cut into ½-inch (1-cm) cubes*
>
> 6 *reduced-fat flour tortillas (each about 7 inches/18 cm in diameter)*
>
> 1½ *teaspoons Oriental sesame oil*
>
> 3 *medium-size onions, chopped*
>
> 6 *cloves garlic, minced or pressed*
>
> 3 *small fresh jalapeño chiles, seeded and finely chopped*
>
> ⅔ *cup (30 g) chopped cilantro*
>
> 2 *teaspoons ground cumin*
>
> 3 *tablespoons (45 ml) lime juice*
>
> 8 *large eggs, beaten to blend*
>
> *About 1½ cups (360 ml) purchased or homemade salsa*
>
> *Salt and pepper*

1. Pour water into a 2- to 3-quart (1.9- to 2.8-liter) pan to a depth of 1 inch (2.5 cm). Add potatoes, cover, and bring to a boil over high heat. Reduce heat and simmer until potatoes are tender when pierced with a fork (10 to 12 minutes). Drain potatoes well.

2. While potatoes are simmering, sprinkle tortillas lightly with water; then stack tortillas, wrap in foil, and heat in a 350°F (175°C) oven until warm (10 to 12 minutes).

3. Meanwhile, heat oil in a wide nonstick frying pan over medium heat. Add onions and garlic. Cook, stirring often, until onions are soft (about 10 minutes); add water, 1 tablespoon (15 ml) at a time, if pan appears dry. Add chiles, cilantro, and cumin; cook, stirring often, for 1 to 2 minutes.

4. Add lime juice and drained potatoes to onion mixture in pan; then spread mixture out to make level. Pour beaten eggs over potatoes. Cook until eggs are set to your liking, using a wide spatula to lift cooked portion from pan bottom to allow uncooked eggs to flow underneath.

5. Spoon egg mixture onto plates; offer salsa, salt, and pepper to add to taste. Serve with tortillas.

Makes 6 servings

NUTRIENTS

Per serving: 323 calories (29% calories from fat), 10 g total fat, 2 g saturated fat, 283 mg cholesterol, 1,028 mg sodium, 43 g carbohydrates, 4 g fiber, 14 g protein, 168 mg calcium, 3 mg iron

VEGETABLE SCRAMBLE POCKETS

Preparation time: **About 10 minutes**
Cooking time: **About 15 minutes**

For breakfast, lunch, or supper, try these warm and satisfying pita pockets filled with egg, vegetables, and cheese.

> 1 *large egg*
>
> 6 *large egg whites*
>
> 1 *teaspoon ground oregano*
>
> 1 *cup (about 4½ oz./130 g) crumbled feta cheese*
>
> 1 *tablespoon (15 ml) olive oil*
>
> 1 *large onion, thinly sliced*
>
> 2 *large red bell peppers (about 1 lb./455 g total), seeded and thinly sliced*
>
> 8 *ounces (230 g) mushrooms, thinly sliced*
>
> 1 *package (about 10 oz./285 g) frozen chopped spinach, thawed and squeezed dry*
>
> *Pepper*
>
> 4 *whole wheat pita breads (each about 6 inches/15 cm in diameter), cut crosswise into halves*

1. In a large bowl, lightly beat whole egg, egg whites, oregano, and cheese until blended. Set aside.

2. Heat oil in a wide nonstick frying pan or wok over medium-high heat. When oil is hot, add onion, bell peppers, and mushrooms; stir-fry until liquid has completely evaporated and mushrooms are tinged with brown (about 7 minutes). Add spinach to pan and stir-fry until heated through (about 3 minutes).

3. Pour egg mixture over vegetables in pan; stir-fry until eggs are softly set and look scrambled (3 to 5 minutes). Season to taste with pepper. Fill pita halves equally with egg mixture.

Makes 4 servings

NUTRIENTS

Per serving: 398 calories (28% calories from fat), 13 g total fat, 5 g saturated fat, 78 mg cholesterol, 813 mg sodium, 54 g carbohydrates, 9 g fiber, 22 g protein, 265 mg calcium, 3 mg iron

EGG, BEAN & POTATO HASH

Preparation time: **About 10 minutes**
Cooking time: **About 35 minutes**

Great at any time of day, this mild hash of diced potatoes and red kidney beans is topped with gently cooked eggs.

1   tablespoon butter or margarine

1   pound (455 g) thin-skinned potatoes, cut into ¼-inch (6-mm) cubes

1   small red onion, cut into thin slivers

1   teaspoon chili powder

1   can (about 15 oz./430 g) red kidney beans, drained and rinsed

1   large tomato, chopped

¾   teaspoon chopped fresh sage

4   large eggs

⅓   cup (15 g) lightly packed cilantro leaves

¾   cup (180 ml) nonfat sour cream

1. Melt butter in a wide nonstick frying pan or wok over medium-high heat. Add potatoes, onion, chili powder, and ¼ cup (60 ml) water. Stir-fry until potatoes are tinged with brown and tender (about 15 minutes; do not scorch). Add water, 1 tablespoon (15 ml) at a time, if pan appears dry.

2. Add beans, tomato, sage, and 2 tablespoons (30 ml) water to pan. Stir-fry gently until heated through, scraping any browned bits free from pan bottom. With a spoon, make 4 depressions in potato mixture; carefully break an egg into each depression. Reduce heat to low, cover, and cook until egg yolks are set to your liking (about 15 minutes for firm but moist yolks). Sprinkle with cilantro and top with sour cream.

Makes 4 servings

NUTRIENTS

Per serving: 328 calories (25% calories from fat), 9 g total fat, 3 g saturated fat, 220 mg cholesterol, 280 mg sodium, 43 g carbohydrates, 8 g fiber, 18 g protein, 125 mg calcium, 3 mg iron

8　diagonal slices French bread (each about 3 by 6 inches/8 by 15 cm and about ⅓ inch/1 cm thick)

1　cup (about 4 oz./115 g) shredded reduced-fat jack cheese

1　can (about 4 oz./115 g) diced green chiles

¼　cup (10 g) finely chopped cilantro

CHERRY TOMATO SALSA:

2　cups (285 g) red cherry tomatoes, cut into halves

⅓　cup (15 g) cilantro leaves

2　small fresh jalapeño chiles, seeded

1　clove garlic, peeled

2　tablespoons (30 ml) lime juice

2　tablespoons thinly sliced green onion

1. In a large bowl, beat egg, egg whites, and milk until well blended. Dip 4 slices of bread into egg mixture; turn to saturate both sides. Arrange slices in a shallow 10- by 15-inch (25- by 38-cm) non-stick baking pan.

2. Top bread in baking pan evenly with cheese, green chiles, and chopped cilantro. Dip remaining 4 bread slices into egg mixture, turning to coat both sides; place atop cheese-covered bread to form 4 sandwiches. Bake sandwiches in a 400°F (205°C) oven until bread begins to brown (about 12 minutes). Then carefully turn sandwiches over with a wide spatula; continue to bake until golden brown (about 10 more minutes).

3. Meanwhile, in a food processor, combine tomatoes, cilantro leaves, jalapeño chiles, and garlic; whirl just until tomatoes are coarsely chopped. Spoon mixture into a small bowl. Add lime juice and onion; stir to mix well.

4. To serve, transfer French toast sandwiches to individual plates. Offer salsa to add to taste.

Makes 4 servings

NUTRIENTS

Per serving: 306 calories (24% calories from fat), 8 g total fat, 4 g saturated fat, 74 mg cholesterol, 811 mg sodium, 37 g carbohydrates, 3 g fiber, 22 g protein, 385 mg calcium, 2 mg iron

CHILE-CHEESE FRENCH TOAST & CHERRY TOMATO SALSA

Preparation time: **About 20 minutes**
Cooking time: **About 25 minutes**

French toast needn't be limited to breakfast time, nor must it be sweet. To reduce the fat content, we've made the batter with extra egg whites, then oven-baked the toast. The cherry tomato salsa is the ideal condiment.

FRENCH TOAST:

1　large egg

4　large egg whites

1　cup (240 ml) nonfat milk

Zucchini Burgers

Preparation time: **About 30 minutes**
Cooking time: **About 12 minutes**

To shred zucchini quickly, you can use a food processor fitted with the shredding disc. Or try a grater.

1½ pounds (680 g) zucchini, shredded

2 tablespoons margarine

1 large onion, finely chopped

¼ cup (25 g) fine dried bread crumbs

2 large eggs, lightly beaten

¼ cup (20 g) grated Parmesan cheese

6 onion bagels, split and toasted

1. Drain zucchini in a colander for 30 minutes; then squeeze to remove moisture. While zucchini is draining, melt 2 teaspoons of the margarine in a wide nonstick frying pan over medium heat. Add onion; stir often until lightly browned (about 10 minutes). Scrape into a bowl.

2. Mix drained zucchini, crumbs, eggs, and cheese with onion in bowl. In frying pan, melt remaining 4 teaspoons margarine over medium-high heat. Ladle three ¼-cup (25-g) mounds of zucchini mixture into pan, spreading each to make a 3-inch-wide (8-cm-wide) patty. Cook until patties are lightly browned on bottom (about 3 minutes). With a wide spatula, turn patties over; continue to cook until browned on other side (about 3 more minutes). Remove from pan and keep warm. Repeat to cook remaining zucchini mixture, making 3 more patties. To serve, place burgers on bagels.
Makes 6 servings

NUTRIENTS

Per serving: 282 calories (25% calories from fat), 8 g total fat, 2 g saturated fat, 73 mg cholesterol, 490 mg sodium, 41 g carbohydrates, 3 g fiber, 13 g protein, 130 mg calcium, 2 mg iron

20 MINUTES OR LESS

1 large egg plus 2 egg whites

1¼ cups (68 g) soft whole wheat bread crumbs

½ cup (48 g) toasted wheat germ

3 tablespoons chopped walnuts

½ cup (50 g) sliced green onions

½ cup (120 ml) small-curd low-fat (1%) cottage cheese

2 tablespoons chopped parsley

1 teaspoon dried basil

½ teaspoon dried oregano

½ teaspoon paprika

Salt

4 thin slices reduced-fat jack cheese (about 2 oz./55 g total)

4 whole wheat hamburger buns, toasted

¼ cup (60 ml) nonfat Thousand Island dressing or mayonnaise

Double Wheat Burgers

1. In a large bowl, beat egg and egg whites to blend. Stir in bread crumbs, wheat germ, walnuts, green onions, cottage cheese, parsley, basil, oregano, and paprika. Season to taste with salt.

2. On an oiled 12- by 15-inch (30- by 38-cm) baking sheet, shape mixture into 4 equal patties, each about ½ inch (1 cm) thick. Broil patties about 3 inches (8 cm) below heat, turning once, until deep golden on both sides (about 6 minutes). Top each patty with a slice of jack cheese and continue to broil just until cheese is melted (about 30 more seconds).

3. To serve, place patties on bottoms of buns. Top with dressing, then with tops of buns. *Makes 4 servings*

Per serving: 346 calories (29% calories from fat), 12 g total fat, 3 g saturated fat, 64 mg cholesterol, 722 mg sodium, 42 g carbohydrates, 7 g fiber, 22 g protein, 225 mg calcium, 4 mg iron

WHEAT GERM BURGERS

Pictured on facing page
Preparation time: **About 20 minutes**
Cooking time: **About 10 minutes**

Toasted wheat germ, and shredded cheese and zucchini, distinguish these winning meatless burgers, which make a delicious lunch or dinner. To save on fat and calories, serve the burgers accompanied by Warm Tortillas (at right), instead of on kaiser rolls or traditional hamburger buns.

2 large eggs

¾ cup (72 g) toasted wheat germ

½ cup (55 g) shredded reduced-fat jack cheese

¼ cup (20 g) chopped mushrooms

3 tablespoons finely chopped onion

½ teaspoon dried thyme, crumbled

½ teaspoon dried rosemary, crumbled

1½ cups (150 g) long zucchini shreds
   Salt and pepper

1 to 2 teaspoons vegetable oil

4 kaiser rolls, hamburger buns, or Warm Tortillas (this page)

½ cup (120 ml) plain nonfat yogurt
   About ¼ cup (60 ml) catsup
   About 2 tablespoons (30 ml) Dijon mustard

4 to 8 butter lettuce leaves, rinsed and crisped

1 large tomato (about 8 oz./230 g), thinly sliced

1. In a large bowl, beat eggs to blend. Stir in wheat germ, cheese, mushrooms, onion, thyme, rosemary, and zucchini. Season to taste with salt and pepper.

2. On sheet of plastic wrap, shape wheat germ mixture into 4 equal patties, each about ¾ inch (2 cm) thick.

3. Heat 1 teaspoon of the oil in a wide nonstick frying pan over medium heat. Add patties and cook until deep golden on bottom (4 to 5 minutes). Turn patties over; add 1 teaspoon more oil to pan, if needed. Cook until deep golden on other side (about 4 more minutes).

4. To serve, place patties on bottoms of buns. Top with yogurt, catsup, mustard, lettuce leaves, and tomato, then with tops of buns.

Makes 4 servings

NUTRIENTS

Per serving: 416 calories (27% calories from fat), 13 g total fat, 4 g saturated fat, 117 mg cholesterol, 885 mg sodium, 54 g carbohydrates, 5 g fiber, 22 g protein, 311 mg calcium, 5 mg iron

WARM TORTILLAS

Cooking time: **About 12 minutes**

Warm corn or flour tortillas are obvious accompaniments for most Mexican-inspired dishes, but don't hesitate to offer them as a low-fat option to rolls or bread with any meal.

6 corn tortillas (each 6 inches/15 cm in diameter) or 6 flour tortillas (each 7 to 9 inches/18 to 23 cm in diameter)

1. Brush tortillas lightly with hot water; then stack, wrap in foil, and heat in a 350°F (175°C) oven until warm (10 to 12 minutes).

Makes 6 tortillas

NUTRIENTS

Per corn tortilla: 56 calories (10% calories from fat), 0.6 g total fat, 0.1 g saturated fat, 0 mg cholesterol, 40 mg sodium, 12 g carbohydrates, 1 g fiber, 1 g protein, 44 mg calcium, 0.4 mg iron

Per flour tortilla: 114 calories (20% calories from fat), 3 g total fat, 0.4 g saturated fat, 0 mg cholesterol, 167 mg sodium, 20 g carbohydrates, 1 g fiber, 3 g protein, 44 mg calcium, 1 mg iron

WHEAT GERM BURGERS (RECIPE ON FACING PAGE)

PINTO BEAN CAKES WITH SALSA (RECIPE ON PAGE 150)

Green Potatoes with Blue Cheese Sauce (recipe on page 153)

Tofu Tacos with Pineapple Salsa (recipe on facing page)

TOFU TACOS WITH PINEAPPLE SALSA

Pictured on facing page
Preparation time: **About 15 minutes**
Cooking time: **About 20 minutes**

Not your standard tacos, these tofu-topped soft tortillas are sure to appeal to the vegetarian crowd. The filling is a combination of bell pepper, corn kernels, and teriyaki-seasoned tofu; a crunchy pineapple and jicama salsa adds a refreshing accent. You can make the flavored oils called for in the marinade (pages 46 and 55) or use purchased equivalents.

3 tablespoons (45 ml) reduced-sodium soy sauce

2 tablespoons (30 ml) honey

1 tablespoon (15 ml) Basil Oil (page 46) or purchased basil oil (or 1 tablespoon/15 ml vegetable oil plus ½ teaspoon dried basil)

1 teaspoon Hot Chile Oil (page 55) or purchased hot chili oil

2 cloves garlic, minced or pressed

12 ounces (340 g) firm tofu, rinsed, drained, and cut into ½-inch (1-cm) cubes

1 cup (155 g) diced fresh or canned pineapple

½ cup (65 g) peeled, shredded jicama

1 teaspoon grated lime peel

3 tablespoons (45 ml) lime juice

2 tablespoons minced fresh basil

4 low-fat flour tortillas (each 7 to 9 inches/18 to 23 cm in diameter)

1 large red bell pepper (about 8 oz./230 g), seeded and finely chopped

1 large onion, finely chopped

1 package (about 10 oz./285 g) frozen corn kernels, thawed and drained

1. In a medium-size bowl, stir together soy sauce, honey, Basil Oil, Hot Chile Oil, and garlic. Add tofu and stir gently to coat. Set aside; stir occasionally to blend.

2. To prepare pineapple salsa, in a large bowl, mix pineapple, jicama, lime peel, lime juice, and basil; set aside.

3. Brush tortillas lightly with hot water; then stack tortillas, wrap in foil, and heat in a 350°F (175°C) oven until warm (10 to 12 minutes).

4. Meanwhile, in a wide nonstick frying pan or wok, combine tofu (and any marinade), bell pepper, and onion. Stir-fry gently over medium-high heat until tofu is browned (about 15 minutes). Add water, 1 tablespoon (15 ml) at a time, if pan appears dry. Add corn and stir-fry until heated through.

5. Top tortillas equally with tofu mixture and pineapple salsa; roll up to enclose.

Makes 4 servings

NUTRIENTS

Per serving: 411 calories (30% calories from fat), 15 g total fat, 2 g saturated fat, 0 mg cholesterol, 761 mg sodium, 57 g carbohydrates, 5 g fiber, 20 g protein, 317 mg calcium, 11 mg iron

Sichuan Tofu with Eggplant

Preparation time: **About 30 minutes**
Cooking time: **About 15 minutes**

Though it is based on two exceptionally mild-flavored foods—tofu and eggplant—this dish will nonetheless win favor with the fire-eaters in your family. Fresh ginger and bottled chili paste with garlic impart spicy overtones.

- 3 tablespoons (45 ml) hoisin sauce
- 2 tablespoons (30 ml) seasoned rice vinegar (or 2 tablespoons/30 ml distilled white vinegar plus ¾ teaspoon sugar)
- 1 tablespoon sugar
- 1 tablespoon chili paste with garlic
- 2 teaspoons Oriental sesame oil
  About 1 pound (455 g) firm tofu, rinsed, drained, and cut into ½-inch (1-cm) cubes
- 10 ounces (285 g) fresh Chinese noodles or linguine
- 1 tablespoon (15 ml) vegetable oil
- 2 medium-size eggplants (about 1½ lbs./680 g total), peeled and cut into ½-inch (1-cm) pieces (about 8 cups)
- 2 teaspoons minced fresh ginger
- 2 green onions, thinly sliced
- ½ cup (20 g) lightly packed cilantro leaves

1. To prepare sauce, in a large bowl, stir together hoisin sauce, vinegar, sugar, chili paste and sesame oil. Add tofu to sauce and stir gently to coat; set aside.

2. In a 5- to 6-quart (5- to 6-liter) pan, cook noodles in about 3 quarts (2.8 liters) boiling water until just tender to bite (3 to 5 minutes); or cook according to package directions. Drain well, transfer to a warm rimmed platter, and keep warm.

3. While noodles are cooking, heat vegetable oil in a wide nonstick frying pan or wok over medium-high heat. Add eggplant and ¼ cup (60 ml) water. Stir-fry until eggplant is soft and tinged with gold (8 to 10 minutes); add more water, 1 tablespoon (15 ml) at a time, if pan appears dry. Add ginger and stir-fry just until fragrant (about 30 seconds; do not scorch). Add tofu mixture and cook, stirring gently, until sauce boils and tofu is heated through (about 3 minutes). Remove from heat and stir in onions.

4. Spoon tofu mixture over noodles and sprinkle with cilantro.   *Makes 4 to 6 servings*

NUTRIENTS

Per serving: 476 calories (30% calories from fat), 16 g total fat, 2 g saturated fat, 54 mg cholesterol, 351 mg sodium, 62 g carbohydrates, 3 g fiber, 24 g protein, 251 mg calcium, 13 mg iron

Sautéed Tofu with Black Bean & Corn Salsa

Preparation time: **About 20 minutes**
Cooking time: **About 15 minutes**

Besides its memorable tangy-spicy-sweet flavor, this dish offers great contrasts of color and texture. Crisp red bell pepper and yellow corn are combined with smooth black beans, then topped with lightly seasoned tofu to make a tempting lunch or dinner.

- 1 pound (455 g) firm tofu, rinsed, drained, and cut into ½-inch (1-cm) cubes
- 1 teaspoon chili powder
- ¼ teaspoon salt
- ½ teaspoon grated lime peel
- 2 tablespoons (30 ml) lime juice
- 2 teaspoons honey
- ¾ teaspoon ground cumin

1   large onion, chopped

1   medium-size red bell pepper (about 6 oz./170 g), seeded and chopped

1   can (about 15 oz./430 g) black beans, drained and rinsed

1   package (about 10 oz./285 g) frozen corn kernels, thawed and drained

1   teaspoon olive oil

1   or 2 cloves garlic, minced or pressed

¼   cup (10 g) lightly packed cilantro leaves

Lime wedges

1. In a large bowl, gently mix tofu, chili powder, and salt; set aside. In a small bowl, stir together lime peel, lime juice, honey, and cumin; set aside.

2. In a wide nonstick frying pan or wok, combine onion, bell pepper, and ¼ cup (60 ml) water. Stir-fry over medium-high heat until onion is soft (about 5 minutes). Add beans, corn, and lime juice mixture; stir-fry gently until beans and corn are heated through (about 3 minutes). Remove bean mixture from pan and keep warm. Wipe pan clean (be careful; pan is hot).

3. Heat oil in pan over medium-high heat. When oil is hot, add tofu and garlic. Stir-fry gently until tofu is heated through (3 to 4 minutes); add water, 1 tablespoon (15 ml) at a time, if pan appears dry.

4. Divide bean mixture among 4 individual plates; top equally with tofu. Sprinkle with cilantro and offer lime wedges for squeezing to taste.

Makes 4 servings

NUTRIENTS

Per serving: 365 calories (28% calories from fat), 12 g total fat, 2 g saturated fat, 0 mg cholesterol, 220 mg sodium, 43 g carbohydrates, 6 g fiber, 27 g protein, 318 mg calcium, 14 mg iron

SWEET & SOUR TOFU

Preparation time: **About 15 minutes**
Cooking time: **About 25 minutes**

The taste-tempting, chile-spiked sweet-sour sauce we use on juicy pork chunks (see Sweet & Sour Pork, page 106) also works well with tender tofu and crunchy, quick-cooked red onion and bell pepper. Hot, fluffy rice is a must with this beautiful dish—it's essential for soaking up the sauce!

1 cup (185 g) long-grain white rice

¼ cup (60 ml) white wine vinegar or distilled white vinegar

4 teaspoons cornstarch

¼ cup (50 g) sugar

1 tablespoon (15 ml) catsup

1 tablespoon (15 ml) reduced-sodium soy sauce

⅛ teaspoon Hot Chile Oil (page 55) or purchased hot chili oil, or to taste

1 pound (455 g) firm tofu, rinsed, drained, and cut into ½-inch (1-cm) cubes

1 teaspoon paprika

1 or 2 cloves garlic, minced or pressed

¼ teaspoon salt

1 teaspoon vegetable oil

1 small red onion, cut into thin wedges

1 large green, red, or yellow bell pepper (about 8 oz./230 g), seeded and cut into 1-inch (2.5-cm) squares

1 medium-size tomato (about 6 oz./170 g), cut into thin wedges

1½ cups (235 g) fresh or canned pineapple chunks, drained

1. In a 3- to 4-quart (2.8- to 3.8-liter) pan, bring 2 cups (470 ml) water to a boil over high heat; stir in rice. Reduce heat, cover, and simmer until liquid has been absorbed and rice is tender to bite (about 20 minutes).

2. Meanwhile, to prepare sweet-sour sauce, in a medium-size bowl, stir together vinegar and cornstarch until blended. Then stir in ¾ cup (180 ml) water, sugar, catsup, soy sauce, and Hot Chile Oil. Set aside.

3. In a large bowl, gently mix tofu, paprika, garlic, and salt; set aside.

4. Heat oil in a wide nonstick frying pan or wok over medium-high heat. When oil is hot, add tofu and stir-fry gently until heated through (3 to 4 minutes). Add water, 1 tablespoon (15 ml) at a time, if pan appears dry. Remove tofu from pan with a slotted spoon; keep warm.

5. Add onion, bell pepper, and 2 tablespoons (30 ml) water to pan. Stir-fry for 1 minute; add water, 1 tablespoon (15 ml) at a time, if pan appears dry. Stir sweet-sour sauce well; pour into pan. Cook, stirring, until sauce boils and thickens slightly (2 to 3 minutes). Stir in tomato, pineapple, and tofu; stir gently just until heated through (about 2 minutes).

6. To serve, spoon rice onto a rimmed platter; top with sweet and sour tofu mixture.

Makes 4 servings

NUTRIENTS

Per serving: 482 calories (22% calories from fat), 12 g total fat, 2 g saturated fat, 0 mg cholesterol, 223 mg sodium, 75 g carbohydrates, 3 g fiber, 23 g protein, 273 mg calcium, 15 mg iron

SIDE DISHES

MEXICAN RICE

Preparation time: **About 10 minutes**
Cooking time: **About 35 minutes**

White rice seasoned with tomatoes and chiles is a superb accompaniment for Mexican-inspired entrées.

1   large can (about 28 oz./795 g) tomatoes

About 3 cups (710 ml) fat-free reduced sodium chicken broth

2   teaspoons butter or margarine

2   cups (370 g) long-grain white rice

1   large onion, chopped

2   cloves garlic, minced or pressed

1   small can (about 4 oz./115 g) diced green chiles

Salt and pepper

¼   cup (10 g) packed cilantro leaves

1. Drain liquid from tomatoes into a glass measure. Add enough of the broth to make 4 cups (950 ml) liquid. Set tomatoes and broth mixture aside.

2. Melt butter in a 4- to 6-quart (3.8- to 6-liter) pan over medium-high heat. Add rice and cook, stirring, until it begins to turn opaque (about 3 minutes). Add onion, garlic, chiles, and ¼ cup (60 ml) water; continue to cook, stirring, for 5 more minutes. Add more water, 1 tablespoon (15 ml) at a time, if pan appears dry.

3. Add tomatoes and broth mixture to pan. Bring to a boil over medium-high heat; then reduce heat, cover, and simmer until liquid has been absorbed and rice is tender to bite (about 25 minutes).

4. To serve, season to taste with salt and pepper; garnish with cilantro.

Makes 10 to 12 servings

NUTRIENTS

Per serving: 161 calories (10% calories from fat), 2 total fat, 0.7 g saturated fat, 2 mg cholesterol, 159 mg sodium, 33 g carbohydrates, 1 g fiber, 4 g protein, 39 mg calcium, 2 mg iron

20 MINUTES OR LESS

1 tablespoon (15 ml) vegetable oil

1 clove garlic, minced or pressed

½ teaspoon minced fresh ginger

½ cup (50 g) thinly sliced green onions

4 ounces (115 g) lean ground pork

8 fresh shiitake mushrooms (about 2 oz./55 g total), stems removed and caps thinly sliced

½ cup (75 g) frozen peas

½ cup (75 g) frozen corn kernels, thawed and drained

½ cup (120 ml) fat-free reduced-sodium chicken broth

2 tablespoons (30 ml) reduced-sodium soy sauce

3 cups (390 g) cooked, cooled long-grain white rice

PORK FRIED RICE

1. Heat oil in a wide nonstick frying pan or wok over medium-high heat. When oil is hot, add garlic, ginger, and onions; then crumble in pork. Stir-fry until pork is browned (about 5 minutes).

2. Add mushrooms, peas, corn, and ¼ cup (60 ml) of the broth to pan; stir-fry until liquid has evaporated (about 2 minutes). Add remaining ¼ cup (60 ml) broth; then stir in soy sauce and rice. Stir-fry until rice is heated through.

Makes 6 servings

Per serving: 234 calories (26% calories from fat), 7 g total fat, 2 g saturated fat, 14 mg cholesterol, 282 mg sodium, 35 g carbohydrates, 1 g fiber, 8 g protein, 25 mg calcium, 2 mg iron

LEMON-CAPER RICE

Preparation time: **About 5 minutes**
Cooking time: **About 25 minutes**

Tangy with lemon and vinegar, this easy-to-make side dish can be paired with any simply cooked main course. You might serve it with Herbed Pork Chops with Apples (page 104) or Hunter's-Style Lamb Stew (page 231), for example.

6 slices bacon

1 cup (200 g) short- or medium-grain rice

1 tablespoon grated lemon peel

2½ cups (590 ml) water

3 tablespoons drained capers

¼ cup (60 ml) seasoned rice vinegar (or ¼ cup/60 ml distilled white vinegar plus 1½ teaspoons sugar)

1. Cook bacon in a 2- to 3-quart (1.9- to 2.8-liter) pan over medium heat until crisp (about 5 minutes). Lift out, drain, crumble, and set aside. Discard all but 1 teaspoon of the drippings.

2. To pan, add rice, lemon peel, and water. Bring to a boil over high heat. Stir; then reduce heat, cover, and simmer until liquid has been absorbed and rice is tender to bite (about 20 minutes). Uncover; stir in crumbled bacon, capers, and vinegar.

Makes 6 to 8 servings

NUTRIENTS

Per serving: 145 calories (21% calories from fat), 3 g total fat, 1 g saturated fat, 5 mg cholesterol, 354 mg sodium, 24 g carbohydrates, 0.3 g fiber, 4 g protein, 3 mg calcium, 1 mg iron

PASTA PILAF

Preparation time: **About 15 minutes**
Cooking time: **About 20 minutes**

Serve this pasta dish with unadorned main dishes, such as roasted chicken, broiled fish steaks, or grilled meat.

1 tablespoon butter or margarine

1 large onion, finely chopped

1 clove garlic, minced or pressed

6 medium-size pear-shaped (Roma-type) tomatoes (about 12 oz./340 g total), peeled, seeded, and chopped

1 tablespoon chopped fresh basil or 1 teaspoon dried basil

8 ounces/230 g (about 1 cup) dried riso, stars, or other small pasta shape

¾ cup (110 g) frozen peas

½ cup (120 ml) half-and-half

½ cup (40 g) freshly grated Parmesan cheese

1. Melt butter in a wide nonstick frying pan over medium heat. Add onion and garlic. Cook, stirring occasionally, until onion is soft but not browned (about 5 minutes).

2. Add tomatoes, basil, and ¼ cup (60 ml) water; reduce heat, cover, and simmer for 10 minutes. Meanwhile, bring 8 cups (1.9 liters) water to a boil in a 4- to 5-quart (3.8- to 5-liter) pan over medium-high heat. Stir in pasta and cook just until tender to bite (8 to 10 minutes); or cook according to package directions. Drain well.

3. Add peas and half-and-half to pan with tomato mixture. Increase heat to high and bring to a boil; stir in pasta. Remove from heat and stir in ¼ cup (20 g) of the cheese. Transfer to a serving dish. Add remaining ¼ cup (20 g) cheese to taste.

Makes 4 to 6 servings

NUTRIENTS

Per serving: 305 calories (25% calories from fat), 9 g total fat, 5 g saturated fat, 21 mg cholesterol, 217 mg sodium, 45 g carbohydrates, 3 g fiber, 12 g protein, 169 mg calcium, 3 mg iron

GOLDEN CURRIED COUSCOUS

Preparation time: **About 15 minutes**
Cooking time: **5 to 10 minutes**

Studded with raisins, sprinkled with pistachios, and spiced with ginger and curry powder, this fluffy couscous will nicely complement pork, chicken, or lamb.

2¼ cups (530 ml) fat-free reduced-sodium chicken broth

¾ cup (110 g) golden raisins

6 tablespoons (90 ml) lemon juice

3 tablespoons finely chopped crystallized ginger

1 tablespoon margarine

¾ teaspoon curry powder

1½ cups (275 g) couscous

½ cup (60 g) thinly sliced celery

⅓ cup (35 g) thinly sliced green onions

3 tablespoons chopped cilantro

¼ cup (30 g) coarsely chopped salted roasted pistachio nuts

Cilantro sprigs

1. In a 2- to 3-quart (1.9- to 2.8-cm) pan, bring broth to a boil over high heat. Stir in raisins, lemon juice, ginger, margarine, curry powder, and couscous. Cover pan and remove from heat; let stand for 5 to 10 minutes. Fluff couscous with a fork. (At this point, you may cover and refrigerate; bring to room temperature before serving.)

2. Serve couscous warm or at room temperature. Just before serving, stir in celery, onions, and chopped cilantro. Mound couscous mixture in a serving dish; sprinkle with pistachio nuts and garnish with whole cilantro sprigs.

Makes 6 servings

NUTRIENTS

Per serving: 318 calories (14% calories from fat), 5 g total fat, 0.7 g saturated fat, 0 mg cholesterol, 330 mg sodium, 61 g carbohydrates, 3 g fiber, 8 g protein, 55 mg calcium, 3 mg iron

LEAN REFRIED BLACK BEANS

Preparation time: **About 15 minutes**
Cooking time: **About 30 minutes**

Deeply browned onions deglazed with chicken broth contribute to the robust flavor of this cumin-seasoned bean dish. You can prepare the beans up to 2 days ahead of time; to serve, simply heat and top with cheese and cilantro.

1 large onion, chopped

2 cloves garlic, minced or pressed

1½ cups (360 ml) fat-free reduced-sodium chicken broth

2 cans (about 15 oz./425 g each) black beans, drained and rinsed

½ teaspoon ground cumin

⅓ cup (43 g) packed feta cheese or *queso fresco* (available in Hispanic markets)

Cilantro sprigs

1. In a wide frying pan (preferably nonstick), combine onion, garlic, and ¾ cup (180 ml) of the broth. Cook over high heat, stirring occasionally, until liquid evaporates and onion begins to brown. To deglaze pan, add 2 to 3 tablespoons (30 to 45 ml) water and stir to loosen browned bits clinging to bottom of pan. Cook, stirring occasionally, until liquid evaporates and onion begins to brown again. Repeat deglazing step, using about 2 tablespoons (30 ml) water each time, until onion is richly browned.

2. Stir in remaining ¾ cup (180 ml) broth; stir to loosen browned bits clinging to bottom of pan. Add beans and cumin. Remove from heat and coarsely mash beans with a large spoon or a potato masher. (At this point, you may cover and refrigerate for up to 2 days.)

3. Bring bean mixture to a simmer over medium heat. Then simmer, stirring often, for about 15 minutes; beans should be thick enough to hold a fork upright (push beans into a mound to test). Spoon into a serving bowl; crumble cheese over top and garnish with cilantro sprigs.

Makes 6 servings

NUTRIENTS

Per serving: 120 calories (20% calories from fat), 3 g total fat, 1 g saturated fat, 6 mg cholesterol, 339 mg sodium, 17 g carbohydrates, 4 g fiber, 8 g protein, 78 mg calcium, 2 mg iron

CERVEZA BEANS

Preparation time: **About 5 minutes**
Cooking time: **About 20 minutes**

Spicy-sweet beans flavored with a hint of beer are just right with meat or poultry entrées. Consider serving them with Turkey Fajitas (page 100).

- 4 slices bacon, coarsely chopped
- 1 large onion, chopped
- 2 cans (about 15 oz./425 g each) pinto beans; or 4 cups cooked (about 2 cups/380 g dried) pinto beans
- 1 can (about 8 oz./230 g) tomato sauce
- ½ cup (120 ml) regular or nonalcoholic beer, or to taste
- 3 tablespoons (45 ml) molasses
- 1½ teaspoons dry mustard
- 1½ teaspoons Worcestershire sauce
- ¼ teaspoon pepper
  Salt

1. In a 3- to 4-quart (2.8- to 3.8-liter) pan, cook bacon and onion over medium heat, stirring often, until browned bits form on pan bottom and onion is soft (8 to 10 minutes). Discard any fat.

2. Drain beans, reserving ¼ cup (60 ml) of the liquid from cans. To pan, add beans and reserved liquid (if using home-cooked beans, use ¼ cup (60 ml) fat-free reduced-sodium chicken broth blended with ½ teaspoon cornstarch). Then stir in tomato sauce, ¼ cup (60 ml) of the beer, molasses, mustard, Worcestershire, and pepper. Bring to a boil; then reduce heat so beans boil gently. Cook, stirring occasionally, until flavors are blended, about 10 minutes. (At this point, you may let cool, then cover and refrigerate for up to 2 days; reheat before continuing.)

3. To serve, stir in remaining ¼ cup (60 ml) beer and season to taste with salt.

Makes 4 to 6 servings

NUTRIENTS

Per serving: 220 calories (14% calories from fat), 3 g total fat, 1 g saturated fat, 4 mg cholesterol, 870 mg sodium, 37 g carbohydrates, 7 g fiber, 10 g protein, 92 mg calcium, 3 mg iron

INDIAN POTATOES

Preparation time: **About 10 minutes**
Cooking time: **About 15 minutes**

Among the flavors of India found in this delicious side dish are cumin, chile, ground coriander, and fresh cilantro.

1¼   pounds (565 g) small red thin-skinned potatoes, scrubbed

2   tablespoons butter or margarine

1   medium-size red bell pepper (about 6 oz./170 g), seeded and cut into thin slivers

1   medium-size onion, cut into thin slivers

1   tablespoon ground cumin

1   teaspoon ground coriander

¼   teaspoon Hot Chile Oil (page 55) or purchased hot chili oil, or to taste

⅓   cup (15 g) chopped cilantro

½   cup (120 ml) nonfat sour cream

Cilantro sprigs

Salt

1. Cut potatoes crosswise into ¼-inch (6-mm) slices. Melt butter in a wide nonstick frying pan or wok over medium-high heat. Add potatoes, bell pepper, onion, cumin, coriander, Hot Chile Oil, and 3 tablespoons (45 ml) water. Stir-fry gently until potatoes are tinged with brown and tender when pierced (about 15 minutes; do not scorch). Add water, 1 tablespoon (15 ml) at a time, if pan appears dry.

2. Remove pan from heat. Sprinkle potato mixture with chopped cilantro and mix gently. Spoon into a serving bowl, top with sour cream, and garnish with cilantro sprigs. Add salt to taste.

Makes 4 servings

NUTRIENTS

Per serving: 220 calories (27% calories from fat), 7 g total fat, 4 g saturated fat, 16 mg cholesterol, 94 mg sodium, 34 g carbohydrates, 4 g fiber, 6 g protein, 67 mg calcium, 2 mg iron

POTATO RISOTTO

Preparation time: **About 10 minutes**
Cooking time: **About 35 minutes**

This rich-tasting dish has the creamy texture of the Italian rice specialty—but it's made with shredded potatoes, cooked gently in chicken broth and finished with evaporated skim milk and a touch of Parmesan cheese.

1   tablespoon margarine

1   small onion, finely chopped

½   teaspoon minced fresh thyme or ¼ teaspoon dried thyme

1   clove garlic, minced or pressed

1¾   cups (420 ml) fat-free reduced-sodium chicken broth

3   medium-size thin-skinned potatoes (about 1¼ lbs./565 g total)

¼   cup (60 ml) evaporated skim milk

¼   cup (20 g) grated Parmesan cheese

Freshly ground nutmeg

Thyme sprigs (optional)

1. Melt margarine in a 2- to 3-quart (1.9- to 2.8-liter) pan over medium heat. Add onion and minced thyme; cook, stirring often, until onion is soft but not browned (3 to 5 minutes). Stir in garlic, then add broth. Increase heat to high and bring mixture to a boil; boil until reduced to 1½ cups/360 ml (about 3 minutes).

2. Peel and shred potatoes. Add to onion mixture; reduce heat to medium-low and cook, uncovered, stirring often, until potatoes are tender to bite (about 25 minutes). Remove from heat and mix in milk and cheese. Season to taste with nutmeg. Spoon into a warm serving bowl; garnish with thyme sprigs, if desired.

Makes 4 to 6 servings

NUTRIENTS

Per serving: 147 calories (23% calories from fat), 4 g total fat, 1 g saturated fat, 4 mg cholesterol, 350 mg sodium, 23 g carbohydrates, 2 g fiber, 6 g protein, 100 mg calcium, 0.9 mg iron

ORANGE & RUM SWEET POTATOES

Preparation time: **About 10 minutes**
Cooking time: **About 20 minutes**

Simmered sweet potato slices in an orange-rum sauce make an easy, interesting side dish that's especially tasty with roast pork or chicken. You might serve the potatoes instead of bulgur with the Pork Tenderloin (page 104), accompanied by a dry white wine.

1 teaspoon vegetable oil

3 medium-size sweet potatoes (about 1¼ lbs./565 g total), peeled and cut into ¼-inch-thick (6-mm-thick) slices

¾ cup (160 ml) fat-free reduced-sodium chicken broth

½ cup (120 ml) orange juice

1 tablespoon (15 ml) rum

   About 2 teaspoons honey, or to taste

2 teaspoons cornstarch

⅛ teaspoon white pepper

   Salt

1 tablespoon minced parsley

1. Heat oil in a wide nonstick frying pan over medium-high heat. Add potatoes and ½ cup (120 ml) of the broth. Bring to a boil over medium-high heat; then reduce heat, cover, and simmer until potatoes are tender when pierced (about 10 minutes). Uncover and continue to cook, stirring occasionally, until liquid has evaporated and potatoes are tinged with brown (about 5 more minutes).

2. In a bowl, mix remaining ¼ cup (60 ml) broth, orange juice, rum, honey, cornstarch, and white pepper. Add cornstarch mixture to pan and bring to a boil over medium heat; boil, stirring, just until thickened. Season to taste with salt and sprinkle with parsley.   *Makes 4 servings*

NUTRIENTS

Per serving: 155 calories (11% calories from fat), 2 g total fat, 0.3 g saturated fat, 0 mg cholesterol, 35 mg sodium, 32 g carbohydrates, 3 g fiber, 2 g protein, 29 mg calcium, 0.7 mg iron

20 MINUTES OR LESS

6 medium-size ears corn (about 3 lbs./1.35 kg total), each about 8 inches (20 cm) long, husks and silk removed

½ cup (120 ml) distilled white vinegar

¼ cup (60 ml) lime juice

1 cup (170 g) minced onion

3 tablespoons sugar

1 small jar (about 2 oz./55 g) diced pimentos

1 teaspoon mustard seeds

¼ to ½ teaspoon crushed red pepper flakes

Salt and pepper

SEASONED SWEET CORN

1. With a sharp, heavy knife, cut corn crosswise into 1-inch (2.5-cm) rounds. In a large pan, bring 4 quarts (3.8 liters) water to a boil over high heat. Add corn, cover, and cook until hot (3 to 4 minutes). Drain corn well and pour into a shallow rimmed dish (about 9 by 13 inches/23 by 33 cm).

2. To prepare vinegar marinade, in a small pan, combine vinegar, lime juice, onion, sugar, pimentos, mustard seeds, and pepper flakes. Bring to a boil over high heat; then boil, stirring, just until sugar is dissolved. Use hot.

3. Pour hot marinade over corn; let stand, frequently spooning marinade over corn, until corn is cool enough to eat out of hand. Season to taste with salt and pepper.   *Makes 6 servings*

Per serving: 115 calories (9% calories from fat), 1g total fat, 0.1 g saturated fat, 0 mg cholesterol, 17 mg sodium, 27 g carbohydrates, 3 g fiber, 3 g protein, 12 mg calcium, 0.7 mg iron

SWEET POTATO STIR-FRY

Pictured on page 183
Preparation time: **About 15 minutes**
Cooking time: **About 15 minutes**

When you're choosing recipes for your holiday table, don't pass up this one. Diced sweet potatoes are stir-fried and sweetened with golden raisins, spices, and coconut; pomegranate seeds, stirred in at the last minute, provide a gleaming, jewel-bright accent.

3 large oranges (about 1¾ lbs./795 g total)

About 24 large spinach leaves (about 2 oz./55 g total), rinsed and crisped

½ cup (120 ml) fat-free reduced-sodium chicken broth or canned vegetable broth

½ cup (75 g) golden raisins

¼ cup (60 ml) orange juice

2 teaspoons honey

⅛ teaspoon ground cloves

⅛ teaspoon ground nutmeg

2 teaspoons vegetable oil

2 large sweet potatoes or yams (about 1 lb./455 g total), peeled and cut into ¼-inch (6-mm) cubes

¼ cup (20 g) sweetened shredded coconut

⅓ cup (55 g) pomegranate seeds

1. Cut off and discard peel and all white membrane from oranges; then cut fruit crosswise into thin slices. Cover and set aside. Arrange spinach leaves on a rimmed platter; cover and set aside. In a bowl, stir together broth, raisins, orange juice, honey, cloves, and nutmeg; set aside.

2. Heat oil in a wide nonstick frying pan or wok over medium-high heat. When oil is hot, add sweet potatoes and 2 tablespoons (30 ml) water; stir-fry until potatoes begin to brown and are just tender-crisp to bite (about 7 minutes). Add some water,

1 tablespoon (15 ml) at a time, if pan appears dry. Add broth mixture to pan; cover and cook until potatoes are just tender to bite (about 5 minutes). Uncover and stir-fry until liquid has evaporated. Remove pan from heat and stir in coconut and ¼ cup (40 g) of the pomegranate seeds.

3. Arrange orange slices over spinach leaves on platter. Spoon potato mixture over oranges; sprinkle with remaining pomegranate seeds.

Makes 4 servings

NUTRIENTS

Per serving: 284 calories (13% calories from fat), 4 g total fat, 2 g saturated fat, 0 mg cholesterol, 117 mg sodium, 61 g carbohydrates, 8 g fiber, 4 g protein, 108 mg calcium, 1 mg iron

CHEESE & APPLE HASH BROWNS

Preparation time: **About 25 minutes**
Cooking time: **About 20 minutes**

Hash browns? Yes, but not the standard kind. True, the potatoes are there—but so are apples, bell pepper, and cumin seeds. Sprinkled with Cheddar cheese, the dish is good alongside grilled Canadian bacon.

2 large Golden Delicious apples (about 1 lb./455 g total), peeled, cored, and finely chopped

1 tablespoon (15 ml) lemon juice

2 teaspoons butter or margarine

2 large russet potatoes (about 1 lb./455 g total), peeled and cut into ¼-inch (6-mm) cubes

1 medium-size onion, chopped

1 medium-size red bell pepper (about 6 oz./170 g), seeded and diced

½ teaspoon cumin seeds

¼ cup (15 g) chopped parsley

½ cup (55 g) shredded reduced-fat sharp Cheddar cheese

Salt and pepper

1. In a medium-size bowl, mix apples and lemon juice. Set aside; stir occasionally.

2. Melt butter in a wide nonstick frying pan or wok over medium heat. Add potatoes, onion, and bell pepper. Stir-fry until potatoes are tinged with brown and tender when pierced (about 15 minutes). Add water, 1 tablespoon (15 ml) at a time, if pan appears dry.

3. Stir in apples and cumin seeds; stir-fry until apples are tender to bite (about 5 minutes). Remove pan from heat and stir in parsley; then spoon potato mixture into a serving bowl. Sprinkle with cheese. Season to taste with salt and pepper.

Makes 4 to 6 servings

NUTRIENTS

Per serving: 178 calories (20% calories from fat), 4 g total fat, 2 g saturated fat, 12 mg cholesterol, 114 mg sodium, 31 g carbohydrates, 4 g fiber, 6 g protein, 119 mg calcium, 1 mg iron

VEGETABLE STIR-FRY WITH SOBA

Preparation time: **About 15 minutes**
Cooking time: **About 10 minutes**

Soft buckwheat noodles tossed with tender-crisp vegetables and topped with roasted cashews make a great complement to grilled pork tenderloin.

- 2 tablespoons (30 ml) oyster sauce
- 2 tablespoons (30 ml) reduced-sodium soy sauce
- 2 tablespoons (30 ml) lemon juice
- 1 teaspoon Oriental sesame oil
- 8 ounces (230 g) dried soba noodles or capellini
- 1 large red or green bell pepper (about 8 oz./230 g), seeded and cut into thin slivers

- ½ cup (60 g) thinly sliced celery
- ½ cup (50 g) thinly sliced green onions
- ½ cup (70 g) salted roasted cashews

1. To prepare sauce, in a small bowl, stir together oyster sauce, soy sauce, and lemon juice. Stir in sesame oil; set aside.

2. In a 4- to 5-quart (3.8- to 5-liter) pan, cook noodles in about 8 cups (1.9 liters) boiling water until just tender to bite (about 5 minutes for soba, about 3 minutes for capellini); or cook according to package directions. Drain well, transfer to a warm wide bowl, and keep warm.

3. In a wide nonstick frying pan or wok, combine bell pepper, celery, and ¼ cup (60 ml) water. Stir-fry over high heat until vegetables are tender-crisp to bite and liquid has evaporated (about 5 minutes). Stir sauce well and pour into pan; bring just to a boil. Pour vegetable mixture over noodles, then add onions and mix gently but thoroughly. Sprinkle with roasted cashews.

Makes 4 servings

NUTRIENTS

Per serving: 329 calories (24% calories from fat), 10 g total fat, 2 g saturated fat, 0 mg cholesterol, 1,225 mg sodium, 54 g carbohydrates, 5 g fiber, 13 g protein, 51 mg calcium, 3 mg iron

SAUTÉED MUSHROOMS WITH APPLE EAU DE VIE

Preparation time: **About 15 minutes**
Cooking time: **About 10 minutes**

Colorless, potent, and redolent of pure ripe fruit, eaux de vie are essentially brandies—but unlike brandies, they aren't aged. A tablespoon of apple eau de vie (or more, if you like) adds a subtle accent to this woodsy-tasting sauté of chanterelle and regular mushrooms. Don't forget the salt—just a pinch really helps bring out the flavors.

8 ounces (230 g) fresh chanterelle mushrooms

8 ounces (230 g) large regular mushrooms

1 teaspoon butter or margarine

4 cloves garlic, minced or pressed

1½ teaspoons chopped fresh thyme or ½ teaspoon dried thyme

About ⅛ teaspoon salt, or to taste

1 tablespoon (15 ml) apple eau de vie or apple brandy, or to taste

1 tablespoon (15 ml) cream sherry, or to taste

Thyme sprigs

Pepper

1. Rinse mushrooms and scrub gently, if needed; pat dry. Cut into ¼- to ½-inch-thick (6-mm- to 1-cm-thick) slices; set aside.

2. Melt butter in a wide nonstick frying pan or wok over medium-high heat. Add garlic and chopped thyme; stir-fry just until fragrant (about 30 seconds; do not scorch). Add mushrooms and ¼ cup (60 ml) water; stir-fry until mushrooms are soft and almost all liquid has evaporated (about 8 minutes). Then add salt and ¼ cup (60 ml) more water; stir-fry until liquid has evaporated (about 2 minutes). Add eau de vie and sherry; stir-fry

until liquid has evaporated. Spoon mushroom mixture into a serving bowl and garnish with thyme sprigs. Season to taste with pepper.

Makes 4 servings

NUTRIENTS

Per serving: 58 calories (23% calories from fat), 1 g total fat, 0.7 g saturated fat, 3 mg cholesterol, 84 mg sodium, 8 g carbohydrates, 2 g fiber, 3 g protein, 17 mg calcium, 2 mg iron

SIMPLY PERFECT EGGPLANT

Preparation time: **About 20 minutes**
Cooking time: **About 25 minutes**

Slices of slender, delicate-flavored Oriental (or Japanese) eggplant bake to tenderness with very little added oil—in fact, you can simply use an olive oil cooking spray.

Olive oil cooking spray

6 Oriental eggplants (1 to 1½ lbs./ 455 to 680 g total)

¼ cup (18 g) sun-dried tomatoes

2 teaspoons olive oil

1 small onion, finely chopped

8 ounces (230 g) mushrooms, finely chopped

1 small red bell pepper (about 5 oz./ 140 g), seeded and chopped

½ teaspoon dried oregano

½ teaspoon dried marjoram

2 cloves garlic, minced or pressed

Salt and pepper

Chopped parsley

1. Spray a shallow rimmed baking pan with cooking spray. Cut eggplants crosswise into ½-inch-thick (1-cm-thick) slices; arrange in a single layer in pan. Spray with cooking spray. Bake in a 425°F (220°C) oven until well browned and very soft when pressed (about 25 minutes).

2. Meanwhile, soak tomatoes in boiling water to cover until soft (about 15 minutes). Drain, discarding liquid; finely chop tomatoes.

3. Heat oil in a wide nonstick frying pan over medium heat. Add tomatoes, onion, mushrooms, bell pepper, oregano, marjoram, and garlic. Cook, stirring often, until mushrooms are lightly browned but mixture is still moist (10 to 15 minutes). Season to taste with salt and pepper.

4. To serve, transfer eggplant slices to a large warm serving platter; top with mushroom mixture and sprinkle with parsley.

Makes 4 to 6 servings

NUTRIENTS

Per serving: 88 calories (24% calories from fat), 3 g total fat, 0.3 g saturated fat, 0 mg cholesterol, 11 mg sodium, 15 g carbohydrates, 4 g fiber, 3 g protein, 55 mg calcium, 1 mg iron

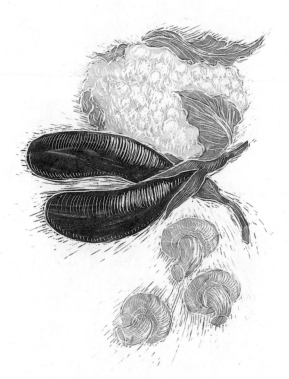

HERBED CAULIFLOWER & ZUCCHINI STIR-FRY

Preparation time: **About 15 minutes**
Cooking time: **About 10 minutes**

If you like cauliflower, zucchini, garlic, and basil, you'll enjoy this robust stir-fry; it's a good addition to a late-summer menu. Diced tomatoes offer a vibrant color contrast to the other vegetables.

- 2 teaspoons olive oil
- 1 large cauliflower (about 2 lbs./965 g) cut into flowerets
- 2 cloves garlic, minced or pressed
- 1 large onion, chopped
- 8 ounces (230 g) small zucchini, cut crosswise into 1/4-inch (6-mm) slices
- 1/3 cup (80 ml) dry white wine
- 3 medium-size firm-ripe pear-shaped (Roma-type) tomatoes (about 8 oz./230 g total), chopped
- 1 tablespoon chopped fresh basil

1. Heat oil in a wide nonstick frying pan or wok over medium-high heat. When oil is hot, add cauliflower, garlic, onion, and zucchini; stir-fry until zucchini is hot and bright in color (2 to 3 minutes).

2. Add wine, tomatoes, and basil to pan. Cover and cook until cauliflower is just tender to bite (about 4 minutes). Uncover and continue to cook until liquid has evaporated (2 to 3 more minutes).

Makes 4 servings

NUTRIENTS

Per serving: 93 calories (27% calories from fat), 3 g total fat, 0.4 g saturated fat, 0 mg cholesterol, 23 mg sodium, 13 g carbohydrates, 4 g fiber, 4 g protein, 56 mg calcium, 1 mg iron

TRICOLOR PEPPER SAUTÉ

Pictured on facing page
Preparation time: **About 15 minutes**
Cooking time: **About 25 minutes**

This colorful side dish is guaranteed to brighten up any menu. Simply spoon ginger-seasoned bell peppers over rice.

1   cup (185 g) long-grain white rice

1   to 2 teaspoons sesame seeds

3   medium-size bell peppers (1 to 1¼ lbs./455 to 565 g total); use 1 each red, yellow, and green bell pepper

1   teaspoon vegetable oil

1   small onion, cut into thin slivers

1   tablespoon minced fresh ginger

1   clove garlic, minced or pressed

1   cup (85 g) bean sprouts

2   teaspoons Oriental sesame oil

    Reduced-sodium soy sauce or salt

1. In a 3- to 4-quart (2.8- to 3.8-liter) pan, bring 2 cups (470 ml) water to a boil over high heat; stir in rice. Reduce heat, cover, and simmer until liquid has been absorbed and rice is tender to bite (about 20 minutes).

2. Meanwhile, in a wide nonstick frying pan or wok, stir sesame seeds over medium heat until golden (about 3 minutes). Pour from pan; set aside.

3. Seed bell peppers and cut into thin slivers, 2 to 3 inches (5 to 8 cm) long. Heat vegetable oil in pan over medium-high heat. When oil is hot, add onion, ginger, and garlic; stir-fry for 1 minute. Add peppers; stir-fry until tender-crisp to bite (about 3 minutes). Add bean sprouts and stir-fry until barely wilted (about 1 minute). Remove from heat and stir in sesame oil.

4. Spoon rice onto a rimmed platter; pour vegetable mixture over rice and sprinkle with sesame seeds. Offer soy sauce to add to taste.

Makes 4 servings

NUTRIENTS

Per serving: 253 calories (16% calories from fat), 5 g total fat, 0.7 g saturated fat, 0 mg cholesterol, 7 mg sodium, 48 g carbohydrates, 3 g fiber, 5 g protein, 43 mg calcium, 3 mg iron

ASPARAGUS SAUTÉ

Preparation time: **About 15 minutes**
Cooking time: **About 10 minutes**

Mandarin oranges add a sweet and surprising accent to this springtime special. Try fresh clementines, a variety of mandarin available in the fall to early winter.

1½   pounds (680 g) asparagus

2   teaspoons olive oil

8   ounces (230 g) mushrooms, thinly sliced

1   clove garlic, minced or pressed

⅓   cup (80 ml) dry white wine

1   tablespoon grated orange peel

⅛   teaspoon crushed red pepper flakes

¼   teaspoon dried tarragon

½   cup (75 g) drained canned mandarin oranges or fresh orange segments

1. Snap off and discard tough ends of asparagus. Cut spears into 1-inch (2.5-cm) diagonal slices.

2. Heat oil in a wide nonstick frying pan or wok over medium-high heat. When oil is hot, add asparagus, mushrooms, and garlic; stir-fry until asparagus is hot and bright green (about 3 minutes).

3. Add wine, orange peel, red pepper flakes, and tarragon. Cover and cook until asparagus is just tender-crisp to bite (about 3 minutes). Uncover and continue to cook until liquid has evaporated (1 to 2 more minutes). Stir in oranges.

Makes 4 servings

NUTRIENTS

Per serving: 90 calories (27% calories from fat), 3 g total fat, 0.4 g saturated fat, 0 mg cholesterol, 7 mg sodium, 12 g carbohydrates, 2 g fiber, 4 g protein, 32 mg calcium, 2 mg iron

Tricolor Pepper Sauté (recipe on facing page)

Mediterranean Squash (recipe on page 190)

SWEET POTATO STIR-FRY (RECIPE ON PAGE 176)

CURRY-GLAZED CARROTS (RECIPE ON FACING PAGE)

CURRY-GLAZED CARROTS

Pictured on facing page
Preparation time: **About 20 minutes**
Cooking time: **About 10 minutes**

These thin-sliced carrots, glazed with orange juice, maple syrup, and curry, are a marvelous choice with fish or chicken. Quick cooking preserves their sweetness.

   1   tablespoon grated orange peel

   ¾   cup (180 ml) orange juice

   2   tablespoons (30 ml) maple syrup

   2   teaspoons cornstarch blended with 2 tablespoons (30 ml) cold water

   1   teaspoon curry powder

1¼   pounds (565 g) carrots, cut diagonally into ¼-inch (6-mm) slices

   2   tablespoons minced parsley

        Salt and pepper

1. In a bowl, stir together orange peel, orange juice, syrup, and cornstarch mixture; set aside.

2. In a wide nonstick frying pan or wok, stir curry powder over medium-high heat just until fragrant (about 30 seconds; do not scorch). Add carrots and ⅓ cup (80 ml) water. Cover and cook just until carrots are tender when pierced (about 4 minutes). Uncover and stir-fry until liquid has evaporated.

3. Stir orange juice mixture well; then pour into pan and cook, stirring, until sauce boils and thickens slightly.

4. Pour carrots and sauce into a serving bowl and sprinkle with parsley. Season with salt and pepper.
Makes 4 servings

NUTRIENTS

Per serving: 117 calories (3% calories from fat), 0.4 g total fat, 0 g saturated fat, 0 mg cholesterol, 52 mg sodium, 28 g carbohydrates, 5 g fiber, 2 g protein, 56 mg calcium, 1 mg iron

COCOA-GLAZED CARROTS & ONIONS

Preparation time: About 15 minutes
Cooking time: 20 to 30 minutes

In Mexico, chocolate isn't just for desserts—it's used in savory dishes, too. Here, a small amount of unsweetened cocoa powder brings mellow, complex flavor to a sauce for baby carrots and pearl onions. Be sure to use unsweetened cocoa powder, not a cocoa mix.

10 ounces (285 g) fresh pearl onions (each about 1 inch/2.5 cm) in diameter); or 1 package (about 10 oz./285 g) frozen pearl onions

1½ pounds (680 g) baby or small carrots, peeled

1 tablespoon butter or margarine

2 tablespoons (30 ml) lemon juice

1 tablespoon (15 ml) honey

1 tablespoon unsweetened cocoa powder

1 teaspoon grated fresh ginger

1. If using fresh onions, place them in a bowl and cover with boiling water. Let stand for 2 to 3 minutes. Drain; then pull or slip off skins and discard them. Also trim root and stem ends of onions.

2. Place peeled fresh onions or frozen onions in a wide nonstick frying pan. Barely cover with water and bring to a boil over high heat. Reduce heat, cover, and simmer gently until onions are tender when pierced (10 to 15 minutes). Drain onions, pour out of pan, and set aside.

3. If using baby carrots, leave whole; if using small carrots, cut diagonally into ¼-inch-thick (6-mm-thick) slices. Place carrots in pan used for onions, barely cover with water, and bring to a boil over high heat. Reduce heat, cover, and simmer gently until carrots are just tender when pierced (7 to 10 minutes). Drain carrots and set aside.

4. In pan, combine butter, lemon juice, 1 tablespoon water, honey, cocoa, and ginger. Stir over medium-high heat until smooth. Add carrots and onions. Stir over high heat until sauce is thick enough to cling to vegetables (2 to 3 minutes).

Makes 6 servings

NUTRIENTS

Per serving: 91 calories (20% calories from fat), 2 g total fat, 1 g saturated fat, 5 mg cholesterol, 61 mg sodium, 18 g carbohydrates, 4 g fiber, 2 g protein, 47 mg calcium, 0.8 mg iron

---

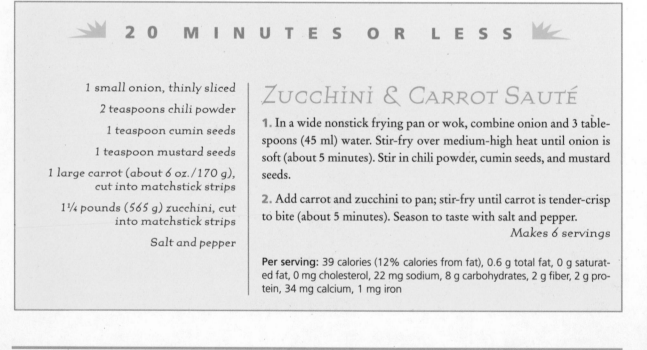

20 MINUTES OR LESS

1 small onion, thinly sliced

2 teaspoons chili powder

1 teaspoon cumin seeds

1 teaspoon mustard seeds

1 large carrot (about 6 oz./170 g), cut into matchstick strips

1¼ pounds (565 g) zucchini, cut into matchstick strips

Salt and pepper

ZUCCHINI & CARROT SAUTÉ

1. In a wide nonstick frying pan or wok, combine onion and 3 tablespoons (45 ml) water. Stir-fry over medium-high heat until onion is soft (about 5 minutes). Stir in chili powder, cumin seeds, and mustard seeds.

2. Add carrot and zucchini to pan; stir-fry until carrot is tender-crisp to bite (about 5 minutes). Season to taste with salt and pepper.

Makes 6 servings

Per serving: 39 calories (12% calories from fat), 0.6 g total fat, 0 g saturated fat, 0 mg cholesterol, 22 mg sodium, 8 g carbohydrates, 2 g fiber, 2 g protein, 34 mg calcium, 1 mg iron

Stir-Fried Spinach with Feta

Preparation time: **About 15 minutes**
Cooking time: **About 10 minutes**

Fresh dill imparts a mild tartness to this attractive side dish. Feta cheese and capers provide zing without a lot of fat.

½ cup (50 g) thinly sliced green onions

1 clove garlic, minced or pressed

1½ teaspoons chopped fresh dill

2 medium-size firm-ripe pear-shaped (Roma-type) tomatoes (about 6 oz./170 g total), chopped

1¼ pounds (565 g) spinach, stems removed, leaves rinsed and drained

3 to 4 tablespoons (25 to 35 g) crumbled feta cheese

1 tablespoon drained capers, or to taste
Pepper

1. In a wide nonstick frying pan, combine onions, garlic, dill, and ¼ cup (60 ml) water. Stir-fry over medium-high heat until onions are soft and almost all liquid has evaporated (about 3 minutes). Transfer to a bowl and stir in tomatoes. Keep warm.

2. Add half the spinach and 1 tablespoon (15 ml) water to pan; stir-fry over medium heat until spinach is just beginning to wilt. Then add remaining spinach; stir-fry just until all spinach is wilted (about 2 more minutes).

3. With a slotted spoon, transfer spinach to a platter and spread out; discard liquid from pan. Top spinach with tomato mixture, then sprinkle with cheese and capers. Season to taste with pepper.

Makes 4 to 6 servings

NUTRIENTS

Per serving: 44 calories (29% calories from fat), 2 g total fat, 0.9 g saturated fat, 5 mg cholesterol, 179 mg sodium, 5 g carbohydrates, 3 g fiber, 4 g protein, 122 mg calcium, 3 mg iron

Sautéed Kale with Cannellini

Preparation time: **About 10 minutes**
Cooking time: **About 20 minutes**

Beautiful, ruffly, bursting with vitamins— once it catches your eye in the produce department, kale can be impossible to resist. But what can you do with it once you've brought it home? We suggest stir-frying the sliced leaves in a small amount of bacon drippings, then serving them with mild cannellini beans to make a robust side dish.

1¼ pounds (565 g) kale

4 slices bacon, chopped

2 large onions, thinly sliced

2 cans (about 15 oz./430 g each) cannellini (white kidney beans), drained and rinsed
Salt and pepper

1. Remove and discard tough stems from kale; then rinse kale, drain, and cut crosswise into ½-inch (1-cm) strips. Set aside.

2. In a wide nonstick frying pan or wok, stir-fry bacon over medium-high heat until crisp (about 3 minutes). Remove from pan with a slotted spoon and set aside. Add onions to drippings in pan and stir-fry until soft (about 5 minutes). Add kale and stir-fry until wilted and bright green (3 to 4 minutes). Transfer to a platter and keep warm.

3. Add beans to pan, reduce heat to medium-low, and stir until heated through (about 4 minutes). Spoon beans over kale; sprinkle beans and kale with bacon. Season to taste with salt and pepper.

Makes 6 servings

NUTRIENTS

Per serving: 190 calories (19% calories from fat), 4 g total fat, 1 g saturated fat, 4 mg cholesterol, 276 mg sodium, 28 g carbohydrates, 11 g fiber, 11 g protein, 125 mg calcium, 3 mg iron

ITALIAN-STYLE SWISS CHARD

Preparation time: **About 15 minutes**
Cooking time: **About 8 minutes**

Balsamic vinegar livens up this simple stir-fry. You can make the dish with red or green Swiss chard; or try a combination of both types.

2½ pounds (1.15 kg) Swiss chard
2 teaspoons olive oil
2 cloves garlic, minced or pressed
2 tablespoons (30 ml) balsamic vinegar
1 tablespoon drained capers

1. Trim and discard discolored stem ends from chard; then rinse and drain chard. Thinly slice chard stems crosswise up to base of leaves; set aside. Use a few whole leaves to line a large platter; cover and set aside. Coarsely chop remaining leaves.

2. Heat oil in a wide nonstick frying pan or wok over medium-high heat. When oil is hot, add garlic and chard stems. Stir-fry until stems are soft (about 2 minutes). Add half the chopped chard leaves to pan, cover, and cook for 2 minutes. Add remaining leaves, cover, and cook until all leaves are wilted (about 2 more minutes). Uncover pan and stir in vinegar and capers; then spoon mixture over whole chard leaves on platter.

Makes 6 servings

NUTRIENTS

Per serving: 51 calories (28% calories from fat), 2 g total fat, 0.2 g saturated fat, 0 mg cholesterol, 440 mg sodium, 8 g carbohydrates, 3 g fiber, 3 g protein, 98 mg calcium, 3 mg iron

ALMOND & ZUCCHINI STIR-FRY

Preparation time: **About 10 minutes**
Cooking time: **About 25 minutes**

If you have a vegetable garden, you probably plant zucchini. And if you do, there's a time—usually at the height of summer—when you're longing for new ways to serve this prolific squash. Here's one delicious choice: a combination of rice and julienned zucchini, seasoned with soy and topped with almonds.

1 cup (185 g) long-grain white rice
½ cup (60 g) slivered almonds
6 large zucchini (about 2 lbs./905 g total), cut into ¼- by 2-inch (6-mm by 5-cm) sticks
2 cloves garlic, minced or pressed
   About 2 tablespoons (30 ml) reduced-sodium soy sauce

1. In a 3- to 4-quart (2.8- to 3.8-liter) pan, bring 2 cups (470 ml) water to a boil over high heat; stir in rice. Reduce heat, cover, and simmer until liquid has been absorbed and rice is tender to bite (about 20 minutes).

2. Meanwhile, in a wide nonstick frying pan or wok, stir almonds over medium heat until golden (4 to 5 minutes). Pour out of pan and set aside. To pan, add zucchini, garlic, and 2 tablespoons (30 ml) water. Increase heat to medium-high; stir-fry until zucchini is tender-crisp to bite and liquid has evaporated (about 9 minutes). Add 2 tablespoons (30 ml) of the soy sauce; mix gently.

3. To serve, spoon rice into a large bowl and pour zucchini on top of it; sprinkle with almonds. Offer more soy sauce to add to taste.

Makes 6 servings

NUTRIENTS

Per serving: 205 calories (27% calories from fat), 6 g total fat, 0.6 g saturated fat, 0 mg cholesterol, 207 mg sodium, 32 g carbohydrates, 2 g fiber, 7 g protein, 64 mg calcium, 2 mg iron

ASIAN-STYLE GREEN BEANS

Preparation time: **About 20 minutes**
Cooking time: **About 15 minutes**

Cooking green beans with mushrooms is not new, but this dish surprises with its seasonings and topping of peanuts.

1 medium-size onion, chopped

8 ounces (230 g) mushrooms, sliced

1 medium-size red bell pepper, cut into ¼-inch-wide (6-mm-wide) strips

1 clove garlic, minced or pressed

3 tablespoons (45 ml) reduced-sodium soy sauce

1 tablespoon (15 ml) honey

1 pound (455 g) slender green beans

¼ cup (36 g) salted roasted peanuts, chopped

1. In a wide nonstick frying pan or wok, combine onion, mushrooms, bell pepper, garlic, and ¼ cup (60 ml) water. Stir-fry over medium-high heat until mushrooms are soft and almost all liquid has evaporated (about 10 minutes). Add water, 1 tablespoon (15 ml) at a time, if pan appears to be dry.

2. Stir soy sauce and honey into mushroom mixture; then transfer to a bowl and keep warm. Wipe pan clean (be careful; pan is hot).

3. To pan, add beans and ⅓ cup (80 ml) water. Cover and cook over medium-high heat just until beans are tender to bite (about 3 minutes). Uncover and stir-fry until liquid has evaporated.

4. Arrange beans on a rimmed serving platter; spoon mushroom mixture over beans and then sprinkle with roasted peanuts.

Makes 4 to 6 servings

NUTRIENTS

Per serving: 118 calories (27% calories from fat), 4 g total fat, 0.5 g saturated fat, 0 mg cholesterol, 400 mg sodium, 18 g carbohydrates, 4 g fiber, 6 g protein, 51 mg calcium, 2 mg iron

20 MINUTES OR LESS

¼ to ½ ounce (8 to 15 g) prosciutto or bacon, chopped

1 or 2 cloves garlic, minced or pressed

1½ teaspoons chopped fresh rosemary or ½ teaspoon dried rosemary

1 pound (455 g) slender green beans, ends removed

About ⅛ teaspoon salt, or to taste

Rosemary sprigs

Pepper

GARLIC & ROSEMARY GREEN BEANS

1. In a wide nonstick frying pan or wok, stir-fry prosciutto over medium-high heat just until crisp (about 1 minute). Remove from pan with a slotted spoon and set aside.

2. Add garlic, chopped rosemary, and 2 tablespoons (30 ml) water to pan. Stir-fry just until garlic is fragrant (about 30 seconds; do not scorch). Add beans, ⅓ cup (80 ml) water, and salt. Cover and cook just until beans are tender to bite (about 3 minutes). Uncover and stir-fry until liquid has evaporated.

3. Arrange beans on a rimmed platter, sprinkle with prosciutto, and garnish with rosemary sprigs. Season to taste with pepper.

Makes 4 servings

Per serving: 39 calories (10% calories from fat), 0.5 g total fat, 0.1 g saturated fat, 2 mg cholesterol, 125 mg sodium, 8 g carbohydrates, 2 g fiber, 3 g protein, 40 mg calcium, 1 mg iron

MEDITERRANEAN SQUASH

Pictured on page 182
Preparation time: **About 25 minutes**
Cooking time: **About 20 minutes**

Bright, cheery, and as bountiful as a summer garden, this handsome dish offers a tempting taste of the Mediterranean. It's seasoned with thyme and plenty of lemon juice.

2 teaspoons olive oil

1 large onion, chopped

1 pound (455 g) mushrooms, thinly sliced

1½ pounds (680 g) yellow crookneck squash or yellow zucchini, cut crosswise into ¼-inch (6-mm) slices

1½ tablespoons fresh thyme leaves or 1½ teaspoons dried thyme

3 tablespoons (45 ml) lemon juice

6 medium-size firm-ripe pear-shaped (Roma-type) tomatoes (about 1 lb./455 g total), cut crosswise into ¼-inch (6-mm) slices

½ cup (50 g) thinly sliced green onions

1 ounce (30 g) feta cheese, crumbled

2 oil-cured black olives, pitted and chopped

1. Heat 1 teaspoon of the oil in a wide nonstick frying pan or wok over medium-high heat. When oil is hot, add half each of the chopped onion, mushrooms, squash, and thyme. Stir-fry until squash is hot and bright in color (about 3 minutes).

2. Add ¼ cup (60 ml) water and 1½ tablespoons (23 ml) of the lemon juice to pan; cover and cook until vegetables are just tender to bite (about 3 minutes). Uncover and continue to cook, stirring, until liquid has evaporated (about 3 more minutes). Remove vegetables from pan and set aside.

3. Repeat to cook remaining chopped onion, mushrooms, squash, and thyme, using remaining 1 teaspoon oil; add ¼ cup (60 ml) water and

remaining 1½ tablespoons (23 ml) lemon juice after the first 3 minutes of cooking.

4. Return all cooked vegetables to pan; gently stir in tomatoes. Transfer vegetables to a serving dish; sprinkle with green onions, cheese, and olives.

Makes 8 servings

NUTRIENTS

Per serving: 78 calories (28% calories from fat), 3 g total fat, 0.8 g saturated fat, 3 mg cholesterol, 72 mg sodium, 12 g carbohydrates, 3 g fiber, 3 g protein, 57 mg calcium, 2 mg iron

SNOW PEAS WITH BACON & MINT

Preparation time: **About 15 minutes**
Cooking time: **About 10 minutes**

A lovely and refreshing choice for a family meal, this emerald-green dish combines sweet snow peas with a light, tart vinegar sauce and a sprinkling of smoky bacon. Be sure to serve it at once; upon standing, the pea pods will lose their bright color.

¼ cup (60 ml) fat-free reduced-sodium chicken broth

¼ cup (60 ml) distilled white vinegar

2 teaspoons sugar

1 teaspoon cornstarch

2 thick slices bacon, finely chopped

1 pound (455 g) fresh Chinese pea pods (also called snow or sugar peas), ends and strings removed; or 3 packages (about 6 oz./170 g each) frozen Chinese pea pods, thawed and drained

1 tablespoon chopped fresh mint

Mint sprigs

1. In a small bowl, stir together broth, vinegar, sugar, and cornstarch; set aside.

2. In a wide nonstick frying pan or wok, stir-fry bacon over medium-high heat until browned and crisp (about 3 minutes). Remove bacon from pan with a slotted spoon and set aside. Pour off and discard drippings from pan. Wipe pan clean (be careful; pan is hot).

3. Add pea pods and ⅓ cup (80 ml) water to pan. Cover and cook over medium-high heat until pea pods are tender-crisp to bite (about 1 minute for fresh pea pods, about 30 seconds for frozen). Uncover and stir-fry until liquid has evaporated. Transfer to a rimmed platter and keep warm.

4. Stir broth mixture and pour into pan. Bring to a boil over high heat; boil, stirring, until slightly thickened. Remove from heat and stir in chopped mint. Pour sauce over pea pods, sprinkle with bacon, and garnish with mint sprigs.

Makes 4 to 6 servings

NUTRIENTS

Per serving: 73 calories (27% calories from fat), 2 g total fat, 0.8 g saturated fat, 4 mg cholesterol, 104 mg sodium, 10 g carbohydrates, 2 g fiber, 4 g protein, 40 mg calcium, 2 mg iron

BROCCOLI & BELL PEPPER WITH COUSCOUS

Preparation time: **About 15 minutes**
Cooking time: **About 15 minutes**

Universally lauded by nutritionists, broccoli is a popular choice at the dinner table these days. In this quick dish, the bright, tender flowerets are teamed with bell pepper and served over couscous.

1½ cups (360 ml) fat-free reduced-sodium chicken broth or canned vegetable broth

¼ to ½ teaspoon dried oregano

1 cup (185 g) couscous

1 tablespoon pine nuts or slivered almonds

4 cups (285 g) broccoli flowerets

1 teaspoon olive oil or vegetable oil

1 small red bell pepper (about 4 oz./ 115 g), seeded and cut into thin slivers

2 tablespoons (30 ml) balsamic vinegar

1. In a 3- to 4-quart (2.8- to 3.8-liter) pan, combine broth and oregano. Bring to a boil over high heat; stir in couscous. Cover, remove from heat, and let stand until liquid has been absorbed (about 5 minutes). Transfer couscous to a rimmed platter and keep warm; fluff occasionally with a fork.

2. While couscous is standing, stir pine nuts in a wide nonstick frying pan or wok over medium-low heat until golden (2 to 4 minutes). Pour out of pan and set aside. To pan, add broccoli and ¼ cup (60 ml) water. Cover and cook over medium-high heat until broccoli is tender-crisp to bite (about 5 minutes). Uncover and stir-fry until liquid has evaporated. Spoon broccoli over couscous and keep warm.

3. Heat oil in pan. When oil is hot, add bell pepper and stir-fry until just tender-crisp to bite (2 to 3 minutes). Add vinegar and remove from heat; stir to scrape any browned bits from pan bottom. Immediately pour pepper mixture over broccoli and couscous; sprinkle with pine nuts and serve.

Makes 4 servings

NUTRIENTS

Per serving: 248 calories (10% calories from fat), 3 g total fat, 0.4 g saturated fat, 0 mg cholesterol, 278 mg sodium, 45 g carbohydrates, 7 g fiber, 12 g protein, 72 mg calcium, 2 mg iron

BROCCOLI WITH RICE & PINE NUTS

Preparation time: **About 5 minutes**
Cooking time: **About 30 minutes**

Golden raisins and chili powder enhance this appealing mixture of white rice and tender broccoli.

¼ cup (35 g) pine nuts or slivered almonds

2 teaspoons olive oil or vegetable oil

⅔ cup (124 g) long-grain white rice

⅓ cup (50 g) golden raisins

2 teaspoons chili powder

2 vegetable bouillon cubes dissolved in 2½ cups (590 ml) hot water

1¼ pounds (565 g) broccoli

1. Toast pine nuts in a wide nonstick frying pan over medium-low heat until lightly browned (about 3 minutes), stirring. Remove from pan and set aside.

2. In same pan, heat oil over medium-high heat. Add rice, raisins, and chili powder. Cook, stirring, until rice begins to turn opaque (about 3 minutes). Stir in bouillon mixture; reduce heat, cover tightly, and simmer for 15 minutes.

3. Meanwhile, cut off and discard tough ends of broccoli stalks. Cut off flowerets in bite-size pieces and set aside. Thinly slice remainder of stalks.

4. Distribute broccoli flowerets and sliced stalks over rice mixture. Cover and continue to cook until broccoli is just tender to bite (7 to 10 more minutes). Mix gently, transfer to a warm serving platter, and sprinkle with pine nuts.

Makes 4 servings

NUTRIENTS

Per serving: 247 calories (26% calories from fat), 8 g total fat, 1 g saturated fat, 0 mg cholesterol, 499 mg sodium, 41 g carbohydrates, 5 g fiber, 8 g protein, 62 mg calcium, 3 mg iron

ROASTED GARLIC & BROCCOLI

Preparation time: **About 15 minutes**
Cooking time: **About 20 minutes**

Serve this combination of sweet roasted garlic and tender-crisp broccoli in a light sesame dressing as a fitting complement to turkey or pork dishes.

3 large heads garlic (about 12 oz./340 g total)

2 teaspoons olive oil

About 1¼ pounds/565 g (about 9 cups) broccoli flowerets

2 tablespoons (30 ml) reduced-sodium soy sauce

1 teaspoon Oriental sesame oil

1. Separate garlic heads into cloves; then peel cloves and place in a lightly oiled 8- to 10-inch-square (20- to 25-cm-square) baking pan. Mix in olive oil. Bake in a 475°F (245°C) oven just until garlic is tinged with brown; do not scorch (about 20 minutes; remove smaller cloves as they brown, if needed). Set aside.

2. While garlic is roasting, in a 5- to 6-quart (5- to 6-liter) pan, bring 3 to 4 quarts (2.8 to 3.8 liters) water to a boil over high heat. Add broccoli and cook until tender-crisp to bite (about 5 minutes). Drain, immerse in ice water until cool, and drain again.

3. In a shallow bowl, mix soy sauce and sesame oil. Add garlic and broccoli; toss gently to mix.

Makes 6 servings

NUTRIENTS

Per serving: 123 calories (18% calories from fat), 3 g total fat, 0.3 g saturated fat, 0 mg cholesterol, 229 mg sodium, 22 g carbohydrates, 4 g fiber, 6 g protein, 127 mg calcium, 2 mg iron

Desserts

Molasses Sugar Cookies

Preparation time: **About 25 minutes**
Cooking time: **About 7 minutes**

Soft, spicy molasses sugar cookies are family favorites all year round. Serve the cookies with cold milk or cider.

2   cups (250 g) all-purpose flour

1½ teaspoons baking powder

1   teaspoon ground ginger

1   teaspoon ground cinnamon

½   teaspoon salt

¼   teaspoon baking soda

½   cup (4 oz./115 g) butter or margarine, at room temperature

½   cup (110 g) firmly packed brown sugar

2   large egg whites

½   cup (120 ml) molasses

2   teaspoons instant espresso powder or coffee powder

    About ⅔ cup (93 g) sugar cubes, coarsely crushed

    About ¼ cup (50 g) granulated sugar

1. In a medium-size bowl, stir together flour, baking powder, ginger, cinnamon, salt, and baking soda; set aside.

2. In a food processor or a large bowl, combine butter, brown sugar, egg whites, molasses, instant espresso powder, and ½ cup (120 ml) water. Whirl or beat with an electric mixer until smooth. Add flour mixture to butter mixture; whirl or beat until dry ingredients are evenly moistened.

3. Spoon rounded 1-tablespoon (15-ml) portions of dough onto lightly greased large nonstick or regular baking sheets, spacing cookies about 2 inches (5 cm) apart.

4. Bake in a 350°F (175°C) oven for 5 minutes. Remove from oven. Working quickly, sprinkle each cookie with about ¾ teaspoon of the crushed

sugar cubes; press in lightly. Return cookies to oven and bake until firm to the touch (about 2 more minutes). Let cookies cool on baking sheets for about 3 minutes. Transfer to racks, sprinkle with granulated sugar, and cool completely.

Makes about 3 dozen cookies

NUTRIENTS

Per cookie: 93 calories (25% calories from fat), 3 g total fat, 2 g saturated fat, 7 mg cholesterol, 91 mg sodium, 17 g carbohydrates, 0.2 g fiber, 0.9 g protein, 26 mg calcium, 0.6 mg iron

Cream Cheese Blond Brownies

Preparation time: **About 15 minutes**
Cooking time: **About 25 minutes**

A swirl of cream cheese enriches these golden brownies. Be sure to buy the nonfat variety of cream cheese.

1   large package (about 8 oz./230 g) nonfat cream cheese, at room temperature

½   cup (100 g) granulated sugar

2   large egg whites

¼   cup (60 ml) nonfat sour cream

1¼ cups (155 g) plus 1 tablespoon all-purpose flour

1   tablespoon (15 ml) vanilla

1   teaspoon baking powder

¼   cup (31 g) chopped walnuts

⅓   cup (80 ml) pure maple syrup

⅓   cup (73 g) firmly packed brown sugar

⅓   cup (76 g) butter or margarine, at room temperature

1   large egg

1. In a small bowl, combine cream cheese, granulated sugar, egg whites, sour cream, 1 tablespoon of the flour, and 1 teaspoon of the vanilla. Beat until smooth; set aside. In another small bowl, stir together remaining 1¼ cups (155 g) flour, baking powder, and walnuts; set aside.

2. In a large bowl, combine syrup, brown sugar, butter, egg, and remaining 2 teaspoons vanilla. Beat until smooth. Add flour mixture; beat until dry ingredients are evenly moistened.

3. Pour two-thirds of the brownie batter into a lightly greased 8-inch-square (20-cm-square) nonstick or regular baking pan; spread to make level. Pour cheese mixture evenly over batter. Drop remaining batter by spoonfuls over cheese mixture; swirl with a knife to blend batter slightly with cheese mixture.

4. Bake in a 350°F (175°C) oven until a wooden pick inserted in center comes out clean (about 25 minutes; pierce brownie, not cheese mixture). Let cool in pan on a rack, then cut into 2-inch (5-cm) squares. *Makes 16 brownies*

NUTRIENTS

Per brownie: 168 calories (30% calories from fat), 6 g total fat, 3 g saturated fat, 25 mg cholesterol, 153 mg sodium, 25 g carbohydrates, 0.4 g fiber, 4 g protein, 76 mg calcium, 0.7 mg iron

ORANGE & COCOA COOKIES

Preparation time: **About 30 minutes**
Cooking time: **About 15 minutes**

To conclude a spicy meal on a sweet note, offer soft cookies filled with orange marmalade and drizzled with a cocoa glaze.

1½ cups all-purpose flour
 1 teaspoon baking powder
 ¼ teaspoon salt
 ⅛ teaspoon ground cloves
 2 tablespoons (30 g) butter or margarine, at room temperature
 ¼ cup (60 ml) smooth unsweetened applesauce

 ½ cup (60 g) powdered sugar
 1 large egg
1½ teaspoons vanilla
    About ⅓ cup (100 g) orange marmalade
 ¼ cup (60 ml) light corn syrup
 1 tablespoon unsweetened cocoa powder

1. In a small bowl, mix flour, baking powder, salt, and cloves. In a food processor (or in a large bowl), whirl (or beat) butter and applesauce until well blended. Add sugar, egg, and 1 teaspoon of the vanilla; whirl (or beat) until smooth. Add flour mixture to egg mixture and whirl (or stir) until blended. Dough will be stiff.

2. With lightly floured fingers, shape 2-teaspoon portions of dough into balls. Set balls 1 inch (2.5 cm) apart on two 12- by 15-inch (30- by 38-cm) nonstick (or lightly greased regular) baking sheets. With floured thumb, press a well in center of each ball (don't press through to baking sheet). Spoon about ½ teaspoon of the marmalade into each well (marmalade should not flow over rim).

3. Bake cookies in a 400°F (205°C) oven until light golden brown (about 15 minutes), switching positions of baking sheets halfway through baking. Let cookies cool on baking sheets for about 3 minutes; then transfer cookies to racks to cool completely.

4. While cookies are cooling, prepare cocoa glaze, in a 1- to 1½-quart (950-ml to 1.4-liter) pan, combine corn syrup and cocoa. Cook over medium heat, stirring, just until mixture comes to a boil. Remove glaze from heat and stir in remaining ½ teaspoon vanilla. Use warm. Stir well before using.

5. Set each rack of cookies over a baking sheet to catch any drips; drizzle warm glaze evenly over cookies. Serve warm; or let stand until glaze hardens (about 2 hours). *Makes about 2 dozen cookies*

NUTRIENTS

Per cookie: 79 calories (14% calories from fat), 1 g total fat, 0.7 g saturated fat, 11 mg cholesterol, 63 mg sodium, 16 g carbohydrates, 0.3 g fiber, 1 g protein, 17 mg calcium, 0.5 mg iron

Currant Biscotti

Preparation time: **About 15 minutes**
Cooking time: **About 25 minutes**

In Italian, the word *biscotti* means "twice baked," and these crunchy cookies do indeed go into the oven twice. First, the log-shaped dough is baked until firm, then the log is sliced and rebaked to produce cookies that are perfect for dunking into coffee or into a dessert wine like sweet marsala.

1   cup (125 g) all-purpose flour

1   teaspoon baking powder

3   tablespoons (43 g) butter or margarine, at room temperature

¼   cup (50 g) granulated sugar

1½ teaspoons grated orange peel

1   large egg

½   teaspoon vanilla

⅓   cup (50 g) dried currants or raisins

1   cup (120 g) powdered sugar

3   to 4 teaspoons (15 to 20 ml) orange juice

1. In a small bowl, stir together flour and baking powder; set aside. In a large bowl, beat butter, granulated sugar, and 1 teaspoon of the orange peel until well blended. Add egg and vanilla and beat well. Add flour mixture to butter mixture and stir to blend thoroughly. Mix in currants.

2. Shape dough into a long log about 1½ inches (3.5 cm) in diameter. Place log in a lightly greased shallow 10- by 15-inch (30- by 38-cm) nonstick or regular baking pan; then flatten log to make a loaf about ½ inch (1 cm) thick. Bake in a 350°F (175°C) oven for 15 minutes.

3. Remove pan from oven. Let loaf cool slightly in pan. Then, using a serrated knife, cut loaf crosswise into slices about ½ inch (1 cm) thick. Tip

---

20 MINUTES OR LESS

½ cup (75 g) dried pitted cherries or raisins

2 tablespoons (30 ml) brandy

About 1 tablespoon (15 ml) kirsch

3 large Golden Delicious apples (about 1½ lbs./680 g total)

1 tablespoon (15 ml) lemon juice

⅓ cup (70 g) firmly packed brown sugar

2 cups (266 g) vanilla nonfat frozen yogurt

Mint sprigs

Cherry & Apple Jubilee

1. In a small bowl, combine cherries, brandy, and 1 tablespoon (15 ml) of the kirsch; let stand until cherries are softened (about 10 minutes), stirring occasionally.

2. Meanwhile, peel and core apples; then cut into ¼- to ½-inch-thick (6-mm- to 1-cm-thick) slices. Place in a large bowl, add lemon juice, and mix gently to coat. Set aside.

3. In a wide nonstick frying pan or wok, combine sugar and 2 tablespoons (30 ml) water. Add apples; stir-fry gently over medium-high heat until apples are almost tender when pierced (4 to 5 minutes). Add cherries (and any soaking liquid) and stir just until heated through.

4. Divide fruit mixture among 4 individual bowls; top equally with frozen yogurt. Garnish with mint sprigs. Offer additional kirsch to drizzle over yogurt, if desired.   *Makes 4 servings*

Per serving: 323 calories (1% calories from fat), 0.5 g total fat, 0.1 g saturated fat, 0 mg cholesterol, 53 mg sodium, 74 g carbohydrates, 3 g fiber, 2 g protein, 122 mg calcium, 0.4 mg iron

slices cut side down in baking pan; return to oven and continue to bake until cookies look dry and are lightly browned (about 10 more minutes). Transfer cookies to racks to cool.

4. Meanwhile, in a small bowl, smoothly blend powdered sugar, remaining ½ teaspoon orange peel, and 1 tablespoon (15 ml) of the orange juice; if necessary, add more orange juice to make icing easy to spread. Spread icing on about 1 inch (2.5 cm) of one end of each cookie. Before serving, return cookies to racks and let stand until icing is completely set.

Makes about 2 dozen cookies

NUTRIENTS

Per cookie: 70 calories (24% calories from fat), 2 g total fat, 1 g saturated fat, 13 mg cholesterol, 38 mg sodium, 13 g carbohydrates, 0.2 g fiber, 0.9 g protein, 16 mg calcium, 0.4 mg iron

CHERRY CHIMICHANGAS

Preparation time: **About 15 minutes**
Baking time: **8 to 10 minutes**

Cherries macerated in berry liqueur and cherry preserves fill these crisp treats; they're excellent with cocoa or coffee.

2 teaspoons berry-flavored liqueur

1 or 2 teaspoons cornstarch

¼ cup (72 g) cherry preserves

1 teaspoon grated lemon peel

2 cups (292 g) pitted, chopped fresh cherries; or 2 cups (225 g) frozen pitted dark sweet cherries, thawed, chopped, and drained well

6 flour tortillas (each 7 to 9 inches / 18 to 23 cm in diameter)

About ⅓ cup (80 ml) nonfat milk

Powdered sugar

1. In a bowl, combine liqueur and cornstarch until smooth (use 1 teaspoon cornstarch if using fresh cherries; use 2 teaspoons cornstarch mixed with 2 teaspoons water if using thawed frozen cherries). Stir in preserves, lemon peel, and cherries.

2. To assemble each chimichanga, brush both sides of a tortilla liberally with milk; let stand briefly to soften tortilla. Place a sixth of the filling on tortilla. Lap ends of tortilla over filling; then fold sides to center to make a packet. Place chimichanga, seam side down, on a lightly oiled 12- by 15-inch (30- to 38-cm) baking sheet; brush with milk. Repeat to make 5 more chimichangas.

3. Bake in a 500°F (260°C) oven, brushing with milk twice, until golden brown (8 to 10 minutes). Cool slightly, dust with sugar, and serve warm.

Makes 6 chimichangas

NUTRIENTS

Per chimichanga: 203 calories (13% calories from fat), 3 g total fat, 0.5 g saturated fat, 0.3 mg cholesterol, 180 mg sodium, 40 g carbohydrates, 2 g fiber, 4 g protein, 71 mg calcium, 1 mg iron

Chocolate Chip Cookies

Preparation time: **About 25 minutes**
Cooking time: **About 10 minutes**

Chewy oat–chip cookies are bound to be winners with your family. Adding applesauce to the batter allows you to cut down on the amount of fat.

1½ cups (185 g) all-purpose flour

1 teaspoon baking powder

½ teaspoon baking soda

½ teaspoon salt

2 tablespoons (30 g) butter or margarine, at room temperature

2 tablespoons (30 ml) vegetable oil

1 cup (220 g) firmly packed dark brown sugar

1 large egg

½ cup (120 ml) smooth unsweetened applesauce

1 teaspoon vanilla

2 cups (160 g) regular rolled oats

1 package (about 6 oz./170 g) semisweet chocolate chips

About 2 tablespoons granulated sugar

1. In a medium-size bowl, stir together flour, baking powder, baking soda, and salt; set aside.

2. In a large bowl, beat butter, oil, and brown sugar with an electric mixer until smooth. Add egg, applesauce, and vanilla; beat until blended. Add flour mixture and beat until smooth. Scrape down sides of bowl; stir in oats and chocolate chips.

3. Shape and bake dough right away; if it is allowed to sit, cookies will be dry. Working quickly, spoon 2-tablespoon (30-ml) portions of dough onto lightly greased large nonstick or regular baking sheets, spacing cookies evenly. Dip fingertips in granulated sugar, then pat cookies into rounds about ⅓ inch (8 mm) thick.

4. Bake in a 350°F (175°C) oven until pale golden (about 10 minutes), switching positions of baking sheets halfway through baking. Let cool for about 3 minutes on baking sheets, then transfer to racks to cool completely. Serve warm or cool.

Makes about 2 dozen cookies

NUTRIENTS

Per cookie: 154 calories (29% calories from fat), 5 g total fat, 2 g saturated fat, 11 mg cholesterol, 109 mg sodium, 26 g carbohydrates, 1 g fiber, 2 g protein, 28 mg calcium, 1 mg iron

CHOCOLATE PISTACHIO COOKIES

Preparation time: **About 20 minutes**
Cooking time: **About 20 minutes**

Nut-topped, chocolaty cookies look pretty on a plate of holiday sweets. If you buy pistachios in the shell, be sure to use those that are opened; unopened nuts are immature. Pistachios are a good source of iron.

- 1 cup (125 g) all-purpose flour
- 2 tablespoons unsweetened cocoa powder
- 1 teaspoon baking powder
- ¼ teaspoon instant espresso or coffee powder
- 1 cup (200 g) granulated sugar
- 2 tablespoons (30 g) butter or margarine, melted
- ⅓ cup (80 ml) smooth unsweetened applesauce
- ½ teaspoon vanilla
- ¼ cup (30 g) shelled pistachio nuts, chopped
- ½ cup (60 g) powdered sugar

1. In a food processor or a large bowl, whirl or stir together flour, cocoa, baking powder, instant espresso, and ¾ cup (150 g) of the granulated sugar. Add butter, applesauce, and vanilla; whirl until dough forms a compact ball. (Or, if not using a processor, stir in butter, applesauce, and vanilla with a fork, then work dough with your hands to form a smooth-textured ball.)

2. With lightly floured fingers, pinch off about 1-inch (2.5-cm) pieces of dough; roll pieces into balls. Set balls 2 inches (5 cm) apart on lightly greased large nonstick or regular baking sheets.

3. Place remaining ¼ cup (50 g) granulated sugar in a shallow bowl. Dip bottom of a lightly greased glass in sugar; use glass to press each ball of dough gently to a thickness of about ½ inch (1 cm). After flattening each ball, dip glass in sugar again to prevent sticking. Sprinkle cookies evenly with pistachios.

4. Bake in lower third of a 300°F (150°C) oven until cookies are firm to the touch and look dry on top (about 20 minutes), switching positions of baking sheets halfway through baking.

5. Let cookies cool on baking sheets for about 3 minutes, then transfer to racks to cool completely. Meanwhile, in a small bowl, smoothly blend powdered sugar with 1½ to 2 teaspoons water, or enough to make icing easy to drizzle. Drizzle icing over cooled cookies.

Makes about 2 dozen cookies

NUTRIENTS

Per cookie: 83 calories (22% calories from fat), 2 g total fat, 0.8 g saturated fat, 3 mg cholesterol, 31 mg sodium, 16 g carbohydrates, 0.5 g fiber, 0.9 g protein, 15 mg calcium, 0.4 mg iron

COCOA PEPPER COOKIES

Pictured on facing page
Preparation time: **About 25 minutes**
Cooking time: **About 20 minutes**

If you like spicy flavors, you'll applaud these unusual cookies. Crushed peppercorns add subtle heat. You can store whole dried peppercorns in a cool, dark place for about a year before they lose their freshness.

1 cup (125 g) all-purpose flour

2 tablespoons unsweetened cocoa powder

1 teaspoon baking powder

1 cup (200 g) sugar

1 teaspoon whole black peppercorns, coarsely crushed

2 tablespoons (30 g) butter, melted

⅓ cup (80 ml) smooth unsweetened applesauce

½ teaspoon vanilla

1. In a food processor (or in a bowl), combine flour, cocoa, baking powder, ¾ cup (150 g) of the sugar, and peppercorns. Whirl (or stir) until blended. Add butter, applesauce, and vanilla; whirl until dough forms a compact ball. (Or stir in butter, applesauce, and vanilla with a fork, then work dough with your hands to form a smooth-textured ball.)

2. With lightly floured fingers, pinch off 1-inch (2.5-cm) pieces of dough and roll into balls. Arrange balls 2 inches (5 cm) apart on two 12- by 15-inch (30- by 38-cm) nonstick (or lightly greased regular) baking sheets. Dip bottom of a lightly greased glass into remaining ¼ cup (50 g) sugar and press each ball gently to a thickness of about ½ inch (1 cm); dip glass again as needed to prevent sticking.

3. Bake in lower third of a 300°F (150°C) oven until cookies are firm to the touch and look dry on top (about 20 minutes), switching positions of baking sheets halfway through baking. Let cookies cool on baking sheets for about 3 minutes; then transfer to racks to cool completely.

Makes about 1½ dozen cookies

N U T R I E N T S

Per cookie: 84 calories (14% calories from fat), 1 g total fat, 0.8 g saturated fat, 3 mg cholesterol, 41 mg sodium, 18 g carbohydrates, 0.3 g fiber, 0.7 g protein, 17 mg calcium, 0.4 mg iron

GINGER BARS

Preparation time: **About 15 minutes**
Cooking time: **20 to 25 minutes**

Bits of crystallized or candied ginger are a piquant surprise in these dark, moist bars. Look for crystallized ginger in Asian markets, where it is much cheaper.

1 cup (120 g) whole wheat flour

¼ cup (50 g) sugar

½ teaspoon baking soda

3 tablespoons coarsely chopped crystallized or candied ginger

¼ cup (60 ml) nonfat milk

¼ cup (60 ml) molasses

2 large egg whites

1. In a large bowl, stir together flour, sugar, baking soda, and ginger. Add milk, molasses, and egg whites; beat until smoothly blended.

2. Spread batter evenly in a lightly greased 8-inch-square (20-cm-square) nonstick or regular baking pan. Bake in a 350°F (175°C) oven until center springs back when lightly pressed (20 to 25 minutes). Serve warm or cool; to serve, cut into 2-inch (5-cm) squares. These bars are best eaten fresh, so serve them the same day you make them.

Makes 16 bars

N U T R I E N T S

Per bar: 67 calories (5% calories from fat), 0.4 g total fat, 0.1 g saturated fat, 0.1 mg cholesterol, 52 mg sodium, 15 g carbohydrates, 0.9 g fiber, 2 g protein, 25 mg calcium, 1 mg iron

Cocoa Pepper Cookies, Lemon Cookies, Mexican Wedding Cookies (recipes on facing page & page 206)

Pear Cobbler with Ginger Crust (recipe on page 214)

SPARKLING JEWELS FRUIT SOUP AND CACTUS PEAR & TREE PEAR SOUP (RECIPES ON PAGES 213 & 212)

Chocolate Shortbread (recipe on facing page)

CHOCOLATE SHORTBREAD

Pictured on facing page
Preparation time: **About 15 minutes**
Cooking time: **About 25 minutes**

A bit softer than traditional shortbread, these ultra-rich treats feature a dark chocolate cookie layer atop a chocolate graham cracker crust. A sweet cocoa glaze is an irresistible topping.

   1   *cup (85 g) chocolate graham cracker crumbs (about twelve 2-inch-square/5-cm-square crackers)*

   ¾   *cup (95 g) all-purpose flour*

   ⅔   *cup (80 g) plus ½ cup (60 g) powdered sugar*

   ½   *cup (43 g) plus 1 tablespoon unsweetened cocoa powder*

   ½   *teaspoon instant espresso or coffee powder*

   ¼   *teaspoon salt*

   ¼   *cup (55 g) butter or margarine, cut into chunks*

   ¼   *teaspoon vanilla*

        About 1 tablespoon (20 ml) nonfat milk

1. In a food processor or a large bowl, whirl or stir together graham cracker crumbs and 1 tablespoon (15 ml) water until crumbs are evenly moistened. Press crumbs evenly over bottom of a lightly greased 9-inch (23-cm) nonstick or regular cheesecake pan with a removable rim; set aside.

2. In food processor or bowl, whirl or stir together flour, the ⅔ cup (80 g) powdered sugar, the ½ cup (43 g) cocoa, 2 teaspoons water, instant espresso, and salt. Add butter; whirl or rub with your fingers until mixture resembles coarse crumbs.

3. Evenly distribute crumbly dough over graham cracker crumbs in pan. With fingers, press out dough firmly to make an even layer that adheres to graham cracker crumbs (if dough is sticky, lightly flour your fingers).

4. Bake in a 325°F (165°C) oven until shortbread smells toasted and feels firm in center when gently pressed (about 25 minutes). Let shortbread cool in pan on a rack for 5 minutes. Then, using a very sharp knife, cut shortbread, still in pan, into 12 equal wedges. Let cool completely in pan on rack.

5. Meanwhile, in a small bowl, stir together remaining ½ cup (60 g) powdered sugar, remaining 1 tablespoon cocoa, vanilla, and 1 tablespoon (15 ml) of the milk. Beat until smooth; if necessary, add more milk to make glaze easy to drizzle. Remove pan rim from shortbread; drizzle glaze over shortbread. Let stand until glaze is set.

Makes 12 servings

NUTRIENTS

Per serving: 148 calories (30% calories from fat), 5 g total fat, 3 g saturated fat, 10 mg cholesterol, 137 mg sodium, 25 g carbohydrates, 2 g fiber, 2 g protein, 9 mg calcium, 1 mg iron

LEMON COOKIES

Pictured on page 201
Preparation time: **About 25 minutes**
Cooking time: **About 15 minutes**

Rolled oats (also known as old-fashioned oats) give these sweet-tart lemon cookies a chewy texture. When you're counting calories, you can make the cookies without the lemony glaze; they're still scrumptious.

½ cup (60 g) all-purpose flour

¼ teaspoon baking soda

¼ teaspoon salt

⅛ teaspoon cream of tartar

2 tablespoons (30 g) butter or margarine, at room temperature

6 tablespoons (72 g) granulated sugar

2 teaspoons lemon peel

2½ teaspoons lemon juice

½ teaspoon vanilla

1 large egg white

½ cup (40 g) regular rolled oats

⅔ cup (66 g) sifted powdered sugar

1. In a small bowl, mix flour, baking soda, salt, and cream of tartar. In a food processor (or in a large bowl), whirl (or beat) butter, granulated sugar, lemon peel, ½ teaspoon of the lemon juice, vanilla, and egg white until well blended. Add flour mixture to egg mixture; whirl (or stir) until combined. Stir in oats.

2. With floured fingers, divide dough into 1½-teaspoon portions (you should have 18); place mounds of dough 2 inches (5 cm) apart on two 12- by 15-inch (30- by 38-cm) nonstick (or lightly greased regular) baking sheets.

3. Bake in a 350°F (175°C) oven until cookies are light golden and firm to the touch (about 15 minutes), switching positions of baking sheets halfway through baking. Let cookies cool on baking sheets for about 3 minutes; then transfer to racks to cool completely.

4. While cookies are baking, prepare lemon icing: In a small bowl, combine powdered sugar, remaining 2 teaspoons lemon juice, and water. Stir until smooth.

5. Set each rack of cookies over a baking sheet to catch any drips; drizzle icing evenly over cookies. Serve; or let stand until icing hardens.

Makes 1½ dozen cookies

NUTRIENTS

Per cookie: 65 calories (20% calories from fat), 1 total fat, 0.8 g saturated fat, 3 mg cholesterol, 64 mg sodium, 12 g carbohydrates, 0.3 g fiber, 0.9 g protein, 3 mg calcium, 0.3 mg iron

MEXICAN WEDDING COOKIES

Pictured on page 201
Preparation time: **About 25 minutes**
Cooking time: **About 15 minutes**

These sugar-coated treats, a more cakelike version of Mexico's famous wedding cookies, will delight guests of all ages.

1½ cups (85 g) all-purpose flour

1 teaspoon baking powder

¼ teaspoon salt

3 tablespoons butter or margarine, at room temperature

⅓ cup (80 ml) unsweetened applesauce

About 1½ cups (180 g) powdered sugar

1 large egg

1 teaspoon vanilla

¼ cup (30 g) chopped pecans

1. In a small bowl, mix flour, baking powder, and salt. In a food processor (or in a large bowl), whirl (or beat) butter and applesauce until well blended. Add ½ cup (60 g) of the sugar, egg, vanilla, and pecans; whirl (or beat) until smooth. Add flour mixture to egg mixture; whirl (or stir) until blended. Dough will be stiff.

2. With lightly floured fingers, shape 2-teaspoon portions of dough into balls; you should have 24. Set balls 1 inch (2.5 cm) apart on two 12- by 15-inch (30- by 38-cm) nonstick (or lightly greased regular) baking sheets. Bake in a 375°F (190°C) oven until cookies are light golden brown (about 15 minutes), switching positions of baking sheets halfway through baking. Let cool on baking sheets until lukewarm.

3. Sift ½ cup (60 g) of the remaining sugar onto a large sheet of wax paper. Roll each cookie gently in sugar. With your fingers, pack more sugar all over each cookie to a depth of about ⅛ inch (3 mm). Place cookies on a rack over wax paper and dust with remaining sugar; let cool.

Makes 2 dozen cookies

NUTRIENTS

Per cookie: 84 calories (26% calories from fat), 2 g total fat, 1 g saturated fat, 13 mg cholesterol, 60 mg sodium, 14 g carbohydrates, 0.3 g fiber, 1 g protein, 15 mg calcium, 0.4 mg iron

MOCHA ALMOND FUDGE TORTE

Preparation time: **About 30 minutes**
Cooking time: **3 to 5 minutes**

Striking to look at and quick to prepare, this majestic torte consists of layers of pound cake and chocolate-flecked cream filling, all cloaked in a mocha-flavored cream cheese frosting.

2 tablespoons slivered almonds

1 large package (about 8 oz./230 g) plus 2 ounces (55 g) nonfat cream cheese, at room temperature

1¾ cups (210 g) powdered sugar

½ teaspoon vanilla

1 cup (240 ml) frozen reduced-fat whipped topping, thawed

1 ounce (30 g) semisweet chocolate, coarsely grated

1 loaf (about 13.6 oz./386 g) purchased nonfat chocolate or regular pound cake, thawed if frozen

2 tablespoons (30 g) butter or margarine, at room temperature

½ teaspoon instant espresso powder or coffee powder

1 to 3 teaspoons nonfat milk

1. Toast almonds in a small nonstick frying pan over medium heat until golden (3 to 5 minutes); stir often. Transfer almonds to a bowl; set aside.

2. In a food processor or a large bowl, combine the 8-ounce (230-g) package cream cheese, ¼ cup (30 g) of the powdered sugar, and vanilla. Whirl or beat with an electric mixer until smooth and fluffy; then gently fold in whipped topping and chocolate. Cover and refrigerate filling until ready to use.

3. With a serrated knife, cut pound cake horizontally into 3 equal layers. Place top cake layer, cut side up, on a rack set over a sheet of wax paper; spread with half the cream cheese filling. Add middle layer and spread with remaining filling; top with remaining cake layer, cut side down.

4. In a clean food processor or large bowl, combine remaining 1½ cups (180 g) powdered sugar, remaining 2 ounces (55 g) cream cheese, butter, instant espresso powder, and 1 teaspoon of the milk. Whirl or beat until smooth and easy to spread; add more milk, if necessary. Frosting will be soft.

5. Spread frosting over top of cake; some of it will flow down sides of cake. Sprinkle top of cake with almonds; scrape up frosting that has dripped onto wax paper and spread it gently on sides of cake. With wide spatulas, carefully transfer cake to a serving platter. Serve immediately; or cover lightly and refrigerate until ready to serve.

Makes 14 servings

NUTRIENTS

Per serving: 194 calories (16% calories from fat), 3 g total fat, 2 g saturated fat, 7 mg cholesterol, 257 mg sodium, 36 g carbohydrates, 0.6 g fiber, 5 g protein, 63 mg calcium, 0.7 mg iron

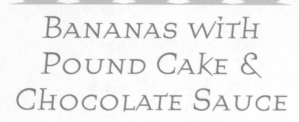

BANANAS WITH POUND CAKE & CHOCOLATE SAUCE

Preparation time: **About 15 minutes**
Cooking time: **About 10 minutes**

For a luscious dessert, top slices of pound cake with warmed banana slices and spoonfuls of rich chocolate sauce.

½ cup (110 g) firmly packed brown sugar

¼ cup (20 g) unsweetened cocoa powder

1 tablespoon cornstarch

¼ teaspoon instant coffee powder

½ cup (120 ml) water

2 tablespoons (30 ml) light corn syrup

2 teaspoons light or dark rum, or to taste

½ teaspoon vanilla

3 large bananas (about 1½ lbs. / 680 g total)

1 tablespoon (15 ml) lemon juice

1 tablespoon sweetened shredded coconut

3 tablespoons granulated sugar

4 slices purchased nonfat pound cake, each about ¾ inch (2 cm) thick

1. To prepare chocolate sauce, in a small pan, combine brown sugar, cocoa, cornstarch, and coffee powder. Add water and corn syrup; stir until smooth. Cook over medium-high heat, stirring until mixture boils and thickens slightly, about 4 minutes. (At this point, you may cover to prevent a film from forming on top, let cool, and refrigerate for up to 3 days.) If preparing ahead, reheat, stirring, before adding rum and vanilla. Otherwise, remove pan from heat and stir in rum and vanilla immediately. Keep warm, stirring occasionally.

2. Cut bananas diagonally into ½-inch-thick (1-cm-thick) slices; place in a large bowl, add lemon juice, and mix gently to coat. Set aside.

3. In a wide nonstick frying pan or wok, stir coconut over medium heat until golden (about 3 minutes). Remove from pan and set aside. To pan, add granulated sugar and 2 tablespoons (30 ml) water. Cook over medium-high heat, stirring, until sugar is dissolved. Add bananas; stir-fry gently until bananas are hot and sauce is thick and bubbly (about 2 minutes). Remove from heat.

4. Place one slice of cake on each of 4 individual plates; spoon banana mixture over cake. Just before serving, stir chocolate sauce well. Drizzle cake with sauce and sprinkle with coconut.

Makes 4 servings

NUTRIENTS

Per serving: 410 calories (3% calories from fat), 2 g total fat, 1 g saturated fat, 0 mg cholesterol, 225 mg sodium, 100 g carbohydrates, 4 g fiber, 4 g protein, 38 mg calcium, 2 mg iron

LEMON POPPY SEED CAKE

Preparation time: About 30 minutes
Cooking time: About 15 minutes

Poppy seeds bring a subtly nutty flavor to this moist lemon layer cake filled with strawberry jam.

3   large eggs

2   large egg whites

1   cup (200 g) granulated sugar

½   cup (120 ml) smooth unsweetened applesauce

1½   cups (185 g) all-purpose flour

¼   cup (23 g) poppy seeds

1   tablespoon baking powder

1   tablespoon plus 1 teaspoon grated lemon peel

½   cup (4 oz./115 g) butter or margarine, melted, plus ⅓ cup (76 g) butter or margarine, at room temperature

3   cups (360 g) powdered sugar

½   cup (120 ml) nonfat sour cream

⅔   cup (200 g) strawberry jam

Thin strips of lemon peel

About 8 cups (1.2 kg) fresh strawberries, hulled and halved

1. In a food processor or a large bowl, combine eggs, egg whites, granulated sugar, and applesauce; whirl or beat with an electric mixer until mixture is thick and lemon-colored. Add flour, poppy seeds, baking powder, 1 tablespoon of the grated lemon peel, and the ½ cup (4 oz./115 g) melted butter; whirl or beat until dry ingredients are evenly moistened. Divide batter equally between 2 greased, floured 8-inch-round (20-cm-round) nonstick or regular baking pans.

2. Bake in a 375°F (190°C) oven until cake layers just begin to pull away from sides of pans and centers spring back when gently pressed (about 15 minutes); halfway through baking, gently rotate each pan one-half turn. Let cakes cool for 10 minutes in pans on racks; then turn out of pans to cool completely.

3. Meanwhile, prepare frosting: In clean food processor or large bowl, combine powdered sugar, sour cream, the ⅓ cup (76 g) butter at room temperature, and remaining 1 teaspoon grated lemon peel. Whirl or beat with electric mixer until frosting is smooth and spreadable; cover and refrigerate until ready to use.

4. To assemble cake, brush all loose crumbs from sides and bottom of each cake layer. Center one layer, top side down, on a serving plate. Using a metal spatula, evenly spread jam to within ½ inch (1 cm) of edge. Top with second layer, top side up.

5. Stir frosting and spread over sides and top of cake; arrange strips of lemon peel decoratively atop cake. To serve, cut cake into slices; offer strawberries alongside.

Makes 10 to 12 servings

NUTRIENTS

Per serving: 528 calories (30% calories from fat), 18 g total fat, 9 g saturated fat, 95 mg cholesterol, 319 mg sodium, 88 g carbohydrates, 4 g fiber, 6 g protein, 169 mg calcium, 2 mg iron

Drunken Cake

Preparation time: **About 10 minutes**
Baking time: **About 20 minutes**

This quick single-layer cake is flecked with orange peel and soaked with a cinnamon-scented orange-rum syrup. It's a perfect warm-weather dessert—and just as tempting in any other season, especially after a spicy meal.

1¼ cups (250 g) sugar

2 tablespoons plus 1 teaspoon grated orange peel

½ cup (120 ml) orange juice

½ teaspoon grated lemon peel

2 tablespoons (30 ml) lemon juice

⅛ teaspoon ground cinnamon

2 to 3 tablespoons (30 to 45 ml) light or dark rum

1 teaspoon vanilla

2 large eggs

¾ cup (95 g) all-purpose flour

1½ teaspoons baking powder

¼ cup (55 g) butter or margarine, melted

Mint sprigs

1. To prepare syrup, in a small pan, mix ¾ cup (150 g) of the sugar, 1 teaspoon of the orange peel, orange juice, lemon peel, lemon juice, and cinnamon. Bring to a boil over medium-high heat. Boil, stirring, just until sugar is dissolved. Remove pan from heat and let cool; then stir in rum and vanilla; set aside.

2. In a food processor, whirl eggs and remaining ½ cup (100 g) sugar until thick and lemon-colored. Add flour, baking powder, butter, and remaining 2 tablespoons orange peel to processor; whirl until well blended. Spread batter in a greased, floured 9-inch (23-cm) cake pan with a removable rim. Bake in a 375°F (190°C) oven until cake just begins to pull away from sides of pan and center springs back when lightly pressed with a finger (about 20 minutes).

3. Set warm cake in pan on a rack; set rack over a plate to catch any drips of syrup. Pierce cake all over with a fork. Slowly pour syrup over cake; let cake cool. Just before serving, remove pan rim. Garnish cake with mint sprigs.

Makes 8 servings

NUTRIENTS

Per serving: 259 calories (27% calories from fat), 8 g total fat, 4 g saturated fat, 69 mg cholesterol, 167 mg sodium, 43 g carbohydrates, 0.3 g fiber, 3 g protein, 66 mg calcium, 0.9 mg iron

20 MINUTES OR LESS

1 tablespoon butter or margarine

5 cups (775 g) ½-inch (1-cm) chunks fresh or canned pineapple

⅓ cup (70 g) firmly packed brown sugar

1 tablespoon finely chopped crystallized ginger

¼ teaspoon grated lime peel

1 tablespoon (15 ml) lime juice

1⅓ cups (100 g) coarsely crushed gingersnaps (about twelve 2-inch/5-cm cookies)

Mint sprigs

Stir-Fried Pineapple with Ginger

1. Melt butter in a wide nonstick frying pan or wok over medium-high heat. Add pineapple, sugar, ginger, lime peel, and lime juice. Stir-fry gently until pineapple is heated through (about 5 minutes).

2. Transfer fruit and sauce to a shallow serving bowl; sprinkle with crushed gingersnaps. Garnish with mint sprigs.

Makes 4 servings

Per serving: 291 calories (17% calories from fat), 6 g total fat, 2 g fat, 8 mg cholesterol, 178 mg sodium, 62 g carbohydrates, 2 g fiber, 2 g protein, 56 mg calcium, 3 mg iron

PEACH SHORTCAKES

Preparation time: About 20 minutes
Baking time: About 15 minutes

These low-fat peach shortcakes are an ideal choice for concluding a midsummer meal (they are also wonderful for breakfast or brunch). If you have a few extra minutes, you can peel the peaches more easily if you score the stem end, then blanch the peaches for about a minute in boiling water. Transfer them to a bowl of cold water, then peel, halve, and pit.

1 cup (125 g) all-purpose flour
2 teaspoons baking powder
¼ teaspoon baking soda
3 tablespoons (43 g) margarine
⅓ cup (80 ml) low-fat buttermilk
1 cup (210 g) low-fat cottage cheese
About 3 tablespoons (45 ml) honey
⅛ teaspoon ground nutmeg
2 large firm-ripe peaches (about 1 lb./455 g total)

1. In a medium-size bowl, stir together flour, baking powder, and baking soda until well blended. Using a pastry blender or your fingers, cut in or rub in margarine until mixture resembles coarse meal. Add buttermilk and stir just until dry ingredients are evenly moistened.

2. Turn dough out onto a lightly floured board and knead gently just until smooth (about 1 minute). Divide dough into fourths. Pat each portion into a 3-inch-diameter/8-cm diameter round; place rounds well apart on an ungreased baking sheet.

3. Bake in a 450°F (230°C) oven until lightly browned (about 15 minutes). Transfer to a rack and let cool slightly.

4. Meanwhile, whirl cottage cheese, 3 tablespoons (45 ml) of the honey, and nutmeg in a blender or food processor until smooth. Peel, then pit and slice peaches.

5. To serve, split each biscuit in half horizontally. Set bottom halves on 4 plates; top each with a fourth of the cottage cheese mixture and a fourth of the peach slices. Cover lightly with biscuit tops. Serve with additional honey, if desired.

Makes 4 servings

NUTRIENTS

Per serving: 345 calories (27% calories from fat), 10 g total fat, 2 g saturated fat, 6 mg cholesterol, 663 mg sodium, 52 g carbohydrates, 2 g fiber, 13 g protein, 212 mg calcium, 2 mg iron

CACTUS PEAR & TREE PEAR SOUP

Pictured on page 203
Preparation time: **About 30 minutes**
Cooking time: **About 15 minutes**

Two fruit purées—one vibrant magenta, the other pale yellow—are poured side by side into individual bowls to create this dramatic dessert. The fruit of a Mexican cactus, prickly pears (also called cactus pears or tunas) are available in the United States in Mexican markets and some well-stocked supermarkets from August through December. If you can't find them, make the raspberry purée instead.

RED PRICKLY PEAR PURÉE:

About 5 pounds (2.3 kg) despined red prickly pears (also called cactus pears or tunas)

⅓ cup (80 ml) lemon juice

2 tablespoons sugar

RASPBERRY PURÉE:

4 cups (490 g) fresh or frozen unsweetened raspberries

1 cup (240 ml) orange juice

⅓ cup (80ml) lemon juice

⅓ cup (70 g) sugar

TREE PEAR PURÉE:

2 cans (about 1 lb./455 g each) pears in extra-light syrup

1 star anise or 1 teaspoon anise seeds

¼ cup (60 ml) lemon juice

1 tablespoon sugar

GARNISH:

6 to 8 star anise (optional)

Mint sprigs (optional)

1. Prepare red prickly pear purée (Step 2) *or* raspberry purée (Step 3), then prepare tree pear purée (Step 4).

2. To prepare red prickly pear purée, wear rubber gloves to protect your hands from hidden needles. Cut prickly pears into halves lengthwise. Using a small knife, pull off and discard outer layer (including peel) from fruit; this layer will separate easily. Place fruit in a food processor (a blender will pulverize seeds). Whirl until puréed, then pour into a fine strainer set over a bowl. Firmly rub purée through strainer into bowl; discard seeds. Add lemon juice and sugar. Pour into a small pitcher. (At this point, you may cover and refrigerate until next day; stir before using.)

3. To prepare raspberry purée, in a food processor, whirl raspberries until smoothly puréed (a blender will pulverize seeds). Pour purée into a fine strainer set over a bowl. Firmly rub purée through strainer into bowl; discard seeds. Add orange juice, lemon juice, and sugar. Pour into a small pitcher. (At this point, you may cover and refrigerate until next day; stir before using.)

4. To prepare tree pear purée, drain pears; reserving 1½ cups (360 ml) of the syrup, discard remainder. In a small pan, combine reserved syrup and 1 star anise or anise seeds. Bring syrup to a boil over high heat; then reduce heat, cover, and simmer very gently until flavors are blended (about 10 minutes). Pour syrup through a fine strainer set over a bowl; discard star anise or seeds. In a food processor or blender, whirl pears until smoothly puréed; then add syrup (if using a blender, add syrup while you are puréeing pears). Stir in lemon juice and sugar. Pour into a small pitcher. (At this point, you may cover and refrigerate until next day; stir before using.)

5. With a pitcher in each hand, simultaneously and gently pour purées into an individual 1½- to 2-cup (360- to 470-ml) soup bowl (wide bowls create the most dramatic effect). Repeat to fill rest of bowls, allowing a total of 1 to 1¼ cups (240 to 300 ml) purée for each serving. Garnish each with a star anise and mint sprigs, if desired.

Makes 6 to 8 servings

NUTRIENTS

Per serving: 187 calories (6% calories from fat), 1 g total fat, 0 g saturated fat, 0 mg cholesterol, 19 mg sodium, 46 g carbohydrates, 0 g fiber, 2 g protein, 150 mg calcium, 1 mg iron

HONEYDEW MELON DESSERT BOWL

Preparation time: **About 30 minutes**

Hollow out two honeydew melons to use as serving bowls for this simple fruit salad. (You'll find canned litchis in Asian markets and some supermarkets.)

FRUIT:

2 medium-size honeydew melons (2½ to 3½ lbs./1.15 to 1.6 kg each)

1 large can (about 20 oz./565 g) or 2 cans (about 11 oz./310 g each) litchis

10 to 16 strawberries, hulled and halved

STRAWBERRY SAUCE:

3 cups (447 g) strawberries, hulled

2 tablespoons (30 ml) lemon juice

1 tablespoon sugar, or to taste

1. Cut off top third of each melon. Scoop out seeds; scoop fruit into balls or chunks from shells and from top slices, removing as much melon as possible. Discard top slices.

2. Place melon pieces in a bowl. Drain litchis, reserving ½ cup (120 ml) of the syrup for the Strawberry Sauce (discard remaining syrup). Add litchis and halved strawberries to melon pieces; mix gently. Spoon fruit into melon shells.

3. To prepare strawberry sauce, in a blender or food processor, combine hulled whole strawberries, the ½ cup (120 ml) reserved litchi syrup, lemon juice, and sugar. Whirl until smooth. (At this point, you may cover and refrigerate fruit salad and sauce separately for up to 4 hours.)

4. Serve fruit in melons with strawberry sauce.

Makes 8 to 10 servings

NUTRIENTS

Per serving: 116 calories (3% calories from fat), 0.5 g total fat, 0 g saturated fat, 0 mg cholesterol, 37 mg sodium, 30 g carbohydrates, 3 g fiber, 1 g protein, 19 mg calcium, 0.7 mg iron

20 MINUTES OR LESS

1 large firm-ripe kiwi fruit (about 4 oz./115 g), peeled and thinly sliced

½ cup (93 g) diced firm-ripe nectarine or peeled peach

⅓ cup (30 g) fresh or frozen unsweetened blueberries

⅓ cup (40 g) thinly sliced hulled strawberries

⅓ cup (50 g) very thinly sliced firm-ripe plums

2 tablespoons (30 ml) lemon juice

2 cups (250 ml) white grape juice

2 tablespoons minced crystallized ginger

3 tablespoons (45 ml) orange-flavored liqueur

Mint sprigs (optional)

SPARKLING JEWELS FRUIT SOUP

PICTURED ON PAGE 203

1. Prepare fruit. Place fruit in a large bowl and mix gently with lemon juice. (At this point, you may cover and refrigerate for up to 2 hours.)

2. In a small pan, bring grape juice and ginger to a boil over high heat. Stir in liqueur; pour over fruit. Ladle soup into bowls; garnish with mint sprigs, if desired.

Makes 4 to 6 servings

Per serving: 145 calories (2% calories from fat) 0.3 g total fat, 0 g saturated fat, 0 mg cholesterol, 15 mg sodium, 33 g carbohydrates, 2 g fiber, 0.5 g protein, 24 mg calcium, 1 mg iron

SAUTÉED PEAR CRISP

Preparation time: **About 20 minutes**
Cooking time: **About 15 minutes**

Cooking pears brings out their natural sweetness. For this recipe, you can use any pear in season, but Boscs would work particularly well because they retain a slight crispness even when ripe. The optional frozen yogurt is a nice added touch.

¾ cup (95 g) all-purpose flour

⅓ cup (30 g) regular rolled oats

3 tablespoons granulated sugar

1 teaspoon ground cinnamon

⅓ cup (76 g) firm butter or margarine (cut into chunks)

1 to 2 teaspoons water

½ cup (75 g) dried cranberries or raisins

3 tablespoons (45 ml) berry liqueur

4 large firm-ripe pears (about 2 lbs./ 905 g total)

4 teaspoons (20 ml) lemon juice

1 teaspoon butter or margarine

⅓ cup (70 g) firmly packed brown sugar

Vanilla nonfat frozen yogurt (optional)

1. To prepare crisp topping, in a food processor or medium-size bowl, whirl or stir together flour, oats, granulated sugar, and cinnamon. Add butter and water; whirl or rub with your fingers until mixture is crumbly.

2. Press oat mixture into ½-inch (1-cm) chunks (some smaller chunks and crumbs are fine, too). Transfer oat chunks to a wide nonstick frying pan or wok. Stir-fry gently over medium-high heat until golden (about 8 minutes; do not scorch). As you stir, gently scrape free any browned bits that stick to pan. Remove from pan. (At this point, you may let cool completely; then cover airtight and store at room temperature for up to 2 days.)

3. In a small bowl, combine cranberries and liqueur; let stand until cranberries are softened (about 10 minutes); stir occasionally. Meanwhile, peel, core, and thinly slice pears. Place in a large bowl, add lemon juice, and mix to coat; set aside.

4. Melt butter in a wide nonstick frying pan or wok over medium-high heat. Add brown sugar and pears. Stir-fry gently until pears are almost tender when pierced (about 4 minutes). Add cranberries (and any soaking liquid) and stir just until heated through.

5. With a slotted spoon, transfer fruit mixture to 4 individual bowls. Strain pan juices, if desired; then pour into a small pitcher. Sprinkle fruit with crisp topping. Top with frozen yogurt, if desired. Drizzle with pan juices to taste.

Makes 4 servings

NUTRIENTS

Per serving: 559 calories (28% calories from fat), 18 g total fat, 10 g saturated fat, 44 mg cholesterol, 173 mg sodium, 96 g carbohydrates, 8 g fiber, 4 g protein, 58 mg calcium, 2 mg iron

PEAR COBBLER WITH GINGER CRUST

Pictured on page 202
Preparation time: **About 20 minutes**
Cooking time: **About 25 minutes**

Fresh pears mingle with maple syrup and lime in a tempting autumn cobbler with a gingersnap cookie crust.

6 large firm-ripe Anjou pears (about 3 lbs./1.35 kg total), peeled, cored, and thinly sliced

2 tablespoons (30 ml) lime juice

¼ cup (60 ml) pure maple syrup

2 cups (170 g) finely crushed gingersnaps (about thirty-five 2-inch/5-cm cookies)

⅔ cup (147 g) firmly packed brown sugar

3 tablespoons all-purpose flour

¼ cup (55 g) butter or margarine, melted

1 teaspoon vanilla

1. In a shallow 1½- to 2-quart (1.4- to 1.9-liter) casserole, combine pears and lime juice. Add syrup; mix gently to coat fruit evenly. Spread out fruit in an even layer; set aside.

2. In a food processor or a medium-size bowl, whirl or stir together crushed gingersnaps, sugar, and flour. Add butter and vanilla; whirl or stir until mixture resembles coarse crumbs. With your fingers, squeeze mixture to form large lumps; then crumble evenly over pear mixture.

3. Set casserole in a larger baking pan to catch any drips. Bake in a 325°F (165°C) oven until fruit is tender when pierced and topping feels firm when gently pressed (about 25 minutes); if topping begins to darken excessively, cover it with foil. Serve warm, spooned into bowls.

Makes 8 servings

NUTRIENTS

Per serving: 370 calories (22% calories from fat), 9 g total fat, 4 g saturated fat, 16 mg cholesterol, 253 mg sodium, 73 g carbohydrates, 4 g fiber, 3 g protein, 64 mg calcium, 3 mg iron

DESSERT NACHOS

Preparation time: **About 20 minutes**
Cooking time: **About 10 minutes**

For a quick and festive dessert that would be just right after a Mexican meal, spoon fruit salsa and a honey-sweetened cream cheese sauce onto crisp flour tortilla chips sprinkled with sugar and cinnamon.

⅓ cup (70 g) sugar

1 teaspoon ground cinnamon

10 flour tortillas (each 7 to 9 inches/ 18 to 23 cm in diameter)

2 cups (275 g) strawberries

2 large kiwi fruit (about 8 oz./230 g total)

1 cup (175 g) diced orange segments

1 large package (about 8 oz./230 g) Neufchâtel or nonfat cream cheese

½ cup (120 ml) orange juice

3 tablespoons (45 ml) honey

1. To prepare nacho chips, in a shallow bowl, combine sugar and cinnamon; set aside. Dip tortillas, one at a time, in water; let drain briefly. Stack tortillas; then cut stack into 6 to 8 wedges. Dip one side of each wedge in sugar mixture. Arrange wedges in a single layer, sugar side up, on lightly oiled 12- by 15-inch (30- by 38-cm) baking sheets; do not overlap wedges. Bake in a 500°F (260°C) oven until crisp and golden, 4 to 5 minutes. (At this point, you may cool; then store airtight at room temperature for up to 3 days.)

2. To prepare fruit salsa, hull strawberries; dice into a bowl. Add kiwi fruit and orange segments. Cover and refrigerate until ready to serve or for up to 4 hours.

3. In a small pan, combine Neufchâtel cheese, orange juice, and honey. Whisk over low heat until sauce is smooth (about 3 minutes).

4. Mound chips on a platter. Offer cheese sauce and salsa to spoon onto chips.

Makes 10 to 12 servings

NUTRIENTS

Per serving: 234 calories (29% calories from fat), 8 g total fat, 3 g saturated fat, 16 mg cholesterol, 236 mg sodium, 37 g carbohydrates, 3 g fiber, 5 g protein, 74 mg calcium, 1 mg iron

HOT PAPAYA SUNDAES

Preparation time: About 15 minutes
Baking time: About 15 minutes

In early spring, before other fresh fruits have reached the marketplace, papayas from the tropics are often abundantly available. Use the luscious golden fruits in this simple, dramatic hot-and-cold dessert.

  1 tablespoon margarine, melted
  ½ teaspoon grated lime peel
  ⅓ cup (80 ml) rum or water
  ¼ cup (60 ml) lime juice
  3 tablespoons (45 ml) honey
  2 small firm-ripe papayas (about 1 lb./455 g each)
  2 cups (470 ml) vanilla low-fat frozen yogurt

1. In a 9- by 13-inch (23- by 33-cm) casserole, stir together margarine, lime peel, rum, lime juice, and honey.

2. Cut unpeeled papayas in half lengthwise; scoop out and discard seeds, then place papaya halves, cut sides down, in honey mixture. Bake in a 375°F (190°C) oven until papayas are heated through and sauce is just beginning to bubble (about 15 minutes).

3. Carefully transfer hot papaya halves, cut sides up, to dessert plates; let stand for about 5 minutes.

4. Meanwhile, stir pan juices in casserole to blend; pour into a small pitcher. Fill each papaya half with small scoops of frozen yogurt; offer pan juices to pour over sundaes to taste.

Makes 4 servings

NUTRIENTS

Per serving: 270 calories (17% calories from fat), 5 g total fat, 2 g saturated fat, 5 mg cholesterol, 101 mg sodium, 46 g carbohydrates, 1 g fiber, 4 g protein, 191 mg calcium, 0.3 mg iron

WEEKEND
COOKING

GRILLED VEGETABLE APPETIZER

Preparation time: **About 25 minutes**
Cooking time: **About 1 hour and 30 minutes,**
including time to heat grill

Vegetables cooked on the grill are a tasty accompaniment for meat, poultry, or fish. Consider starting early; you can prepare the vegetables up to 2 hours in advance of serving. A grill topper (page 10) will keep the vegetables from falling through the grill rack.

2   long, slender baguettes (each about 8 oz./230 g, about 25 inches/63 cm long), cut diagonally into slices about 1 inch (2.5 cm) thick

4   medium-size slender eggplants, such as Asian or Italian (about 12 oz./340 g total)

3   medium-size sweet potatoes or yams (about 1¼ lbs./565 g total), scrubbed

1   large onion

3   tablespoons (45 ml) olive oil

2   large red bell peppers (about 1¼ lbs./565 g total), seeded

3   large heads garlic (about 12 oz./340 g total), unpeeled (leave heads whole)

1½ teaspoons chopped fresh rosemary or ½ teaspoon dried rosemary, crumbled

1½ teaspoons chopped fresh sage or ½ teaspoon dried rubbed sage

    Rosemary sprigs

    Fresh sage leaves

    Salt and pepper

1. Arrange bread slices in a single layer (overlapping as little as possible) in shallow 10- by 15-inch (25- by 38-cm) baking pans. Bake in a 325°F (165°C) oven until crisp and tinged with brown (15 to 20 minutes). Transfer toast to a rack to cool.

2. While bread is toasting, ignite 70 charcoal briquets in a large barbecue with dampers open. Spread coals out in a solid layer and let burn until

medium-low to low; if fire is too hot, vegetables will scorch.

3. Cut ends from eggplants and sweet potatoes; cut unpeeled onion into quarters. Brush cut surfaces of onion with a little of the oil. Place eggplants, sweet potatoes, onion, bell peppers, and garlic on a greased grill 4 to 6 inches (10 to 15 cm) above coals. Cover barbecue. Cook until vegetables are very tender when pressed, watching carefully to prevent scorching; allow about 40 minutes for eggplant and peppers, 50 to 60 minutes for onion and garlic, and 1 hour for sweet potatoes. During the first 30 minutes of grilling, turn vegetables every 5 minutes; after 30 minutes, add 10 more briquets to the fire and turn vegetables every 10 minutes. Remove vegetables from grill as they are cooked.

4. Remove peel from sweet potatoes, onion, and bell peppers. Cut heads of garlic in half horizontally. Coarsely chop eggplants, peppers, and sweet potatoes. Squeeze half the garlic cloves from skins and finely chop.

5. On a platter, arrange chopped eggplants, peppers, and sweet potatoes; onion quarters; and whole garlic cloves. Place chopped garlic in center of platter.

6. Drizzle vegetables with remaining oil; sprinkle with chopped rosemary and sage. Garnish with rosemary sprigs and sage leaves. Place toast in a basket. (At this point, you may cover lightly and let stand for up to 2 hours.)

7. To serve, top toast with garlic (either chopped or whole cloves); then spoon other vegetables on top. Season to taste with salt and pepper.

Makes 8 servings

NUTRIENTS

Per serving: 376 calories (17% calories from fat), 7 g total fat, 1 g saturated fat, 0 mg cholesterol, 365 mg sodium, 70 g carbohydrates, 7 g fiber, 10 g protein, 157 mg calcium, 3 mg iron

Greek-Style Chicken & Potato Salad

Preparation time: **About 15 minutes**
Chilling time: **At least 15 minutes**
Cooking time: **About 30 minutes**

This Greek-inspired potato salad improves on standing. If you prefer to use fresh rather than canned olives, buy Greek calamata olives, available at gourmet stores.

2 pounds (905 g) small red thin-skinned potatoes (each about 1½ inches/ 3.5 cm in diameter), scrubbed

1 skinless, boneless chicken breast half (about 6 oz./170 g)

1 jar (about 6 oz./170 g) marinated artichoke hearts

1 large jar (about 4 oz./115 g) sliced pimentos

1 can (about 2¼ oz./63 g) sliced ripe olives, drained

½ cup (50 g) thinly sliced green onions

¼ cup (60 ml) lemon juice

4 large romaine lettuce leaves, rinsed and crisped

½ cup (65 g) crumbled feta cheese

Pepper

1. In a 4- to 5-quart (3.8- to 5-liter) pan, bring 8 cups (1.9 liters) water to a boil over medium-high heat. Add potatoes; reduce heat, cover, and simmer until potatoes are tender when pierced with a fork (about 25 minutes). Drain potatoes and let stand until cool enough to handle; then cut into quarters.

2. While potatoes are cooking, rinse chicken and pat dry. Then, in a 3- to 4-quart (2.8- to 3.8-liter) pan with a tight-fitting lid, bring 8 cups (1.9 liters) water to a rolling boil over high heat. Remove pan from heat and immediately add chicken. Cover pan tightly and let stand until meat in thickest part is no longer pink; cut to test (15 to 20 minutes; do not uncover until ready to test). If chicken is not done, return it to hot water, cover, and steep for 2 to 3 more minutes.

3. Lift chicken from pan and let stand just until cool enough to handle; then cut into bite-size pieces. Place in a large bowl and add potatoes, artichokes and their marinade, pimentos, olives, onions, and lemon juice. Mix gently but thoroughly. Cover and refrigerate for at least 15 minutes or up to 4 hours before serving.

4. To serve, place a lettuce leaf on each of 4 plates; divide chicken mixture among plates. Sprinkle salads with cheese; season to taste with pepper.

Makes 4 servings

NUTRIENTS

Per serving: 361 calories (26% calories from fat), 11 g total fat, 4 g saturated fat, 44 mg cholesterol, 651 mg sodium, 50 g carbohydrates, 5 g fiber, 19 g protein, 150 mg calcium, 4 mg iron

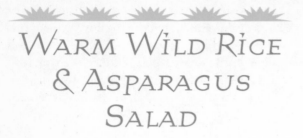

WARM WILD RICE & ASPARAGUS SALAD

Preparation time: About 15 minutes
Cooking time: About 1 hour and 20 minutes

Balsamic vinegar lends a sweet-tart accent to a warm salad of wild rice, lentils, mushrooms, and fresh asparagus.

1   cup (170 g) wild rice, rinsed and drained

1   cup (200 g) lentils

1   pound (455 g) mushrooms, thinly sliced

1   large onion, chopped

    About 2½ cups (590 ml) vegetable broth

1   pound (455 g) slender asparagus

3   tablespoons (45 ml) balsamic vinegar

1   tablespoon (15 ml) olive oil

½   cup (40 g) grated Parmesan cheese

1. In a 5- to 6-quart (5- to 6-liter) pan, combine rice and 8 cups (1.9 liters) water. Bring to a boil over high heat; then reduce heat, cover, and simmer for 30 minutes. Meanwhile, sort through lentils, discarding any debris; rinse lentils, drain, and set aside.

2. Add lentils to rice and continue to simmer until both rice and lentils are tender to bite (about 25 more minutes). Drain and let cool.

3. In a wide nonstick frying pan, combine mushrooms, onion, and ¾ cup (180 ml) of the broth. Cook over medium-high heat, stirring often, until liquid evaporates and browned bits stick to pan bottom (about 10 minutes). To deglaze pan, add ⅓ cup (80 ml) of the broth, stirring to loosen browned bits; continue to cook until browned bits form again. Repeat deglazing step about 3 more times or until vegetables are browned, using ⅓ cup (80 ml) more broth each time.

4. Snap off and discard tough ends of asparagus; thinly slice stalks. Add asparagus and ⅓ cup (80 ml) more broth to mushroom mixture; cook, stirring often, until asparagus is tender-crisp to bite (about 2 minutes).

5. Spoon rice-lentil mixture into a large bowl. Add asparagus mixture, vinegar, and oil; mix gently but thoroughly. Sprinkle with cheese.

Makes 8 servings

NUTRIENTS

Per serving: 236 calories (16% calories from fat), 4 g total fat, 1 g saturated fat, 4 mg cholesterol, 413 mg sodium, 27 g carbohydrates, 6 g fiber, 15 g protein, 106 mg calcium, 4 mg iron

CURRIED SHRIMP & SHELL SALAD

Preparation time: About 25 minutes
Cooking time: About 15 minutes
Chilling time: At least 30 minutes

Make this salad ahead of time to enjoy on a warm summer day, along with fresh fruit and crisp toast.

¼   cup (60 ml) nonfat or reduced-calorie mayonnaise

1   tablespoon (15 ml) Dijon mustard

½   teaspoon grated lemon peel

1   tablespoon (15 ml) lemon juice

1   teaspoon dried dill weed

1   teaspoon honey

½   teaspoon curry powder

¼   teaspoon pepper

2   ounces/55 g (about ½ cup) dried small shell-shaped pasta

12   ounces (340 g) tiny cooked shrimp

1   cup (145 g) coarsely chopped cucumber

3   tablespoons sun-dried tomatoes packed in oil, drained well and coarsely chopped

    Salt

4 to 8 large butter lettuce leaves, rinsed and crisped

Lemon wedges

1. To prepare curry dressing, in a small nonmetal bowl, combine mayonnaise, mustard, lemon peel, lemon juice, dill weed, honey, curry powder, and pepper. Mix until blended; cover and refrigerate for up to 1 hour.

2. Bring 4 cups (950 ml) water to a boil in a 3- to 4-quart (2.8- to 3.8-liter) pan over medium-high heat. Stir in pasta and cook just until tender to bite (8 to 10 minutes); or cook according to package directions. Drain, rinse with cold water until cool, and drain well.

3. Transfer pasta to a large nonmetal bowl. Add shrimp, cucumber, and sun-dried tomatoes; stir dressing and add to bowl. Mix thoroughly but gently. Season to taste with salt. Cover and refrigerate at least 30 minutes or for up to 4 hours; stir occasionally to mix.

4. Place lettuce on 4 individual plates. Spoon pasta mixture onto lettuce. Offer lemon to add to taste.

Makes 4 servings

NUTRIENTS

Per serving: 226 calories (28% calories from fat), 7 g total fat, 1 g saturated fat, 166 mg cholesterol, 395 mg sodium, 19 g carbohydrates, 2 g fiber, 21 g protein, 51 mg calcium, 4 mg iron

Spiced Purée of Carrot Soup

Preparation time: **About 25 minutes**
Cooking time: **About 25 minutes**
Chilling time: **At least 7 hours**

As an extra convenience to the cook, this curry-seasoned soup can be made a day in advance of serving and refrigerated. Indeed, it's flavor improves on standing. A colorful watercress purée garnishes the flavorful blend of carrots, onions, and potatoes.

1 tablespoon (15 ml) olive oil

1½ pounds (680 g) carrots, thinly sliced

1 pound (455 g) onions, chopped

1 cup (120 g) chopped celery

1 pound (455 g) russet potatoes, peeled and cut into ½-inch (1-cm) cubes

1 teaspoon ground cumin

1 teaspoon curry powder

6 cups (1.4 liters) fat-free reduced-sodium chicken broth

3 tablespoons (45 ml) lemon juice

1 cup (40 g) lightly packed watercress sprigs

¼ cup (60 ml) plain nonfat yogurt

1. Heat oil in a 4- to 5-quart (3.8- to 5-liter) pan over medium-high heat. Add carrots, onions, and celery. Cover and cook, stirring often, until vegetables begin to brown (about 12 minutes). Add potatoes, cumin, curry powder, and broth. Bring to a boil over high heat; then reduce heat, cover, and simmer until potatoes are tender when pierced (about 10 minutes). Stir in lemon juice.

2. In a blender or food processor, whirl soup, a portion at a time, until puréed. Let cool slightly, then cover and refrigerate until cold (at least 7 hours) or until next day.

3. To prepare watercress purée, in a blender, combine watercress and yogurt. Whirl until puréed.

4. To serve, pour soup into 6 individual bowls; drizzle with watercress purée.

Makes 6 servings

NUTRIENTS

Per serving: 183 calories (13% calories from fat), 3 g total fat, 0.4 g saturated fat, 0.2 mg cholesterol, 721 mg sodium, 34 g carbohydrates, 7 g fiber, 8 g protein, 86 mg calcium, 2 mg iron

Mexican Shellfish Chowder

Preparation time: **About 45 minutes**
Cooking time: **About 45 minutes**

One might call this hearty seafood soup a Mexican-style bouillabaisse. For the fish, use all one kind or a combination of two or more types.

2½ quarts (2.4 liters) fat-free reduced-sodium chicken broth

½ cup (120 ml) dry white wine

1 dried bay leaf

2 cloves garlic, minced or pressed

⅛ teaspoon powdered saffron

4 to 6 small fresh jalapeño chiles, seeded and finely chopped

3 large tomatoes (1¼ to 1½ lbs./565 to 680 g total), chopped

2 pounds (905 g) white-fleshed fish steaks or fillets such as rockfish, halibut, or lingcod

8 ounces (230 g) sea scallops, rinsed and patted dry

18 small hard-shell clams suitable for steaming, scrubbed

8 ounces (230 g) medium-large raw shrimp (36 to 42 per lb.), shelled and deveined

Salt and pepper

¼ cup (10 g) chopped cilantro

Lime wedges

1. In a 6- to 8-quart (6- to 8-liter) pan, combine broth, wine, bay leaf, garlic, saffron, and chiles. Cover and bring to a boil over medium-high heat; reduce heat and simmer for 30 minutes. Meanwhile, in a food processor or blender, whirl tomatoes until coarsely puréed; set aside. Rinse fish, pat dry, and cut into chunks. Cut scallops into ½-inch-thick (1-cm-thick) slices.

2. Stir tomatoes into broth mixture. Cover, increase heat to medium, and bring to a boil. Add clams, reduce heat to medium-low, cover, and simmer for 5 minutes. Add fish, scallops, and shrimp. Cover and simmer until clams pop open and fish, scallops, and shrimp are opaque in center; cut to test (3 to 5 minutes). Season to taste with salt and pepper; sprinkle with cilantro. Serve with lime wedges to squeeze into soup to taste.

Makes 8 to 10 servings

NUTRIENTS

Per serving: 199 calories (12% calories from fat), 3 g total fat, 0.5 g saturated fat, 85 mg cholesterol, 872 mg sodium, 7 g carbohydrates, 1 g fiber, 36 g protein, 48 mg calcium, 6 mg iron

Citrus Chicken Soup

Preparation time: **About 25 minutes**
Cooking time: **About 1 hour**

This vibrant chicken soup is easy to prepare. To make it, you'll need mild fresh chiles, such as the New Mexico variety.

4 chicken breast halves (about 2 lbs./905 g total)

6 cups (1.4 liters) fat-free reduced-sodium chicken broth

1 medium-size onion, finely chopped

1 can (about 14½ oz./415 g) diced tomatoes

½ teaspoon dried oregano

1 teaspoon grated lemon peel

¼ teaspoon pepper

2 medium-size thin-skinned potatoes (about 10 oz./285 g total), scrubbed and diced

1 medium-size ear corn (about 10 oz./285 g)

⅓ cup (15 g) coarsely chopped cilantro

2 medium-size fresh mild red or green chiles, seeded and finely chopped

1 small firm-ripe avocado

2 tablespoons (30 ml) lime juice

Lime wedges

1. Rinse chicken, pat dry, and place in a 5- to 6-quart (5- to 6-liter) pan. Add broth, onion, tomatoes and their liquid, oregano, lemon peel, and pepper; bring to a boil over medium-high heat. Then reduce heat, cover, and simmer until meat in thickest part is no longer pink; cut to test (about 25 minutes). Lift out chicken and set aside until cool enough to touch.

2. While chicken is cooling, add potatoes to pan; cover and cook over medium-low heat until potatoes are tender to bite (25 to 30 minutes). Meanwhile, remove and discard skin and bones from chicken; tear meat into bite-size pieces and set aside. Discard husk and silk from corn; cut corn kernels from cob.

3. Skim and discard fat from soup. Add chicken, corn, cilantro, and chiles. Cook just until heated through (3 to 5 minutes). Meanwhile, pit, peel, and dice avocado; mix gently with lime juice. Offer avocado to sprinkle into soup and lime wedges to squeeze into each serving to taste.

Makes 6 servings

NUTRIENTS

Per serving: 245 calories (20% calories from fat), 6 g total fat, 1 g saturated fat, 57 mg cholesterol, 831 mg sodium, 21 g carbohydrates, 3 g fiber, 29 g protein, 43 mg calcium, 2 mg iron

LIGHT CASSOULET

Preparation time: **About 30 minutes**

Cooking time: **About 1 hour and 30 minutes**

Here is a low-fat version of the traditional French cassoulet. It contains chicken instead of duck and turkey sausage rather than the typical fatty pork sausage.

1 large onion, chopped

2 medium-size carrots (about 6 oz./ 170 g total), thinly sliced

1 medium-size red bell pepper (about 6 oz./170 g), seeded and thinly sliced

3 cloves garlic, minced or pressed

1 can (about 14½ oz./415 g) low-sodium stewed tomatoes

1¾ cups (420 ml) vegetable broth

⅔ cup (160 ml) dry red wine

1 teaspoon dried thyme

1 dried bay leaf

¼ teaspoon pepper

¼ teaspoon liquid hot pepper seasoning

2 cans (about 15 oz./425 g each) cannellini (white kidney beans), drained and rinsed

1½ pounds (680 g) skinless, boneless chicken breast, cut into 1-inch (2.5-cm) pieces

4 ounces (115 g) turkey kielbasa (Polish sausage), thinly sliced

¼ cup (15 g) finely chopped parsley

1. In a 5- to 6-quart (5- to 6-liter) pan, combine onion, carrots, bell pepper, garlic, and ½ cup (120 ml) water. Cook over medium-high heat, stirring often, until liquid evaporates and browned bits stick to pan bottom (about 10 minutes). To deglaze pan, add ⅓ cup (80 ml) water, stirring to loosen browned bits from bottom of pan; continue to cook until browned bits form again. Repeat deglazing step about 2 more times or until vegetables are browned, using ⅓ cup (80 ml) water each time. Stir in tomatoes and their liquid, broth, wine, thyme, bay leaf, pepper, and hot pepper seasoning. Bring to a boil; then reduce heat, cover, and simmer for 45 minutes.

2. Stir in beans; simmer, uncovered, for 10 minutes. Stir in chicken and sausage. Continue to simmer, uncovered, until chicken is no longer pink in center; cut to test (about 10 more minutes). Just before serving, remove and discard bay leaf. To serve, ladle cassoulet into 8 individual serving bowls and sprinkle with parsley.

Makes 8 servings

NUTRIENTS

Per serving: 240 calories (12% calories from fat), 3 g total fat, 1 g saturated fat, 59 mg cholesterol, 557 mg sodium, 24 g carbohydrates, 7 g fiber, 29 g protein, 75 mg calcium, 3 mg iron

Chicken with Chanterelle & Tarragon Sauce

Preparation time: **About 35 minutes**
Soaking time: **30 minutes**
Cooking time: **About 25 minutes**

You will need dried chanterelle mushrooms for this recipe. Chanterelles are trumpet-shaped wild mushrooms with a nutty flavor and a slightly chewy texture. If you can't find dried ones at the supermarket, just substitute economical button mushrooms.

½ ounce/15 g (about 1 cup) dried chanterelle mushrooms; or 8 ounces (230 g) fresh regular mushrooms, thinly sliced

1½ cups (280 g) long-grain white rice

2 teaspoons butter or olive oil

1 pound (455 g) skinless, boneless chicken breast, cut into ½- by 2-inch (1- by 5-cm) strips

¾ cup (180 ml) fat-free reduced-sodium chicken broth

¼ cup (60 ml) Chardonnay

2 teaspoons chopped fresh tarragon or 1 teaspoon dried tarragon

2 tablespoons (30 ml) half-and-half

1. If using chanterelles, place them in a 1½- to 2-quart (1.4- to 1.9-liter) pan and add 1½ cups (360 ml) water. Bring to a boil over high heat; then reduce heat, cover tightly, and simmer gently until mushrooms are very tender when pierced (about 30 minutes). Remove from heat and let stand for 30 minutes. Then lift chanterelles from water, squeezing liquid from them into pan; reserve water. Set chanterelles aside.

2. In a 4- to 5-quart (3.8- to 5-liter) pan, bring 3 cups (710 ml) water to a boil over high heat; stir in rice. Reduce heat, cover, and simmer until liquid has been absorbed and rice is tender to bite (about 20 minutes).

3. Meanwhile, melt butter in a wide nonstick frying pan or wok over medium-high heat. Add chicken and stir-fry until no longer pink in center; cut to test (3 to 4 minutes). Remove chicken from pan with a slotted spoon and keep warm.

4. Add chanterelles or regular mushrooms to pan; stir-fry until tinged a darker brown (about 5 minutes). Carefully pour reserved cooking water into pan, taking care not to add any grit from mushrooms. Add broth, wine, and tarragon. Bring to a boil; then boil, stirring, until liquid is reduced to ⅓ cup (80 ml). Add half-and-half; cook, stirring, until mixture returns to a boil. Remove from heat and stir in chicken.

5. To serve, spoon rice onto a rimmed platter; spoon chicken mixture over rice.

Makes 4 servings

NUTRIENTS

Per serving: 563 calories (8% calories from fat), 5 g total fat, 2 g saturated fat, 74 mg cholesterol, 226 mg sodium, 89 g carbohydrates, 2 g fiber, 36 g protein, 63 mg calcium, 5 mg iron

ROAST TURKEY WITH APPLE ORZO

Pictured on page 238
Preparation time: **About 20 minutes**
Cooking time: **About 2 hours and 15 minutes**

Turkey and cranberries have long been traditional partners. Here they're combined in an entirely new way. Lean turkey breast is served with orzo rather than fatty stuffing. And instead of offering fresh cranberry sauce, dried cranberries are added to the orzo for a colorful presentation.

2 tablespoons chopped pecans

1 boned turkey breast half (3 to 3½ lbs./1.35 to 1.6 kg), trimmed of fat

⅓ cup (100 g) apple jelly

1 tablespoon (15 ml) raspberry vinegar or red wine vinegar

¼ teaspoon ground sage

2 cups (470 ml) apple juice

   About 2¾ cups (650 ml) fat-free reduced-sodium chicken broth

10 ounces/285 g (about 1⅔ cups) dried orzo or other rice-shaped pasta

½ cup (45 g) dried cranberries or raisins

¼ teaspoon ground coriander

1 tablespoon cornstarch mixed with 3 tablespoons (45 ml) cold water

⅓ cup (20 g) chopped parsley or green onions

   Sage sprigs

   Salt and pepper

1. Toast pecans in a small frying pan over medium heat, shaking pan often, until golden (about 4 minutes). Remove from pan and set aside.

2. Place turkey skin side up. Fold narrow end under breast; pull skin to cover as much breast as possible. Tie snugly lengthwise and crosswise with string at 1-inch (2.5-cm) intervals. Place in a non-stick or lightly oiled square 8-inch (20-cm) pan.

3. Combine jelly, vinegar, and ground sage in a 1- to 1½-quart (950-ml to 1.4-liter) pan. Cook over medium-low heat, stirring, until jelly is melted. Baste turkey with some of the mixture, reserving remaining mixture.

4. Roast turkey in a 375°F (190°C) oven, basting with pan drippings and remaining jelly mixture, until a meat thermometer inserted in thickest part registers 160°F/70°C (about 2 hours); if drippings start to scorch, add ⅓ cup (80 ml) water to pan, stirring to loosen browned bits.

5. Meanwhile, combine apple juice and 1⅓ cups (320 ml) of the broth in a 4- to 5-quart (3.8- to 5-liter) pan. Bring to a boil over high heat. Stir in pasta, cranberries, and coriander. Reduce heat, cover, and simmer, stirring occasionally, until almost all liquid is absorbed (about 15 minutes); do not scorch. Remove from heat and keep warm, stirring occasionally.

6. Transfer turkey to a warm platter; cover and let stand for 10 minutes.

7. Meanwhile, pour pan drippings and accumulated juices into a 2-cup (470-ml) glass measure; skim off and discard fat. Stir cornstarch mixture and blend into drippings. Add enough of the remaining broth to make 1½ cups (360 ml). Pour into a 1- to 1½-quart (950-ml to 1.4-liter) pan and cook over medium-high heat, stirring, until boiling. Pour into a serving container.

8. Remove strings from turkey. Slice meat and arrange on individual plates. Stir parsley into pasta and mound beside turkey; sprinkle with nuts. Garnish with sage sprigs. Offer gravy, salt, and pepper to add to taste.

Makes 8 to 10 servings

NUTRIENTS

Per serving: 436 calories (25% calories from fat), 12 g total fat, 3 g saturated fat, 93 mg cholesterol, 123 mg sodium, 40 g carbohydrates, 1 g fiber, 41 g protein, 45 mg calcium, 3 mg iron

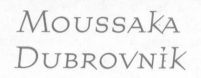

MOUSSAKA DUBROVNIK

Preparation time: **About 30 minutes**
Cooking time: **About 1 hour and 30 minutes**

For an ideal make-ahead dinner, try this streamlined version of a famous eggplant casserole. The eggplant slices are oven-browned, not fried; the meat sauce is a spicy, super-lean blend of ground turkey breast, garlic, and browned onions. And in place of the usual cream sauce, we've substituted a simple combination of broth and light sour cream.

2 large eggplants (2½ to 3 lbs./1.15 to 1.35 kg total)

Olive oil cooking spray

2 large onions, finely chopped

1 clove garlic, minced or pressed

2 teaspoons olive oil

1 cup (240 ml) water

1½ pounds (680 g) skinless, boneless turkey breast, cut into 1-inch (2.5-cm) chunks

¼ teaspoon fennel seeds

¼ teaspoon ground cinnamon

¼ teaspoon ground cumin

¼ teaspoon ground cardamom

About ⅛ teaspoon freshly grated or ground nutmeg

2 tablespoons plus 4 teaspoons cornstarch

3 cups (710 ml) fat-free reduced-sodium chicken broth

Salt and pepper

½ cup (120 ml) light sour cream or plain nonfat yogurt

2 tablespoons grated Parmesan cheese (optional)

1. Cut unpeeled eggplants lengthwise into ½-inch-thick (1-cm-thick) slices. Spray 2 shallow rimmed baking pans with cooking spray. Divide eggplant slices equally between pans in a single layer, overlapping slices slightly; spray eggplant with cooking spray. Bake in a 450°F (230°C) oven for 20 minutes; turn slices over and continue to bake until lightly browned and very soft when pressed (about 10 more minutes). Line a 9- by 13- by 2-inch (23- by 33- by 5-cm) casserole with half the eggplant; set remaining pan of eggplant aside.

2. In empty baking pan, combine onions, garlic, oil, and ½ cup (120 ml) of the water. Bake until water has evaporated and onions are dark brown, stirring often with a wide spatula (30 to 35 minutes). Meanwhile, whirl turkey in a food processor, about half at a time, until minced.

3. Add remaining ½ cup (120 ml) water to onion mixture, stirring to scrape up browned bits. Scatter turkey over onion mixture. Return to oven and bake until turkey is opaque throughout (about 6 minutes). Set turkey mixture aside.

4. In a 2-quart (1.9-liter) pan, mix fennel seeds, cinnamon, cumin, cardamom, ⅛ teaspoon of the nutmeg, and 4 teaspoons of the cornstarch. Blend in 1½ cups (360 ml) of the broth. Bring to a boil over high heat, stirring constantly; stir into turkey mixture. Season to taste with salt and pepper.

5. Spread turkey mixture over eggplant in casserole. Cover with remaining eggplant; set aside.

6. Rinse the 2-quart (1.9-liter) pan; in it, smoothly blend remaining 2 tablespoons cornstarch and ¼ cup (60 ml) of the broth. Blend in sour cream, then remaining 1¼ cups (300 ml) broth. Bring to a boil over high heat, stirring. Spoon over eggplant. (At this point, you may cover and refrigerate casserole for up to a day.)

7. Sprinkle casserole with cheese, if used; then sprinkle lightly with additional nutmeg. Bake, uncovered, in a 425°F (220°C) oven until heated through (15 to 20 minutes; 30 to 40 minutes if casserole has been refrigerated).

Makes 8 to 10 servings

NUTRIENTS

Per serving: 192 calories (18% calories from fat), 4 g total fat, 1 g saturated fat, 51 mg cholesterol, 266 mg sodium, 17 g carbohydrates, 3 g fiber, 23 g protein, 70 mg calcium, 2 mg iron

ITALIAN SAUSAGE LASAGNE

Preparation time: **About 25 minutes**
Cooking time: **About 2 hours**

Because this slimmed-down version of Italian lasagne is not layered like traditional lasagne, it is assembled quickly.

1 pound (455 g) pork tenderloin or boned pork loin, trimmed of fat

¼ cup (60 ml) dry white wine

2 tablespoons chopped parsley

1½ teaspoons crushed fennel seeds

½ teaspoon crushed red pepper flakes

2 cloves garlic, minced or pressed

3 large onions (about 1½ lbs./680 g total), chopped

2 large stalks celery (about 8 oz./230 g total), chopped

2 medium-size carrots (about 6 oz./170 g total), chopped

5 cups (1.2 liters) beef broth

1 can (about 6 oz./170 g) tomato paste

1½ teaspoons dried basil

½ teaspoon dried rosemary

¼ teaspoon ground nutmeg

12 ounces (340 g) dried lasagne

3 tablespoons cornstarch

1½ cups (360 ml) nonfat milk

2 cups (about 8 oz./230 g) shredded fontina cheese

½ cup (40 g) freshly grated Parmesan cheese

1. Cut pork into 1-inch (2.5-cm) chunks. Whirl in a food processor, about half at a time, until coarsely chopped (or put through a food chopper fitted with a medium blade). In a large bowl, combine pork, wine, parsley, fennel seeds, pepper flakes, and garlic. Mix well; cover and refrigerate. (At this point, you may refrigerate sausage until next day.)

2. Combine onions, celery, carrots, and 1½ cups (360 ml) of the broth in a 5- to 6-quart (5- to 6-liter) pan (preferably nonstick). Bring to a boil over high heat and cook, stirring occasionally, until liquid has evaporated and vegetables begin to brown (12 to 15 minutes). To deglaze pan, add ¼ cup (60 ml) water, stirring to loosen browned bits. Continue to cook, stirring often, until mixture begins to brown again. Repeat deglazing step, adding ¼ cup (60 ml) more water each time, until mixture is richly browned.

3. Crumble sausage into pan; add ½ cup (120 ml) more water. Cook, stirring occasionally, until liquid has evaporated and meat begins to brown (about 10 minutes). Add ⅓ cup (80 ml) more water and cook, stirring, until meat is browned (2 to 4 more minutes). Reduce heat to medium-low and add 2½ cups (590 ml) more broth, stirring to loosen browned bits. Add tomato paste, basil, rosemary, and nutmeg. Bring to a boil; reduce heat, cover, and simmer, stirring occasionally, until flavors have blended (about 20 minutes).

4. Meanwhile, bring 12 cups (2.8 liters) water to a boil in a 5- to 6-quart (5- to 6-liter) pan over medium-high heat. Stir in pasta and cook just until barely tender to bite (about 8 minutes). Drain well and keep warm.

5. Blend remaining 1 cup (240 ml) broth with cornstarch and milk until smooth. Add to meat mixture. Cook over medium-high heat, stirring, until bubbling and thickened. Stir in 1 cup (115 g) of the fontina; remove from heat. Gently stir in pasta. Transfer to a shallow 3-quart (2.8-liter) baking dish; swirl pasta. Sprinkle with Parmesan and remaining 1 cup (115 g) fontina. (At this point, you may cool, cover, and refrigerate for up to a day.)

6. Bake in a 375°F (190°C) oven until bubbling (about 30 minutes; 35 to 40 minutes if chilled).

Makes 8 servings

NUTRIENTS

Per serving: 480 calories (27% calories from fat), 14 g total fat, 7 g saturated fat, 76 mg cholesterol, 1,625 mg sodium, 53 g carbohydrates, 4 g fiber, 32 g protein, 376 mg calcium, 4 mg iron

¼ cup (32 g) cornstarch mixed with
⅓ cup (80 ml) water

2 cups (about 8 oz./230 g) shredded
fontina cheese

¾ to 1 pound (340 to 455 g) cooked
crabmeat

1. Slice fennel thinly crosswise, reserving feathery tops. Mix fennel, onions, and mushrooms in
a 12- by 14-inch (30- by 35.5-cm) baking pan.
Bake in a 475°F (245°C) oven, stirring occasionally, until browned bits stick to pan bottom (about
45 minutes); do not scorch. To deglaze pan, add
½ cup (120 ml) of the broth, stirring to loosen
browned bits. Continue to bake until browned
bits form again (about 20 more minutes). Repeat
deglazing step, adding ½ cup (120 ml) more broth,
and bake until vegetables are well browned. Add
½ cup (120 ml) more broth, stirring to loosen
browned bits. Keep warm.

2. Bring 12 cups (2.8 liters) water to a boil in a
5- to 6-quart (5- to 6-liter) pan over medium-high
heat. Stir in pasta and cook just until tender to bite
(8 to 10 minutes); or cook according to package
directions. Drain well; blot dry.

3. Mince enough of the reserved fennel tops to
make ¼ cup (8 g). In a wide nonstick frying pan,
combine minced fennel tops, milk, sherry, and remaining ½ cup (120 ml) broth. Bring to a boil
over high heat. Stir cornstarch mixture and add to
pan. Cook, stirring, until sauce comes to a boil.
Remove from heat, add half the cheese, and stir
until smooth. Keep hot.

4. Arrange a third of the pasta in a 9- by 13-inch
(23- by 33-cm) baking pan. Spread with vegetables and half the sauce. Cover with a third more
of the pasta, crab, and all but ½ cup (120 ml) of
the sauce. Top with remaining pasta, sauce, and
cheese. Bake in a 450°F (230°C) oven until bubbling (about 10 minutes). Broil 4 to 6 inches
(10 to 15 cm) below heat until browned (4 to 5
minutes). Let stand for 5 minutes.

Makes 6 to 8 servings

NUTRIENTS

Per serving: 427 calories (29% calories from fat), 13 g total fat, 7 g
saturated fat, 97 mg cholesterol, 610 mg sodium, 45 g carbohydrates, 4 g fiber, 30 g protein, 407 mg calcium, 4 mg iron

CRAB LASAGNE

Preparation time: **About 30 minutes**
Cooking time: **About 1 hour and 45 minutes**

Try lasagne with sweet, succulent crabmeat
and fennel for an elegant casserole. In this
recipe, you use both the fennel bulbs and
the frondlike leaves (which resemble the herb
dill). Be sure to buy fennel bulbs that are firm and
clean, with straight stalks and fresh green leaves.

2¼ pounds (1.02 kg) fennel, ends trimmed

2 large onions (about 1 lb./455 g total),
thinly sliced

12 ounces (340 g) mushrooms, sliced

2 cups (470 ml) fat-free reduced-sodium
chicken broth

8 ounces (230 g) dried lasagne

2 cups (470 ml) low-fat (1%) milk

¼ cup (60 ml) dry sherry

OVEN-BAKED PAELLA

Preparation time: **About 25 minutes**
Cooking time: **About 1 hour and 5 minutes**

A light variation on the Spanish classic, this paella calls for reduced-fat Italian sausage instead of the fattier chorizo. If you use saffron threads, be sure to crush them just before adding them.

> 2   cups (370 g) long-grain brown rice
>
> 6   ounces (170 g) reduced-fat mild or hot Italian sausage, casings removed
>
> 4   cups (950 ml) vegetable broth
>
> 2   cloves garlic, minced or pressed
>
> ⅛   teaspoon ground saffron or a large pinch of saffron threads, or to taste
>
> 1   can (about 15 oz./425 g) cannellini (white kidney beans), drained and rinsed
>
> 1   package (about 10 oz./285 g) frozen tiny peas, thawed and drained
>
> 1   large tomato (about 8 oz./230 g), coarsely chopped and drained
>
> ½   cup (50 g) thinly sliced green onions
>
> 8   ounces (230 g) small cooked shrimp
>
>   Lemon wedges

1. Spread rice in a shallow 3- to 3½-quart (2.8- to 3.3-liter) casserole, about 9 by 13 inches (23 by 33 cm). Bake in a 350°F (175°C) oven, stirring occasionally, until rice is golden brown (about 25 minutes).

2. Meanwhile, coarsely chop or crumble sausage; then place in a 3- to 4-quart (2.8- to 3.8-liter) pan and cook over medium-high heat, stirring often, until no longer pink (5 to 7 minutes). Remove sausage from pan and set aside; pour off and discard any fat from pan.

3. In same pan, combine 3½ cups (830 ml) of the broth, 2½ cups (590 ml) water, garlic, and saffron. Bring just to a boil over medium-high heat.

Leaving casserole on oven rack, carefully stir broth mixture and sausage into rice. Cover tightly and bake until almost all liquid has been absorbed (about 40 minutes); stir after 20 and 30 minutes, covering casserole tightly again each time.

4. Uncover casserole; stir in remaining ½ cup (120 ml) broth, beans, peas, and tomato. Bake, uncovered, for 5 more minutes. Remove casserole from oven; stir in onions, then sprinkle with shrimp. Garnish with lemon wedges.

Makes 8 servings

NUTRIENTS

Per serving: 322 calories (15% calories from fat), 5 g total fat, 1 g saturated fat, 61 mg cholesterol, 905 mg sodium, 51 g carbohydrates, 3 g fiber, 18 g protein, 49 mg calcium, 3 mg iron

PORK STEW WITH SPAETZLE

Preparation time: **About 10 minutes**
Cooking time: **About 2 hours**

In Germany, spaetzle is often paired with sauerkraut, as in this delicious pork stew flavored with a touch of caraway.

1   pound (455 g) boned pork shoulder or butt, trimmed of fat, cut into 1-inch (2.5-cm) cubes

1   can (about 1 lb./455 g) sauerkraut, drained

¼   cup (65 g) tomato paste

3   tablespoons paprika

2   tablespoons sugar

1   pound (455 g) carrots, cut diagonally ¼ inch (6 mm) thick

    About 10 ounces/285 g (about 2 cups) dried spaetzle or fettuccine

¼   cup (15 g) chopped parsley

½   teaspoon caraway seeds, or to taste

1. Place pork and ¼ cup (60 ml) water in a 5- to 6-quart (5- to 6-liter) pan. Cover and cook over medium-high heat for 10 minutes. Uncover, increase heat to high, and bring to a boil. Cook, stirring often, until liquid has evaporated and drippings are well browned.

2. Add sauerkraut, tomato paste, paprika, sugar, and 3 cups (710 ml) more water. Bring to a boil; reduce heat, cover, and simmer for 1 hour.

3. Stir in carrots. Cover and cook until pork is tender (about 30 more minutes). Meanwhile, bring 12 cups (2.8 liters) water to a boil in a 5- to 6-quart (5- to 6-liter) pan over medium-high heat. Stir in pasta and cook just until tender to bite (about 10 minutes for spaetzle, 8 to 10 minutes for fettuccine); or cook according to package directions. Drain well. Stir in 2 tablespoons of the parsley and caraway seeds. Arrange pasta and stew on individual plates. Sprinkle with remaining parsley.

Makes 4 to 6 servings

NUTRIENTS

Per serving: 454 calories (21% calories from fat), 11 g total fat, 3 g saturated fat, 117 mg cholesterol, 420 mg sodium, 63 g carbohydrates, 6 g fiber, 28 g protein, 72 mg calcium, 6 mg iron

GINGERED BUTTERFLIED LAMB WITH YAMS

Preparation time: **About 25 minutes**
Marinating time: **At least 4 hours**
Roasting time: **About 1 hour**

A tart and spicy marinade infuses every ingredient in this entrée—oven-roasted yam wedges, tender onion halves, and thinly sliced boned leg of lamb.

⅓   cup (38 g) chopped fresh ginger

8   cloves garlic

¼   teaspoon pepper

1½   tablespoons (23 ml) soy sauce

¾   cup (180 ml) red wine vinegar

2   to 2½ pounds (905 g to 1.15 kg) boneless butterflied leg of lamb

2   teaspoons sugar

¼   cup (38 g) raisins

    Vegetable oil cooking spray

8   to 10 small yams or sweet potatoes (3½ to 4 lbs./1.6 to 1.8 kg total), scrubbed

8   to 10 small onions (each about 2 inches/5 cm in diameter), unpeeled, cut into halves lengthwise

1   cup (240 ml) beef broth

1. In a food processor or blender, combine ginger, garlic, pepper, soy sauce, and 2 tablespoons (30 ml) of the vinegar. Whirl until mixture forms a paste; set aside.

2. Trim and discard surface fat covering lamb. Lay lamb flat in a 9- by 13-inch (25- by 33-cm)

baking dish; spoon ginger mixture around lamb. Mix sugar, raisins, and remaining 10 tablespoons (150 ml) vinegar; pour over lamb. Cover and refrigerate for at least 4 hours or up to a day.

3. Spray a roasting pan (12 by 17 inches/30 by 43 cm or larger) with cooking spray. Cut unpeeled yams lengthwise into 1-inch-thick (2.5-cm-thick) wedges. Arrange yams and onion halves, cut sides down, in pan. Spray all vegetables with cooking spray. Roast on lower rack of a 425°F (220°C) oven for 15 minutes.

4. Meanwhile, lift lamb from dish, reserving marinade. Place lamb, boned side down, on a rack in a shallow baking pan. Insert a meat thermometer in thickest part.

5. After vegetables have roasted for 15 minutes, place lamb in oven on middle rack. Continue to roast both lamb and vegetables, basting lamb occasionally with marinade, for 30 minutes. Lift raisins from marinade and sprinkle over lamb. Drizzle vegetables with all but 3 tablespoons (45 ml) of the remaining marinade. Continue to roast until vegetables are tender when pierced and thermometer registers 140° to 145°F (60° to 63°C) for medium-rare (10 to 15 more minutes).

6. Transfer lamb, onions, and yams to a platter; cover lightly with foil and keep warm. To lamb cooking pan, add broth and reserved 3 tablespoons (45 ml) marinade; cook over medium heat, stirring to scrape up browned bits, until reduced to about ¾ cup (180 ml).

7. Cut lamb across the grain into thin slices; serve with onions, yams, and sauce to add to taste.

Makes 8 to 10 servings

NUTRIENTS

Per serving: 379 calories (15% calories from fat), 6 g total fat, 2 g saturated fat, 73 mg cholesterol, 450 mg sodium, 53 g carbohydrates, 6 g fiber, 27 g protein, 59 mg calcium, 3 mg iron

HUNTER'S-STYLE LAMB STEW

Preparation time: **About 25 minutes**
Cooking time: **About 1 hour and 30 minutes**

This meaty lamb-mushroom stew is bound to win compliments at your next large gathering.

2 pounds (905 g) boneless loin or leg of lamb, trimmed of fat and cut into 1-inch (2.5-cm) chunks

1½ cups (360 ml) dry white wine

12 ounces (340 g) mushrooms, quartered

2 cloves garlic, minced or pressed

2 tablespoons fresh rosemary
Lemon-Caper Rice (page 171)

¾ teaspoon cornstarch blended with 1 tablespoon (15 ml) cold water

2 tablespoons (30 ml) red wine vinegar
Salt and pepper

1. In a wide 3½- to 4-quart (3.3- to 3.8-liter) pan, combine lamb and ¾ cup (180 ml) of the wine. Place over medium-low heat, cover, and cook gently for 30 minutes. Add mushrooms, garlic, and rosemary; cook, uncovered, stirring occasionally, until almost all liquid has evaporated and juices are browned (25 to 30 minutes). Meanwhile, prepare Lemon-Caper Rice.

2. Add remaining ¾ cup (180 ml) wine to pan, stirring to scrape up browned bits. Reduce heat, cover, and continue to simmer until lamb is very tender when pierced (25 to 30 more minutes). Stir cornstarch mixture and pour into pan; cook, stirring, until liquid is bubbly. Stir in vinegar, then season to taste with salt and pepper.

Makes 8 servings

NUTRIENTS

Per serving with Lemon-Caper Rice: 307 calories (30% calories from fat), 10 g total fat, 3 g saturated fat, 79 mg cholesterol, 391 mg sodium, 25 g carbohydrates, 0.8 g fiber, 28 g protein, 34 mg calcium, 4 mg iron

GRILLED
LEG OF LAMB
& PEARS

Preparation time: **About 30 minutes**
Marinating time: **At least 2 hours**
Cooking time: **About 1 hour and 5 minutes**

A combination of butterflied leg of lamb and pears is certain to make any barbecue memorable. Before grilling, both meat and fruit are soaked in a piquant orange-onion marinade that doubles as a tart relish.

1   medium-size orange (about 8 oz./ 230 g)

1   large red onion, minced

2   cups (470 ml) dry red wine

½   cup (120 ml) beef broth

½   cup (75 g) golden or dark raisins

¼   cup (60 ml) raspberry vinegar

¼   cup (60 ml) balsamic vinegar

2   tablespoons minced fresh ginger

¼   cup (50 g) sugar

1   tablespoon (15 ml) Dijon mustard

5   or 6 large firm-ripe pears (about 8 oz./230 g each), peeled, halved, and cored

1   leg of lamb (about 6 lbs./2.7 kg), boned and trimmed of fat

    Salt and pepper

1. To prepare onion relish marinade, with a vegetable peeler or sharp knife, remove peel (colored part only) from orange. Finely chop peel and place in a 4- to 5-quart (3.8- to 5-liter) pan. Cut off and discard remaining peel and white pith. Holding orange over pan, cut between membranes to free segments; drop segments into pan. Squeeze juice from membranes into pan; discard membranes.

2. To pan, add onion, wine, broth, raisins, raspberry and balsamic vinegars, ginger, sugar, and mustard; bring to a boil over high heat. Add pears;

reduce heat, cover, and simmer, turning fruit over occasionally, until tender when pierced (about 10 minutes).

3. With a slotted spoon, gently transfer pears to a bowl. Pour about a fourth of the pan liquid through a strainer over pears; return solids in strainer to pan. Cover pears and refrigerate for at least 2 hours or until next day, turning fruit over occasionally.

4. Meanwhile, place lamb, boned side up, on a board; cut long, deep slashes through thickest sections and press apart to give meat an even thickness. Place lamb in a large bowl; add remaining onion relish marinade from pear cooking pan. Cover and refrigerate for at least 2 hours or until next day, turning lamb over several times.

5. Lift lamb from marinade; shake off seasonings. Set lamb aside. Transfer marinade left in bowl to a 4- to 5-quart (3.8- to 5-liter) pan; then drain liquid from pears into pan. Bring to a boil over high heat; boil, uncovered, stirring often, until mixture is reduced to about 2½ cups (590 ml) and almost all liquid has evaporated (about 10 minutes). Pour this onion relish into a small bowl; set aside at room temperature.

6. Lay lamb out flat, boned side up, on a grill over a solid bed of hot coals. Scatter 10 charcoal briquets onto coals. Cook, turning as needed, until lamb is evenly browned and done to your liking; cut in thickest part to test (about 45 minutes for medium-rare).

7. About 15 minutes before lamb is done, thread pear halves, cut sides up, onto parallel thin metal skewers (this keeps fruit from spinning). Lay pears on grill and cook, turning several times, until warm (about 15 minutes).

8. Transfer lamb and pears to a large warm platter. Slice lamb; serve with pears and onion relish. Season to taste with salt and pepper.

Makes 10 to 12 servings

NUTRIENTS

Per serving: 350 calories (25% calories from fat), 10 g total fat, 3 g saturated fat, 106 mg cholesterol, 194 mg sodium, 31 g carbohydrates, 4 g fiber, 35 g protein, 420mg calcium, 3 mg iron

CURRIED LAMB WITH GRAPE CHUTNEY

Preparation time: **About 35 minutes**
Cooking time: **About 1 hour and 30 minutes**

If you want to add interest to a simple lamb curry, serve it with warm homemade grape-apple chutney. While the chutney simmers, you can easily cook the meat and a pan of fluffy couscous. To save time, make the chutney in advance and reheat it before serving if desired.

- 1   large onion, finely chopped
- 1   large tart apple such as Newtown Pippin or McIntosh (about 8 oz./ 230 g), peeled, cored, and finely chopped
- 2   cups (320 g) seedless red or green grapes
- ⅓   cup (75 g) firmly packed brown sugar
- ⅓   cup (80 ml) red wine vinegar
- ⅛   teaspoon pepper
      Salt
- 1   pound (455 g) lean boneless leg of lamb, trimmed of fat and cut into 1-inch (2.5-cm) cubes
- 10 ounces (285 g) tiny onions (each about ¾ inch/2 cm in diameter), peeled
- 2½ teaspoons curry powder
- 1½ cups (360 ml) fat-free reduced-sodium chicken broth
- 1   cup (185 g) couscous
- 1   tablespoon (15 ml) olive oil
- 1   tablespoon chopped fresh mint, or to taste
      Mint sprigs

1. To prepare grape chutney, in a wide nonstick frying pan or wok, combine onion and ¼ cup (60 ml) water. Cook over medium-high heat, stirring occasionally, until liquid evaporates and onion begins to brown and stick to pan bottom.

To deglaze pan, add ¼ cup (60 ml) more water and stir to scrape browned bits free from pan bottom. Then continue to cook, stirring often, until liquid evaporates and browned bits stick to pan again. Deglaze with ¼ cup (60 ml) more water; then cook, stirring often, until onion is richly browned. (Total cooking time will be 10 to 15 minutes.)

2. To pan, add apple, grapes, ½ cup (120 ml) water, sugar, vinegar, and pepper. Bring to a boil; then reduce heat, cover, and simmer until grapes begin to split (about 10 minutes).

3. Uncover pan. Increase heat to medium-high and cook, stirring often, until mixture is thick and almost all liquid has evaporated (about 20 minutes); as mixture thickens, watch carefully and stir more often to prevent scorching. Season to taste with salt. (At this point, you may cool, then cover and refrigerate for up to 3 days. Reheat before serving, if desired. Makes about 2¼ cups /530 ml.)

4. When chutney is almost done, combine lamb, onions, curry powder, and ½ teaspoon salt in a large bowl; turn meat and onions to coat with seasonings. Set aside.

5. In a 3- to 4-quart (2.8- to 3.8-liter) pan, bring broth to a boil over high heat; stir in couscous. Cover, remove from heat, and let stand until liquid has been absorbed (about 5 minutes). Keep warm; fluff occasionally with a fork.

6. While couscous is standing, heat oil in a wide nonstick frying pan or wok over medium-high heat. When oil is hot, add lamb and onions. Stir-fry just until onions are heated through and meat is done to your liking; cut to test (5 to 7 minutes for medium-rare). Add water, 1 tablespoon (15 ml) at a time, if pan appears dry.

7. Spoon couscous onto a rimmed platter. Spoon meat and onions over couscous; sprinkle with chopped mint. Garnish with mint sprigs. Offer grape chutney on side to add to taste.

Makes 4 servings

NUTRIENTS

Per serving with ¼ cup grape chutney: 543 calories (17% calories from fat), 10 g total fat, 2 g saturated fat, 73 mg cholesterol, 607 mg sodium, 83 g carbohydrates, 6 g fiber, 33 g protein, 79 mg calcium, 4 mg iron

BRAISED VEAL SHANKS

Preparation time: **About 10 minutes**
Cooking time: **About 2 hours and 15 minutes**

Oven-browning and long baking ensure meat that's both tender and richly flavored. Gravy made from the seasoned pan juices is a delicious extra; allow guests to serve it for themselves.

6   veal shanks, each about 6 inches (15 cm) long (about 6 lbs./2.7 kg total); have your butcher split each shank in half crosswise

1   lemon (unpeeled), chopped

4   cups (950 ml) beef broth

1   teaspoon dried marjoram

1   dried bay leaf

½   teaspoon whole black peppercorns

¼   teaspoon coriander seeds

2   tablespoons (30 ml) balsamic or red wine vinegar

1   tablespoon cornstarch mixed with 2 tablespoons (30 ml) cold water

1. Lay veal in a single layer in a 9- by 13-inch (23- by 33-cm) baking pan. Bake in a 400°F (205°C) oven until browned (about 35 minutes). Remove pan from oven; turn veal over. Then add lemon, broth, marjoram, bay leaf, peppercorns, and coriander seeds to pan. Cover tightly with foil, return to oven, and bake until meat is so tender it pulls apart easily (about 1½ hours). With a slotted spoon, lift veal shanks gently to a warm platter; keep warm.

2. Pour pan juices through a fine strainer into a 1-quart (950-liter) measure; press residue in strainer to extract any liquid. Discard residue. (At this point, you may cover and refrigerate veal and pan juices separately until next day. Before continuing, reheat veal, covered, in a 400°F (205°C) oven until warm, 15 to 20 minutes. Place on a warm platter; keep warm.)

3. Skim and discard fat from pan juices (or lift off and discard solidified fat from chilled juices). Pour pan juices into a wide frying pan; add vinegar and bring to a boil over high heat. Boil, uncovered, until reduced to 1½ to 2 cups/360 to 470 ml (8 to 12 minutes). Stir in cornstarch mixture and return to a boil, stirring.

4. Pour gravy into a small pitcher; offer at the table to pour over meat to taste.

Makes 6 servings

NUTRIENTS

Per serving: 267 calories (16% calories from fat), 4 g total fat, 1 g saturated fat, 177 mg cholesterol, 1,240 mg sodium, 4 g carbohydrates, 0.1 g fiber, 49 g protein, 27 mg calcium, 3 mg iron

BRAISED VEAL WITH ESCAROLE & PASTA

Preparation time: **About 15 minutes**
Cooking time: **About 1 hour and 20 minutes**

If desired, substitute boneless veal shoulder for the roast. Look for heads of escarole that are crisp, with no yellowing.

2   tablespoons (30 ml) olive oil

2   pounds (905 g) veal tip roast, trimmed of fat, cut into 1-inch (2.5-cm) cubes

2   ounces (55 g) thinly sliced prosciutto, shredded

1   large onion, finely chopped

1   large carrot, finely chopped

1   cup (240 ml) dry white wine

14   to 16 ounces (400 to 455 g) fresh fettuccine

18   cups lightly packed shredded escarole (about 1½ lbs./680 g)

4   teaspoons cornstarch mixed with ½ cup (120 ml) water

1. Heat 1 tablespoon of the oil in a 5- to 6-quart (5- to 6-liter) pan (preferably a nonstick pan) over medium-high heat. Add half the veal and cook, turning often, until browned (about 5 minutes); remove from pan. Repeat with remaining oil and veal. Set aside.

2. Add prosciutto, onion, and carrot to pan. Cook, stirring often, until soft (about 5 minutes). Return veal to pan. Add wine and 1 cup (240 ml) water. Bring to a boil; reduce heat, cover, and simmer, stirring occasionally, until veal is tender when pierced (about 1 hour).

3. Meanwhile, bring 4 quarts (3.8 liters) water to a boil in a 6- to 8-quart (6- to 8-liter) pan. Stir in pasta and cook just until tender to bite (1 to 3 minutes; or according to package directions). Drain well and transfer to a deep platter; keep warm.

4. Add escarole to veal, a portion at a time if needed, and cook, stirring, until wilted (about 3 minutes). Stir cornstarch mixture and add to veal. Increase heat to high and cook, stirring, until mixture comes to a boil. Spoon over pasta.

Makes 6 servings

NUTRIENTS

Per serving: 454 calories (24% calories from fat), 12 g total fat, 3 g saturated fat, 198 mg cholesterol, 352 mg sodium, 43 g carbohydrates, 5 g fiber, 42 g protein, 106 mg calcium, 5 mg iron

VEAL CHOPS & SAGE DRESSING

Preparation time: **About 15 minutes**
Cooking time: **About 45 minutes**

Treat family and friends to this tempting meal. Juicy veal chops topped with a sage-seasoned apple dressing are simmered to tenderness in white wine and chicken broth.

1   large onion, chopped

1½   cups (360 ml) fat-free reduced-sodium chicken broth

4   cups (120 g) cubed whole wheat bread (½-inch/1-cm cubes)

2   stalks celery, thinly sliced

1   large tart green apple such as Granny Smith or Newtown Pippin (about 8 oz./230 g), cored and chopped

1   cup (145 g) raisins

1   teaspoon dried sage

4   veal loin chops (about 1½ lbs./680 g total)

½   cup (120 ml) dry white wine

1. Place onion and ½ cup (120 ml) of the broth in a wide nonstick frying pan. Cook over high heat, stirring often, until onion is soft and liquid has evaporated (about 5 minutes). Scrape onion into a large bowl; add ½ cup (120 ml) more broth, bread, celery, apple, raisins, and sage. Mix until well blended.

2. Add veal chops to pan and cook over medium-high heat, turning once, until well browned on both sides (about 5 minutes). Pile dressing evenly over chops. Pour wine and remaining ½ cup (120 ml) broth around chops; bring to a boil. Reduce heat to low, cover, and simmer until veal is very tender when pierced (about 35 minutes).

Makes 4 servings

NUTRIENTS

Per serving: 369 calories (20% calories from fat), 8 g total fat, 3 g saturated fat, 57 mg cholesterol, 496 mg sodium, 58 g carbohydrates, 6 g fiber, 20 g protein, 81 mg calcium, 3 mg iron

VEAL CHOPS WITH NOODLE PUDDING

Pictured on facing page
Preparation time: **About 15 minutes**
Cooking time: **About 3 hours and 5 minutes**

Moist and rich noodle pudding enhances these veal chops. The pudding bakes in the oven with the chops during the last 40 minutes.

8 large veal loin chops (about 4 lbs./ 1.8 kg total), trimmed of fat

About ¼ cup (30 g) all-purpose flour

2 teaspoons olive oil

16 sage leaves

1½ cups (360 ml) dry white wine

⅓ cup (70 g) plus 3 tablespoons granulated sugar

¼ cup (60 g) butter or margarine

½ teaspoon ground cinnamon

1½ cups (40 g) corn flake cereal

5 ounces/140 g (about 4 cups) dried wide egg noodles

1 cup (240 ml) peach or apricot nectar

½ cup (122 g) smooth applesauce

½ cup (105 g) low-fat (1%) cottage cheese

2 large egg whites

1 teaspoon cornstarch mixed with 1 tablespoon (15 ml) water

½ cup (75 g) raisins

2 teaspoons brown sugar, or to taste

2 tablespoons minced parsley

2 tablespoons chopped green onion

4 teaspoons (20 ml) white wine vinegar, or to taste

Sage sprigs

1. Coat chops lightly with flour. Heat oil in a wide nonstick frying pan over medium heat. Add sage leaves. Cook, stirring, until darker in color (about 2 minutes). With a slotted spoon, remove from pan and set aside. Add chops, half at a time, and cook, turning, until browned on both sides (about 6 minutes). Place in a lightly oiled 12- by 17-inch (30- by 43-cm) roasting pan, overlapping chops as little as possible. Top with sage leaves. Pour in wine. Cover tightly and bake in a 375°F (190°C) oven until tender when pierced and slightly pink in center; cut to test (about 2 hours).

2. Meanwhile, prepare noodle pudding. To prepare crunch topping, in a food processor or bowl, combine ⅓ cup (70 g) of the granulated sugar, butter, and cinnamon. Whirl or beat well. Add corn flakes. Mix gently. Press into lumps; set aside.

3. Bring 8 cups (1.9 liters) water to a boil in a 5-quart (5-liter) pan over medium-high heat. Stir in noodles and cook just until tender to bite (8 to 10 minutes), or according to package directions.

4. Meanwhile, combine nectar, applesauce, cheese, the remaining 3 tablespoons granulated sugar, and egg whites in a blender. Stir cornstarch mixture and add to blender. Whirl until smooth.

5. Drain noodles well and transfer to a nonstick or lightly oiled 8-inch-square (20-cm-square) baking pan. Stir in raisins and cheese mixture. Crumble topping over pudding. Bake in a 375°F (190°C) oven until a knife inserted in center comes out clean and top is golden (about 40 minutes); check to be sure top does not overbrown.

6. Lift out chops and keep warm. Skim and discard fat from pan drippings and measure. If less than 1 cup (240 ml), add water and bring to a boil in a 1- to 1½-quart (950-ml to 1.4-liter) pan over high heat; if more, pour drippings into pan and boil until reduced to 1 cup (240 ml). Add brown sugar and cook, stirring, until melted; remove from heat. Stir in parsley, onion, and vinegar.

7. To serve, arrange veal chops and noodle pudding on 8 individual plates. Drizzle gravy over chops. Garnish with sage sprigs.

Makes 8 servings

NUTRIENTS

Per serving: 452 calories (25% calories from fat), 13 g total fat, 6 g saturated fat, 138 mg cholesterol, 313 mg sodium, 52 g carbohydrates, 1 g fiber, 33 g protein, 114 mg calcium, 4 mg iron

VEAL CHOPS WITH NOODLE PUDDING (RECIPE ON FACING PAGE)

Roast Turkey with Apple Orzo (recipe on page 225)

Capellini with Tomatoes & White Beans (recipe on page 244)

GRILLED BEEF & PEPPERS WITH ORZO (RECIPE ON FACING PAGE)

Grilled Beef & Peppers with Orzo

Pictured on facing page
Preparation time: **About 20 minutes**
Marinating time: **At least 30 minutes**
Cooking time: **About 25 minutes**

This appealing dinner, cooked on the grill, features skewers of multicolored bell peppers and pounded, marinated top round steak. Accompany the grilled meat with rice-shaped pasta dotted with toasted pine nuts.

  1 tablespoon (15 ml) lemon juice

  1 tablespoon (20 ml) plus 1 teaspoon olive oil

 ⅓ cup (80 ml) dry red wine

1½ pounds (680 g) boneless beef top round (about ½ inch/1 cm thick), trimmed of fat

  1 small green bell pepper (about 5 oz./140 g)

  1 small red bell pepper (about 5 oz./140 g)

  1 small yellow bell pepper (about 5 oz./140 g)

 12 rosemary sprigs, each about 12 inches (30 cm) long

  2 tablespoons pine nuts

  2 cloves garlic, minced or pressed

  1 teaspoon dried basil

 ½ teaspoon dried marjoram

  1 cup (5 to 7 oz./170 to 200 g) orzo

  1 tablespoon (15 ml) tarragon vinegar

   Salt and pepper

1. Set a large heavy-duty plastic bag in a shallow pan. In bag, combine lemon juice, 1 teaspoon of the oil, and wine.

2. Cut beef across the grain into 6 strips; place between sheets of plastic wrap, then pound until

each piece is about ¼ inch (6 mm) thick. Cut peppers lengthwise into sixths; remove and discard seeds. Add beef and peppers to marinade; seal bag and turn to coat beef and peppers with marinade. Refrigerate for at least 30 minutes or up to a day.

3. Lift beef strips and peppers from bag, reserving marinade. On each of 6 metal skewers (at least 10 inches/25 cm long), weave one beef strip and 3 bell pepper pieces (one of each color), rippling beef slightly around peppers. For each skewer, tuck 2 rosemary sprigs between meat and skewer. Set skewers aside.

4. To prepare orzo, toast pine nuts in a small non-stick frying pan over medium-low heat until lightly browned (about 3 minutes), stirring. Remove from pan and let cool. Heat remaining 1 tablespoon (15 ml) olive oil in same pan; add garlic, basil, and marjoram. Cook, stirring, until garlic is soft but not browned (about 2 minutes). Set aside.

5. In a 3- to 4-quart (2.8- to 3.8-liter) pan, cook orzo in 2 quarts (1.9 liters) boiling water until tender to bite (about 10 minutes); or cook according to package directions. Drain well, transfer to a warm bowl, and mix gently with garlic mixture, pine nuts, and vinegar.

6. Place skewers on a lightly greased grill 4 to 6 inches (10 to 15 cm) above a bed of hot coals. Cook, turning and brushing with marinade, until meat is browned and done to your liking; cut to test (6 to 8 minutes for rare). Season to taste with salt and pepper. Serve with orzo.

Makes 6 servings

NUTRIENTS

Per serving: 335 calories (27% calories from fat), 10 g total fat, 2 g saturated fat, 72 mg cholesterol, 58 mg sodium, 27 g carbohydrates, 1 g fiber, 32 g protein, 75 mg calcium, 5 mg iron

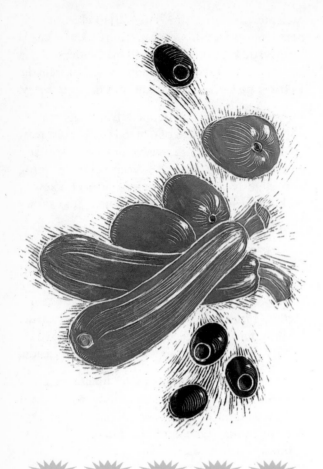

1 small red or yellow bell pepper (about 5 oz./140 g), seeded and finely chopped

8 ounces (230 g) mushrooms, thinly sliced

1 cup (45g) finely diced unpeeled eggplant

2 to 4 canned peperoncini peppers, drained, seeded, and minced

1 pound (455 g) pear-shaped (Roma-type) tomatoes, cut lengthwise into eighths

2 small zucchini (about 5 oz./140 g total), thinly sliced

6 large pitted ripe olives, thinly sliced

1 pound (455 g) dried spaghetti

Salt and pepper

Grated Parmesan cheese (optional)

1. Soak sun-dried tomatoes in hot water to cover until very soft (about 1 hour).

2. About 30 minutes before serving, heat oil in a 4- to 5-quart (3.8- to 5-liter) pan over medium heat. Add onion, garlic, carrot, bell pepper, mushrooms, and eggplant; cook, stirring often, until all liquid has evaporated and vegetables are soft (about 20 minutes).

3. Drain soaked tomatoes, discarding liquid; chop tomatoes and add to eggplant mixture along with peperoncini, pear-shaped tomatoes, zucchini, and olives. Increase heat to high and cook, stirring often, until almost all liquid has evaporated (8 to 10 minutes).

4. Meanwhile, in a 6- to 8-quart (6- to 7.6-liter) pan, cook spaghetti in 4 quarts (3.8 liters) boiling water just until tender to bite (10 to 12 minutes); or cook according to package directions. Drain well and place in a warm wide serving bowl.

5. Season vegetable sauce to taste with salt and pepper; spoon over pasta. If desired, serve with Parmesan cheese to add to taste.

Makes 6 servings

Spaghetti alla Calabrese

Preparation time: **About 25 minutes**
Soaking time: **About 1 hour**
Cooking time: **About 30 minutes**

In Calabria—a region at the "toe" of boot-shaped Italy—local produce plays a major role in many traditional dishes. This bright sauce combines sun-dried tomatoes with a variety of fresh vegetables; it's best over spaghetti or other pasta. Adjust the number of piquant peperoncini to suit your taste.

⅓ cup (40 g) sun-dried tomatoes

2 tablespoons (30 ml) olive oil

1 medium-size onion, chopped

3 cloves garlic, minced or pressed

1 medium-size carrot (about 3 oz./85 g), diced

NUTRIENTS

Per serving: 404 calories (15% calories from fat), 7 g total fat, 0.9 g saturated fat, 0 mg cholesterol, 291 mg sodium, 74 g carbohydrates, 6 g fiber, 14 g protein, 46 mg calcium, 4 mg iron

Eggplant & Zucchini Lasagne

Preparation time: **About 45 minutes**
Cooking time: **About 1 hour and 15 minutes**

Slices of eggplant and zucchini replace the typical wide noodles in this variation on an old favorite. The filling includes tofu and chewy brown rice.

- 2 medium-size eggplants (about 2½ lbs./1.15 kg total)
- 4 small zucchini (about 1 lb./455 g total)
- 1 tablespoon (15 ml) olive oil
- 10 ounces (285 g) firm reduced-fat tofu, rinsed and drained
- 1½ cups (360 ml) nonfat cottage cheese
- 1½ cups (about 6 oz./170 g) shredded part-skim mozzarella cheese
- 1 cup (145 g) cooked brown rice
- ½ teaspoon fennel seeds, crushed
- ½ teaspoon crushed red pepper flakes
- 2½ cups (590 ml) purchased reduced-fat spaghetti sauce
- 2 tablespoons grated Parmesan cheese

1. Cut unpeeled eggplants crosswise into ½-inch (1-cm) slices; cut zucchini lengthwise into ¼-inch (6-mm) slices. Brush 3 shallow 10- by 15-inch (25- by 38-cm) baking pans with oil; arrange vegetable slices in a single layer in pans. Bake in a 400°F (205°C) oven for 15 minutes; then turn vegetables over and continue to bake until tinged with brown (about 15 more minutes).

2. Meanwhile, slice tofu; place between paper towels and press gently to release excess liquid. Place tofu in a medium-size bowl and mash well. Mix in cottage cheese, mozzarella cheese, rice, fennel seeds, and red pepper flakes.

3. Spread ½ cup (120 ml) of the spaghetti sauce in a 9- by 13-inch (23- by 33-cm) baking pan. Top evenly with half each of the eggplant, zucchini, and tofu mixture; spread with 1 cup (240 ml) more spaghetti sauce. Repeat layers. Sprinkle with Parmesan cheese. Bake in a 400°F (205°C) oven until heated through (about 45 minutes). Let stand for about 10 minutes before serving.

Makes 8 servings

NUTRIENTS

Per serving: 228 calories (26% calories from fat), 7 g total fat, 3 g saturated fat, 17 mg cholesterol, 560 mg sodium, 26 g carbohydrates, 4 g fiber, 17 g protein, 282 mg calcium, 2 mg iron

HARVEST GRATIN

Preparation time: **About 15 minutes**
Cooking time: **About 1 hour and 50 minutes**

Sweet potatoes are paired with apples in this early-fall dish. You can use a gratin pan if you have one.

3 large sweet potatoes or yams (about 1½ lbs./680 g total), peeled

1 cup (240 ml) apple juice

About ½ teaspoon cider vinegar

2 large tart apples such Newtown Pippin or Granny Smith (about 1 lb./455 g total)

1 tablespoon firmly packed brown sugar

4 ounces (115 g) prosciutto, cut into thin strips about 1 inch (2.5 cm) long

1 tablespoon chopped fresh oregano

1 cup (240 ml) plain nonfat yogurt

1. In a 4- to 5-quart (3.8- to 5-liter) pan, bring 8 cups (1.9 liters) water to a boil over medium-high heat. Add potatoes; then reduce heat, cover, and simmer for 20 minutes. Meanwhile, in a small pan, bring apple juice to a boil over high heat. Boil until reduced to ⅔ cup/160 ml (about 8 minutes). Stir in vinegar and set aside.

2. Drain potatoes well and let stand until cool enough to handle; then peel and cut into slices about ½ inch (1 cm) thick. Set aside. Peel and core apples; cut into slices about ½ inch (1 cm) thick.

3. Decoratively arrange potato and apple slices in a greased oval 2-quart (1.9-liter) casserole, about 8 by 12 inches (20 by 30 cm). Pour apple juice mixture over potato mixture and sprinkle with sugar. Cover tightly and bake in a 375°F (190°C) oven for 45 minutes.

4. Uncover casserole and spoon pan juices over potatoes and apples. Return to oven and bake, uncovered, basting occasionally with pan juices, until potatoes and apples are very soft and almost all liquid has evaporated (30 to 40 more minutes). Ten minutes before casserole is done, sprinkle

prosciutto on top; when vegetables are done, prosciutto should be crisp and light brown. Sprinkle with oregano; offer yogurt to add to taste.

Makes 4 servings

NUTRIENTS

Per serving: 328 calories (16% calories from fat), 6 g total fat, 2 g saturated fat, 24 mg cholesterol, 586 mg sodium, 58 g carbohydrates, 6 g fiber, 14 g protein, 154 mg calcium, 2 mg iron

CAPELLINI WITH TOMATOES & WHITE BEANS

Pictured on page 239
Preparation time: **About 15 minutes**
Cooking time: **About 1 hour and 15 minutes**

As the vegetables for this hearty pasta dish brown slowly in the oven, they caramelize, giving a rich, sweet flavor.

1 medium-size red onion, cut into ¾-inch (2-cm) chunks

1 tablespoon (15 ml) olive oil

6 tablespoons (90 ml) balsamic vinegar

14 medium-size pear-shaped (Roma-type) tomatoes (about 1¾ lbs./ 795 g total), halved lengthwise

Salt

8 ounces (230 g) dried capellini

2 cans (about 15 oz./425 g each) cannellini (white kidney beans)

3 tablespoons chopped fresh thyme

3 tablespoons chopped fresh basil

Thyme sprigs

1. Mix onion, 1 teaspoon of the oil, and 2 tablespoons (30 ml) of the vinegar in a lightly oiled 8-inch-square (20-cm-square) baking pan. Arrange tomatoes, cut sides up, in a lightly oiled 9- by 13-inch (23- by 33-cm) baking pan; rub with remaining 2 teaspoons oil and season with salt.

2. Bake onion and tomatoes in a 475°F (245°C) oven, switching pan positions halfway through baking, until edges of vegetables are well browned (40 to 50 minutes for onion, about 1 hour and 10 minutes for tomatoes); if drippings begin to burn, add 4 to 6 tablespoons (60 to 90 ml) water to each pan, stirring to loosen browned bits. Meanwhile, bring 8 cups (1.9 liters) water to a boil in a 4- to 5-quart (3.8- to 5-liter) pan over medium-high heat. Stir in pasta and cook just until tender to bite (about 4 minutes); or cook according to package directions.

3. Drain pasta well and keep warm. Pour beans and their liquid into pan. Add chopped thyme. Bring to a boil; reduce heat and simmer, stirring often, for 3 minutes. Add pasta; lift with 2 forks to mix. Remove from heat; keep warm.

4. Chop 10 of the tomato halves. Add to pasta with chopped basil, onion, and remaining ¼ cup (60 ml) vinegar. Transfer pasta to a wide, shallow serving bowl. Arrange remaining tomato halves around edge. Garnish with thyme sprigs.

Makes 4 to 6 servings

NUTRIENTS

Per serving: 401 calories (12% calories from fat), 6 g total fat, 0.8 g saturated fat, 0 mg cholesterol, 616 mg sodium, 73 g carbohydrates, 15 g fiber, 17 g protein, 111 mg calcium, 6 mg iron

BLACK BEANS WITH VEGETABLES

Preparation time: **About 30 minutes**
Soaking time: **1 hour**
Cooking time: **About 3 hours**

Black beans mingle with brown rice, bell peppers, and chiles in this hearty, nourishing soup-stew. To save time, you could use canned black beans.

1 pound (455 g) dried black beans

2 tablespoons (30 ml) olive oil or vegetable oil

2 large red onions (about 1½ lbs./680 g total), finely chopped

2 large green bell peppers (1 to 1¼ lbs./455 to 565 g total), seeded and chopped

2 large red bell peppers (1 to 1¼ lbs./455 to 565 g total), seeded and chopped

1 small can (about 4 oz./115 g) diced green chiles

1 large head garlic (about 2½ oz./70 g), separated into cloves, peeled, and minced or pressed

1½ tablespoons dried oregano

3 vegetable bouillon cubes

¼ cup (60 ml) dry sherry (optional)

Salt and pepper

4 to 6 cups (580 g) hot cooked brown rice

1. Rinse and sort beans, discarding any debris; drain. In a 6- to 8-quart (6- to 7.6-liter) pan, bring beans and 2 quarts (1.9 liters) water to a boil; boil for 5 minutes. Cover; remove from heat. Let stand for 1 hour. Drain; set aside.

2. In same pan, heat oil over medium-high heat. Add onions, bell peppers, chiles, garlic, and oregano. Cook, stirring often, until vegetables are soft and tinged with brown (25 to 30 minutes).

3. Add beans, 6 cups (1.4 liters) water, and bouillon cubes to pan. Bring to a boil; reduce heat, cover, and simmer until beans are soft to bite (about 2½ hours), adding more water as needed to keep beans from drying out. Mash some of the beans to thicken mixture slightly. Stir in sherry, if desired. Season to taste with salt and pepper. Mound rice in 8 to 10 wide, shallow bowls; spoon bean mixture over rice.

Makes 8 to 10 servings

NUTRIENTS

Per serving: 368 calories (12% calories from fat), 5 g total fat, 0.8 g saturated fat, 0 mg cholesterol, 402 mg sodium, 68 g carbohydrates, 11 g fiber, 16 g protein, 126 mg calcium, 4 mg iron

FIERY OVEN STRATA

Preparation time: **About 20 minutes**
Chilling time: **At least 8 hours**
Cooking time: **About 55 minutes**

This version of strata—a layered casserole of bread, cheese, and eggs—gets a kick from chiles and hot pepper seasoning.

OVEN STRATA:

12 slices firm-textured whole wheat bread

2 cups (140 g) thinly sliced mushrooms

1 cup (100 g) sliced green onions

1 large can (about 7 oz./200 g) diced green chiles

3 cups (about 12 oz./340 g) shredded reduced-fat sharp Cheddar cheese

3 large eggs

4 large egg whites

2½ cups (590 ml) nonfat milk

1 tablespoon dry mustard

About 1 teaspoon liquid hot pepper seasoning, or to taste

1 cup (115 g) coarsely crushed low-fat baked tortilla chips

TOMATO SALSA:

2 medium-size tomatoes (about 12 oz./340 g total), chopped

½ small onion, finely chopped

1 can (about 4 oz./115 g) diced green chiles

4 teaspoons (20 ml) distilled white vinegar

1 tablespoon chopped cilantro

Sugar

1. Line bottom of a 9- by 13-inch (23- by 33-cm) baking pan with a single layer of bread; use about half the bread slices, trimming them to fit and reserving scraps. Top bread with half the mushrooms and green onions, half the large can of chiles, and half the cheese. Repeat, starting with bread (and any scraps) and ending with cheese.

2. In a large bowl, beat eggs and egg whites until blended. Add milk, mustard, and hot pepper seasoning; beat to blend well. Pour egg mixture slowly over ingredients in pan; cover and refrigerate for at least 8 hours or up to 24 hours. Then uncover, sprinkle with tortilla chips, and bake in a 350°F (175°C) oven until golden (about 55 minutes). Let stand for about 15 minutes before serving.

3. Meanwhile, to prepare tomato salsa, in a medium-size bowl, stir together tomatoes, chopped onion, the 4-ounce (115-g) can of chiles, vinegar, and cilantro. Season to taste with sugar.

4. To serve, cut strata into squares or spoon it from pan. Offer tomato salsa to add to taste.

Makes 10 servings

NUTRIENTS

Per serving: 297 calories (29% calories from fat), 10 g total fat, 5 g saturated fat, 89 mg cholesterol, 759 mg sodium, 32 g carbohydrates, 5 g fiber, 22 g protein, 439 mg calcium, 2 mg iron

CRANBERRY & TOMATO RELISH IN LEMON SHELLS

Preparation time: **About 20 minutes**
Cooking time: **About 50 minutes**

For a festive presentation, you can turn the lemons into serving containers for this unusual cranberry-tomato relish.

4 lemons or ½ cup (120 ml) fresh lemon juice

1 large can (about 28 oz./795 g) tomatoes

1 large onion, finely chopped

1 cup (200 g) sugar

2 tablespoons minced fresh ginger

1 package (about 12 oz./340 g) fresh or frozen cranberries

1. If using lemons for serving containers, cut them in half crosswise (cut decorative zigzag edges, if desired). Squeeze out juice and set aside; then scoop out and discard pulp and membranes from lemon shells. Trim a thin slice from base of each shell so it will sit steadily upright. Wrap shells in paper towels, enclose in a plastic bag, and refrigerate; use within 2 days.

2. Measure ½ cup (120 ml) of the lemon juice and pour into a wide frying pan or 5-quart (5-liter) pan. Cut up tomatoes; add tomatoes and their liquid to pan. Then add onion, sugar, and ginger. Bring to a boil over medium-high heat; boil, uncovered, stirring often, for 20 minutes.

3. Add cranberries and continue to cook, uncovered, stirring often, until relish is reduced to about 3½ cups/830 ml (about 30 more minutes). As relish thickens, watch carefully and stir more often to prevent scorching. Let cool. (At this point, you may cover and refrigerate for up to 3 weeks.)

4. To serve, divide relish equally among lemon shells (if using); or spoon into small (about ⅓-cup/80-ml size) cups or bowls.

Makes 8 to 10 servings

NUTRIENTS

Per serving: 136 calories (2% calories from fat), 0.3 g total fat, 0 g saturated fat, 0 mg cholesterol, 145 mg sodium, 34 g carbohydrates, 2 g fiber, 1 g protein, 32 mg calcium, 0.7 mg iron

PICKLED VEGETABLES

Preparation time: **About 15 minutes**
Cooking time: **About 15 minutes**
Marinating time: **At least 12 hours**

This colorful combination of pickled carrots, chiles, and onion is known down in Mexico as vegetables *en escabeche*; it makes a superb condiment for fajitas or sandwiches. If you like, you can make the pickled vegetables up to a week in advance of serving.

5 cloves garlic, peeled

2 medium-size carrots (about 8 oz./ 230 g total), cut into ¼-inch-thick (6-mm-thick) slices

4 fresh jalapeño chiles or 6 large serrano chiles (about 2 oz./55 g total), halved and seeded

1 small onion, thinly sliced

½ cup (120 ml) cider vinegar

2 dried bay leaves

½ teaspoon dried oregano

½ teaspoon dried thyme

4 whole black peppercorns, crushed

1. In a wide frying pan, combine garlic and 2 tablespoons (30 ml) water. Cook over medium-high heat, stirring often, until garlic is fragrant and just tinged with brown (3 to 4 minutes). Remove garlic from pan and set aside.

2. Add carrots, chiles, onion, and ¼ cup (60 ml) water to pan. Cook, stirring often, until onion is soft and liquid has evaporated (about 5 minutes).

3. Return garlic to pan; then add ½ cup (120 ml) water, vinegar, bay leaves, oregano, thyme, and peppercorns. Bring to a boil; then reduce heat, cover, and simmer until carrots and chiles are just tender to bite (about 7 minutes).

4. Transfer vegetables and cooking liquid to a nonmetal bowl and let cool to room temperature. Cover and refrigerate until next day; then serve. Or, to store, put pickles in a 3-cup (710-ml) jar, pressing down to fill jar compactly; cover with liquid. Apply lid and refrigerate for up to 1 week.

Makes about 3 cups

NUTRIENTS

Per ¼ cup: 16 calories (2% calories from fat), 0.1 g total fat, 0 g saturated fat, 0 mg cholesterol, 7 mg sodium, 4 g carbohydrates, 0.7 g fiber, 0.4 g protein, 13 mg calcium, 0.4 mg iron

CHOCOLATE BANANA CAKE

Preparation time: About 25 minutes
Cooking time: 50 to 60 minutes

This terrific cake has only a gram of fat per serving. A surprising ingredient is cholesterol-free tofu, which allows the use of egg whites instead of whole eggs.

- 1½ cups (185 g) all-purpose flour
- ½ cup (43 g) unsweetened cocoa powder
- 1 tablespoon baking powder
- 1½ teaspoons baking soda
- ½ teaspoon instant espresso powder or ¾ teaspoon instant coffee powder
- 1½ cups (330 g) firmly packed brown sugar
- 8 ounces (230 g) soft tofu, rinsed and drained
- 1 cup (226 g) mashed ripe bananas
- 2 large egg whites
- 2 teaspoons vanilla
- 1 cup (100 g) sifted powdered sugar
  Mint sprigs

1. In a small bowl, stir together flour, cocoa, baking powder, baking soda, and espresso powder. Set aside. In a food processor or a large bowl, combine brown sugar, tofu, bananas, egg whites, and vanilla; whirl or beat with an electric mixer until smoothly blended. Add flour mixture; whirl or beat until well blended.

2. Spoon batter evenly into a well-greased, floured 3- to 3½-quart (2.8- to 3.3-liter) fluted tube pan; smooth top. Bake in a 350°F (175°C) oven until top of cake springs back when gently pressed and sides begin to pull away from pan (50 to 60 minutes).

3. Let cake cool in pan on a rack for about 15 minutes. Carefully slide a thin knife between edge of cake and pan to loosen cake; then carefully invert cake onto rack, lift off pan, and let cool.

4. In a small bowl, stir together powdered sugar and 3 to 4 teaspoons (15 to 20 ml) water, or enough to make a glaze that drizzles easily. Drizzle glaze evenly over cooled cake. Garnish with mint sprigs.
Makes 10 to 12 servings

NUTRIENTS

Per serving: 256 calories (4% calories from fat), 1 g total fat, 0.4 g saturated fat, 0 mg cholesterol, 329 mg sodium, 59 g carbohydrates, 2 g fiber, 4 g protein, 114 mg calcium, 2 mg iron

SOUR CREAM POUND CAKE

Preparation time: About 20 minutes
Cooking time: About 1 hours and 30 minutes

Fine-grained and delicate, this streamlined pound cake is as tempting as the traditional version. Try it plain or topped with fresh fruit: either raspberries, strawberries, or orange slices (or a combination) would make a pretty presentation.

- 3 cups (354 g) cake flour
- 1 teaspoon baking powder
- ¼ teaspoon baking soda
- 6 large egg whites, at room temperature
- 2½ cups (500 g) sugar
- ¼ cup (55 g) butter or margarine, at room temperature
- 3 large eggs
- 1 carton (about 1 lb./455 g) nonfat sour cream
- 1 teaspoon almond extract
- 1 teaspoon vanilla

1. In a small bowl, stir together flour, baking powder, and baking soda; set aside.

2. In a large bowl, beat egg whites with an electric mixer on high speed until frothy. Gradually add ½ cup (100 g) of the sugar, beating until whites hold soft peaks. Set aside.

3. In another large bowl, beat remaining 2 cups (400 g) sugar and butter until well blended. Add eggs, one at a time, beating well after each addition and scraping sides of bowl occasionally. Then beat in sour cream, almond extract, and vanilla. Add flour mixture, 1 cup at a time, beating until blended after each addition and scraping sides of bowl often. Fold a fourth of the beaten egg whites into batter to lighten it; then fold in remaining whites until no streaks remain.

4. Spread batter in a greased, floured 10-inch (25-cm) nonstick or regular plain or fluted tube pan. Bake in a 300°F (150°C) oven until cake springs back at edge when gently pressed (about 1½ hours). Let cool in pan on a rack for 10 minutes. Run a knife between cake and edge of pan; turn cake out onto rack to cool completely.

Makes 16 to 20 servings

NUTRIENTS

Per serving: 263 calories (14% calories from fat), 4 g total fat, 2 g saturated fat, 48 mg cholesterol, 132 mg sodium, 50 g carbohydrates, 0 g fiber, 6 g protein, 64 mg calcium, 2 mg iron

LIME CHEESECAKE

Preparation time: **About 20 minutes**
Cooking time: **45 to 55 minutes**
Cooling & chilling time: **At least 4 hours**

This easy cheesecake is rich—but refreshing, too, thanks to plenty of tangy fresh lime peel and juice.

1½ cups (128 g) graham cracker crumbs (about eighteen 2-inch-square/5-cm-square crackers)

1 cup (200 g) plus 1 tablespoon sugar

¼ cup (55 g) butter or margarine, at room temperature

2 large packages (about 8 oz./230 g each) nonfat cream cheese, at room temperature

2 cups (470 ml) nonfat sour cream

2 large eggs

2 large egg whites

1 tablespoon grated lime peel

¼ cup (60 ml) lime juice

3 tablespoons all-purpose flour
Lime slices

1. In a food processor or a large bowl, whirl or stir together graham cracker crumbs, 2 tablespoons of the sugar, and butter until mixture resembles coarse crumbs. Press mixture firmly over bottom and ½ inch (1 cm) up sides of a 9-inch (23-cm) nonstick or regular cheesecake pan with a removable rim. Bake in a 350°F (175°C) oven until lightly browned (about 10 minutes).

2. Meanwhile, in clean food processor or large bowl, combine ¾ cup plus 2 tablespoons (175 g) of the sugar, cream cheese, 1 cup (240 ml) of the sour cream, eggs, egg whites, lime peel, lime juice, and flour. Whirl or beat with an electric mixer until smooth.

3. Pour cream cheese filling into crust. Return to oven and bake until filling jiggles only slightly in center when pan is gently shaken (35 to 45 minutes). Let cool in pan on a rack for 30 minutes. Meanwhile, in a small bowl, gently stir together remaining 1 cup (240 ml) sour cream and remaining 1 tablespoon sugar; cover and refrigerate.

4. Spread cooled cheesecake with sour cream topping. Cover and refrigerate until cold (at least 4 hours) or until next day. Before serving, remove pan rim and garnish cheesecake with lime slices.

Makes 12 to 16 servings

NUTRIENTS

Per serving: 211 calories (21% calories from fat), 5 g total fat, 2 g saturated fat, 43 mg cholesterol, 305 mg sodium, 31 g carbohydrates, 0.4 g fiber, 9 g protein, 141 mg calcium, 0.5 mg iron

Fresh Strawberry Pie

Preparation time: **About 35 minutes**
Cooking time: **About 30 minutes**
Chilling time: **At least 1 hour**

Glazed whole strawberries glisten like jewels in this special springtime treat, infused with an orange liqueur, such as curaçao or Cointreau.

Pie Pastry:

1 cup plus 2 tablespoons (141 g) all-purpose flour

¼ teaspoon salt

6 tablespoons (75 g) solid vegetable shortening or 6 tablespoons (85 g) butter or margarine, cut into chunks

Filling:

¾ cup (150 g) sugar

3 tablespoons cornstarch

1 teaspoon grated orange peel

7 cups (1 kg) fresh strawberries, hulled

2 tablespoons (30 ml) orange-flavored liqueur or orange juice, or to taste

Topping:

3 large oranges (about 1½ lbs./680 g total)

¼ cup (50 g) sugar

1. To prepare pastry, stir together flour and salt in a medium-size bowl. Using a pastry blender or your fingers, cut or rub in shortening until mixture resembles fine crumbs. Sprinkle with 2 to 3 tablespoons (30 to 45 ml) cold water, stirring with a fork until pastry holds together. On a lightly floured board, pat pastry into a flat, smooth round. Then roll pastry into a 12-inch (30-cm) circle; ease into a lightly greased 9-inch (23-cm) non-stick or regular pie pan. Fold edge of pastry under; flute rim decoratively. Prick pastry all over with a fork to prevent puffing.

2. Bake pastry shell on lowest rack of a 425°F (220°C) oven until golden (12 to 15 minutes). Let cool completely on a rack.

3. Meanwhile, in a small pan, stir together the ¾ cup (150 g) sugar, cornstarch, and orange peel. In a blender or food processor, combine 2 cups (298 g) of the least perfect strawberries and 6 tablespoons (90 ml) water; whirl until smoothly puréed. Pour purée into pan with sugar mixture and stir well. Then cook over medium-high heat, stirring often, until mixture comes to a full boil and thickens slightly (about 4 minutes). Remove pan from heat and stir in liqueur.

4. Working quickly, arrange remaining strawberries, tips up, in pastry shell; evenly spoon hot glaze over berries, covering them completely. Refrigerate, uncovered, until glaze is cool and set (at least 1 hour); then cover and refrigerate until ready to serve or until next day.

5. While pie is chilling, make topping. Cut peel (colored part only) from oranges; cut peel into thin slivers. Squeeze oranges to extract juice; set juice aside. Place slivered peel in a small pan and add enough water to cover; bring to a boil. Drain, then cover with water and bring to a boil again. Drain well; add orange juice and the ¼ cup (50 g) sugar. Bring to a boil over high heat; boil, stirring often and watching closely to prevent scorching, until almost all liquid has evaporated and syrup forms big bubbles (about 10 minutes). Remove from heat; let cool, stirring occasionally to separate slivers of peel. (At this point, you may cover and refrigerate until next day.)

6. Just before serving, sprinkle about a third of the candied orange peel over pie. Offer additional candied peel to accompany individual servings.

Makes 8 servings

NUTRIENTS

Per serving: 337 calories (27% calories from fat), 10 g total fat, 2 g saturated fat, 0 mg cholesterol, 70 mg sodium, 58 g carbohydrates, 4 g fiber, 3 g protein, 35 mg calcium, 1 mg iron

CHOCOLATE CREAM PIE

Preparation time: **About 30 minutes**
Cooking time: **About 25 minutes**
Chilling time: **At least 4 hours**

Silky smooth chocolate mousse covers a rich chocolate graham cracker crust in this chocolate-lover's special.

2½ cups (213 g) chocolate or honey graham cracker crumbs (about thirty 2-inch-square/5-cm-square crackers)

2 tablespoons granulated sugar

1 tablespoon all-purpose flour

½ to 1 teaspoon instant espresso powder or coffee powder

½ cup (144 g) apple jelly, melted and cooled slightly

1 envelope unflavored gelatin

½ cup (120 ml) nonfat milk

1 large package (about 8 oz./230 g) nonfat cream cheese, at room temperature

1 jar (about 7 oz./200 g) marshmallow fluff (marshmallow creme)

½ cup (43 g) unsweetened cocoa powder

¼ cup (30 g) powdered sugar

1 teaspoon vanilla

½ cup (120 ml) half-and-half

¼ cup (43 g) semisweet chocolate chips

2 cups (470 ml) frozen reduced-fat whipped topping, thawed

1. In a food processor or a large bowl, whirl or stir together 2 cups (170 g) of the graham cracker crumbs, granulated sugar, flour, and ¼ to ½ teaspoon of the espresso powder. Add jelly; whirl or stir until mixture is moistened. Press mixture firmly over bottom and ½ inch (1 cm) up sides of a lightly greased 10-inch (25-cm) nonstick or regular pie pan. Bake in a 350°F (175°C) oven until crust turns a slightly darker brown (about 15 minutes). Let cool completely on a rack.

2. Meanwhile, in a small bowl, sprinkle gelatin over milk; let stand for about 5 minutes to soften gelatin. In a clean food processor or large bowl, combine cream cheese, marshmallow fluff, cocoa, powdered sugar, vanilla, and remaining ¼ to ½ teaspoon espresso powder. Whirl or beat with an electric mixer until smooth; set aside.

3. In a 1- to 1½-quart (950-ml to 1.4-liter) pan, bring half-and-half to a boil over medium heat. Add gelatin mixture; reduce heat to low and stir until gelatin is dissolved (about 5 minutes). Remove pan from heat, add chocolate chips, and stir until melted and smooth.

4. With food processor running, slowly pour gelatin mixture into cream cheese mixture; whirl until smooth. (Or beat with electric mixer until smooth.) With a spatula, gently fold in whipped topping. Pour filling into cooled crust; smooth top. Cover pie, making sure cover does not touch filling (hold a "tent" of plastic wrap above pie with wooden picks, or cover pie with a cake cover). Refrigerate until filling is firm (at least 4 hours) or for up to 8 hours.

5. Just before serving, sprinkle remaining ½ cup (43 g) graham cracker crumbs around edge of pie.
Makes 8 to 10 servings

NUTRIENTS

Per serving: 365 calories (19% calories from fat), 8 g total fat, 4 g saturated fat, 8 mg cholesterol, 311 mg sodium, 68 g carbohydrates, 2 g fiber, 8 g protein, 112 mg calcium, 2 mg iron

INDEX

A

Albóndigas soup, turkey, 30
All-vegetable chili, 146
Almond & zucchini stir-fry, 188
Appetizers, 16–26
  black bean salsa with crisp vegetables, 25
  cherry tomato salsa, 22
  corn pancakes with black bean salsa, 18
  corn salsa, 24
  creamy guacamole, 24
  cucumber & jicama salsa, 20
  curry beef in lettuce, 20
  favas with herbs, 18
  garlic chicken bites with tomato-raisin sauce, 17
  grilled vegetable appetizer, 218
  lime salsa, 21
  Mexican-style corn nachos, 23
  nachos with pita chips, 21
  North Beach bruschetta, 17
  spinach-bean roll-ups, 22
  sweet potatoes with caviar, 26
  tomato-crab quesadillas, 16
  water-crisped tortilla chips, 25
  white bean pâté with tomato relish, 19
Apple(s)
  cheese &, hash browns, 176
  cherry &, jubilee, 196
  chicken &, stir-fry, 96
  herbed pork chops with, 104
  pork &, stir-fry, 109
  sautéed lamb with, 110
Artichoke(s)
  pasta with, & anchovies, 120
  pesto pasta, 118
Asian-style green beans, 189
Asparagus
  sauté, 180
  shrimp & watercress soup, 28
  stir-fried beef &, 111
  warm wild rice &, salad, 220
Avocado
  creamy guacamole, 24
  shrimp &, tostadas with papaya salsa, 81

B

Baked quesadillas, 148
Balsamic-broiled salmon with mint, 64
Banana(s)
  chocolate, cake, 248
  couscous, peanut stew with, 144
  with pound cake & chocolate sauce, 208
Basil oil, 46
Bean(s)
  all-vegetable chili, 146
  black. See Black bean(s)
  blackened steak with, & greens, 114
  burritos, 151
  cerveza, 173
  couscous, paella, 144
  egg, & potato hash, 157
  favas with herbs, 18
  garbanzos, Swiss chard with, & Parmesan, 149
  green. See Green bean(s)
  kidney Cobb salad, 40
  light cassoulet, 223
  pinto, cakes with salsa, 150
  vegetable-bean chili, 147
  white. See White bean(s)
Beef
  blackened steak with beans & greens, 114
  chile, burritos, 114
  curry, in lettuce, 20
  garlic, in pita bread with cool yogurt sauce, 112
  grilled, & peppers with orzo, 241
  marsala, & couscous, 113
  stir-fried, & asparagus, 111
Beet borscht, creamy, 32
Biscotti, currant, 196
Black bean(s)
  bucatini &, 133
  & corn salsa, sautéed tofu with, 166
  & jicama salad, 43
  lean refried, 172
  roasted bell pepper &, salad, 40
  salsa, corn pancakes with, 18
  salsa with crisp vegetables, 25
  soup, 32
  with vegetables, 245
Blackened steak with beans & greens, 114
Blue cheese sauce, green potatoes with, 153
Borscht, creamy beet, 32
Bow-tie pasta with broccoli pesto, 129
Braised veal shanks, 234
Braised veal with escarole & pasta, 234
Broccoli
  & bell pepper with couscous, 191
  pesto, bow-tie pasta with, 129
  roasted garlic &, 192
  rotini with, & ricotta, 130
  scallops with, & bell pepper, 76
  with rice & pine nuts, 192

Brownies, cream cheese blond, 194
Bruschetta, North Beach, 17
Bucatini & black beans, 133
Bulgur
  pork tenderloin with, 104
  scrambled eggs &, 154
Burger(s)
  chicken chutney, 96
  double wheat, 159
  turkey & mushroom, 101
  wheat germ, 160
  zucchini, 159
Burritos
  bean, 151
  chile beef, 114
  vegetable, 148

C

Cactus pear & tree pear soup, 212
Cake(s)
  chocolate banana, 248
  drunken, 210
  lemon poppy seed, 209
  lime cheesecake, 249
  mocha almond fudge torte, 207
  pound, bananas with, & chocolate sauce, 208
  sour cream pound, 248
Cannellini. See White bean(s)
Cantaloupe
  melon, papaya & cucumber salad, 37
Capellini with cilantro pesto & white beans, 124
Capellini with tomatoes & white beans, 244
Carrot(s)
  cocoa-glazed, & onions, 186
  curry-glazed, 185
  soup, spiced purée of, 221
  zucchini &, sauté, 186
Cassoulet, light, 223
Cauliflower, herbed, & zucchini stir-fry, 179
Caviar, sweet potatoes with, 26
Cerveza beans, 173
Chanterelle & tarragon sauce, chicken with, 224
Cheese
  & apple hash browns, 176
  quesadillas, fruit &, 152
Cheesecake, lime, 249
Cherry(ies)
  & apple jubilee, 196
  chimichangas, 197
  lamb chops with, & orecchiette, 110
Cherry tomato salsa, 22
Chicken
  & apple stir-fry, 96
  bites, garlic, with tomato-raisin sauce, 17
  breasts Calvados, 94
  chutney burgers, 96
  citrus, soup, 222
  curry in pita bread, 93

Chicken (cont'd.)
  jalapeño, with mole poblano, 88
  lemon, 86
  litchi, penne &, salad, 39
  & mushrooms with couscous, 98
  noodle soup, 31
  pasta with, & prosciutto, 138
  peanut, with rice, 87
  & potato salad, Greek-style, 219
  salad, warm Chinese, 36
  salsa, 95
  sesame, with stir-fried vegetables, 94
  tortas, spicy, 97
  with chanterelle & tarragon sauce, 224
Chile beef burritos, 114
Chile(s)
  beef burritos, 114
  -cheese French toast & cherry tomato salsa, 158
  green, dressing, 56
  hot, oil, 55
  jalapeño chicken with mole poblano, 88
  red, dressing, 53
  roasted, with eggs, 155
Chili
  all-vegetable, 146
  -mac, spicy, 146
  vegetable-bean, 147
Chili shrimp, 82
Chinese chicken salad, warm, 36
Chips, water-crisped tortilla, 25
Chocolate
  banana cake, 248
  chip cookies, 198
  cream pie, 251
  mocha almond fudge torte, 207
  pistachio cookies, 199
  sauce, bananas with pound cake &, 208
  shortbread, 205
Chowder
  crab & rice, 26
  Mexican shellfish, 222
Chutney, grape, curried lamb with, 233
Cioppino salad, warm, 45
Citrus chicken soup, 222
Cobb salad, kidney, 40
Cobbler, pear, with ginger crust, 214
Cocoa pepper cookies, 200
Cocoa-glazed carrots & onions, 186
Coconut couscous, island pork with, 107
Coconut rice, curried turkey with, 100
Cookies
  chocolate chip, 198
  chocolate pistachio, 199
  chocolate shortbread, 205
  cocoa pepper, 200

Cookies (cont'd.)
cream cheese blond
brownies, 194
currant biscotti, 196
ginger bars, 200
lemon, 206
Mexican wedding, 206
molasses sugar, 194
orange & cocoa, 195
Coriander-curry shrimp, 84
Corn
nachos, Mexican-style, 23
pancakes with black bean
salsa, 18
salsa, 24
salsa, black bean &, sautéed
tofu with, 166
seasoned sweet, 175
stew, triple 108
Couscous
bean paella, 144
broccoli & bell pepper
with, 191
chicken & mushrooms
with, 98
golden curried, 172
island pork with coconut,
107
lemon shrimp over caper, 78
marsala beef &, 113
Mediterranean turkey
with, 102
paella, 134
peanut stew with banana,
144
with ratatouille & feta
cheese, 145
Crab
cracked, with onion, 68
lasagne, 228
mizuna, fennel &, salad, 44
quesadillas, tomato-, 16
& rice chowder, 26
tacos, soft, with tomatillo
& lime salsa, 73
with emerald sauce, 68
Cracked crab with onion, 68
Cranberry & tomato relish in
lemon shells, 246
Cream cheese blond
brownies, 194
Creamy beet borscht, 32
Creamy guacamole, 24
Crisp, sautéed pear, 214
Cucumber(s)
& jicama salsa, 20
melon, papaya &, salad, 37
Currant biscotti, 196
Curry/curried food
beef in lettuce, 20
chicken, in pita bread, 93
coriander-, shrimp, 84
-glazed carrots, 185
golden, couscous, 172
lamb with grape chutney, 233
oil, 55
shrimp & shell salad, 220
turkey with coconut rice,
100
Custard, shrimp, 80

D
Desserts, 194–216. See also
Cakes; Cookies; Pies
cactus pear & tree pear
soup, 212
cherry & apple jubilee, 196
cherry chimichangas, 197
dessert nachos, 215
honeydew melon dessert
bowl, 213
hot papaya sundaes, 216
peach shortcakes, 211
pear cobbler with ginger
crust, 214
sautéed pear crisp, 214
sparkling jewels fruit soup,
213
stir-fried pineapple with
ginger, 210
Dips and spreads. See also
Salsa
creamy guacamole, 24
favas with herbs, 18
white bean pâté with
tomato relish, 19
Double wheat burgers, 159
Dressings
green chile, 56
pesto, 46
red chile, 53
shallot, 45
strawberry tarragon, 41
Drowned eggs, 154
Drunken cake, 210

E
East-West hash, 156
Eggplant
moussaka Dubrovnik, 226
Sichuan tofu with, 166
simply perfect, 178
& zucchini lasagne, 243
Egg(s)
bean & potato hash, 157
drowned, 154
East-West hash, 156
fiery oven strata, 246
roasted chiles with, 155
scrambled, & bulgur, 154
vegetable scramble
pockets, 156
Escarole
braised veal with, & pasta,
234
stir-fried pork &, salad, 38
tortellini &, soup, 34

F
Fajitas, turkey, 100
Farfalle with chard, garlic
& ricotta, 119
Farfalle with smoked salmon
& vodka, 138
Favas with herbs, 18
Fennel, mizuna & crab
salad, 44
Feta
couscous with ratatouille &,
145

Feta (cont'd.)
stir-fried spinach with, 187
ziti with turkey, & sun-
dried tomatoes, 135
Fettuccine with shrimp
& Gorgonzola, 141
Fiery oven strata, 246
Fish. See also specific fish
& pea soup, 27
poached, with horseradish
sauce, 58
soup, salsa, 27
French toast, chile-cheese,
& tomato salsa, 158
Fresh strawberry pie, 250
Fruit. See also specific fruits
& cheese quesadillas, 152
fruited quinoa salad, 42
& ricotta pizza, quick 152
soup, sparkling jewels, 213

G
Garbanzo beans, Swiss chard
with, & Parmesan, 149
Garlic
beef in pita bread with cool
yogurt sauce, 112
chicken bites with tomato-
raisin sauce, 17
oil, 54
roasted, & broccoli, 192
& rosemary green beans,
189
shrimp with rice, 80
Ginger(ed)
bars, 200
butterflied lamb with
yams, 230
oil, 56
pork with Asian pears, 108
Goat cheese
orecchiette with lentils &,
132
& spinach pasta, 122
Golden curried couscous, 172
Gorgonzola
fettuccine with shrimp &,
141
ravioli with, 120
Grape chutney, curried lamb
with, 233
Greek-style chicken & potato
salad, 219
Green bean(s)
Asian-style, 189
garlic & rosemary, 189
sea bass with, & sesame-
orange sauce, 59
Green chile dressing, 56
Green potatoes with blue
cheese sauce, 153
Grilled beef & peppers with
orzo, 241
Grilled leg of lamb & pears,
232
Grilled scallops with
pear-ginger coulis, 74
Grilled vegetable appetizer,
218
Guacamole, creamy, 24

H
Halibut
piccata with lemon
linguine, 60
with tomato & cilantro
linguine, 60
Harvest gratin, 244
Hash
East-West, 156
egg, bean & potato, 157
Herbed cauliflower &
zucchini stir-fry, 179
Herbed pork chops with
apples, 104
Honeydew melon dessert
bowl, 213
Horseradish sauce, poached
fish with, 58
Hot chile oil, 55
Hot papaya sundaes, 216
Hunter's-style lamb stew, 231

I-K
Indian potatoes, 174
Island pork with coconut
couscous, 107
Italian garden pasta, 118
Italian sausage lasagne, 227
Italian-style Swiss chard, 188
Jalapeño chicken with mole
poblano, 88
Jicama
black bean &, salad, 43
cucumber &, salsa, 20
Kale, sautéed, with cannellini,
187
Kidney Cobb salad, 40

L
Lamb
chops with cherries &
orecchiette, 110
curried, with grape
chutney, 233
gingered butterflied, with
yams, 230
grilled leg of, & pears, 232
sautéed, with apples, 110
stew, hunter's-style, 231
Lasagne
crab, 228
eggplant & zucchini, 243
Italian sausage, 227
Lean refried black beans, 172
Lemon(y)
-caper rice, 171
chicken, 86
cookies, 206
poppy seed cake, 209
shrimp over caper
couscous, 78
shrimp tostadas, 79
Lentils, orecchiette with, &
goat cheese, 132
Lettuce, watercress & shrimp
salad, 47
Light cassoulet, 223
Lime cheesecake, 249
Lime salsa, 21

Linguine with creamy shrimp, 142
Linguine with red & yellow tomatoes, 133
Litchi, penne & chicken salad, 39
Lo mein, low-fat, 137

M

Mango relish, swordfish with, 61
Maritata soup, 31
Marsala beef & couscous, 113
Meats, 104–116. See Beef; Lamb; Pork; Veal
Mediterranean squash, 190
Mediterranean turkey with couscous, 102
Melon
  honeydew, dessert bowl, 213
  papaya & cucumber salad, 37
Mexican rice, 170
Mexican shellfish chowder, 222
Mexican-style corn nachos, 23
Mexican wedding cookies, 206
Mizuna
  fennel & crab salad, 44
  sautéed, & shells, 122
Mocha almond fudge torte, 207
Molasses sugar cookies, 194
Mole poblano, jalapeño chicken with, 88
Moussaka Dubrovnik, 226
Mushroom(s)
  burgers, turkey &, 101
  chicken &, with couscous, 98
  pasta with shrimp & shiitakes, 140
  sautéed, with apple eau de vie, 178
  veal with, 116

N

Nachos
  Mexican-style corn, 23
  with pita chips, 21
Nectarine, plum & basil salad-salsa, 37
Noodle pudding, veal chops with, 236
North Beach bruschetta, 17
Nutritional data, about our, 5

O

Oil(s)
  basil, 46
  curry, 55
  garlic, 54
  ginger, 56
  hot chile, 55
  thyme, 48

Onion(s)
  cocoa-glazed carrots &, 186
  cracked crab with, 68
  orange-, salad with red chile dressing, 53
Orange(s)
  & cocoa cookies, 195
  -onion salad with red chile dressing, 53
  & rum sweet potatoes, 175
  wilted spinach salad with, 43
Orecchiette with lentils & goat cheese, 132
Oriental salad, 54
Oriental-style red snapper stir-fry, 62
Oven-baked paella, 229

P

Paella
  couscous, 134
  couscous bean, 144
  oven-baked, 229
Papaya(s)
  salad, with melon & cucumber, 37
  salsa, shrimp & avocado tostadas with, 81
  scallop & pea pod stir-fry with, 74
  sundaes, hot, 216
Pasta, 118–142. See also Couscous; Lasagne
  artichoke pesto, 118
  bow-tie, with broccoli pesto, 129
  bucatini & black beans, 133
  capellini with cilantro pesto & white beans, 124
  capellini with tomatoes & white beans, 244
  farfalle with chard, garlic & ricotta, 119
  farfalle with smoked salmon & vodka, 138
  fettuccine with shrimp & Gorgonzola, 141
  goat cheese & spinach, 122
  Italian garden, 118
  linguine with creamy shrimp, 142
  linguine with red & yellow tomatoes, 133
  low-fat lo mein, 137
  orecchiette with lentils & goat cheese, 132
  peanut, & tofu, 131
  penne with turkey sausage, 136
  pie, 121
  pilaf, 171
  ravioli with Gorgonzola, 120
  rotini with broccoli & ricotta, 130
  rotini with scallops, 139
  sausage, basil & port fettuccine, 134

Pasta (cont'd.)
  sautéed mizuna & shells, 122
  Southwestern fettuccine, 123
  spaghetti alla Calabrese, 242
  spinach, and scallops, 140
  Thai tofu & tagliatelle, 130
  vermicelli with turkey, 136
  with artichokes & anchovies, 120
  with chicken & prosciutto, 138
  with shrimp & shiitakes, 140
  ziti with turkey, feta & sun-dried tomatoes, 135
Pâté, white bean, with tomato relish, 19
Peach shortcakes, 211
Peanut(s)
  chicken with rice, 87
  pasta & tofu, 131
  stew with banana couscous, 144
Pear(s)
  cobbler with ginger crust, 214
  gingered pork with Asian, 108
  grilled leg of lamb &, 232
  -ginger coulis, grilled scallops with, 74
  sautéed, crisp, 214
  warm spinach, & sausage salad, 38
Pea(s). See also Snow peas
  salad, split pea & green, 48
  soup, fish &, 27
Penne with turkey sausage, 136
Pepper(s)
  broccoli &, with couscous, 191
  grilled beef &, with orzo, 241
  red & yellow, salad, 36
  roasted, & black bean salad, 40
  scallops with broccoli &, 76
  tricolor, sauté, 180
Pesto
  artichoke, pasta, 118
  bow-tie pasta with broccoli, 129
  capellini with cilantro, & white beans, 124
  shrimp & orzo with, dressing, 46
  shrimp with parsley, & linguine, 83
Pickled vegetables, 247
Pies
  chocolate cream, 251
  fresh strawberry, 250
  pasta, 121
Pine nuts, broccoli with rice &, 192

Pineapple
  salsa, tofu tacos with, 165
  stir-fried, with ginger, 210
Pinto bean cakes with salsa, 150
Pistachio cookies, chocolate, 199
Pizza
  quick fruit & ricotta, 152
  Thai, with shrimp, 82
Plum, nectarine, & basil salad-salsa, 37
Poached fish with horseradish sauce, 58
Poppy seed cake, lemon, 209
Pork
  & apple stir-fry, 109
  chops, herbed, with apples, 104
  chops, smoked, with ruote, 105
  fried rice, 170
  gingered, with Asian pears, 108
  island, with coconut couscous, 107
  stew with spaetzle, 230
  stir-fried, & escarole salad, 38
  sweet & sour, 106
  tenderloin with bulgur, 104
Potato(es)
  cheese & apple hash browns, 176
  green, with blue cheese sauce, 153
  hash, East-West, 156
  hash, egg, bean &, 157
  Indian, 174
  risotto, 174
  salad, Greek-style chicken &, 219
Pound cake
  bananas with, & chocolate sauce, 208
  sour cream, 248

Q

Quesadillas
  baked, 148
  fruit & cheese, 152
  tomato-crab, 16
Quick cooking. See 20 Minutes or Less recipes
Quick fruit & ricotta pizza, 152
Quinoa salad, fruited, 42

R

Raspberry-glazed turkey sauté, 98
Ratatouille & feta cheese, couscous with, 145
Ravioli with Gorgonzola, 120
Red chile dressing, 53
Red & yellow pepper salad, 36
Red snapper, Oriental-style, stir-fry, 62

Relish. *See also* Chutney
    cranberry & tomato, in
        lemon shells, 246
    mango, swordfish with, 61
    tomato-orange, tuna with,
        66
    tomato, white bean pâté
        with, 19
Rice
    broccoli with, & pine nuts,
        192
    crab &, chowder, 26
    curried turkey with
        coconut, 100
    garlic shrimp with, 80
    lemon-caper, 171
    Mexican, 170
    peanut chicken with, 87
    pork fried, 170
Ricotta
    farfalle with chard, garlic
        &, 119
    pizza, quick fruit &, 152
    rotini with broccoli &, 130
Roast turkey with apple orzo,
    225
Roasted bell pepper & black
    bean salad, 40
Roasted chiles with eggs, 155
Roasted garlic & broccoli, 192
Rotini with broccoli &
    ricotta, 130
Rotini with scallops, 139

S

Salads, 36–56. *See also*
    Dressings
    black bean & jicama, 43
    curried shrimp & shell, 220
    fruited quinoa, 42
    Greek-style chicken &
        potato, 219
    kidney Cobb, 40
    litchi, penne & chicken, 39
    melon, papaya & cucumber,
        37
    mizuna, fennel & crab, 44
    nectarine, plum & basil,
        -salsa, 37
    orange-onion, with red
        chile dressing, 53
    Oriental, 54
    red & yellow pepper, 36
    roasted bell pepper & black
        bean, 40
    shrimp & orzo, with pesto
        dressing, 46
    shrimp & spinach slaw, 44
    split pea & green pea, 48
    stir-fried pork & escarole, 38
    warm Chinese chicken, 36
    warm cioppino, 45
    warm spinach, pear &
        sausage, 38
    warm wild rice &
        asparagus, 220
    watercress, butter lettuce &
        shrimp, 47
    wilted spinach, with
        oranges, 43

Salmon
    balsamic-broiled, with
        mint, 64
    sauté with citrus sauce, 64
    with creamy tomatillo
        sauce, 63
Salsa
    black bean, corn pancakes
        with, 18
    black bean & corn, sautéed
        tofu with, 166
    black bean, with crisp
        vegetables, 25
    cherry tomato, 22
    cherry tomato, chile-cheese
        French toast &, 158
    cherry tomato, tuna &, 65
    chicken, 95
    corn, 24
    cucumber & jicama, 20
    fish soup, 27
    lime, 21
    papaya, shrimp & avocado
        tostadas with, 81
    pineapple, tofu tacos with
        165
    pinto bean cakes with, 150
    tomatillo & lime, soft crab
        tacos with, 73
Sandwiches
    chicken chutney burgers, 96
    chicken curry in pita bread,
        93
    double wheat burgers, 159
    garlic beef in pita bread with
        cool yogurt sauce, 112
    spicy chicken tortas, 97
    turkey & mushroom
        burgers, 101
    vegetable scramble
        pockets, 156
    wheat germ burgers, 160
    zucchini burgers, 159
Sauces. *See also* Dressings;
        Pesto; Salsa
    blue cheese, green potatoes
        with, 153
    chanterelle & tarragon,
        chicken with, 224
    chocolate, bananas with
        pound cake &, 208
    citrus, salmon sauté with,
        64
    emerald, crab with, 68
    horseradish, poached fish
        with, 58
    mole poblano, jalapeño
        chicken with, 88
    pear-ginger coulis, grilled
        scallops with, 74
    sesame-orange, sea bass
        with green beans &, 59
    tomatillo, creamy, salmon
        with, 63
    tomato-raisin, garlic
        chicken bites with, 17
    yogurt, cool, 113
Sausage(s)
    basil & port fettuccine, 134
    Italian, lasagne, 227

Sausage(s) (cont'd.)
    penne with turkey, 136
    warm spinach, pear &,
        salad, 38
Sautéed kale with cannellini, 187
Sautéed lamb with apples, 110
Sautéed mizuna & shells, 122
Sautéed mushrooms with
    apple eau de vie, 178
Sautéed pear crisp, 214
Sautéed scallops with spinach
    & farfalle, 76
Sautéed tofu with black bean
    & corn salsa, 166
Sautéed turkey with
    provolone & sage, 99
Scallop(s)
    grilled, with pear-ginger
        coulis, 74
    & pea pod stir-fry with
        papaya, 74
    rotini with, 139
    sautéed, with spinach &
        farfalle, 76
    scampi, 75
    spinach pasta and, 140
    with broccoli & bell
        pepper, 76
Scrambled eggs & bulgur, 154
Sea bass with green beans &
    sesame-orange sauce, 59
Seafood, 58–84. *See also*
    specific fish and shellfish
    Mexican shellfish chowder,
        222
    warm cioppino salad, 45
Seasoned sweet corn, 175
Sesame chicken with stir-fried
    vegetables, 94
Sesame-orange sauce, sea bass
    with green beans &, 59
Shallot dressing, 45
Shiitakes, pasta with shrimp
    &, 140
Shortbread, chocolate, 205
Shortcakes, peach, 211
Shrimp
    asparagus, & watercress
        soup, 28
    & avocado tostadas with
        papaya salsa, 81
    chili, 82
    coriander-curry, 84
    curried, & shell salad, 220
    custard, 80
    fettuccine with, &
        Gorgonzola, 141
    garlic, with rice, 80
    gingered, & capellini soup, 29
    lemon, over caper couscous,
        78
    lemony, tostadas, 79
    linguine with creamy, 142
    & orzo with pesto dressing, 46
    pasta with, & shiitakes, 140
    sauté, 79
    & spinach slaw, 44
    Thai pizza with, 82
    watercress, butter lettuce
        &, salad, 47

Shrimp (cont'd.)
    & white bean soup, 29
    with parsley pesto &
        linguine, 83
Sichuan tofu with eggplant, 166
Simply perfect eggplant, 178
Slaw, shrimp & spinach, 44
Smoked pork chops with
    ruote, 105
Smoked salmon & vodka,
    farfalle with, 138
Snow peas with bacon &
    mint, 190
Soft crab tacos with tomatillo
    & lime salsa, 73
Soups, 26-34. *See also* Chowder
    asparagus, shrimp &
        watercress, 28
    black bean, 32
    cactus pear & tree pear, 212
    chicken noodle, 31
    citrus chicken, 222
    creamy beet borscht, 32
    fish & pea, 27
    gingered shrimp &
        capellini, 29
    Maritata, 31
    salsa fish, 27
    shrimp & white bean, 29
    sparkling jewels fruit, 213
    spiced purée of carrot, 221
    spring vegetable, with
        shells, 33
    sweet potato, 33
    tortellini & escarole, 34
    turkey Albóndigas, 30
Sour cream pound cake, 248
Southwestern fettuccine, 123
Spaetzle, pork stew with, 230
Spaghetti alla Calabrese, 242
Sparkling jewels fruit soup, 213
Spiced purée of carrot soup,
    221
Spicy chicken tortas, 97
Spicy chili-mac, 146
Spinach
    -bean roll-ups, 22
    pear & sausage salad, warm
        38
    salad, wilted, with oranges, 43
    slaw, shrimp &, 44
    stir-fried tuna on, 67
    stir-fried, with feta, 187
Spinach pasta and scallops, 140
Split pea & green pea salad, 48
Spring vegetable soup with
    shells, 33
Squash, Mediterranean, 190
Stews
    all-vegetable chili, 146
    hunter's-style lamb, 231
    light cassoulet, 223
    peanut, with banana
        couscous, 144
    pork, with spaetzle, 230
    spicy chili-mac, 146
    triple corn, 108
    vegetable-bean chili, 147
    white bean tagine, 150
Stir-fried beef & asparagus, 111

Stir-fried pineapple with ginger, 210
Stir-fried pork & escarole salad, 38
Stir-fried spinach with feta, 187
Stir-fried tuna on spinach, 67
Stir-fried veal piccata, 115
Strata, fiery oven, 246
Strawberry(ies)
  pie, fresh, 250
  tarragon dressing, 41
Sun-dried tomatoes, ziti with turkey, feta &, 135
Sundaes, hot papaya, 216
Sweet & sour pork, 106
Sweet & sour tofu, 168
Sweet potato(es)
  with caviar, 26
  harvest gratin, 244
  orange & rum, 175
  soup, 33
  stir-fry, 176
Swiss chard
  farfalle with, garlic & ricotta, 119
  Italian-style, 188
  with garbanzos & Parmesan, 149
Swordfish with mango relish, 61

T

Tacos
  soft crab, with tomatillo & lime salsa, 73
  tofu, with pineapple salsa, 165
Tagine, white bean, 150
Thai pizza with shrimp, 82
Thai tofu & tagliatelle, 130
Thyme oil, 48
Tilapia, whole, with onion & lemon, 58
Tofu
  peanut pasta &, 131
  sautéed, with black bean & corn salsa, 166
  Sichuan, with eggplant, 166
  sweet & sour, 168
  tacos with pineapple salsa, 165
  Thai, & tagliatelle, 130
Tomatillo(s)
  & lime salsa, soft crab tacos with, 73
  sauce, creamy, salmon with, 63
Tomato(es)
  capellini with, & white beans, 244
  -crab quesadillas, 16
  cranberry &, relish in lemon shells, 246
  linguine with red & yellow, 133
  -orange relish, tuna with, 66
  -raisin sauce, garlic chicken bites with, 17
  relish, white bean pâté with, 19
  salsa, cherry, 22

Tomato(es) (cont'd.)
  salsa, cherry, chile-cheese French toast &, 158
  salsa, cherry, tuna &, 65
Tortas, spicy chicken, 97
Torte, mocha almond fudge, 207
Tortellini & escarole soup, 34
Tortilla(s)
  warm, 160
  water-crisped, chips, 25
Tostada(s)
  lemony shrimp, 79
  shrimp & avocado, with papaya salsa, 81
Tree pear, cactus pear &, soup, 212
Tricolor pepper sauté, 180
Triple corn stew, 108
Tuna
  & cherry tomato salsa, 65
  stir-fried, on spinach, 67
  with tomato-orange relish, 66
Turkey
  Albóndigas soup, 30
  curried, with coconut rice, 100
  fajitas, 100
  Mediterranean, with couscous, 102
  & mushroom burgers, 101
  raspberry-glazed, sauté, 98
  roast, with apple orzo, 225
  sautéed, with provolone & sage, 99
  vermicelli with, 136
  ziti with, feta & sun-dried tomatoes, 135
20 Minutes or Less recipes
  baked quesadillas, 148
  black bean & jicama salad, 43
  blackened steak with beans & greens, 114
  cherry & apple jubilee, 196
  chicken chutney burgers, 96
  creamy beet borscht, 32
  creamy guacamole, 24
  double wheat burgers, 159
  favas with herbs, 18
  garlic & rosemary green beans, 189
  garlic shrimp with rice, 80
  halibut with tomato & cilantro linguine, 60
  linguine with red & yellow tomatoes, 133
  marsala beef & couscous, 113
  nectarine, plum & basil salad-salsa, 37
  pasta with artichokes & anchovies, 120
  pasta with shrimp & shiitakes, 140
  pork fried rice, 170
  rotini with broccoli & ricotta, 130
  sautéed turkey with provolone & sage, 99

20 Minutes or Less recipes (cont'd.)
  seasoned sweet corn, 175
  sparkling jewels fruit soup, 213
  spinach pasta and scallops, 140
  stir-fried pineapple with ginger, 210
  zucchini & carrot sauté, 186

V

Veal
  braised, with escarole & pasta, 234
  chops & sage dressing, 235
  chops with noodle pudding, 236
  piccata, stir-fried, 115
  shanks, braised, 234
  with mushrooms, 116
Vegetable(s). See also specific vegetables
  -bean chili, 147
  black beans with, 245
  burritos, 148
  chili, all-, 146
  grilled, appetizer, 218
  pickled, 247
  scramble pockets, 156
  soup, spring, with shells, 33
  stir-fry with soba, 177
Vermicelli with turkey, 136

W

Warm Chinese chicken salad, 36
Warm cioppino salad, 45
Warm spinach, pear & sausage salad, 38
Warm tortillas, 160
Warm wild rice & asparagus salad, 220
Water-crisped tortilla chips, 25
Watercress
  asparagus, shrimp &, soup, 28
  butter lettuce & shrimp salad, 47
Weekend Cooking, 218–251
  black beans with vegetables, 245
  braised veal shanks, 234
  braised veal with escarole & pasta, 234
  capellini with tomatoes & white beans, 244
  chicken with chanterelle & tarragon sauce, 224
  chocolate banana cake, 248
  chocolate cream pie, 251
  citrus chicken soup, 222
  crab lasagne, 228
  cranberry & tomato relish in lemon shells, 246
  curried lamb with grape chutney, 233
  curried shrimp & shell salad, 220
  eggplant & zucchini lasagne, 243

Weekend Cooking (cont'd.)
  fiery oven strata, 246
  fresh strawberry pie, 250
  gingered butterflied lamb with yams, 230
  Greek-style chicken & potato salad, 219
  grilled beef & peppers with orzo, 241
  grilled leg of lamb & pears, 232
  grilled vegetable appetizer, 218
  harvest gratin, 244
  hunter's-style lamb stew, 231
  Italian sausage lasagne, 227
  light cassoulet, 223
  lime cheesecake, 249
  Mexican seafood chowder, 222
  moussaka Dubrovnik, 226
  oven-baked paella, 229
  pickled vegetables, 247
  pork stew with spaetzle, 230
  roast turkey with apple orzo, 225
  sour cream pound cake, 248
  spaghetti alla Calabrese, 242
  spiced purée of carrot soup, 221
  veal chops & sage dressing, 235
  veal chops with noodle pudding, 236
  warm wild rice & asparagus salad, 220
Wheat germ burgers, 160
White bean(s)
  capellini with cilantro pesto &, 124
  capellini with tomatoes &, 244
  pâté with tomato relish, 19
  sautéed kale with cannellini, 187
  soup, shrimp &, 29
  spinach-bean roll-ups, 22
  tagine, 150
Whole tilapia with onion & lemon, 58
Wild rice, warm, & asparagus salad, 220
Wilted spinach salad with oranges, 43

Y-Z

Yogurt sauce, cool, 113
Ziti with turkey, feta & sun-dried tomatoes, 135
Zucchini
  almond &, stir-fry, 188
  burgers, 159
  & carrot sauté, 186
  eggplant &, lasagne, 243
  herbed cauliflower &, stir-fry, 179